# ISLAND to ISLAND

# ISLAND

## *From Somerset to Seychelles*

*A collection of photographs – the pictures behind the story*

# SALLY MILLS

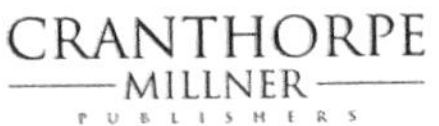

First published by Cranthorpe Millner Publishers (2023)

ISBN 978-1-80378-142-6 (Paperback)

www.cranthorpemillner.com

Cranthorpe Millner Publishers

Front cover image © Melvyn Yeandle

# The Story Behind the Photographs

As I look back on my career in nature conservation, I feel extremely fortunate to have been able to follow my lifelong passion for the natural world throughout my working life. Although filled with many remarkable experiences, one of the exceptional highlights has to be when, after 25 years of conservation employment in the UK, my partner Melvyn and I earned the opportunity to manage the prestigious Aride Island Nature Reserve in Seychelles. The unique experience of living and working on a small, remote tropical island with only six other human inhabitants, no electricity or running water and an array of incredible wildlife was both cathartic and inspirational. Some years later, I decided to share the highs and lows of this life changing experience through an illustrated memoir, *Island to Island*.

Living amongst a million seabirds and some of the rarest wildlife in the world, life on Aride left a lasting impression, and the aim of my memoir was to share an honest and authentic account of what island life was truly like. Following the release of *Island to Island* in August 2022, I received frequent requests for the publication of a collection of photographs to complement the existing story and illustrations. Thus, *Island to Island: Photographic Collection* was born.

Featuring images taken by myself, Melvyn, and others, alongside text from the book, it is hoped that this collection will offer a unique glimpse into the realities of living on a small remote island in the middle of the Indian Ocean, both for those who have read the memoir and for those who are new to our story.

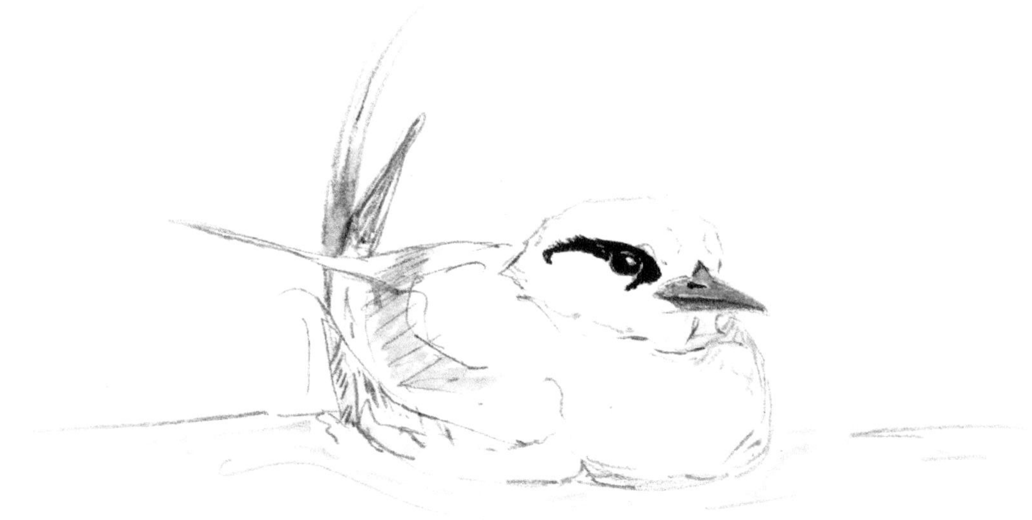

*White-tailed tropicbird*

# Chapter 1

## From Somerset to Seychelles

The opportunity to spend two years working as nature reserve wardens for the Island Conservation Society on Aride Island, Seychelles first appeared in an email. For three years, it remained nothing more than a dream. I kept the message in my inbox just in case, opening up the advert once in a while and imagining what it would be like. Never did I think it would ever become a reality.

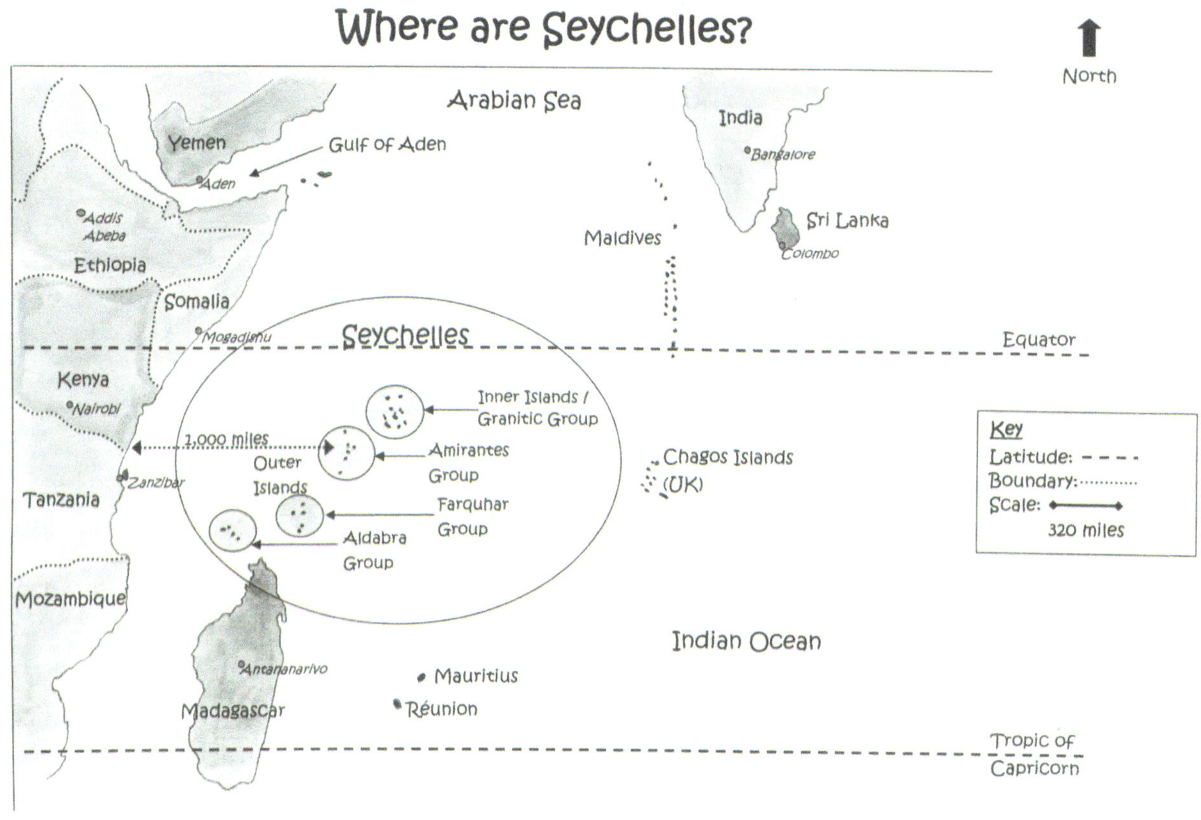



The Seychelles archipelago is approximately a thousand miles off the East African coast, and a thousand miles north of Mauritius. Made up of one hundred and fifty-five islands in total, they are located in three main groups. There are forty-two granitic and one hundred and thirteen coralline, the geology and substrate determining their habitation, vegetation and shape. This basically means the granite islands are hilly and the coral islands are flat.

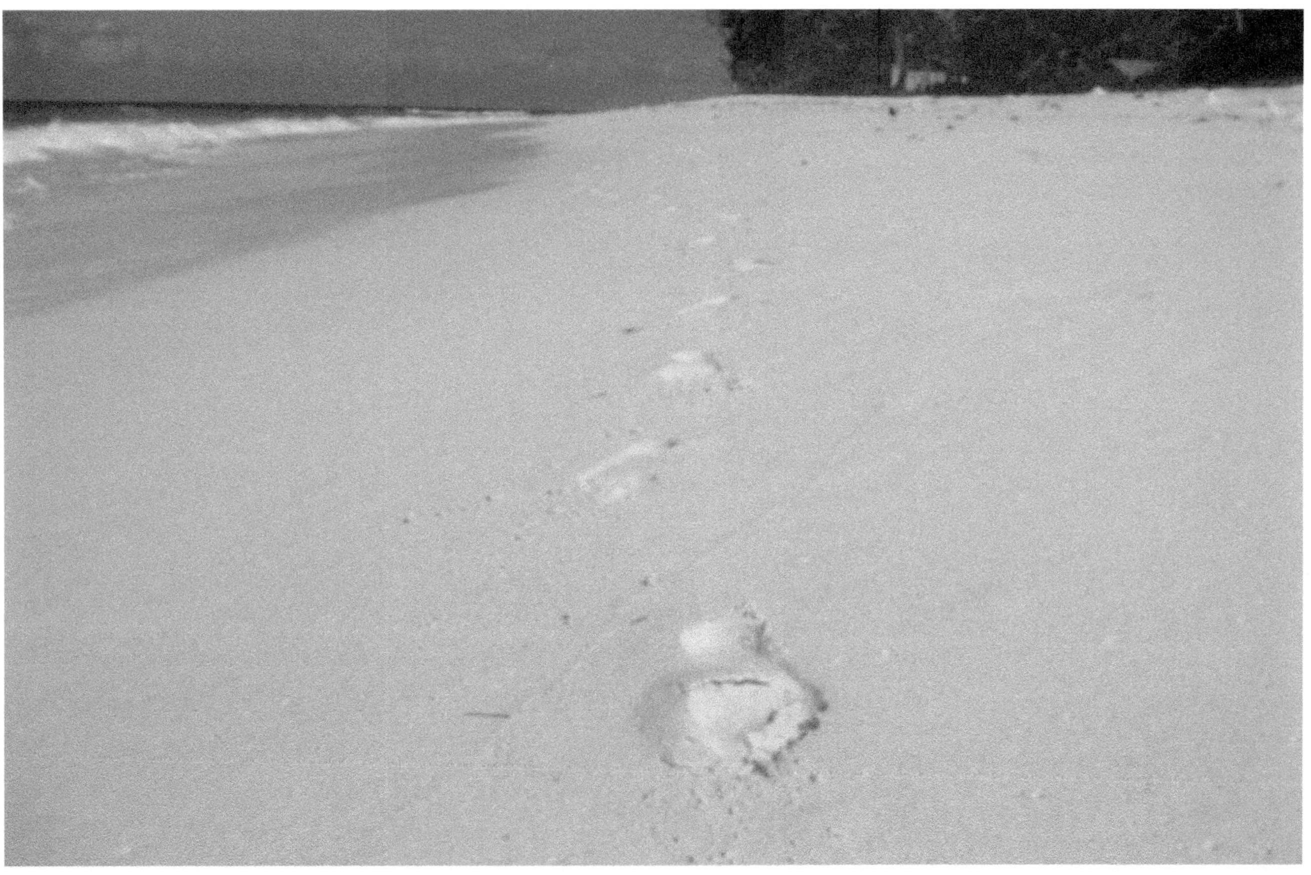

With only a comparatively recent history of human presence and interference, a number of the islands are still very rich in wildlife. Despite Aride's chequered past – once a coconut plantation, then later harvested for sooty tern eggs – it was never invaded by rats or cats (the non-native species that spell disaster for island wildlife), and so remains the richest of the granitic islands, and home to over a million seabirds.

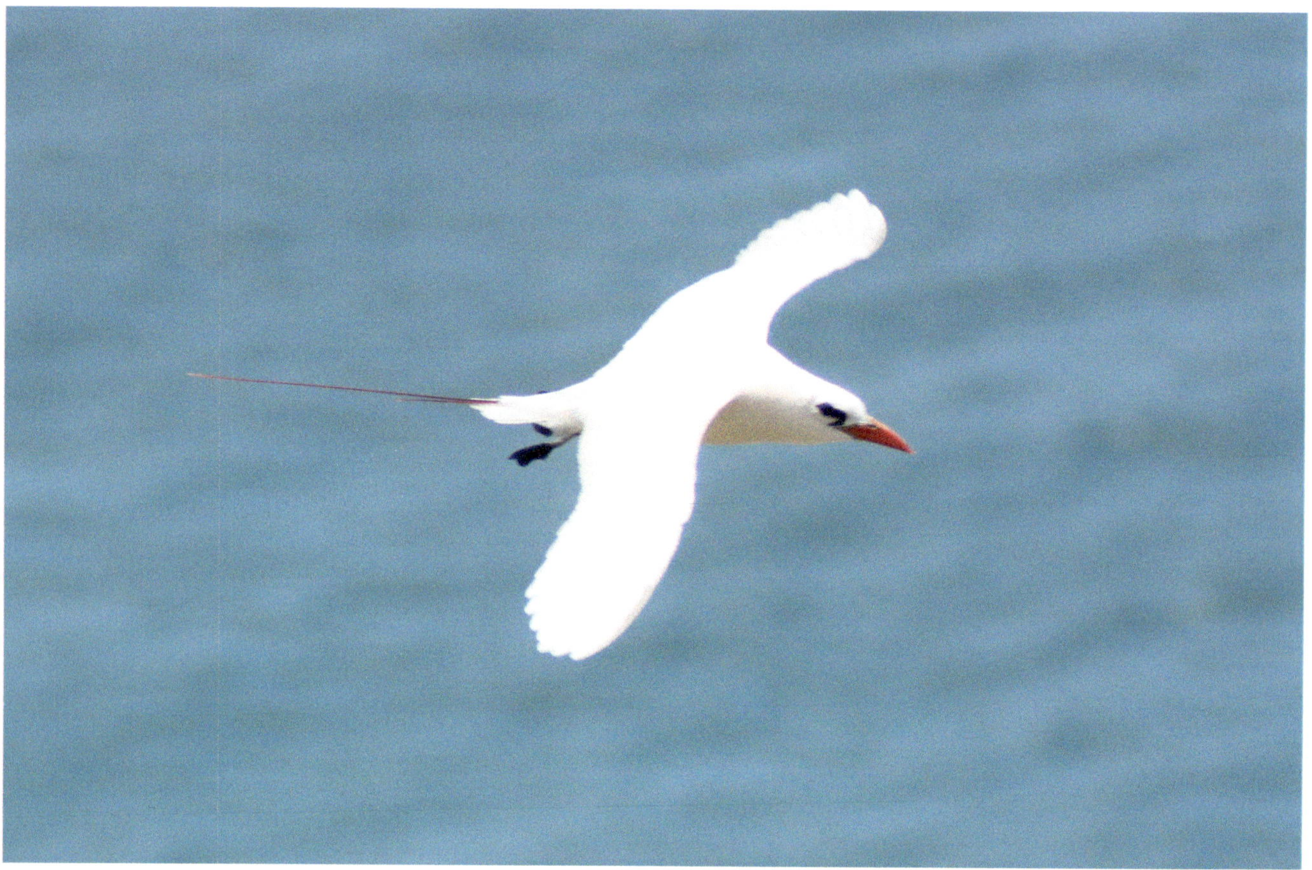

© Jean Cheadle

Dr Christopher Cadbury, whose father was the creator of the Cadbury squiggle that we all know from bars of chocolate, purchased Aride in the 1970s to safeguard it for wildlife, which included the rare red-tailed tropicbird. With the desire and intention for Aride to be under the management of the local people of Seychelles, the Cadbury's ultimately handed over Aride to a young Seychelles' non-governmental organisation, the Island Conservation Society, who were to be our future employers.

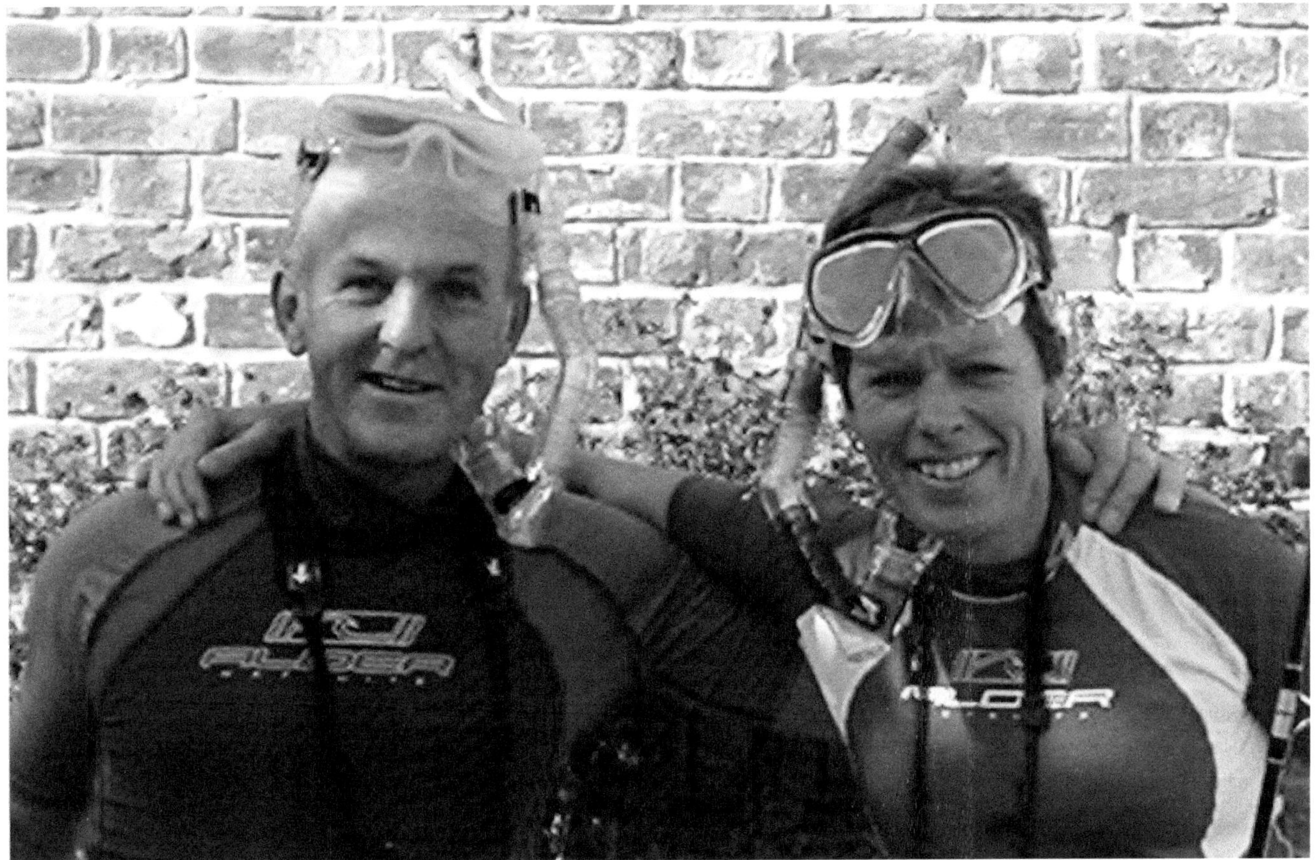

© Kate Wright

I'm still not quite sure how, but we managed to get the Aride positions in March, ready to start in November. The seven months that followed were a rollercoaster of emotion, packed with nervous excitement, as Melv and I prepared to embark on the most adventurous journey either of us had ever chosen. We prepared rigorously; it was like we were training for the London Marathon, but without the exercise!

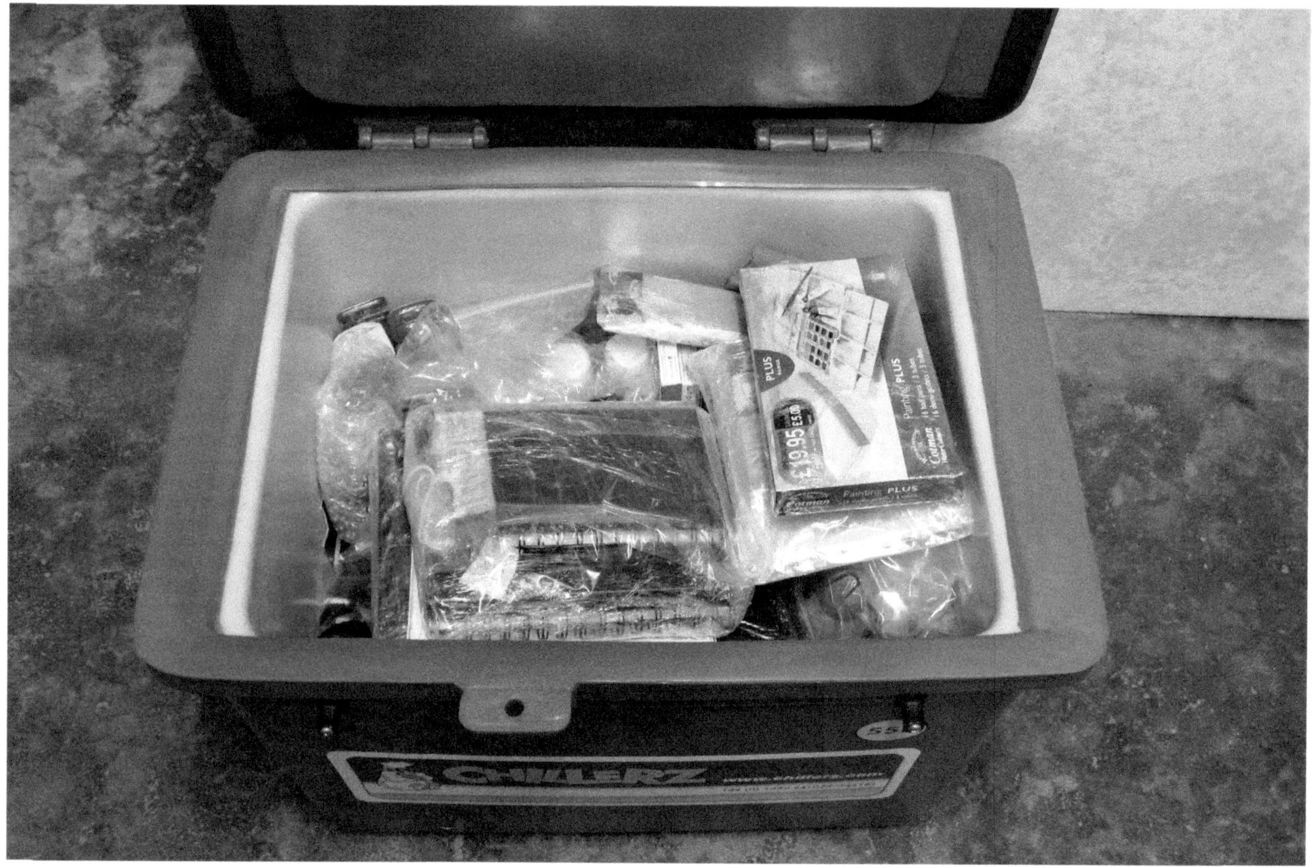

There was an opportunity to ship out a crate, which would meet us there, providing a chance to send out a few home comforts. About the size of a coffin, our crate was filled with a carefully collated two-year survival kit: pillows, towels, a ukulele, enough fishing gear to feed a family of ten for two years, batteries, art materials, toothpaste, Tupperware and tampons.

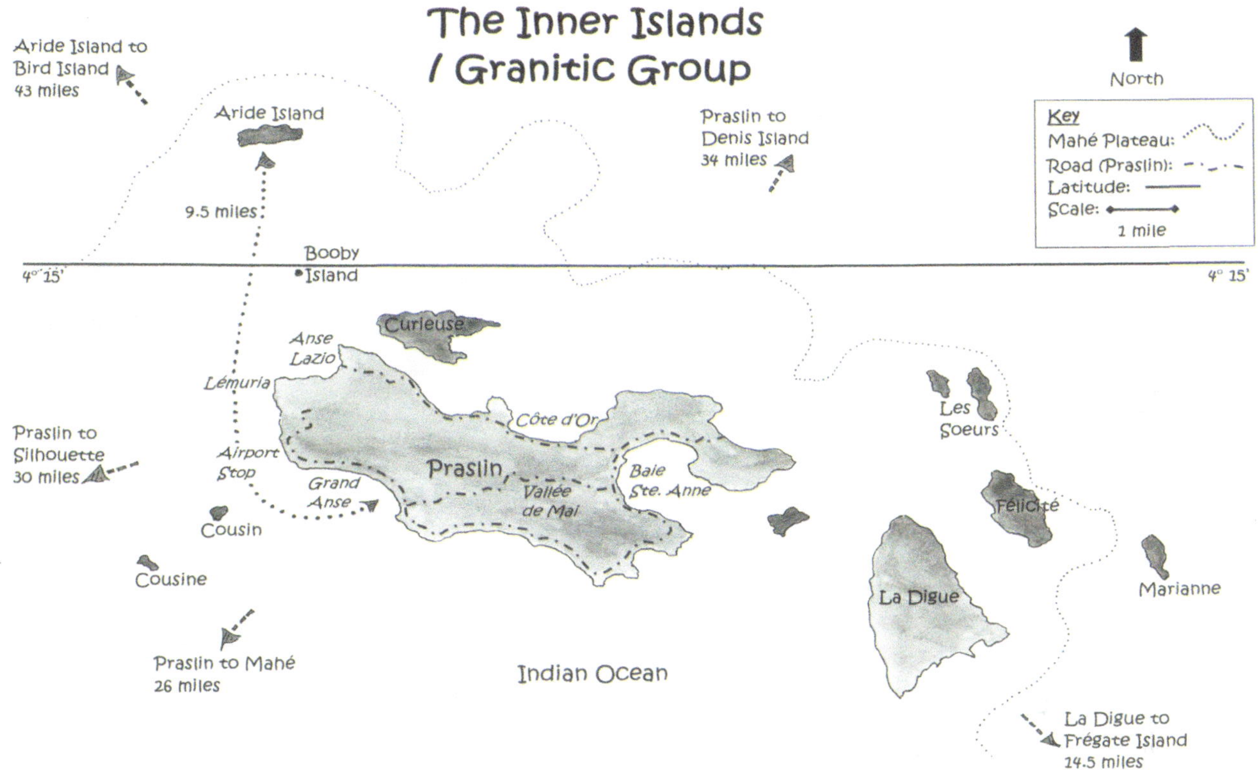


Aride is in the most northern of the Seychelles' granitic group of islands, situated six nautical miles off Praslin and forty nautical miles from Mahé, the home of the capital city Victoria.

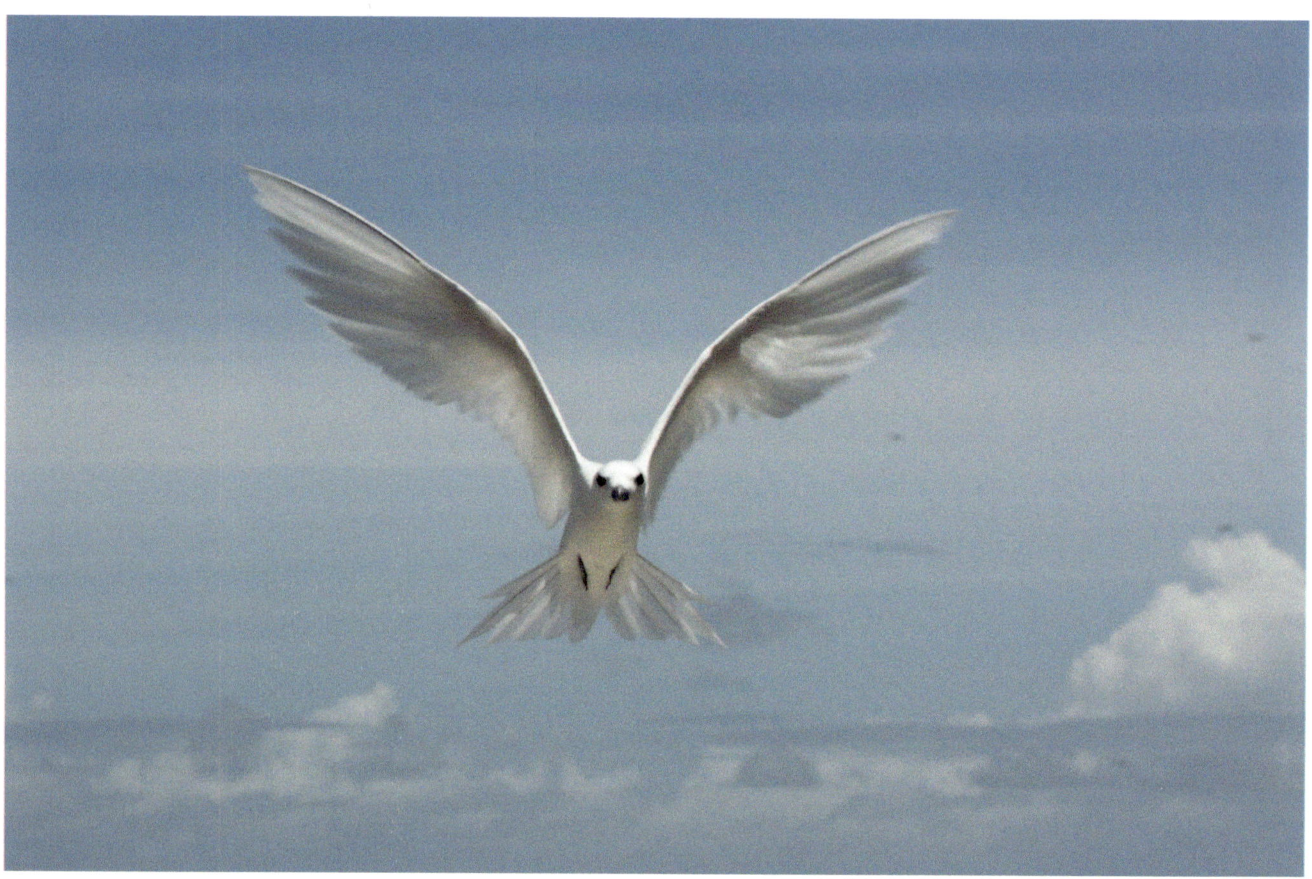

*© Jean Cheadle*

The island remains a special place where fairy terns hover around your head, shearwaters wail under the cover of darkness and Seychelles magpie robins join you for breakfast.

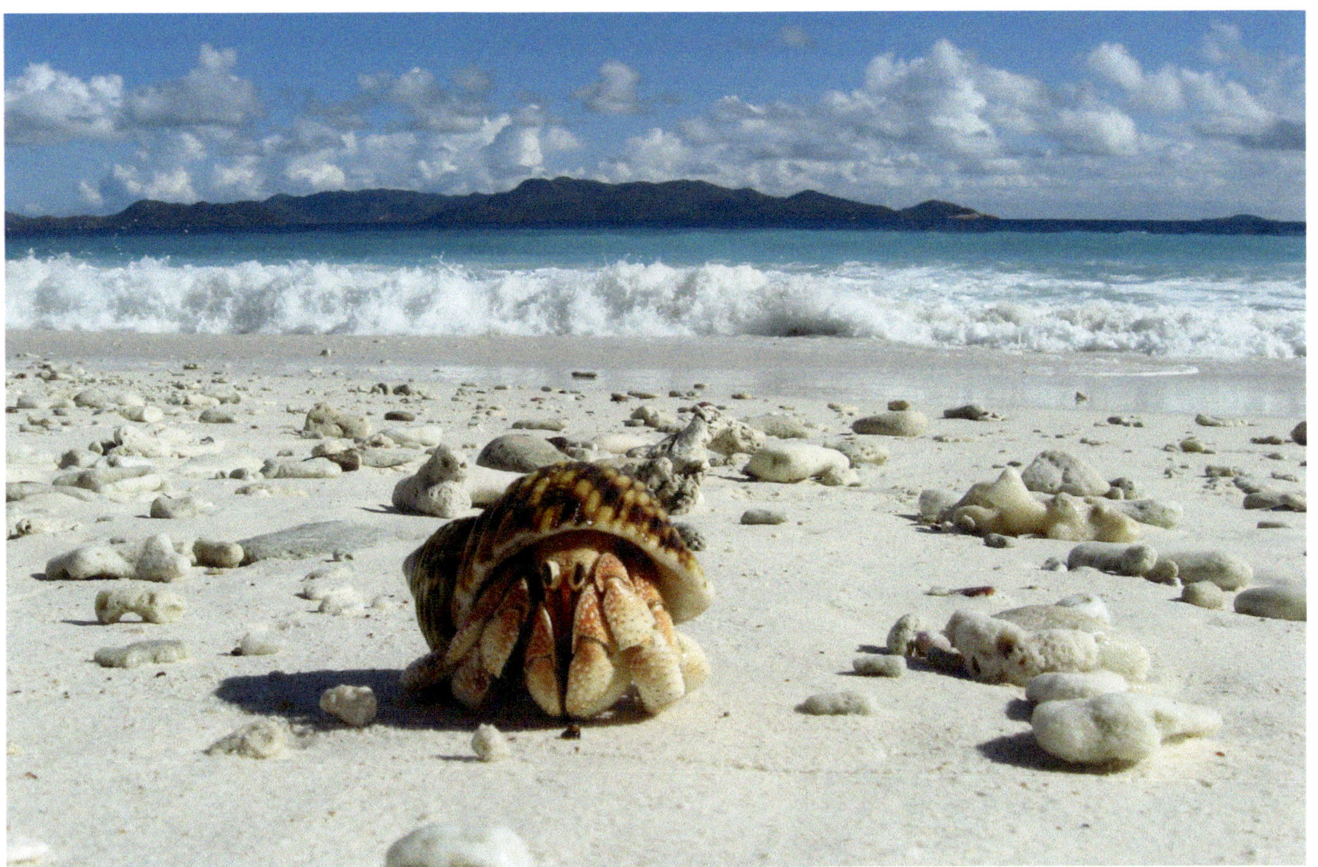

*© Chloe Prehn-Arnold*

Aride's south-facing beach provides egg-laying sites for green and hawksbill turtles, the sand-covered ground is crawling with crabs, and it is home to the world's highest density of skinks (a type of lizard), with over one per square metre. A nature lover's dream, and we had the chance to spend two years there.

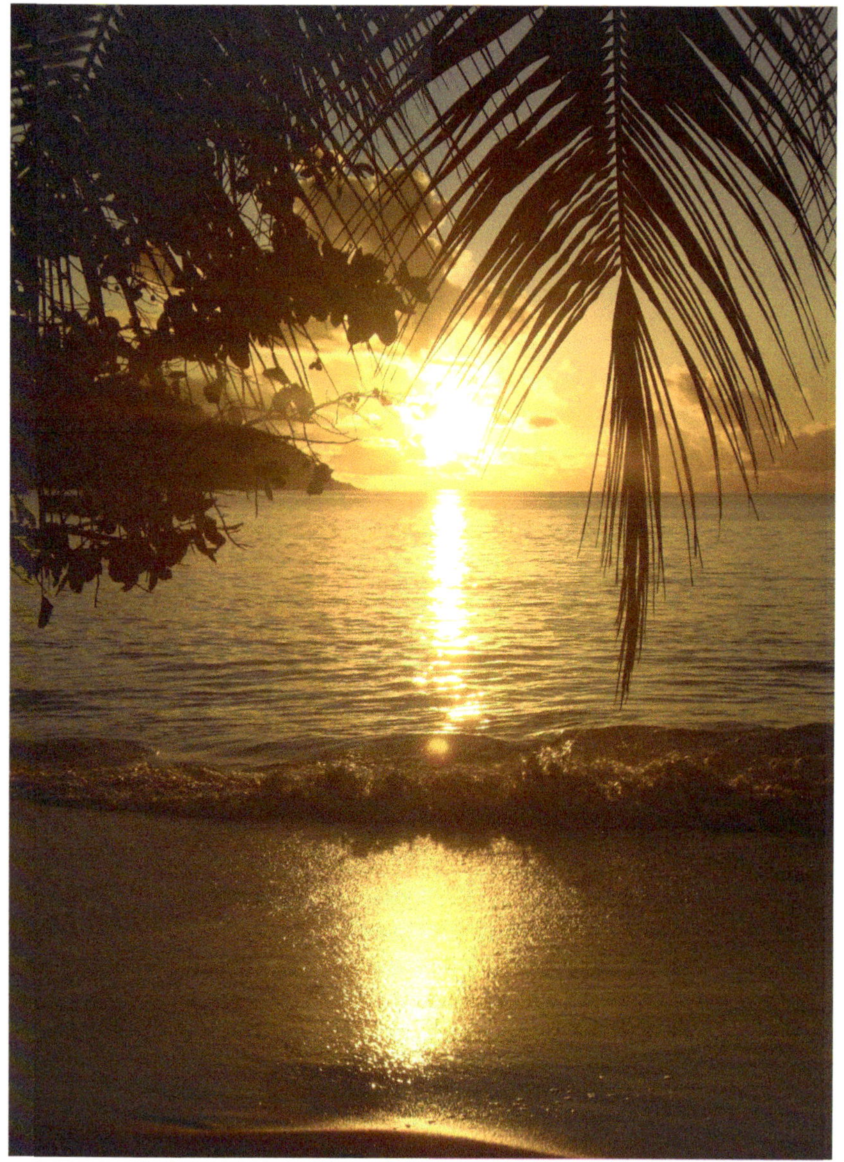

© *Chloe Prehn-Arnold*

Our journey to Aride was busy and intense. It began with flying into Mahé, the main island, where we spent two days dealing with all the paperwork, getting residency cards, having medicals and opening bank accounts. We then flew across to Praslin, which would be our closest main island, where we were shown the ropes for dealing with money, shopping, and getting supplies. It all felt rather tortuous and we secretly took any opportunity to gain a glimpse of Aride on the horizon, but to no avail. We had to patiently wait for what lay in store.

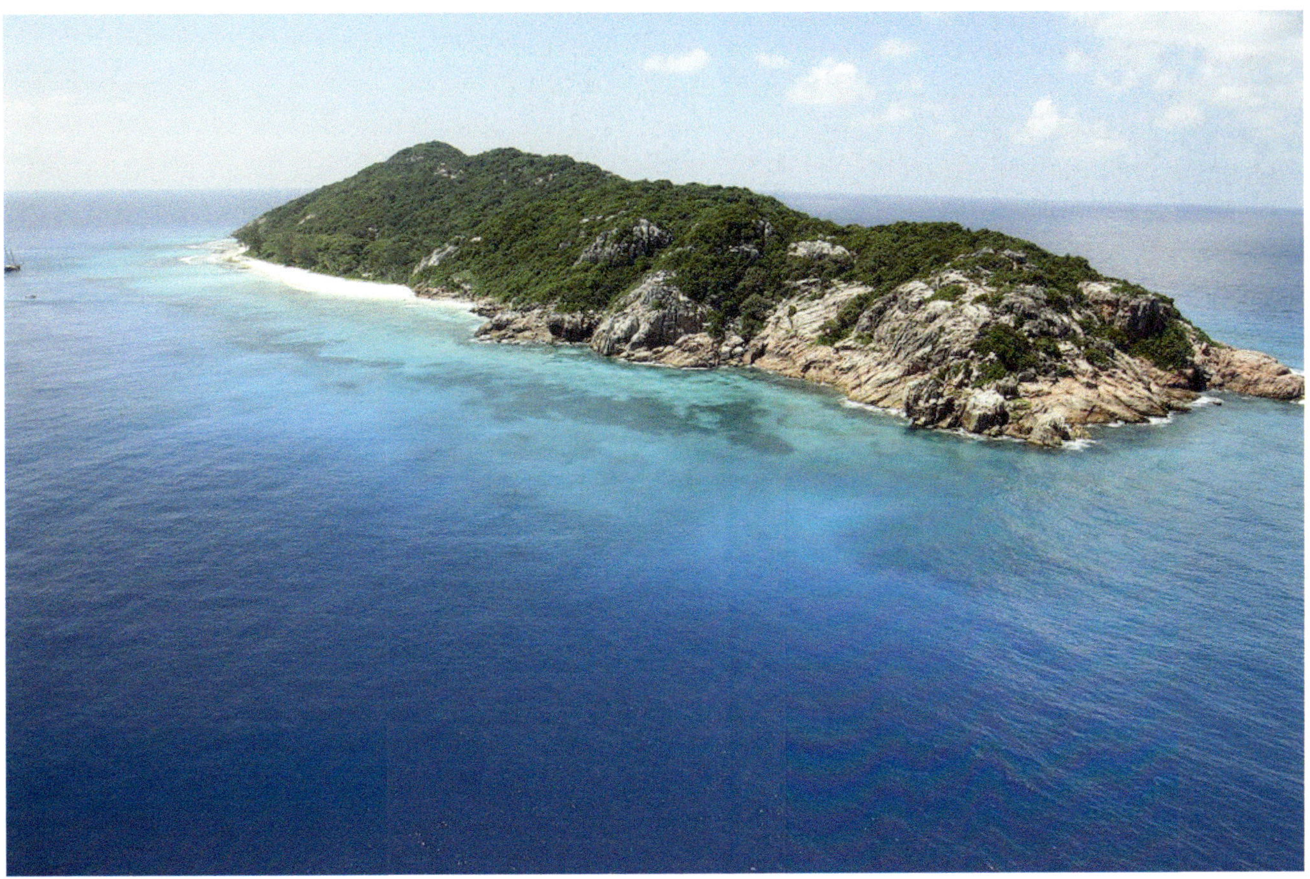

*© Colin Bell*

Finally, we boarded the boat to make the forty-minute journey from Praslin to Aride, and as we powered past the northwest shores of the mainland we were rewarded by our first view of our long-awaited destination. The Indian Ocean seemed to welcome us as we glided effortlessly over the clear, calm, azure blue water to our new home.

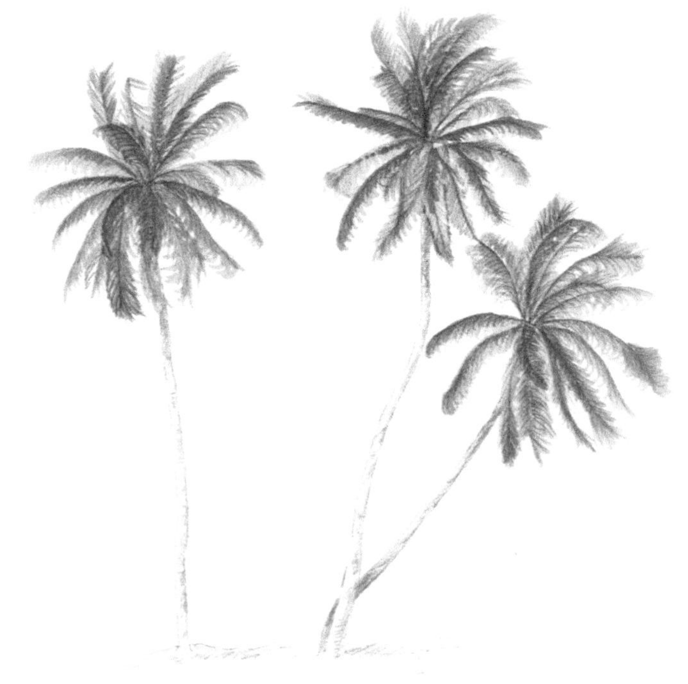



# Chapter 2

## Showering in Death Water

'The day-to-day life on Aride is so different to back home,' Melv wrote in one of our first blog posts, 'which you may well think is bloody obvious: Somerset Levels to tropical island, duh! Of course, we knew it would be different, but although we had researched the jobs in great depth for some months before our departure, there are some things you only find out by actually experiencing them.'

# Aride Island

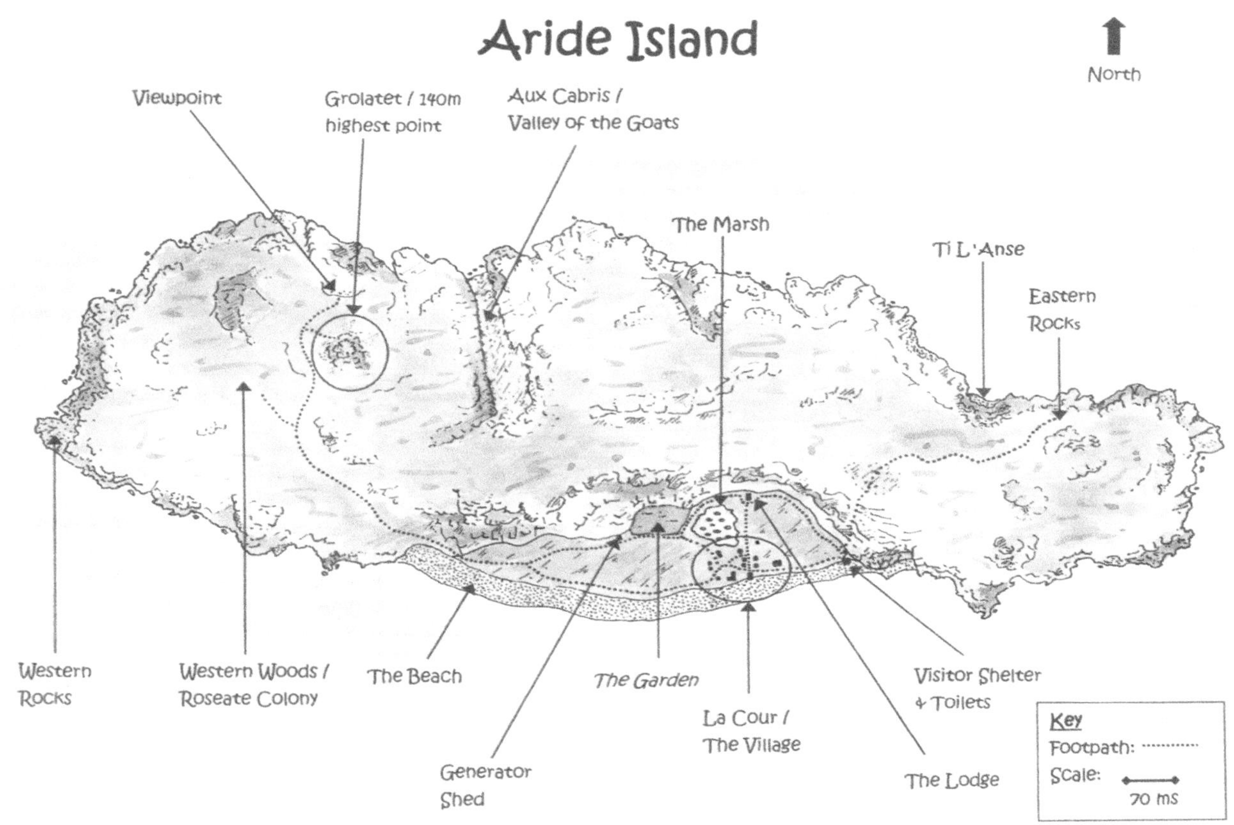



Approximately one mile long (east to west) by half a mile wide (north to south), Aride is a small, linear, densely wooded granitic outcrop in the middle of the Indian Ocean. The island is split into three distinct areas, or four if you count the sea alongside the beach, plateau and hill, and with a total island area of just sixty-eight hectares (equivalent to one hundred and twenty-six football pitches), it is dwarfed by the vast expanse of water surrounding it.

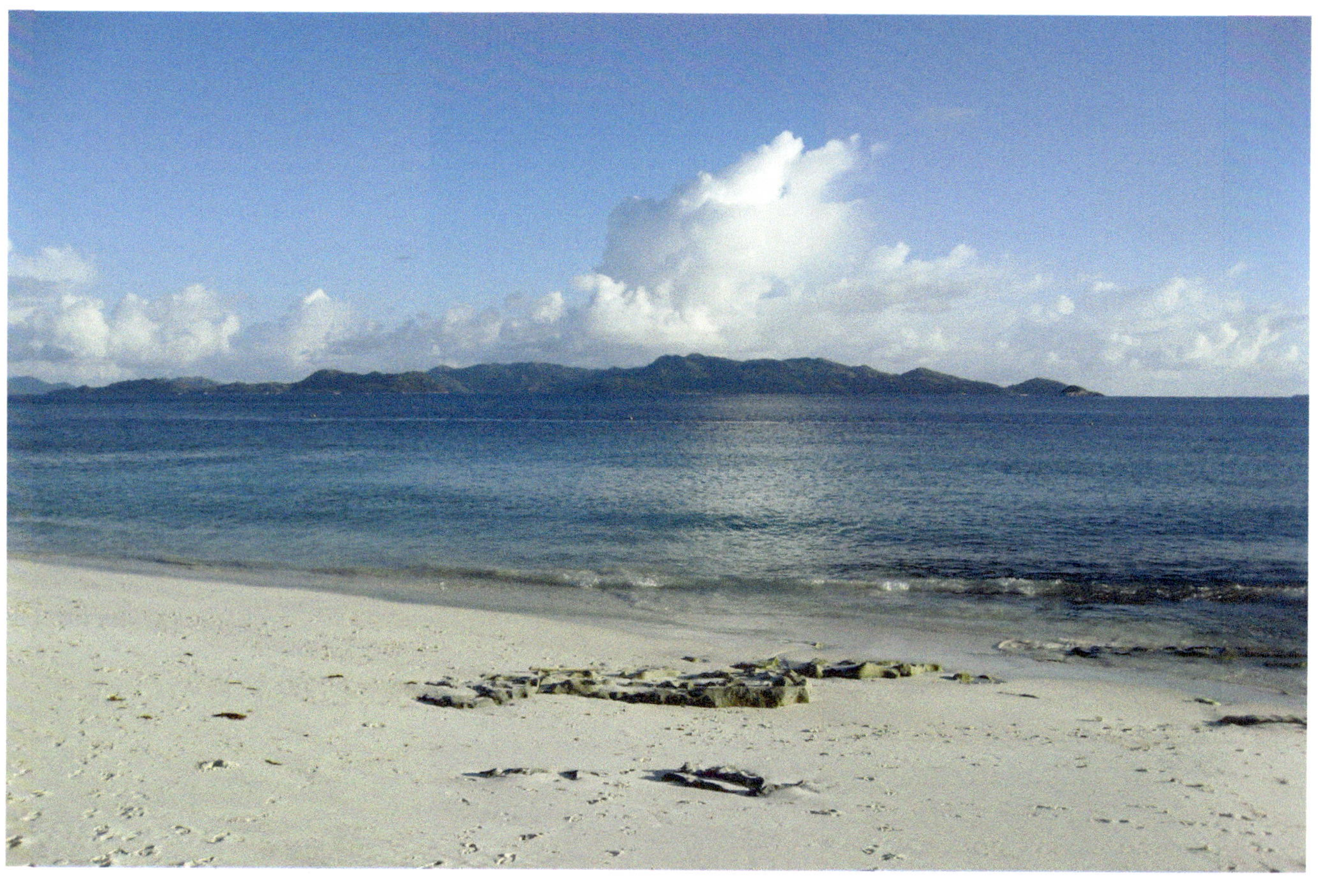

Looking out from Aride's beach, Praslin is approximately six nautical miles away and the main landmark. It changes colour and mood depending on the weather; clouds hang over it, casting it in shadow, or blue skies illuminate it, highlighting its gentle, green undulating topography.

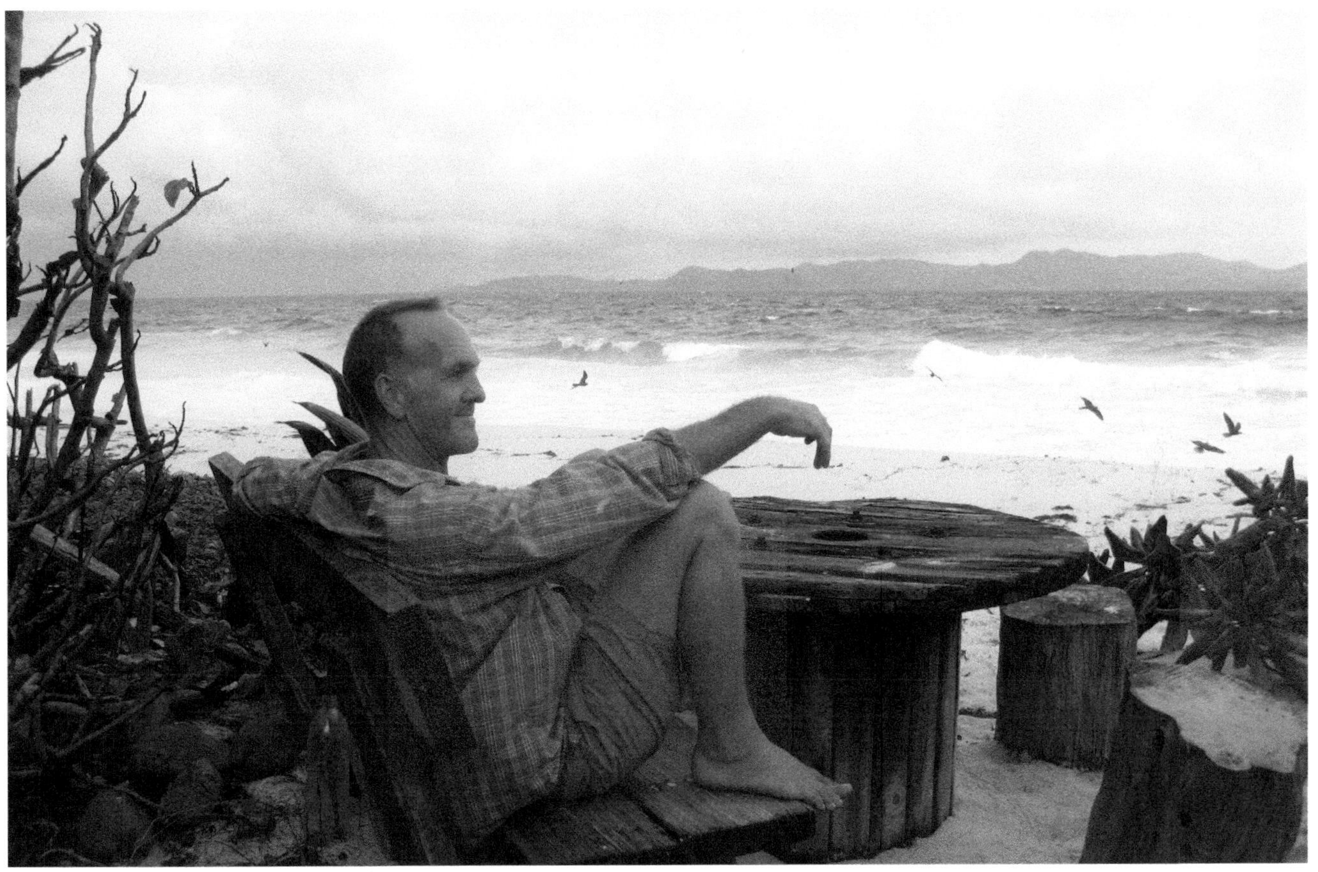

To avoid the mosquitoes and to take in the evening, we would sit on what felt like our own private section of beach crest. It didn't matter that our seating facility was not quite as luxurious as the location warranted. Comprising a rickety wooden bench and a table fashioned from a large cable reel, perfect to support a much needed but rather shabby cotton umbrella, it still felt fit for purpose.

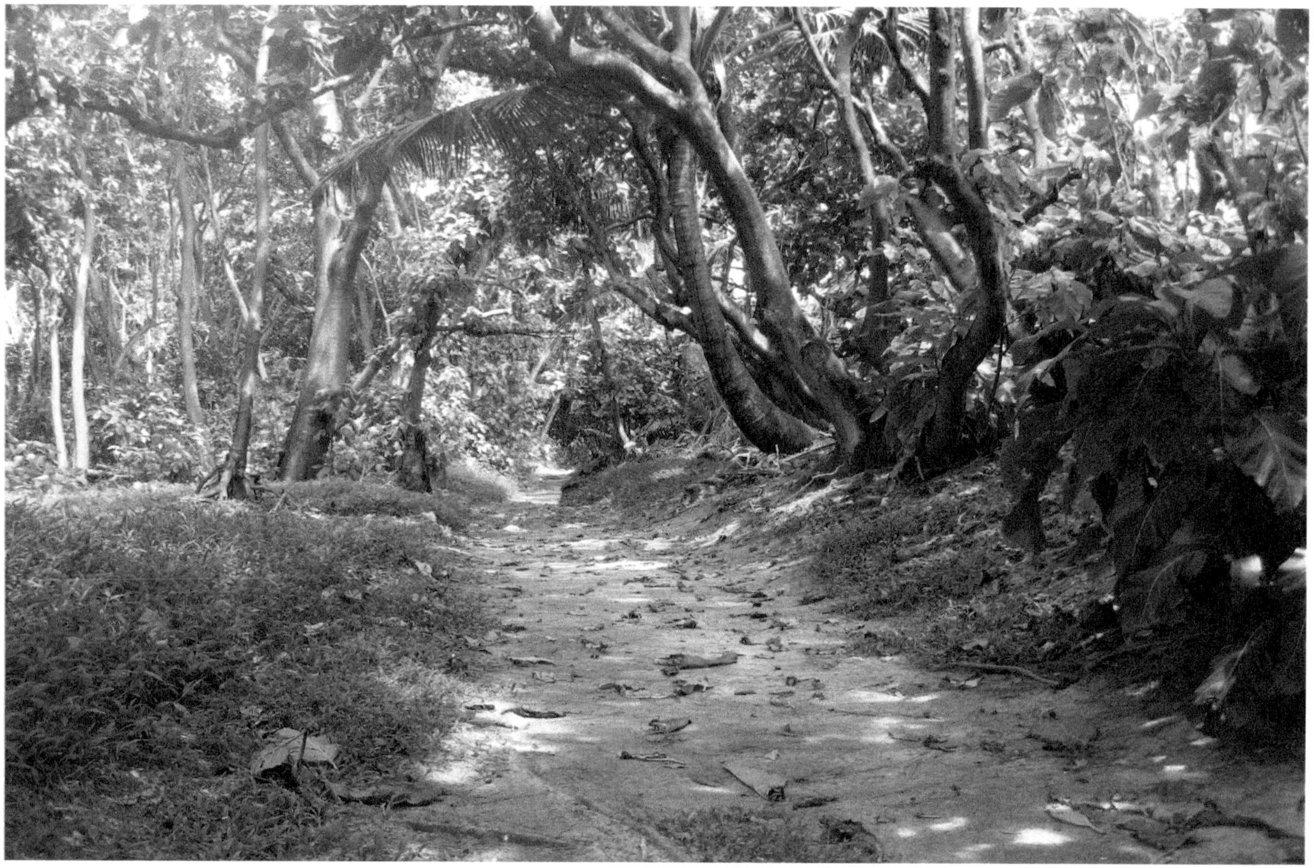

The plateau runs along the length of the beach crest, dominated by woodland but intersected by a network of sandy paths used as visitor trails and access routes. It is the focal point for all human activity and where the houses, the visitors' centre and the water well are situated.

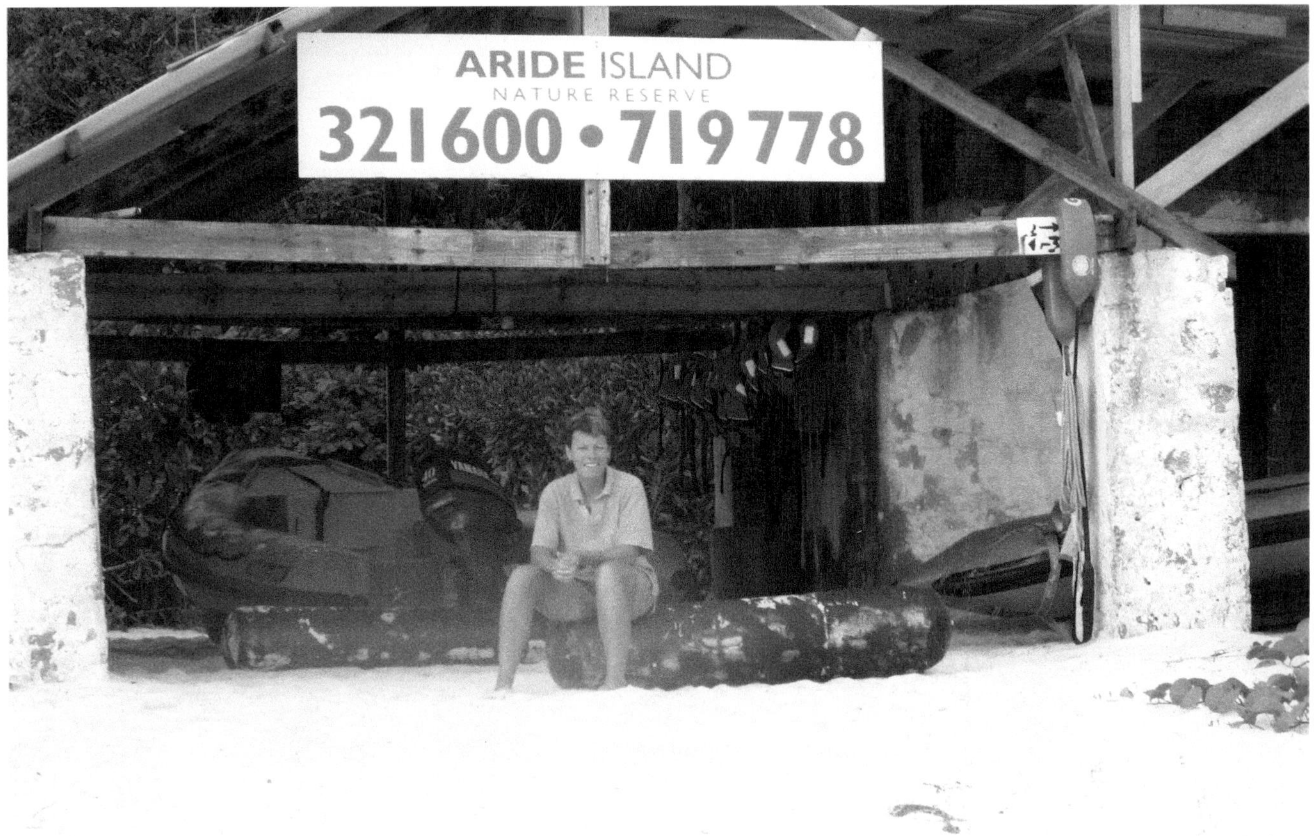


*© Melvyn Yeandle*

The boatshed on the beach was the gateway to the island. During our time there, the building was in a very bad state of repair, and comprised of a small workshop, rat-proof room and two lean-to shelters, supported by pillars that held up the corrugated tin roof, which housed two 12ft inflatable boats.

# La Cour / The Village

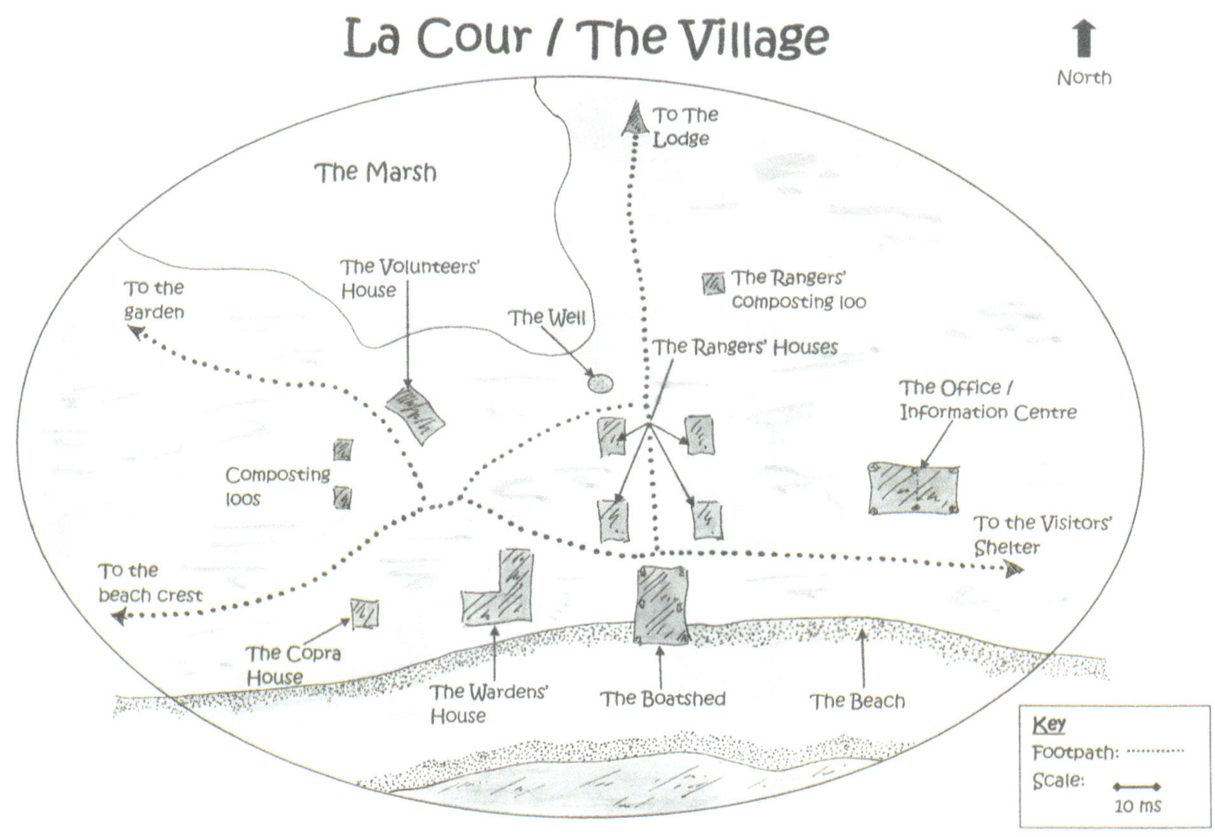


An open-ended building, the back entrance of the boatshed led to the main village area, or 'La Cour' (French for 'the courtyard') as it was known. Here, there were four rangers' houses, all detached, each with two bedrooms, a kitchen, a shower room and veranda. The open area in the middle of the collection of houses, onto which each veranda looked, was our main meeting place, where we gathered for morning meetings, BBQ's and general get-togethers.

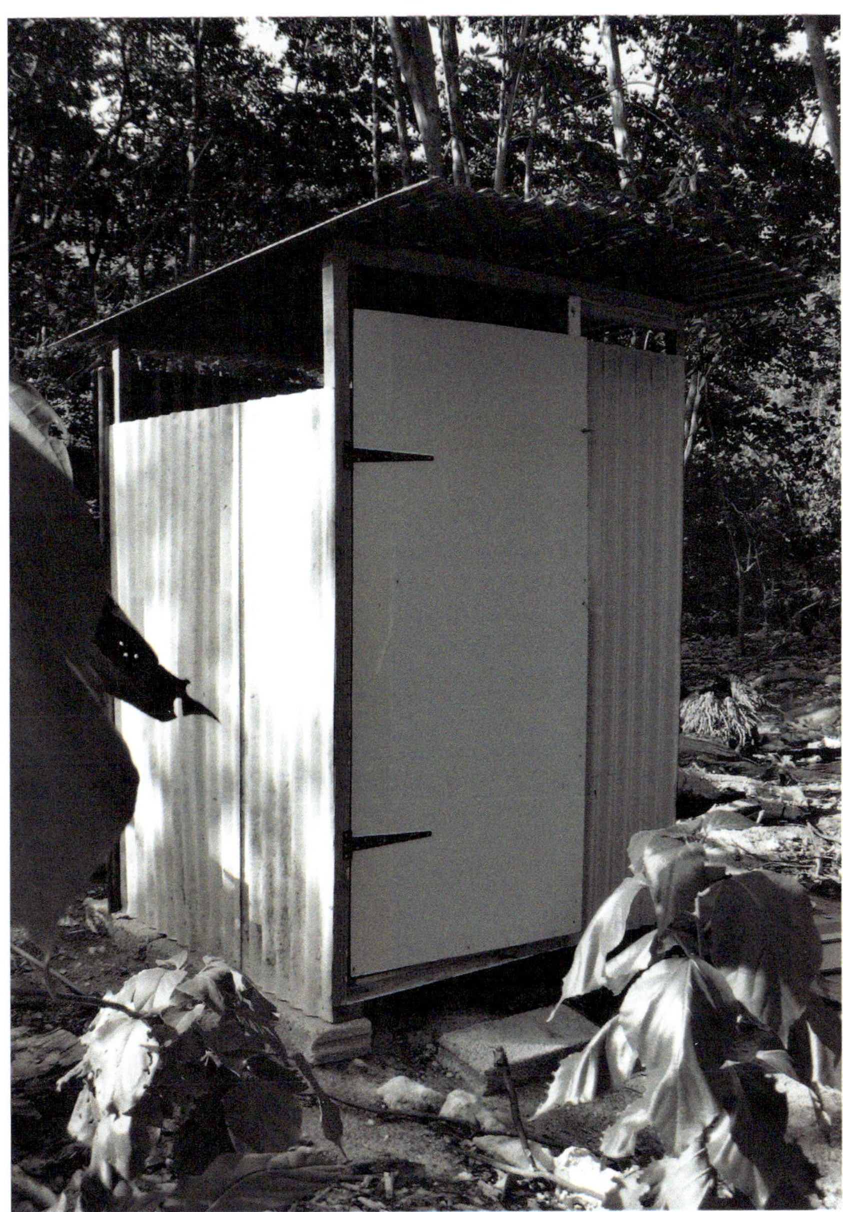

*New composting loo*

Listening to the dawn chorus from the toilet was a great way to start the day. The small tin shacks that surrounded the long drops were built for ventilation, which meant if air could get in and out, so too could sound. There was something very special and memorable about sitting, pants down, with just a sheet of corrugated iron between me and the outside world, whilst I waited for the laxatives that mum and dad had sent through to work.

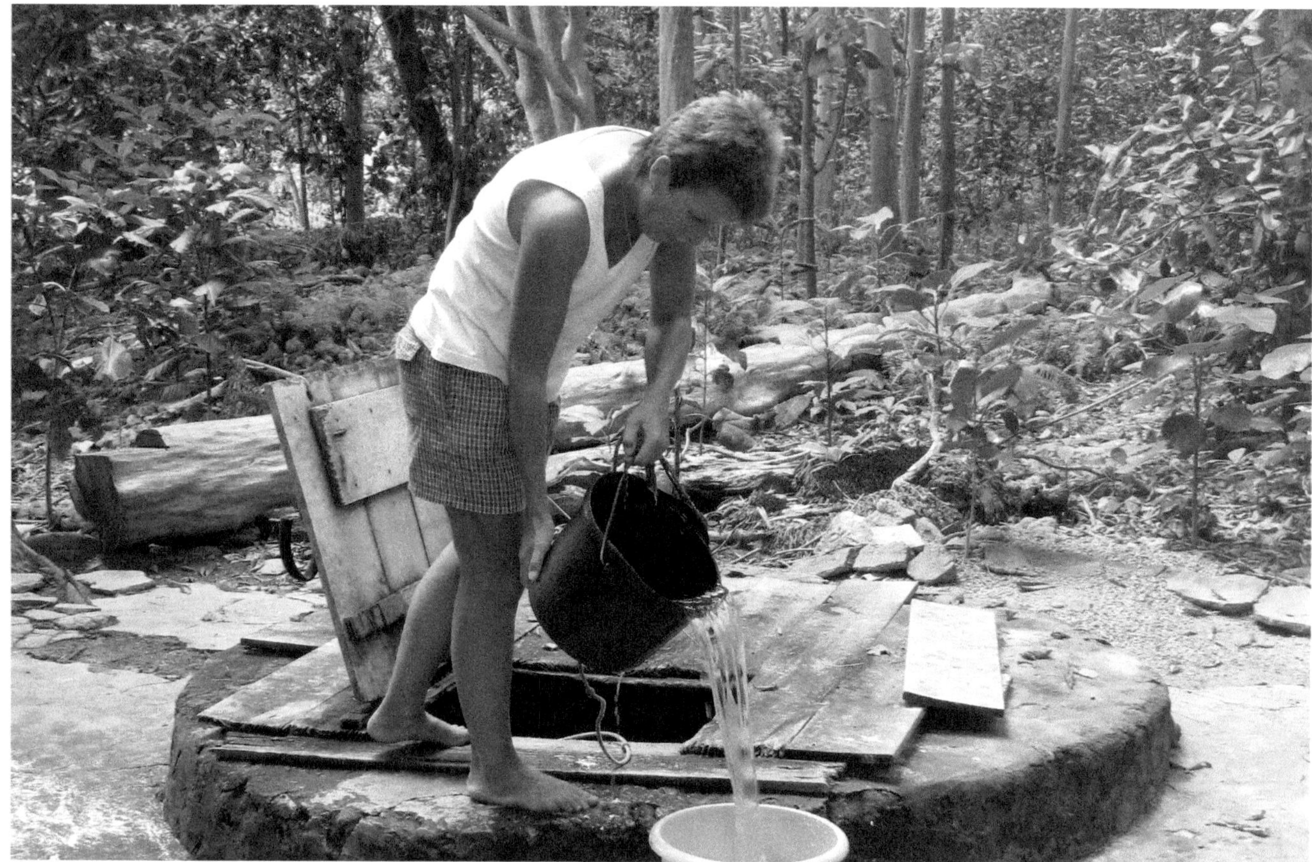

© *Melvyn Yeandle*

The well was a magical place for wildlife, much like an oasis to which all were attracted. The equivalent of the Aride laundrette, it was often the place where humans and wildlife mixed, which was a delight to see. All washing was done in large buckets, which we left our clothes to soak in during the heat of the day before going to the well to scrub and rinse them.

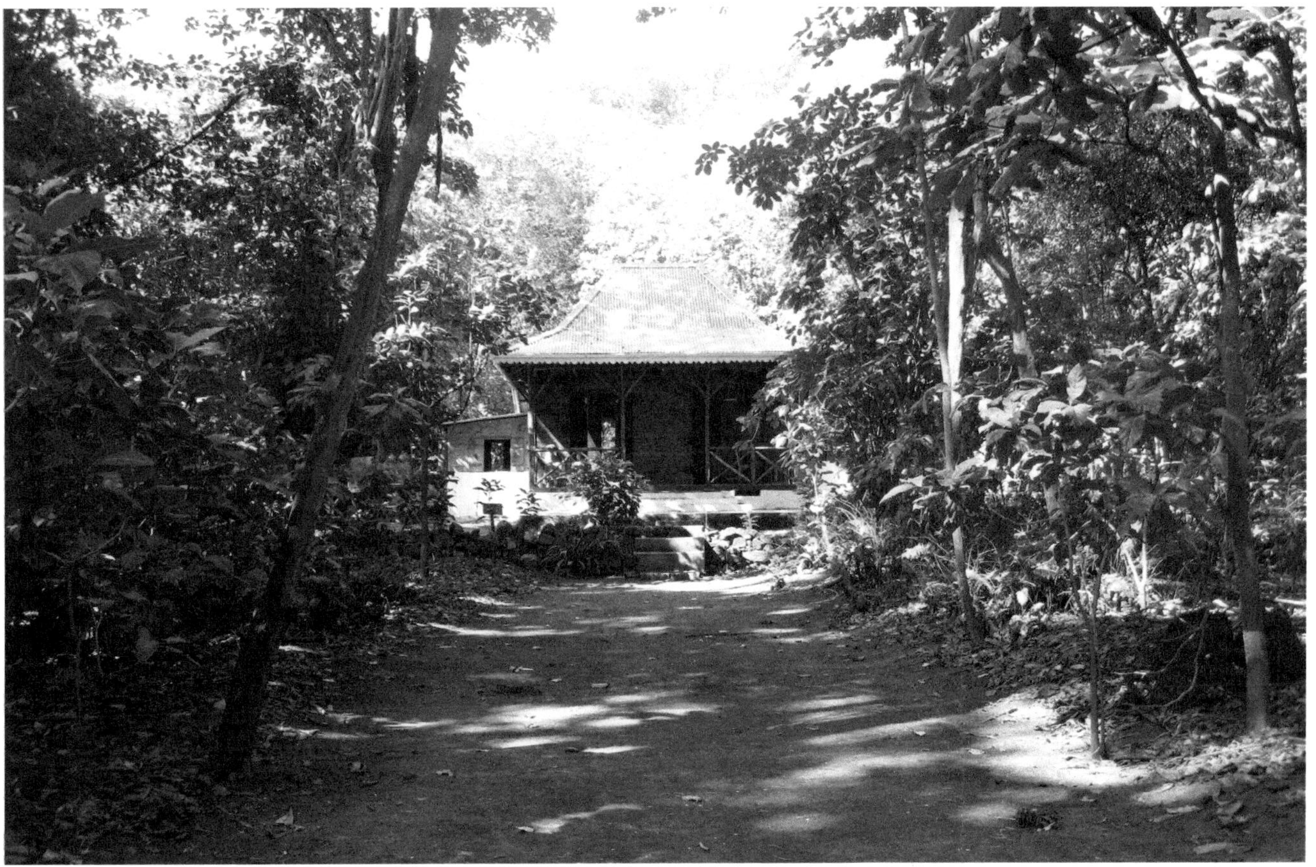

Leading from La Cour was a grand pathway through an avenue of trees to 'the lodge': the old coconut plantation lodge where the manager of the island once lived when Aride joined the coconut industry, processing coconuts into copra and oil to generate an income.

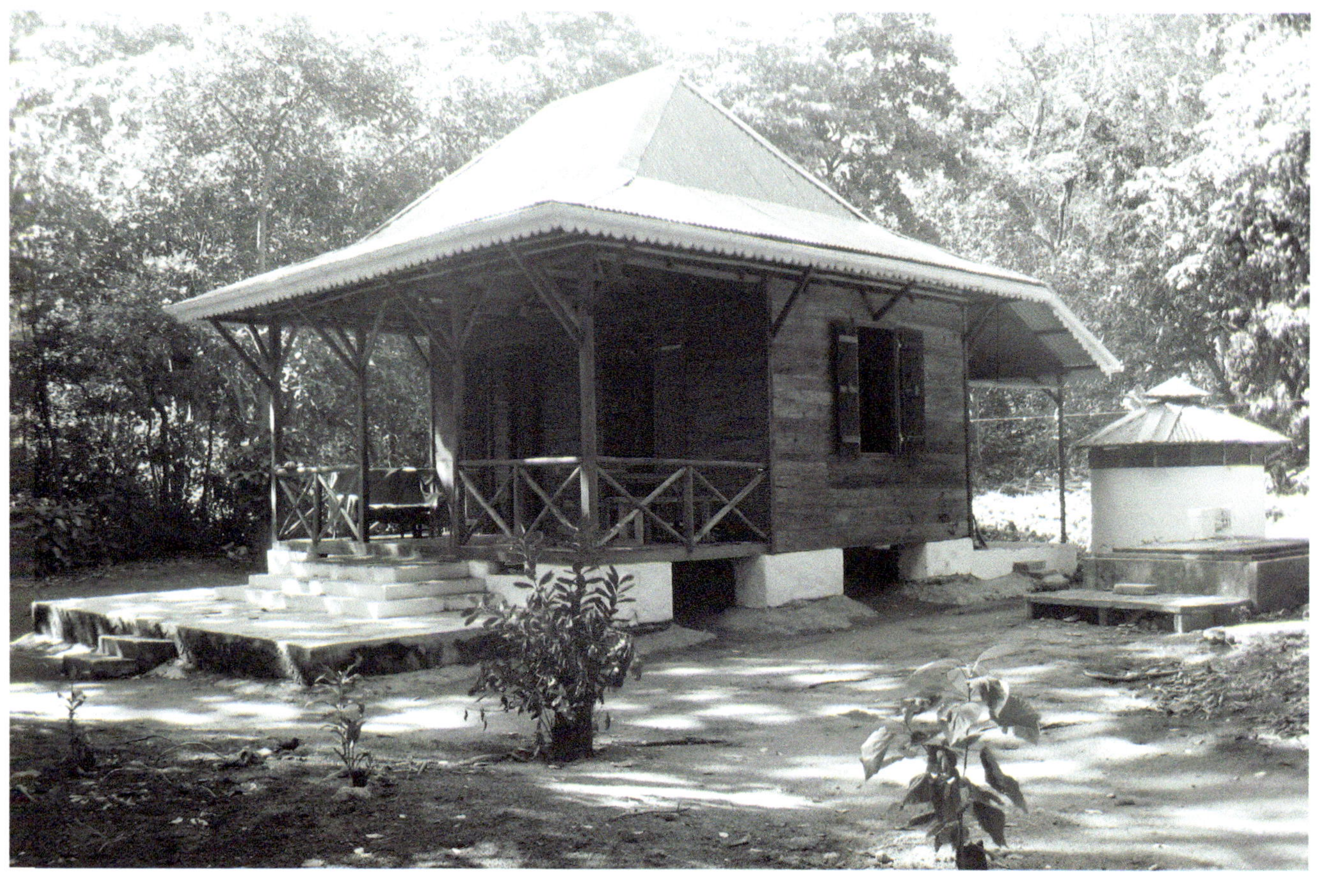

The lodge was the best accommodation on the island, with two bedrooms, its own kitchen and shower, a veranda at the front and back, no ceilings and a high roof, specially constructed for ventilation. Its only downside was its location; being set back from the main village and beach crest, it was a popular spot for mosquitos.

***Sprouting coconut on the beach crest***

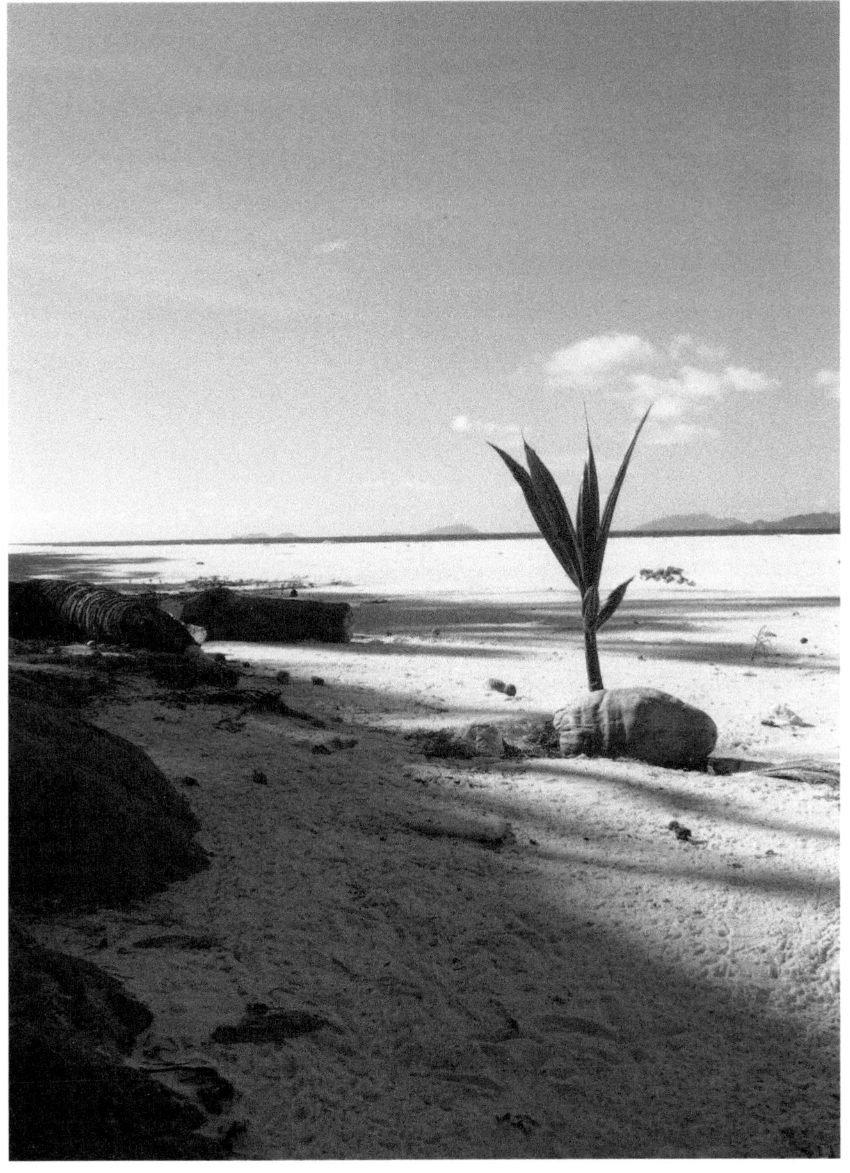

*© Chloe Prehn-Arnold*

The processing of coconuts became big business, both to produce virgin coconut oil from the fresh meat of the coconut and copra from the dried kernel, which was preserved through drying or smoking for future oil extraction. Although Aride succumbed to this practice in the 1920s and 1930s, the island did not, like many others, become a blanket coconut plantation from beach to mountaintop, due to the hostile nature of the hill.

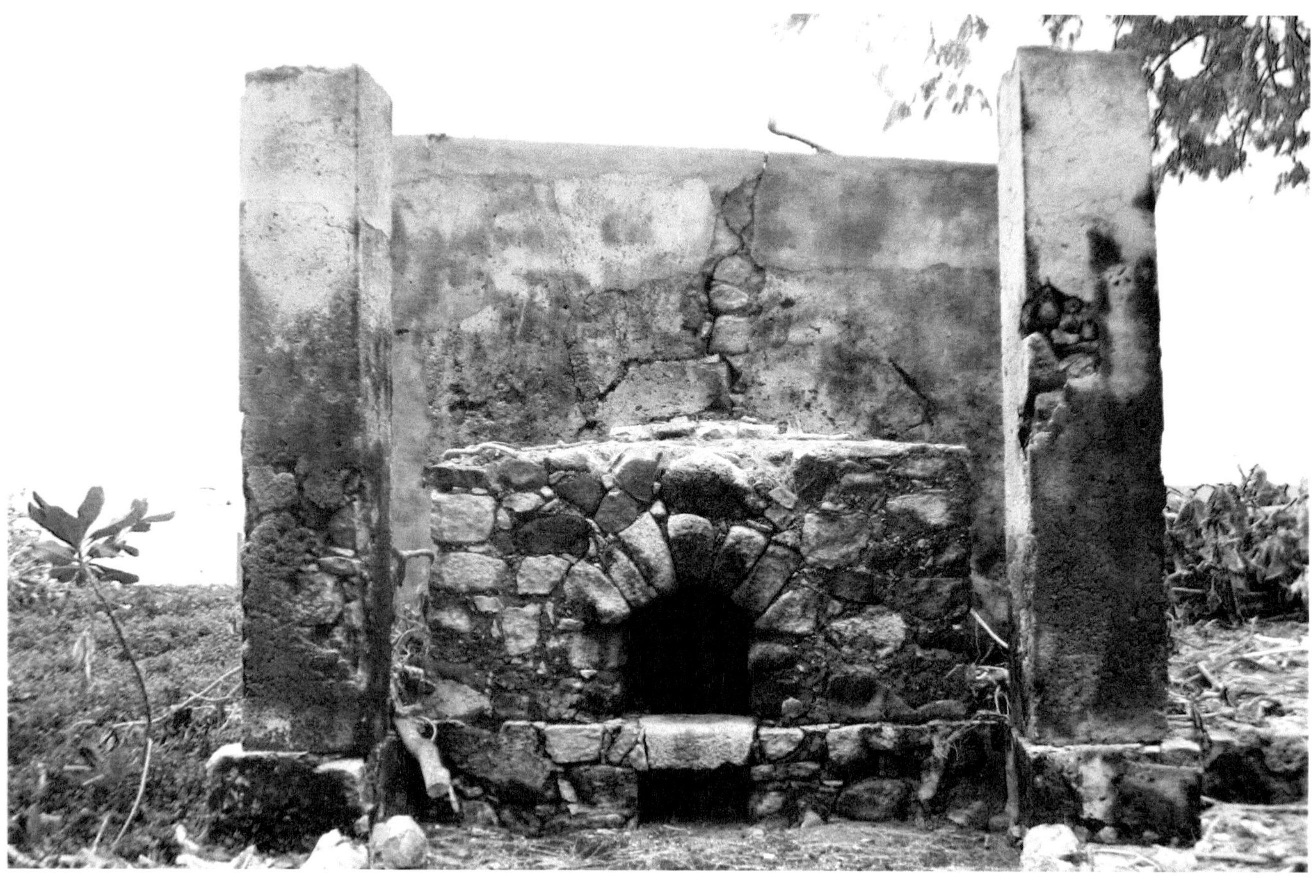

The copra house stood on the beach crest. Although a very shabby and rough little place, it had a certain charm and a significant story to tell about the history of the island. In the early 1900s, when Seychelles entered the age of the coconut, copra and coconut oil became the islands' major exports. What remains of the copra house displays an external stone oven on the northern face, perfectly shaped and in excellent condition. The oven would have been lit to provide heat to release the oil from the coconuts, evidence from which could still be seen upon the scorched stones.

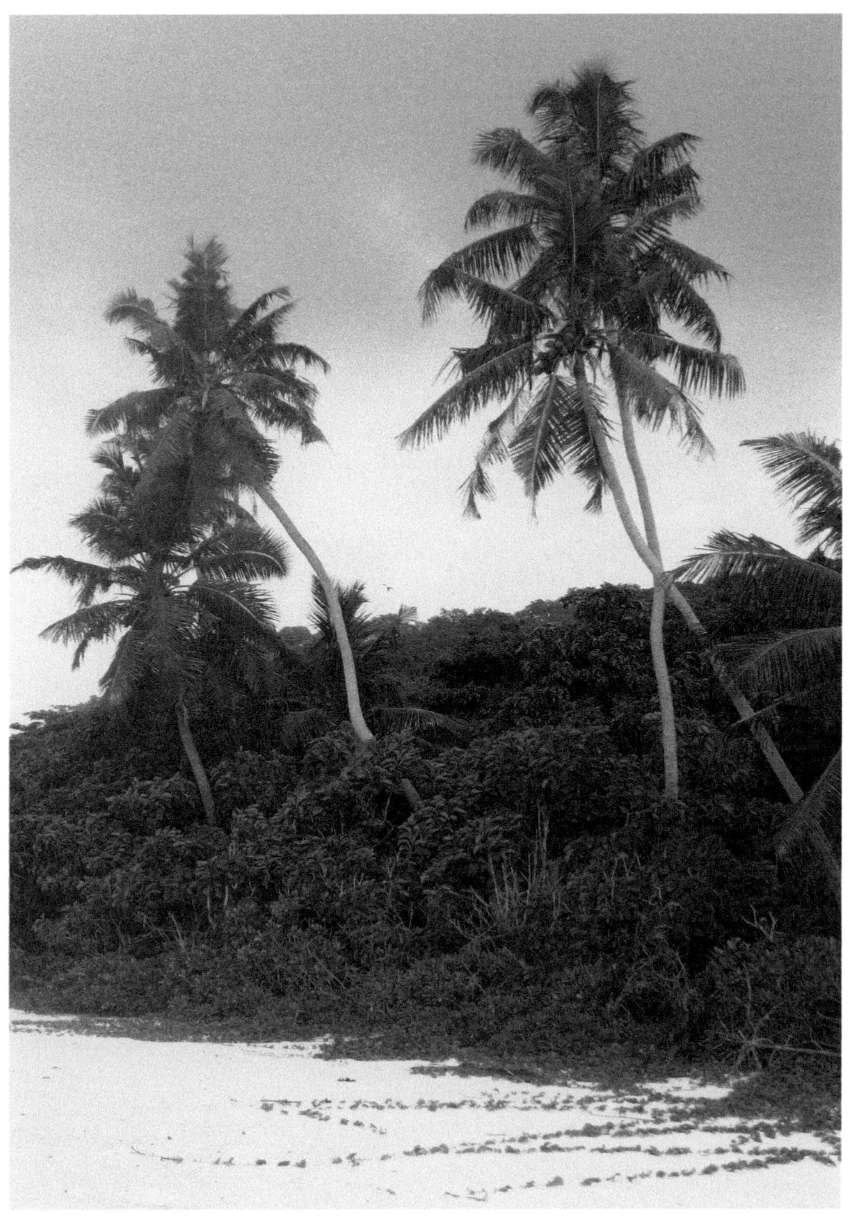

In the late 1800s, Aride was known as a barren place, and an island which suffered from the scorching rays of the sun. As a result, only the fertile, flat land of the plateau was able to accommodate the coconut palms, which were found growing amongst tropical fruits such as bananas, watermelons and pineapples.

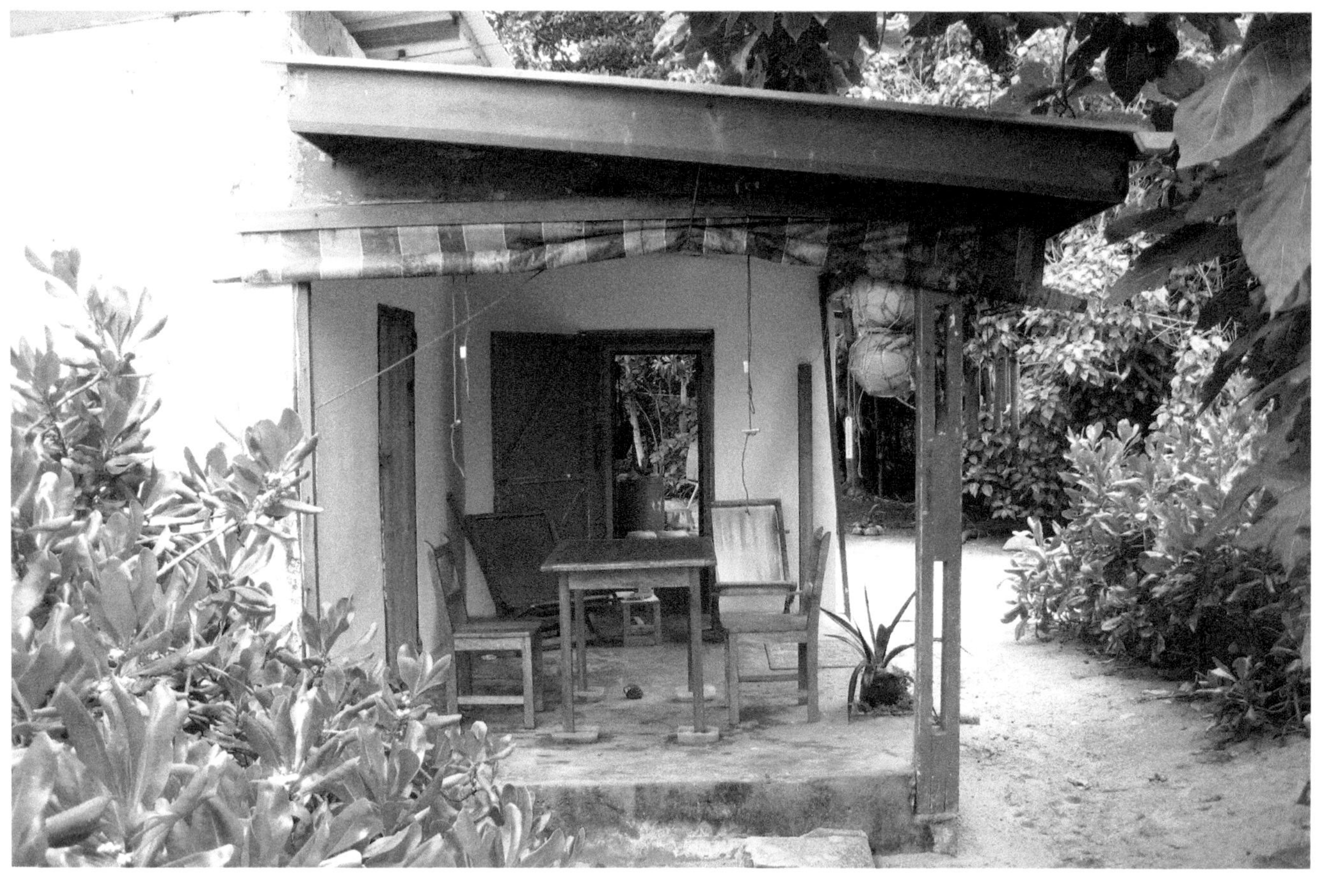

Following the path over a bridge to the west of La Cour is the house where Melv and I lived. The largest of all the concrete dwellings, it comprised a kitchen, bedroom, shower room, large central storage room, back office, workshop and two verandas.

***Our salubrious shower!***

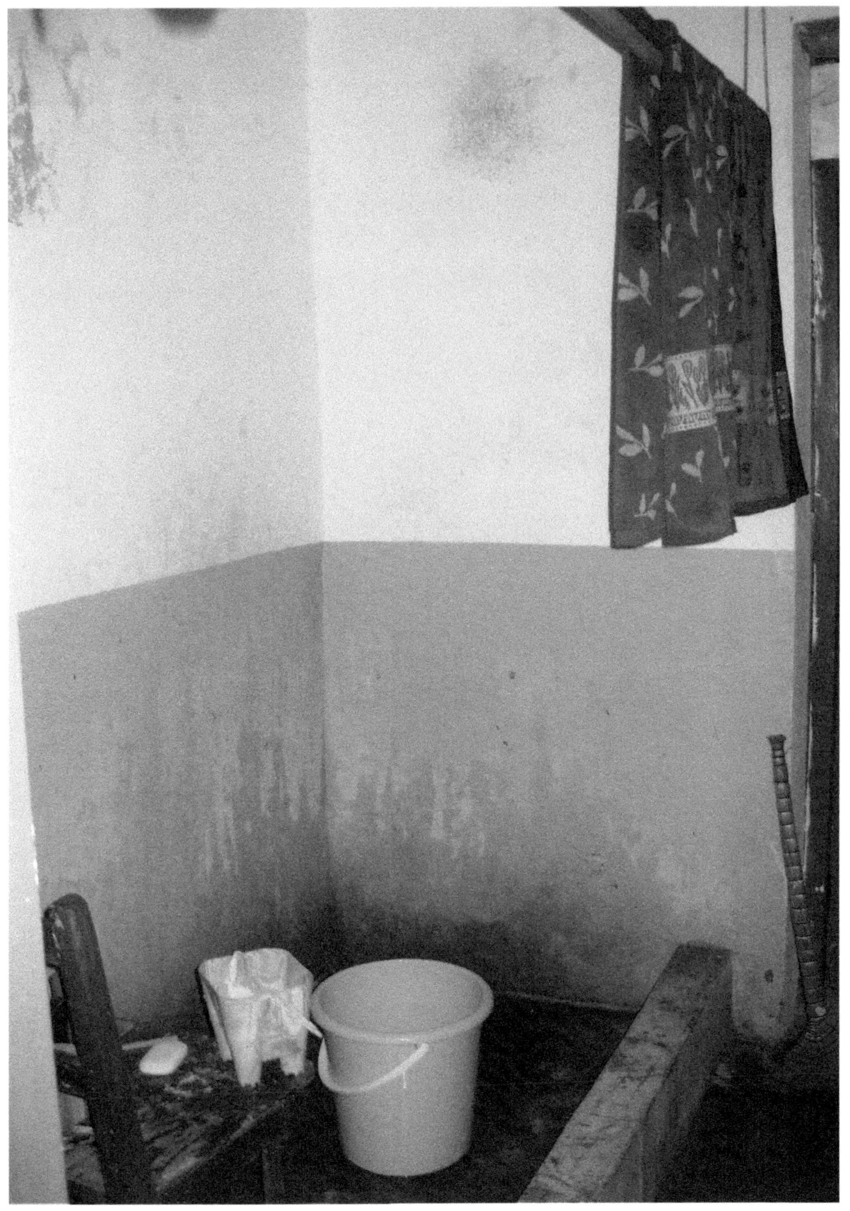

Just a room with a small concrete area to wash in, the shower was basically a bucket of water that one tipped over one's head, as James Cadbury described so beautifully at our interview. Having not been recently painted, it was rather grubby, and the concrete floor attracted sand. The room was dark, for though it had a window with glass louvers, which faced the beach, these grimed up regularly.

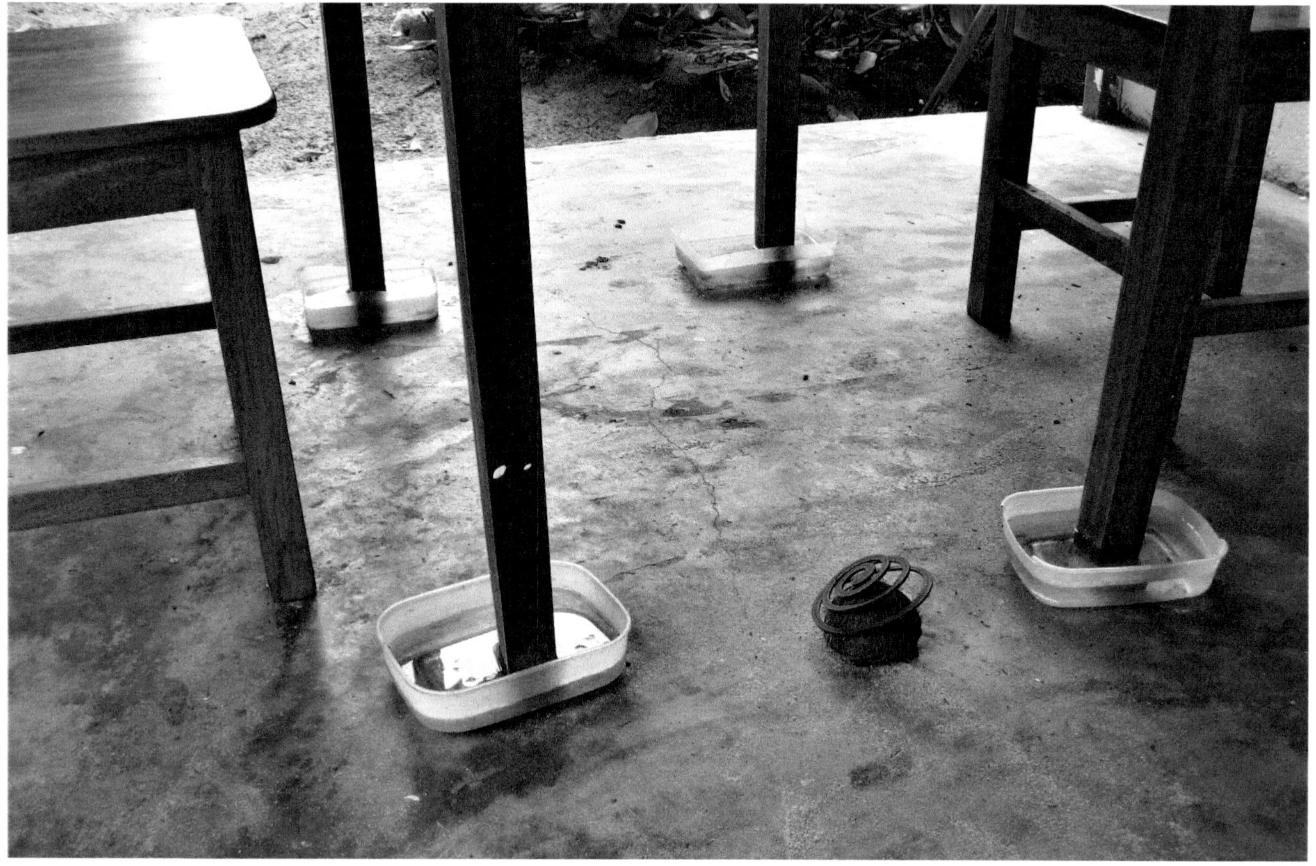

The house was certainly never our own; we shared it with a whole array of creatures, from ants to crabs, but neither of us were bothered by this. Ants were just part of everyday life, often drawn to the warmth of our bodies, and crabs scurried round our feet at night; so too did mice and skinks.

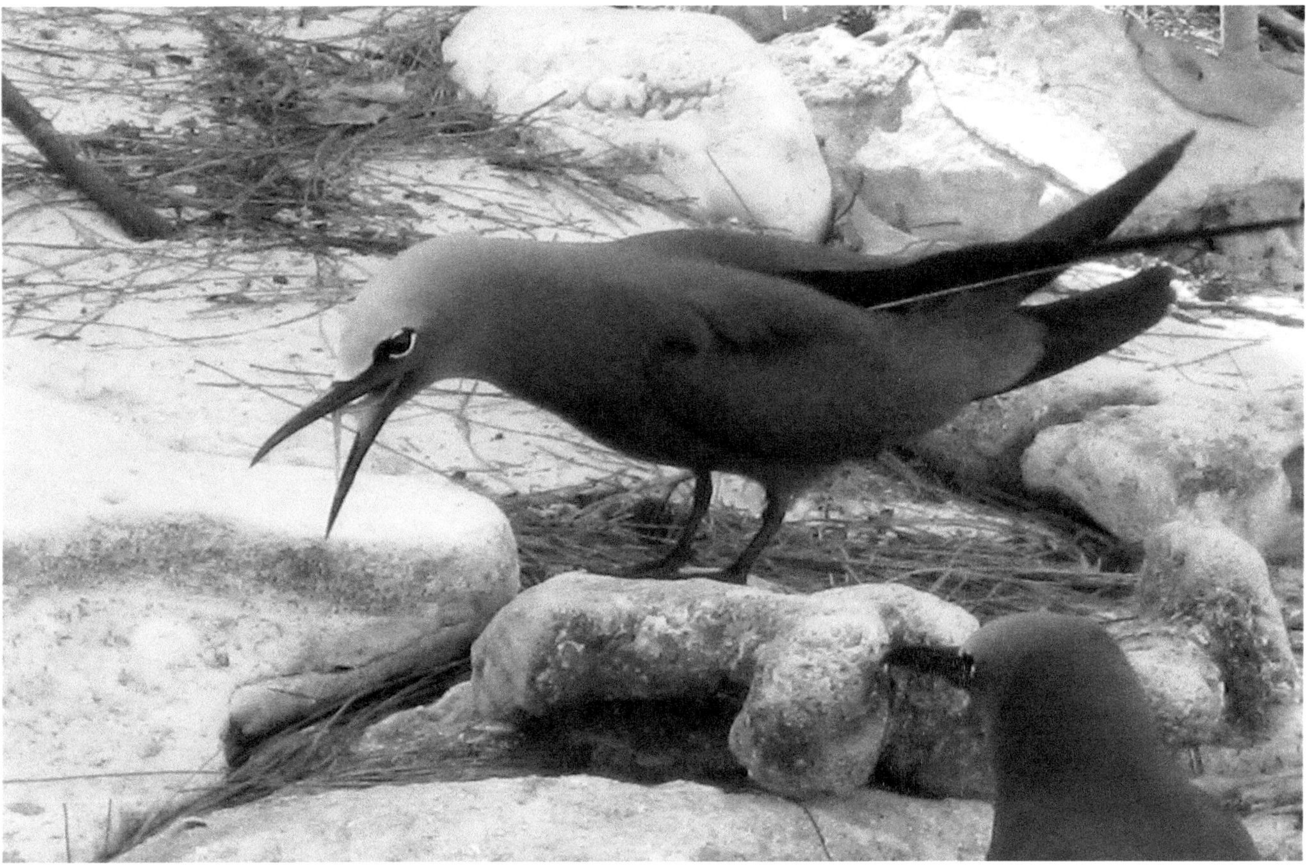

The provision of drinking water was a challenge. Unable to drink from the well, we collected rainwater off the roof, but the roof wasn't the cleanest place and attracted a variety of wildlife. It seemed particularly appealing to brown noddies, unless Melv could get there first, and on a number of occasions he found himself pitting his wits against a heavy-footed rogue individual determined to take up residency.

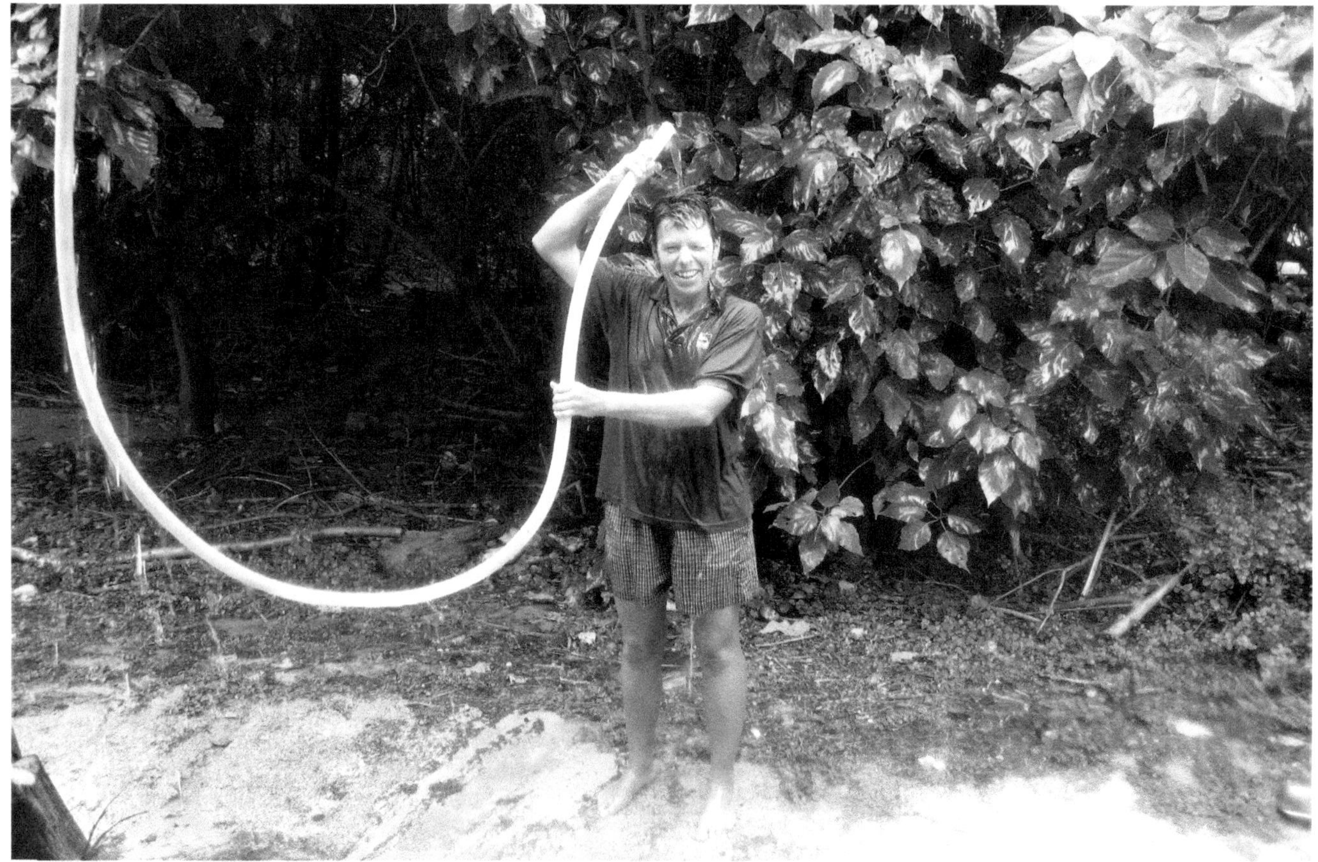

© Melvyn Yeandle

We always got excited about heavy rain, especially when we had a full drinking supply; it was the only time we ever had running water, so with buckets and soap powder at the ready it was a chance to do the washing. I would then replenish all our other water stocks, so no carrying from the well would be needed. If there was plenty of rain to go around for everything, after I had finished all the dirty clothes I could lay my hands on, I moved on to the dishes, the floor and the dive boots.

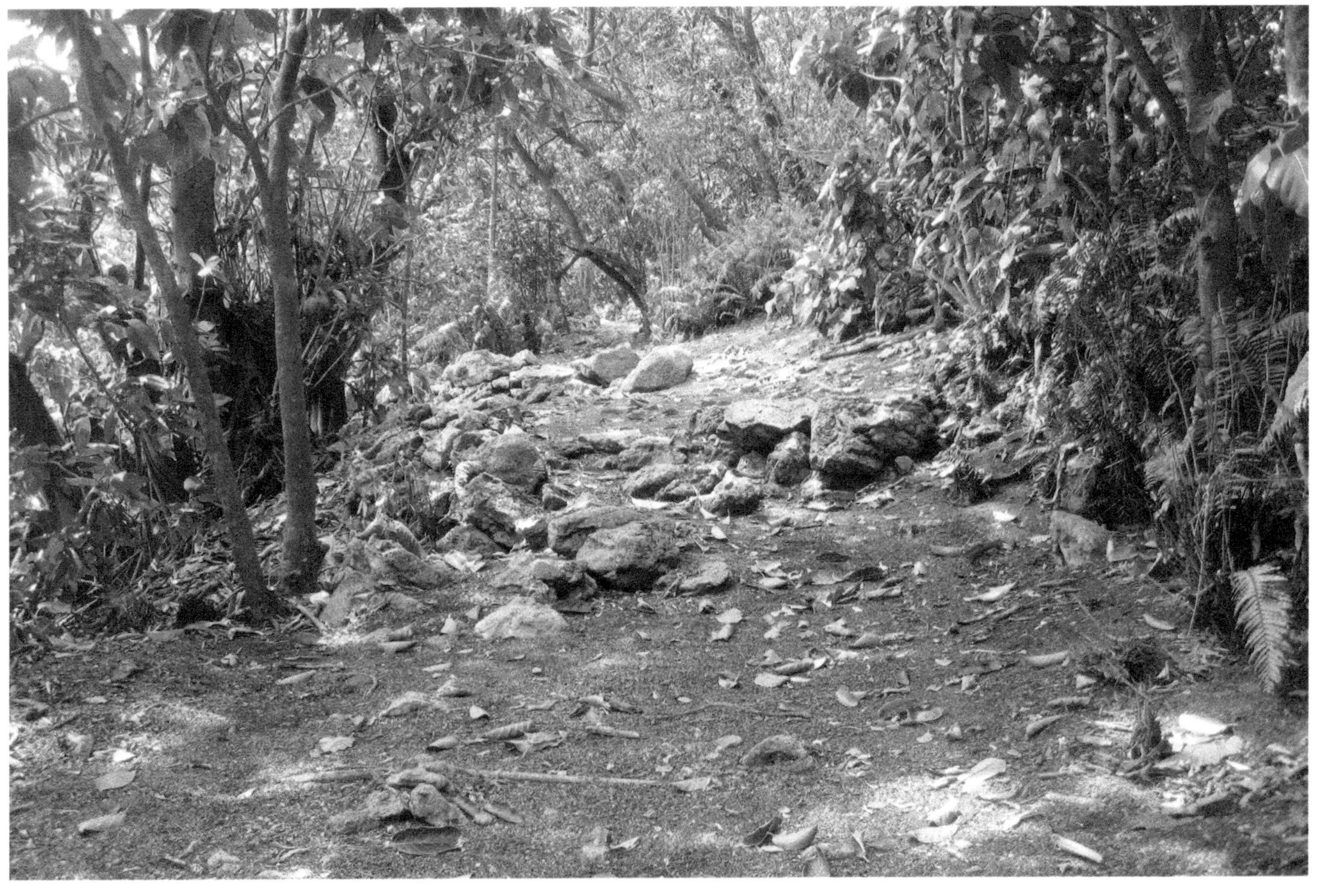

The hill is an inhospitable, rocky outcrop which occupies over 85% of Aride's surface and is covered in trees. There are many routes up the hill, but the tourist trail is a 140m climb up a rugged path, which twists and turns up the wooded incline, towering over the plateau below to the south.

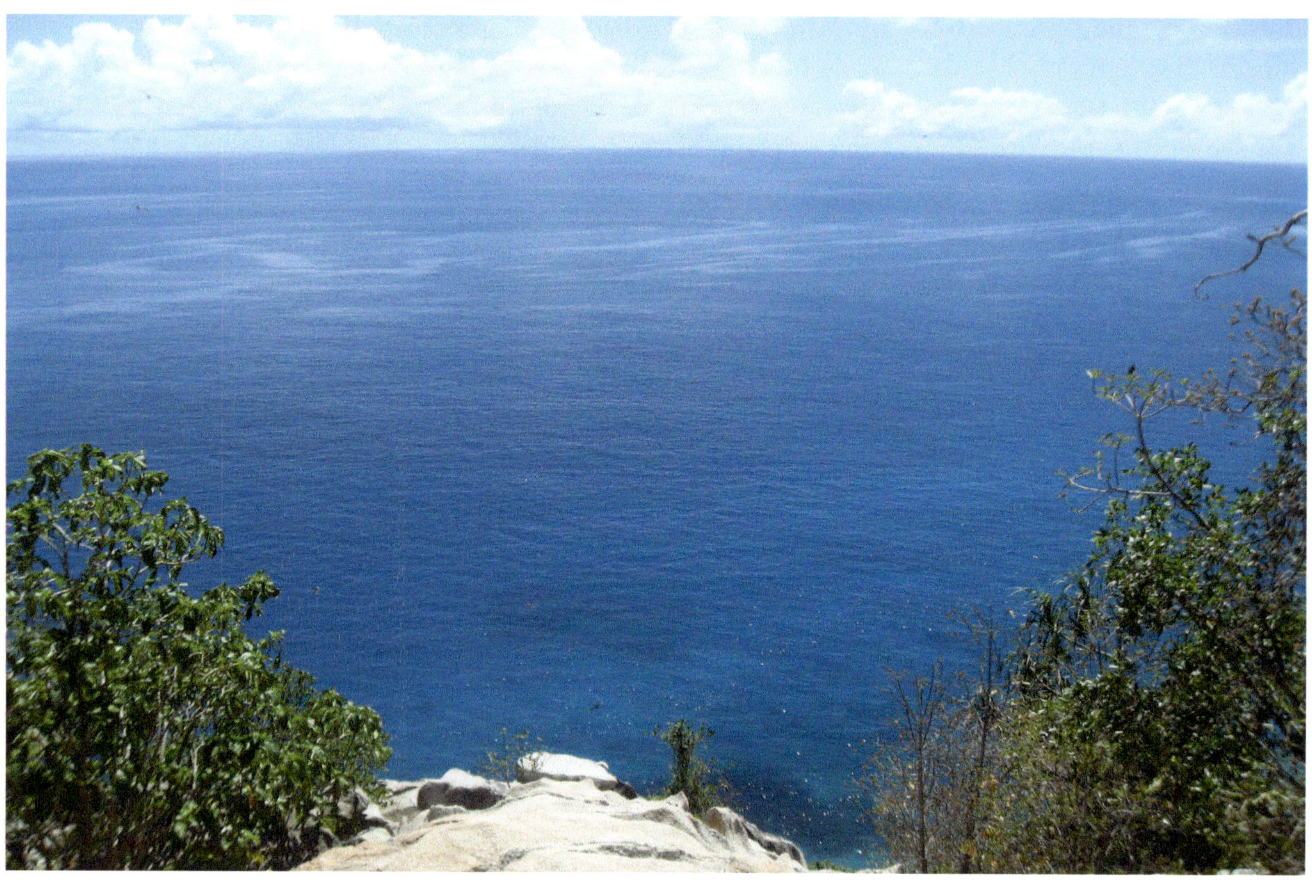

The path leads to a viewpoint at the top, a clearing in the trees from which you can see the curvature of the earth. It reveals a breath-taking expanse of Indian Ocean, only interrupted on super clear days by the tiny bumps of Denis and Bird Islands many miles away. The elevated position enables you to get a rare eye-to-eye view of frigate birds like nowhere else in Seychelles.

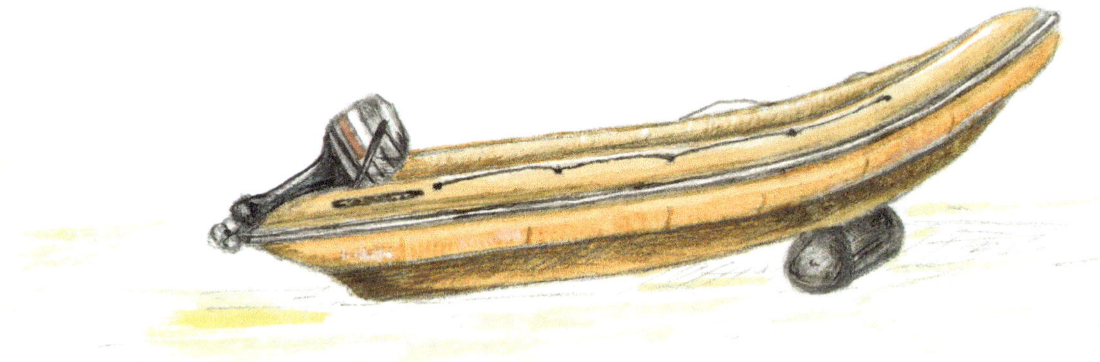

*Tornado rib*

## Chapter 3

## The Team

Living on an island with just eight people, it was essential that we all worked together as a team to do our jobs, raise money, preserve our sanity and reach the mainland for supplies and medical care. When this didn't happen, which seemed to occur rather frequently, everything all fell apart. The team was made up of two wardens (myself and Melv), four Seychellois rangers and typically two volunteers, who could be from anywhere, but during our time they were British.

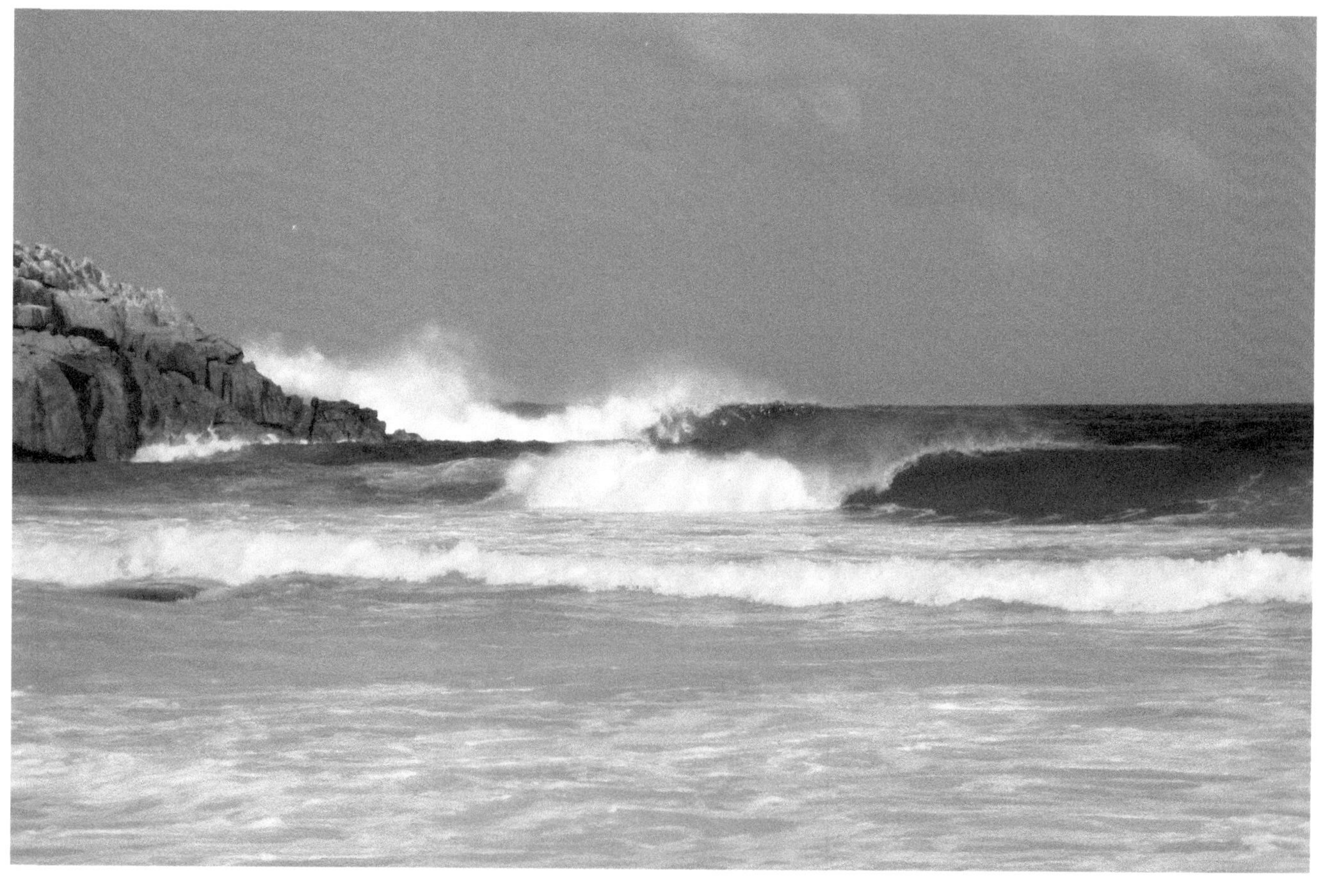

As we expected, due to their life experiences, each of the rangers portrayed a slightly different presentation of the Seychellois culture, which added further complexity to our time on Aride. They were as changeable as the weather and a little like the sea, turbulent and volatile one minute, calm and quiet the next.

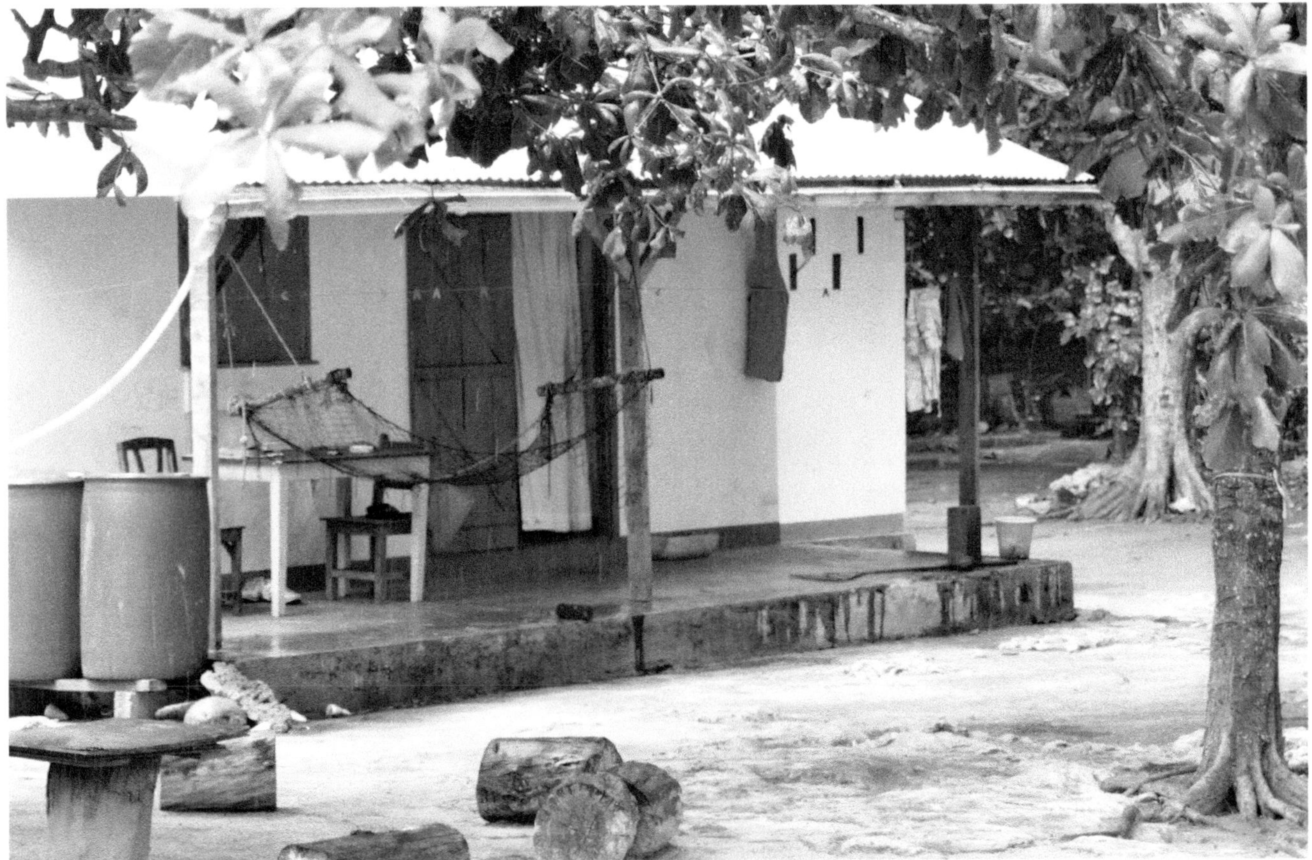

© *Jean Cheadle*

Although reasonably paid, the role of ranger was not considered a prospective career, and turnover of staff was abnormally high. We appreciated that there were significant drawbacks, such as basic accommodation in a bad state of repair, and as partners were not permitted to be on the island permanently, working as a ranger meant being away from friends and family.

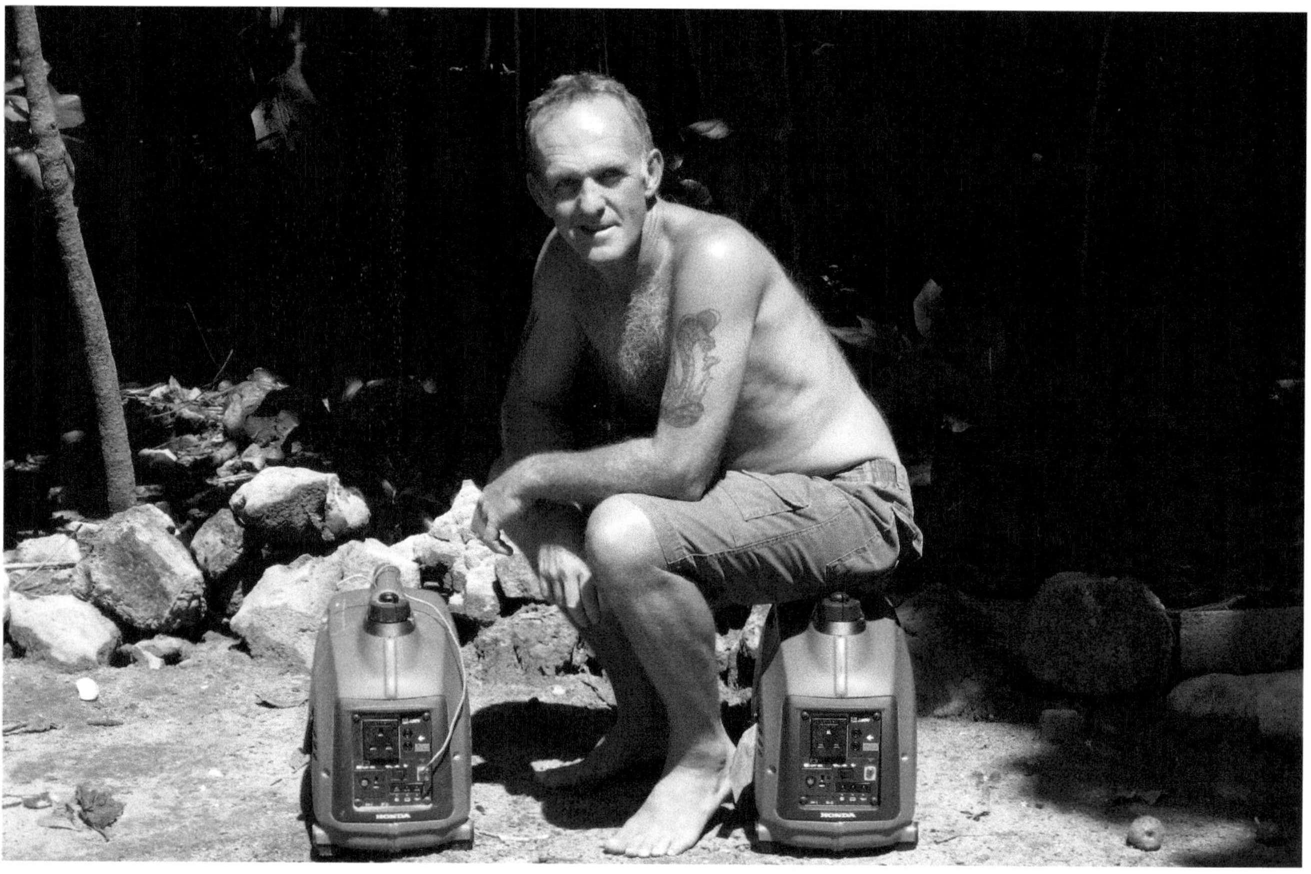

Rangers were expected to live in very poor conditions with no running water and associated facilities, and often no electricity. When we did have electricity, it was very unreliable, and often didn't last for long.

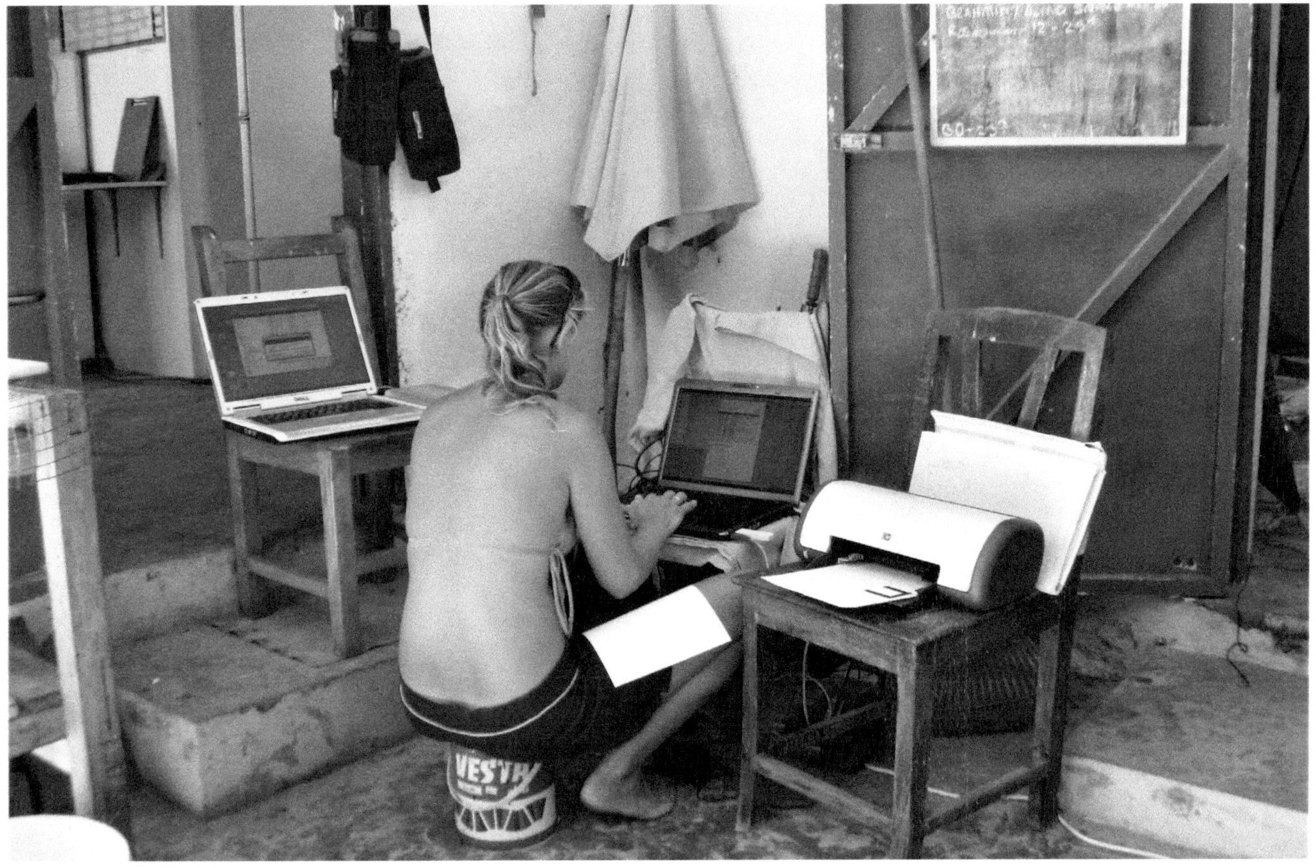

The office had to move depending on where the portable generator was working, and although no electricity  quickly became the norm, the lack of light in the evening made for short days and long nights.

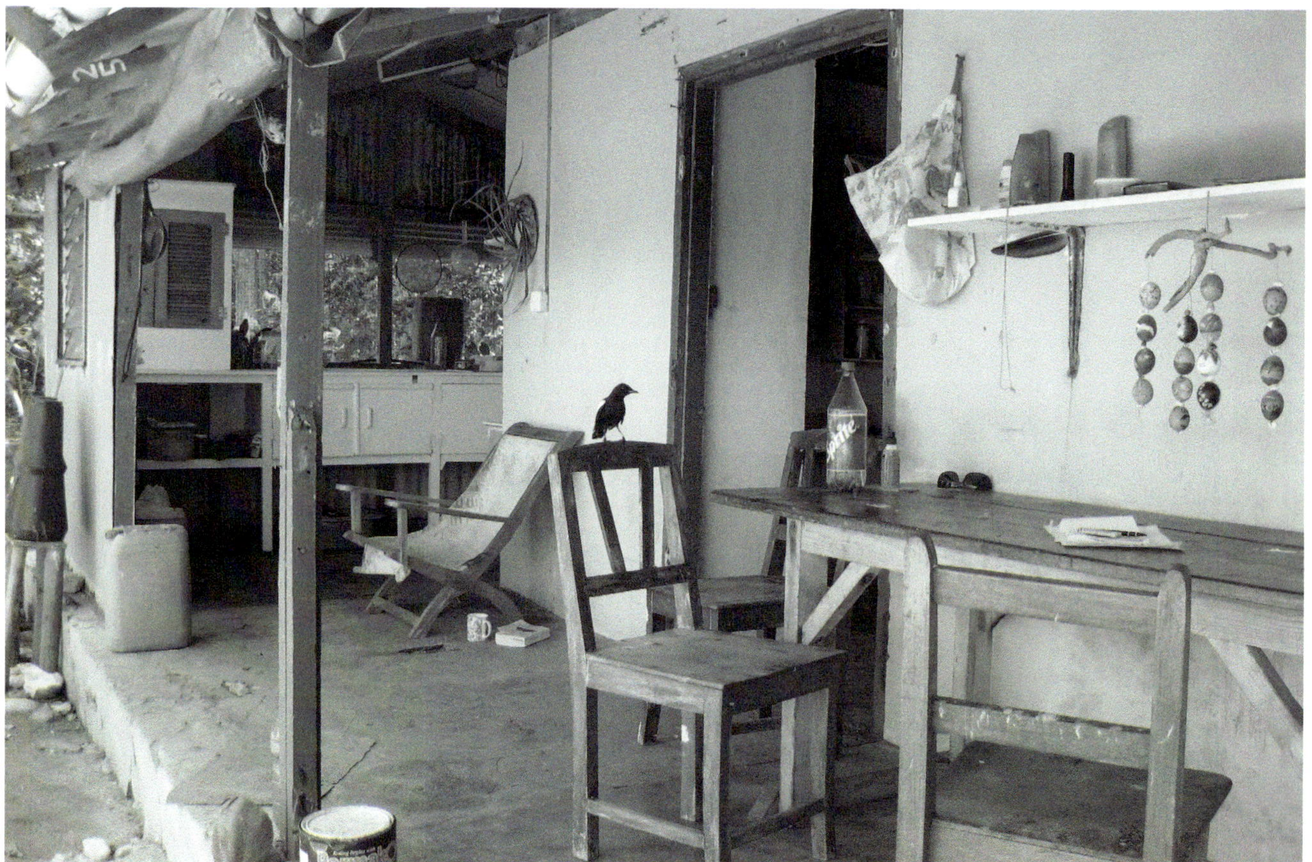

*© Chloe Prehn-Arnold*

Recruiting the right volunteers for Aride was no easy task; it takes a certain type of person to want to live on a remote island, share accommodation (and rough accommodation at that) with somebody you have never met before, learn to work in a completely different culture, cope with ailments quite unheard of in the UK and work long hours without being paid.

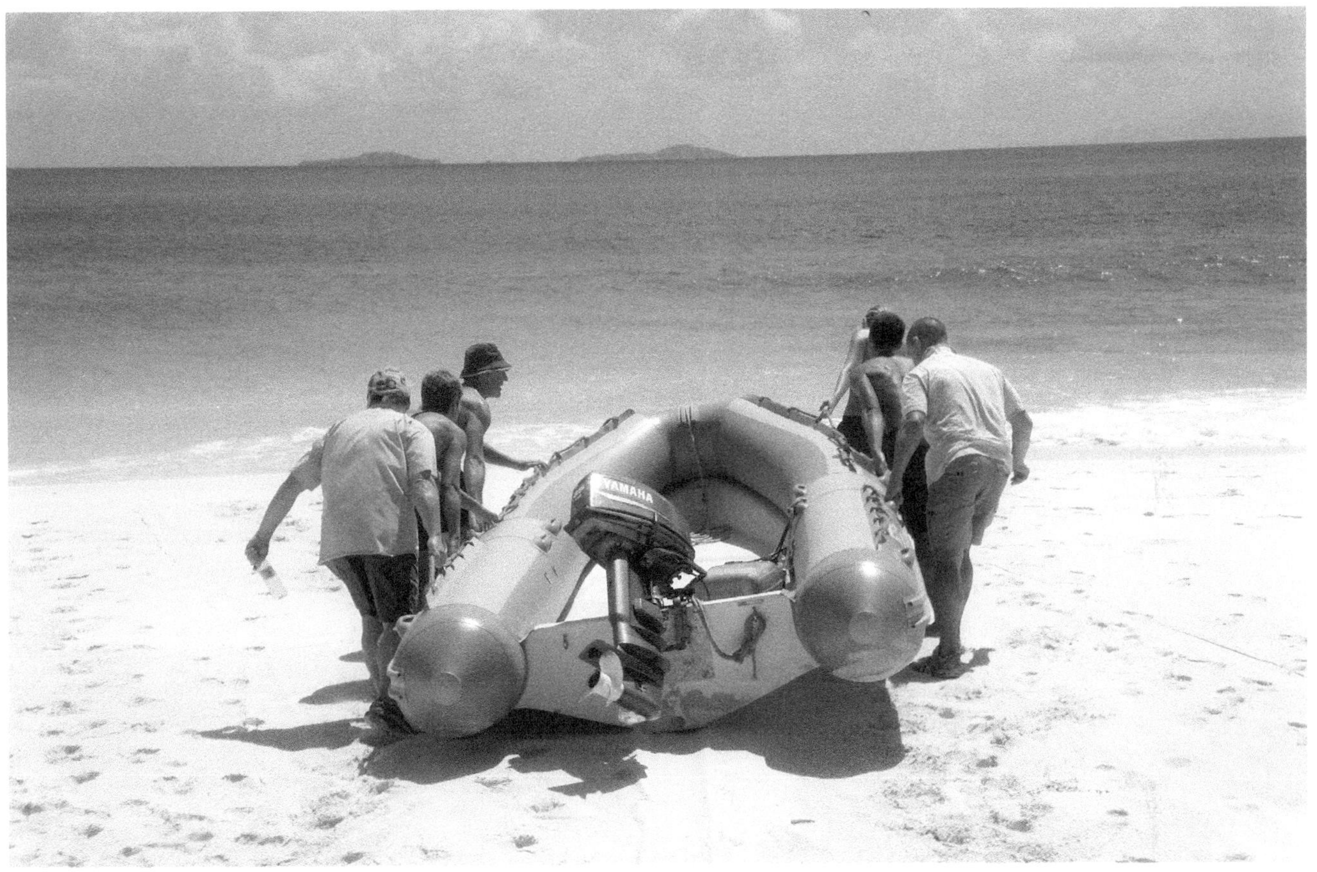

© Caroline Arnold

The changeover of volunteers had to be slick as the reduction in the number of hands had a significant effect on all our lives. Island life was a very physical one and extremely demanding on the body; everything involved hard manual work, from pulling the boat up the beach to carrying water from the well.

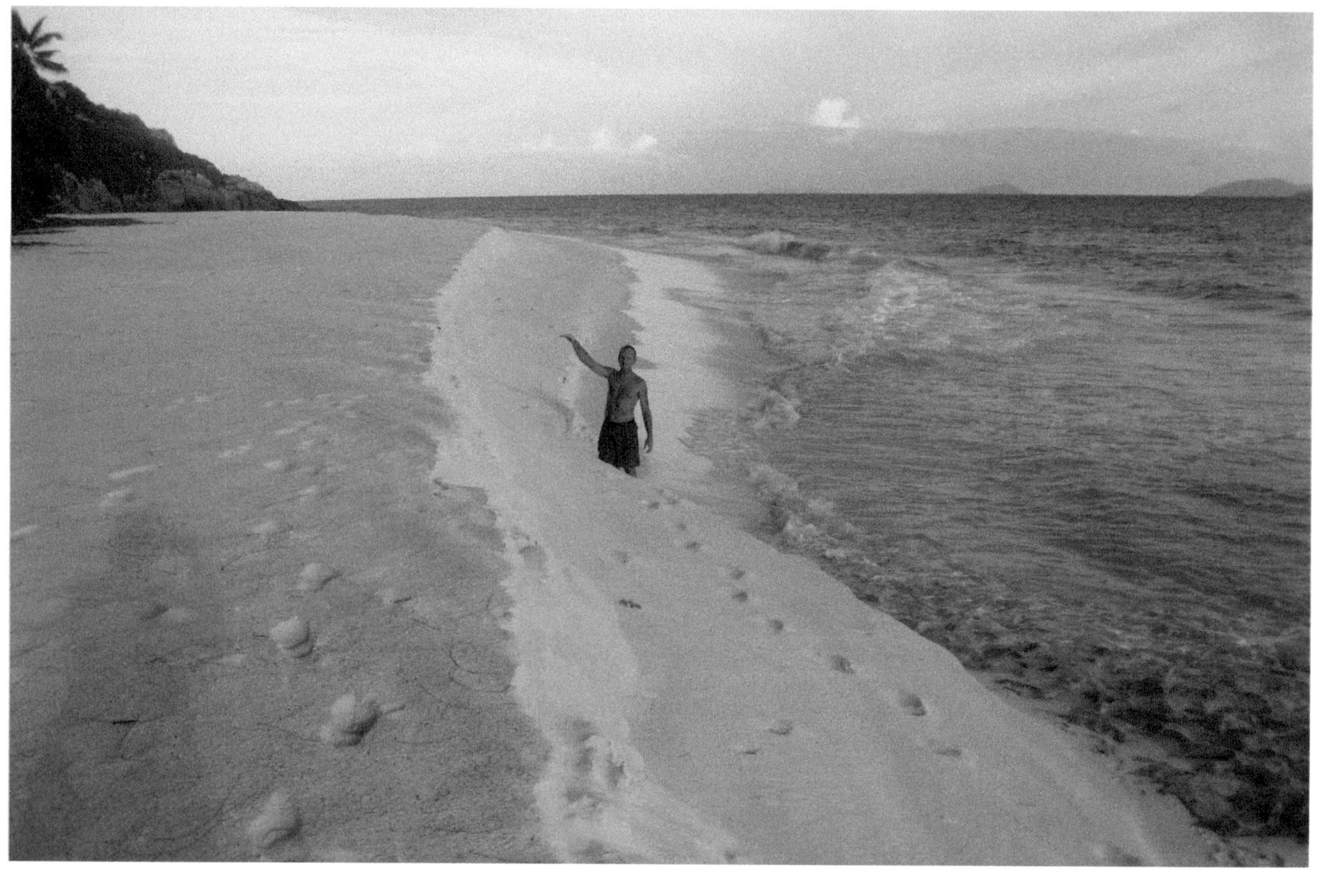

Without mechanical assistance and with a small number of people, putting the boat in the boatshed at the end of the day was exhausting, particularly when the beach worked against us and we didn't have the full compliment of staff. Hauling a 6m Tornado rib together with a 40hp engine up metre high sand-cliffs was gruelling, and many a time I felt sick from the pure physical effort.

## *Melv's fiftieth birthday party*

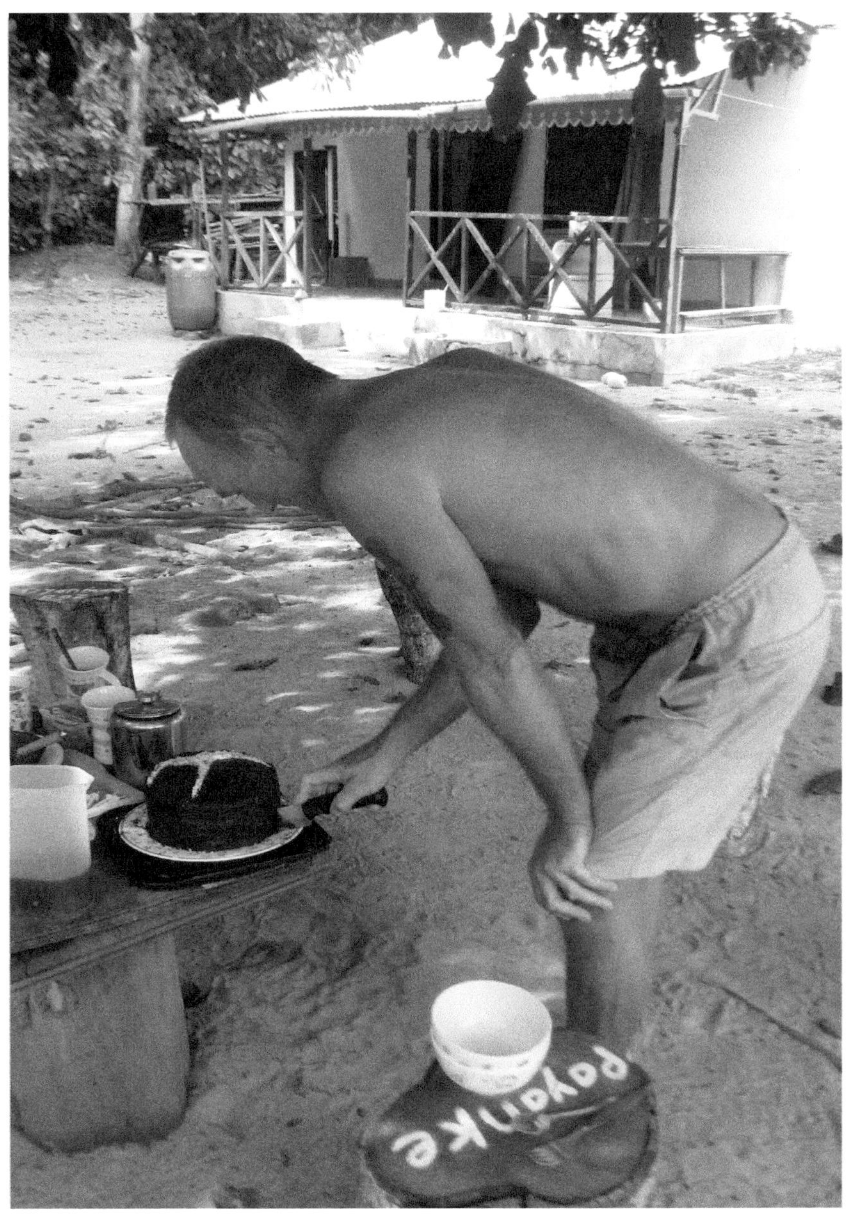


Another hectic week on the island began with a significant fiftieth birthday for Melv, which we celebrated with a civilised get-together involving tea and cake. The cake was excellent – a triple layer chocolate cake made by Lara, one of the volunteers – and provided a much needed sugar rush for all. There were some alcoholic beverages later, but all rather reserved due to limited supplies and the thought of a hangover in 36˚C.

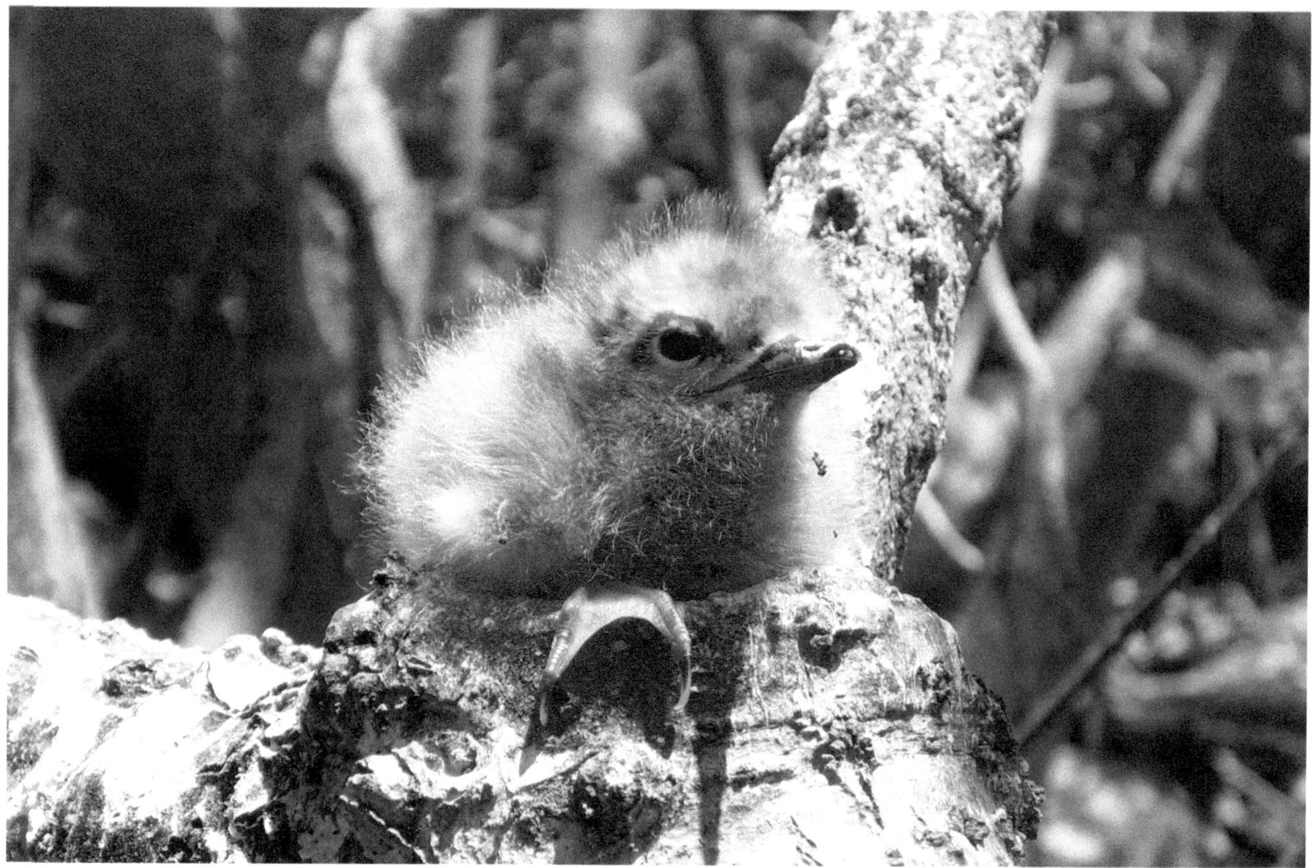

*© Chloe Prehn-Arnold*

With team management becoming increasingly demanding on our time, and many hours devoted to managing the high staff turnover and training new recruits, Melv and I were always keen to make time for our conservation work. One of our favourite tasks was the weekly monitoring of the fairy tern population and checking on the progress of the incubating adults and the small chicks.

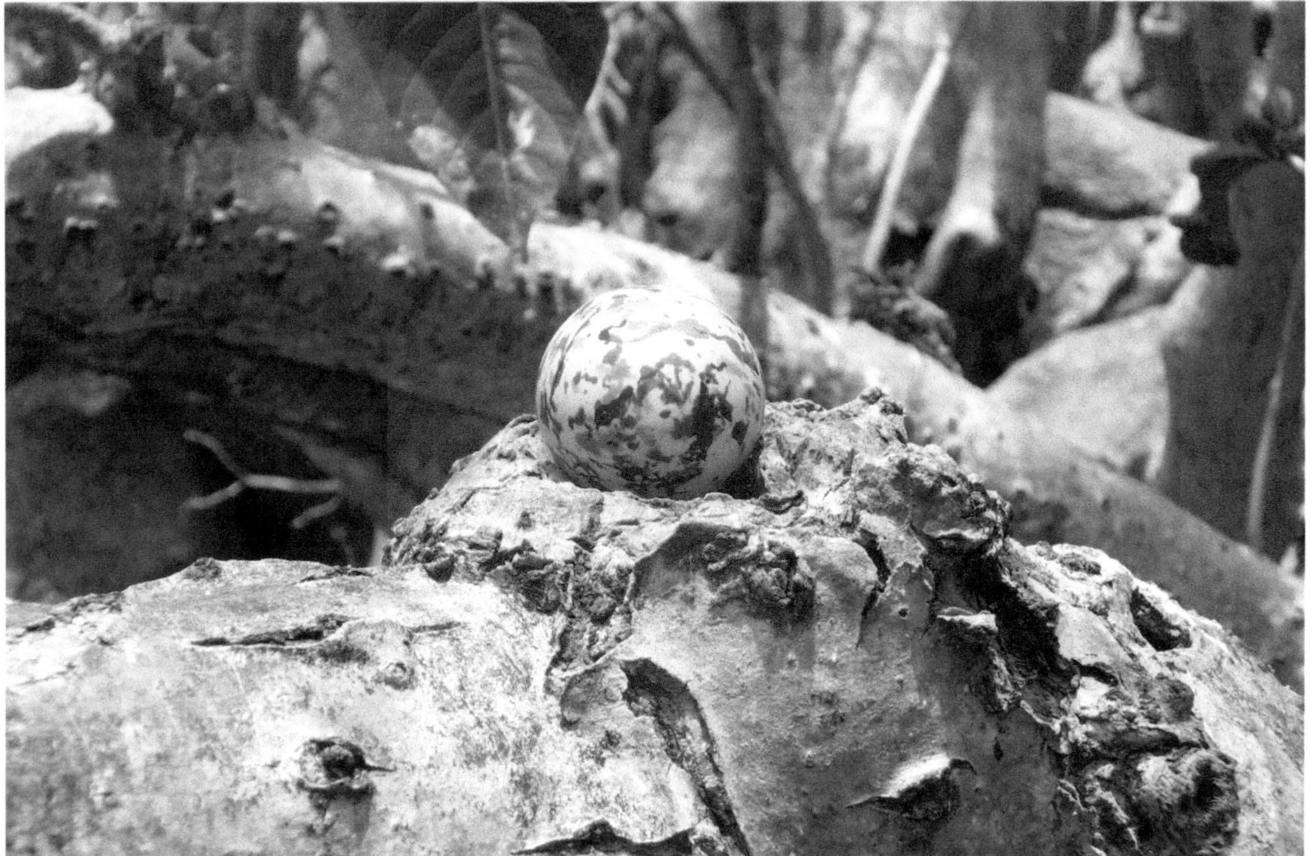

*© Chloe Prehn-Arnold*

The eggs of these magical birds are beautiful: cream and patterned with brown-tinged squiggles. Perched precariously on the nub of a branch, it still amazes me how they manage to successfully rear their young in such perilous circumstances.

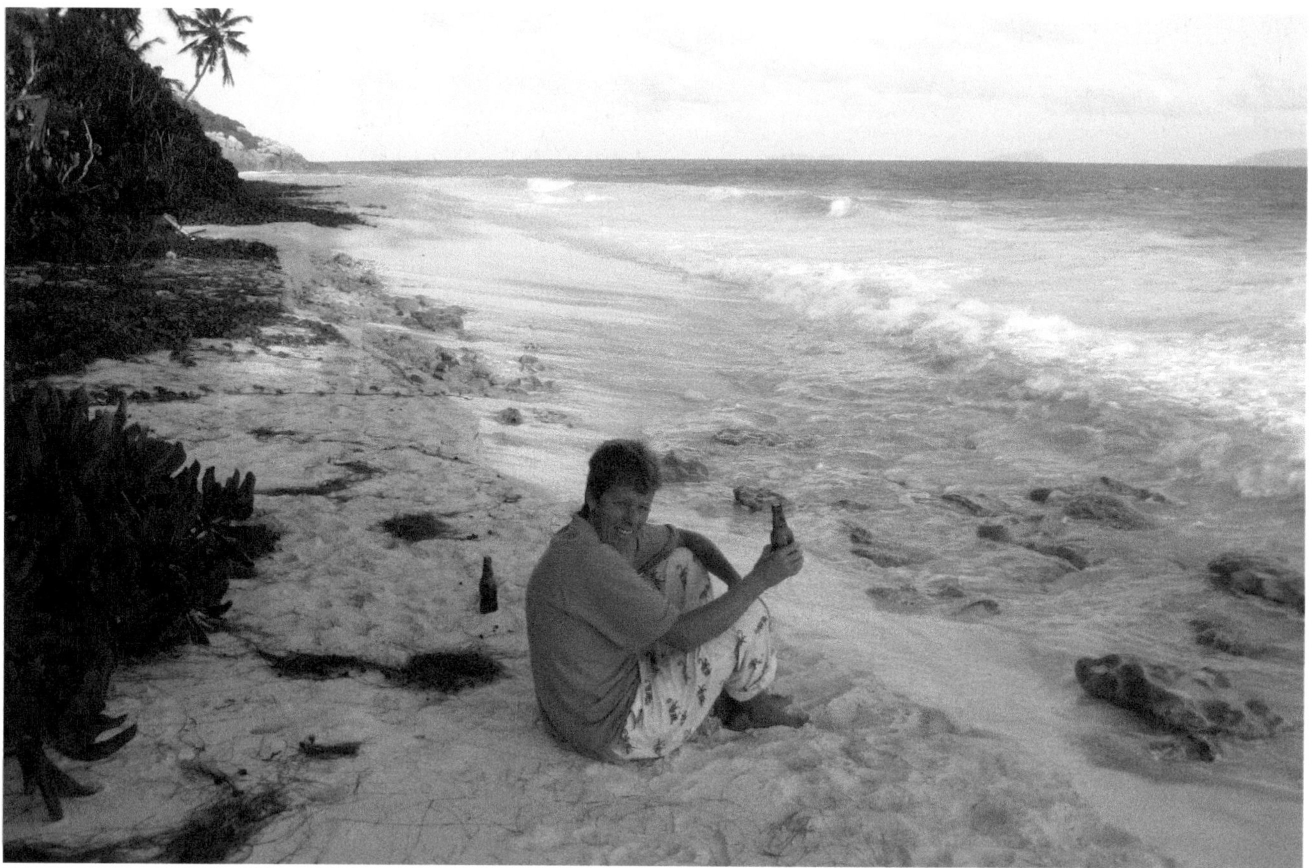

*© Melvyn Yeandle*

It had been a difficult week all round when this photograph was taken, and I was glad to see two of our rangers disappear home for the weekend. I was digging deep for my best people management skills at this time, and as they left, the tension was lifted, and the island returned back to peace and quiet. I joined Melv on the beach to watch the waves. The sea was still very rough, and as the tide came in it was compelling. We sat on the sand watching the water as bit by bit the waves nibbled at the beach.

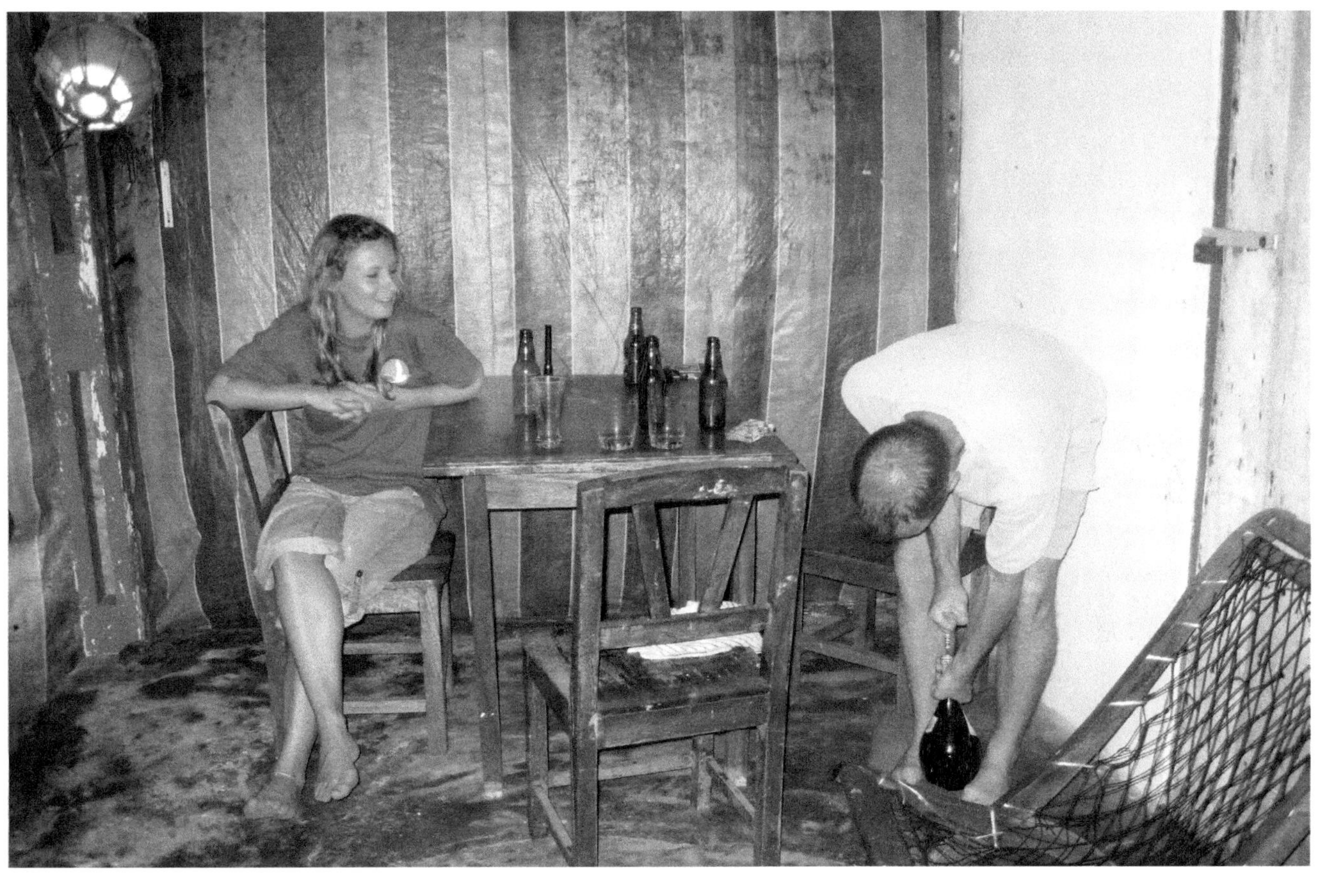

Enjoying each others company was important to us and sharing a beer over supper was a great way to start the weekend. Volunteer Lara became my right-hand girl, an honest, reliable, organised and determined young lady. Although very sensitive, she was extremely hard-working and tough, all the essential ingredients for survival on Aride. And survive she did, for a further twelve months after her initial three-month placement.

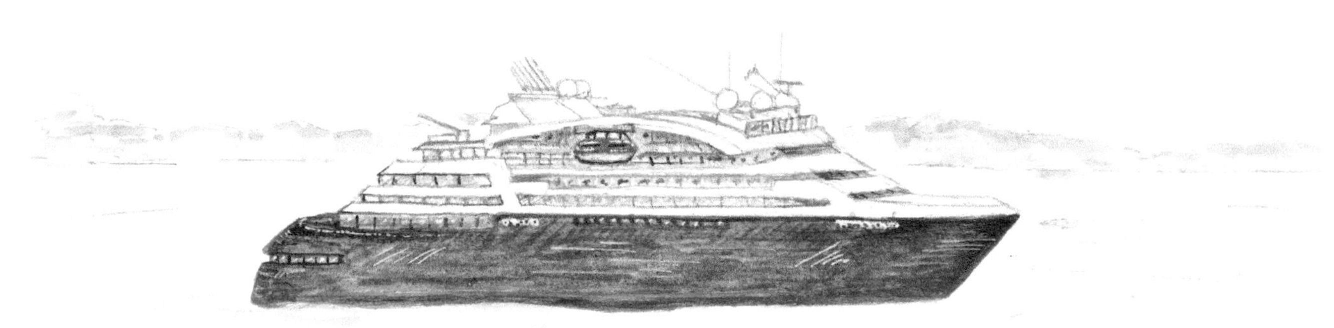

*Le Ponant cruise ship*

# Chapter 4

## Our Bread and Butter

'One of the jobs I was least looking forward to before we went out to Aride was dealing with tourists,' Melv wrote in our weekly blog. 'I'd seen those poxy TV fly-on-the-wall programmes about tour operators and facilitators in holiday resorts getting continual grief from people who shouldn't have been given a passport until they could prove they'd learnt some manners or knew when to shut up. But to my relief and surprise, our experience was quite the opposite. We met so many interesting people during our time on Aride, all of them fascinated by our primitive way of life.'

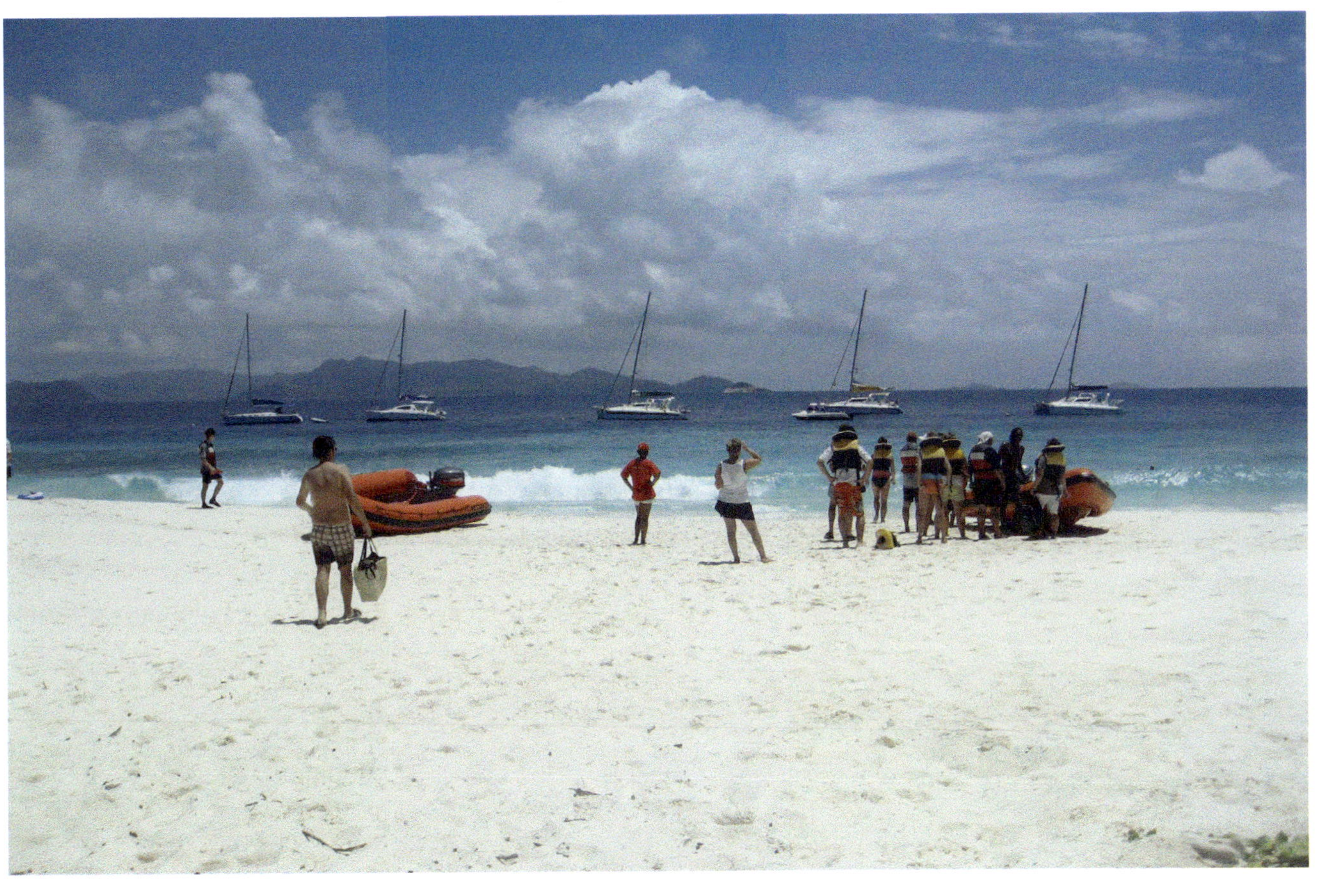

'The money from tourists funded our conservation work,' Melv continued, 'so it was desperately important that we improved on our visitor numbers. We dealt with three main types of client: people from hotels who had hired a boat to get to us; people who had hired damned expensive yachts and were sailing aimlessly around trying to find something to do, and cruise ship passengers. No matter how they got to us, all boats and ships had to moor offshore and we would then go out and pick them up in our rib.'

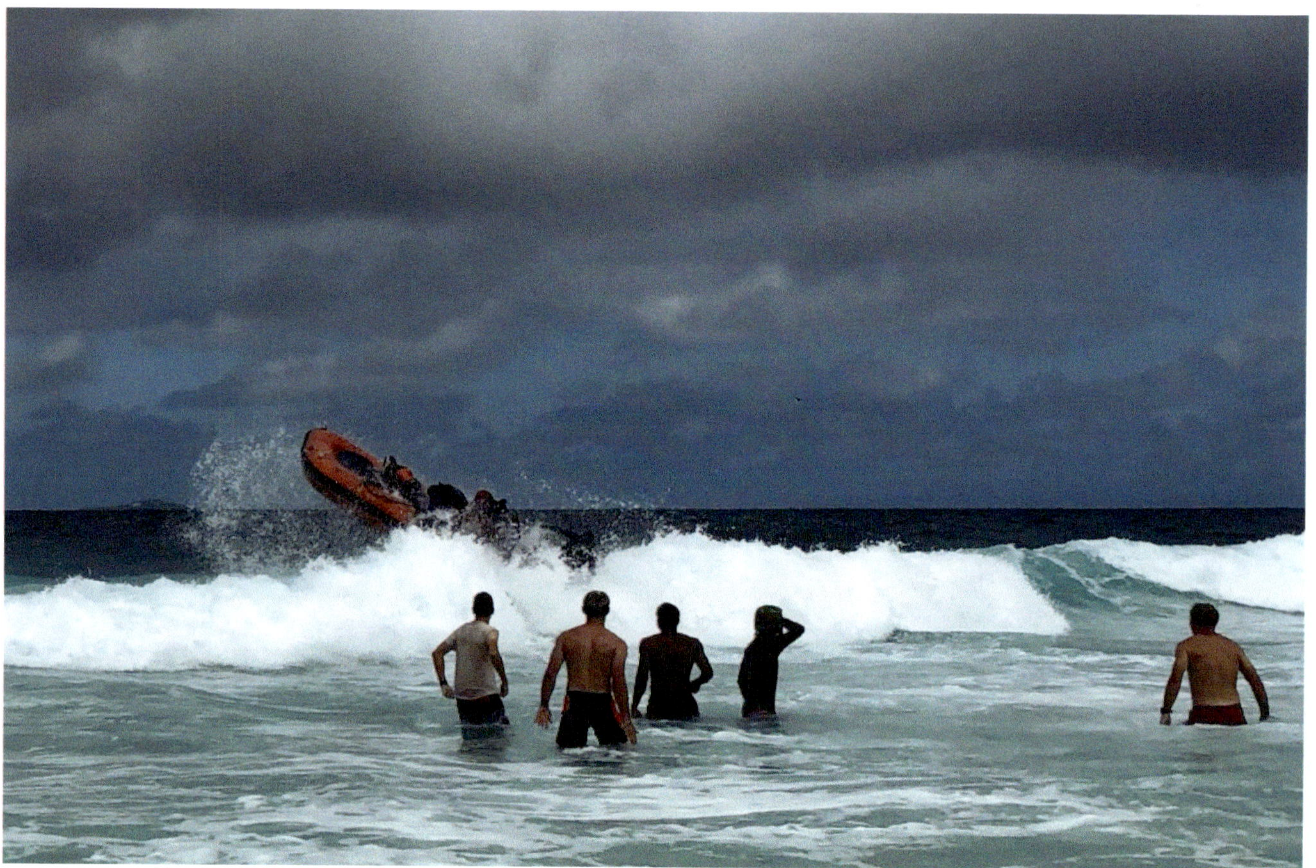

© Colin Taylor

Welcoming guests to the island was a very important part of our work — it literally paid the wages — but their arrival and departure was completely governed by the elements as the weather conditions affected the boat landing and launching dramatically. Even in the northwest monsoon, when conditions made the sea a little calmer, getting on and off the island could be very uncertain, and during the southeast monsoon it was nigh on impossible. With no jetty, launching was done by hand, and pulling the boat out through the surf was one of the hardest jobs we did.

### *New Seychelles magpie robin sponsorship display*

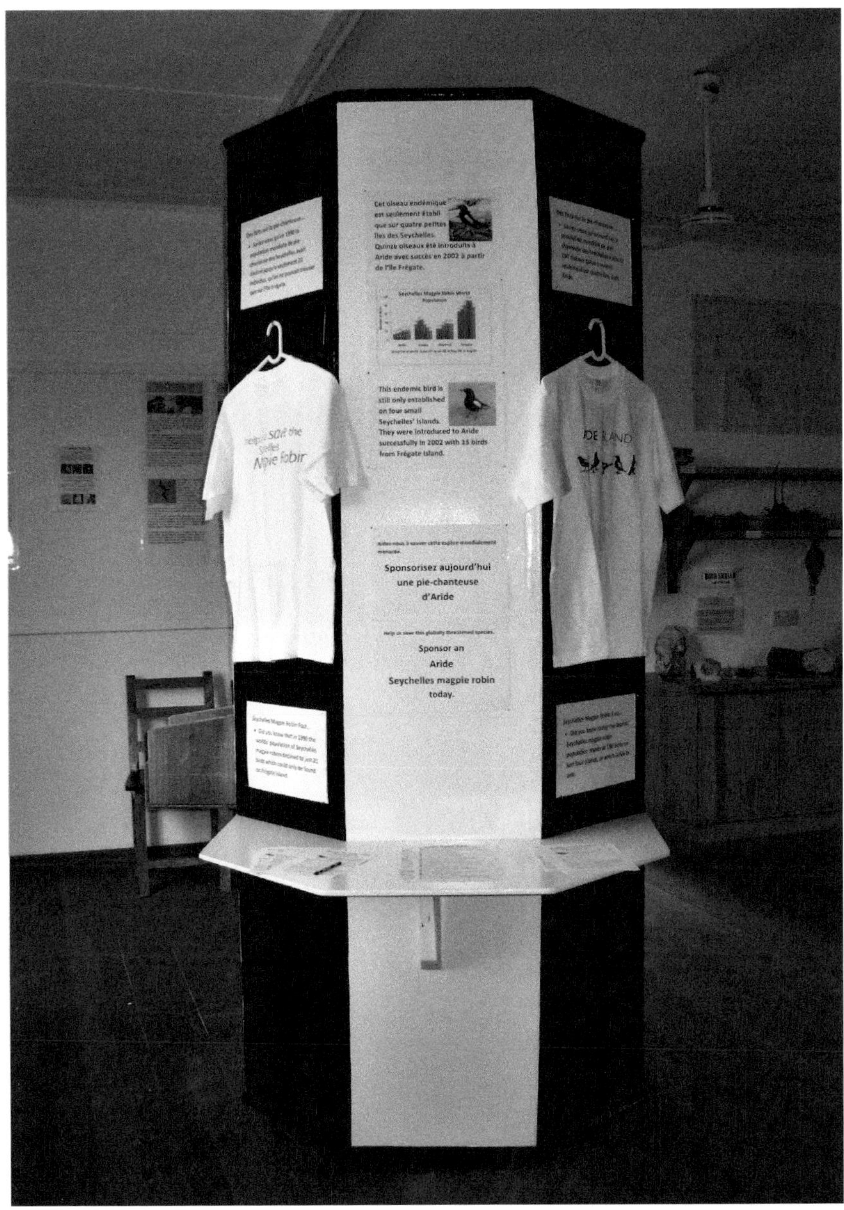

Having guests on the island provided important social interaction; it was a chance to talk to people from all over the world, and 90% of them were very interested in what we did. Aride ran a project which involved paying a sum to sponsor an individual Seychelles magpie robin, and in return people received a newsletter, certificate and a t-shirt. It was an excellent way to raise funds.

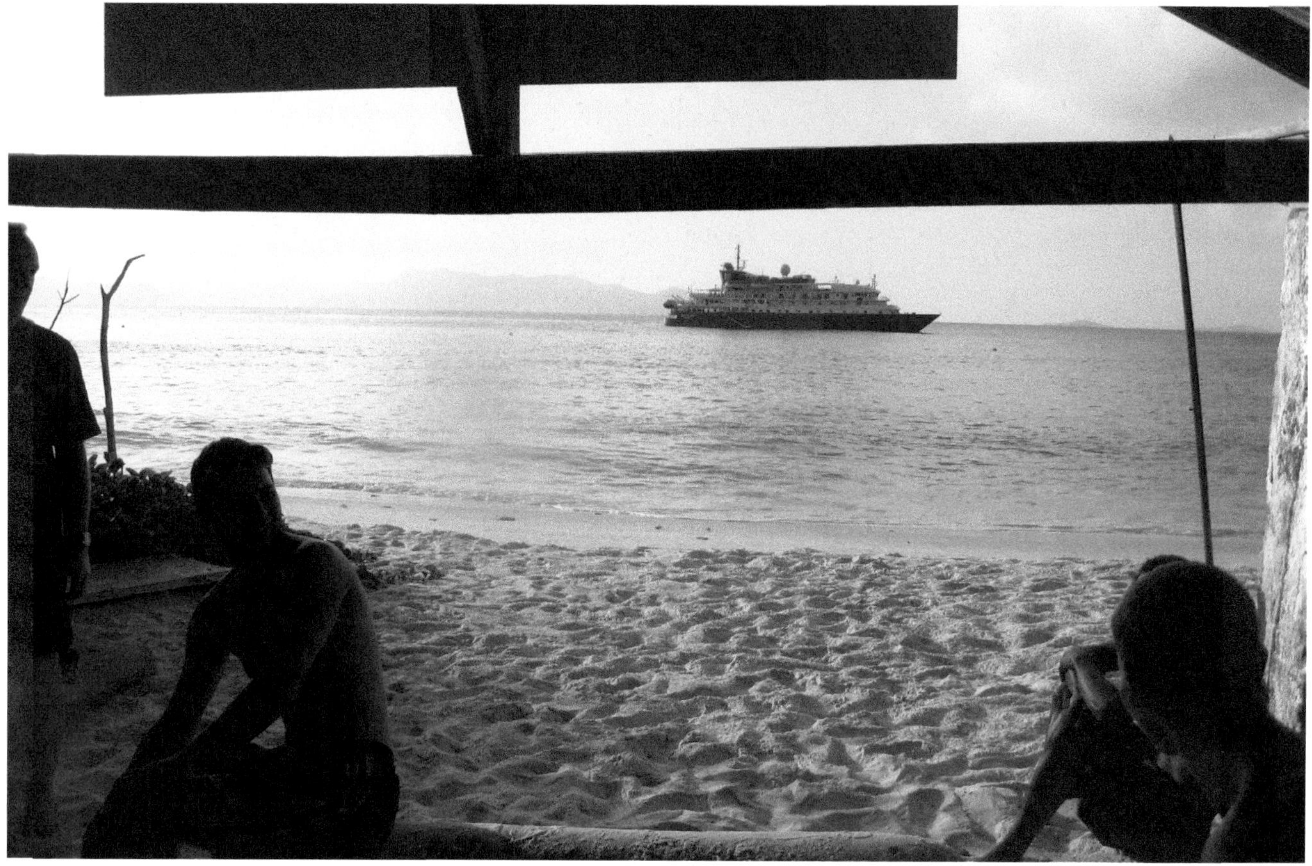

Visitors arrived in all shapes and sizes of vessels: we regularly entertained cruise ships which were financially lucrative, but hard work. *Island Sky*, one of our regular cruise ships, would appear on the horizon the night before and head over to Aride in the morning.

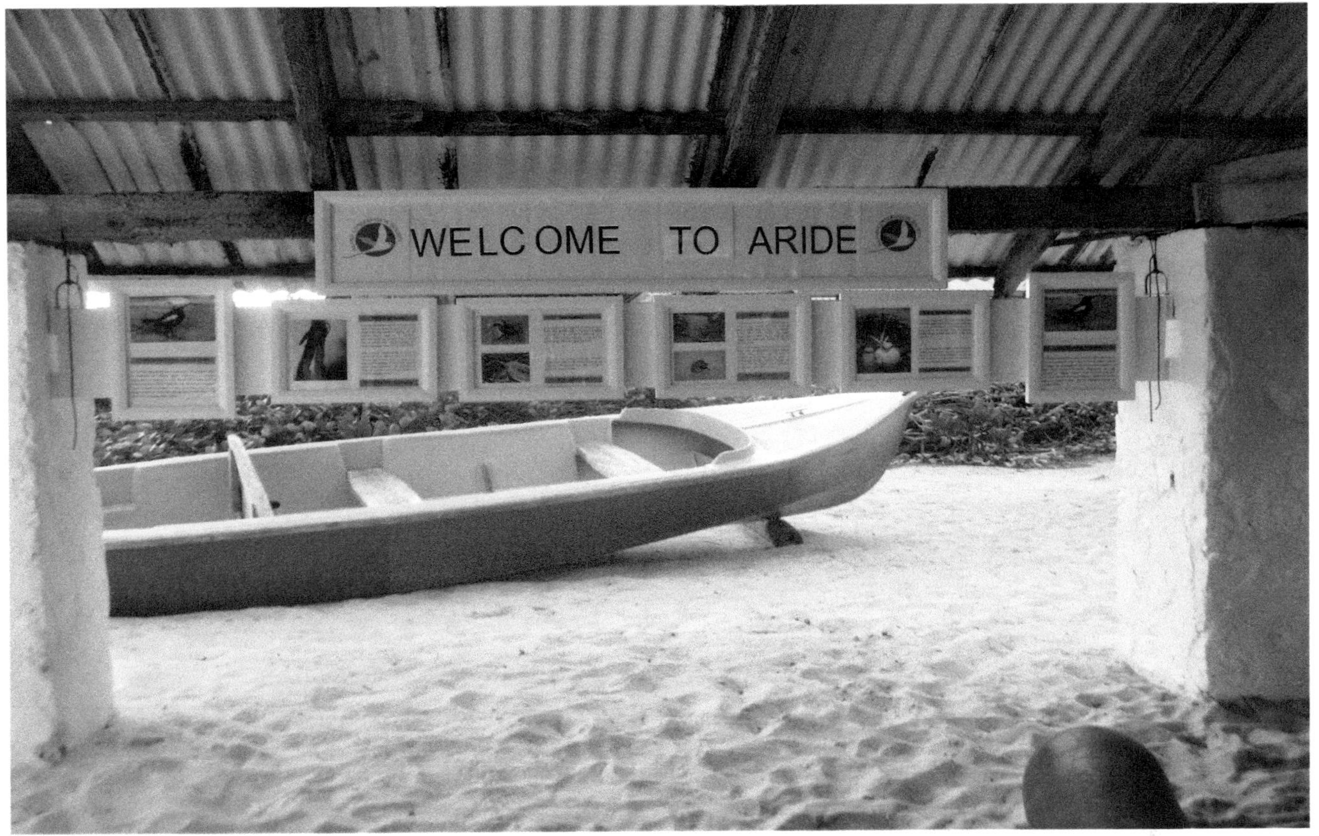


After a successful visit by ninety-nine cruise ship passengers, everyone was high on success. The rangers were rewarded with good tips and a box of cigarettes, and we gratefully received a bottle of wine. It was lovely to see the proud expressions on the rangers' faces and for them to take satisfaction from the service they had provided. That day, I reflected on when we had first arrived, and how little training we had received when it came to dealing with tourists. It certainly helped that we came from a society where the need to be on time, polite, reliable and to provide a good service was the culture we had been brought up in.

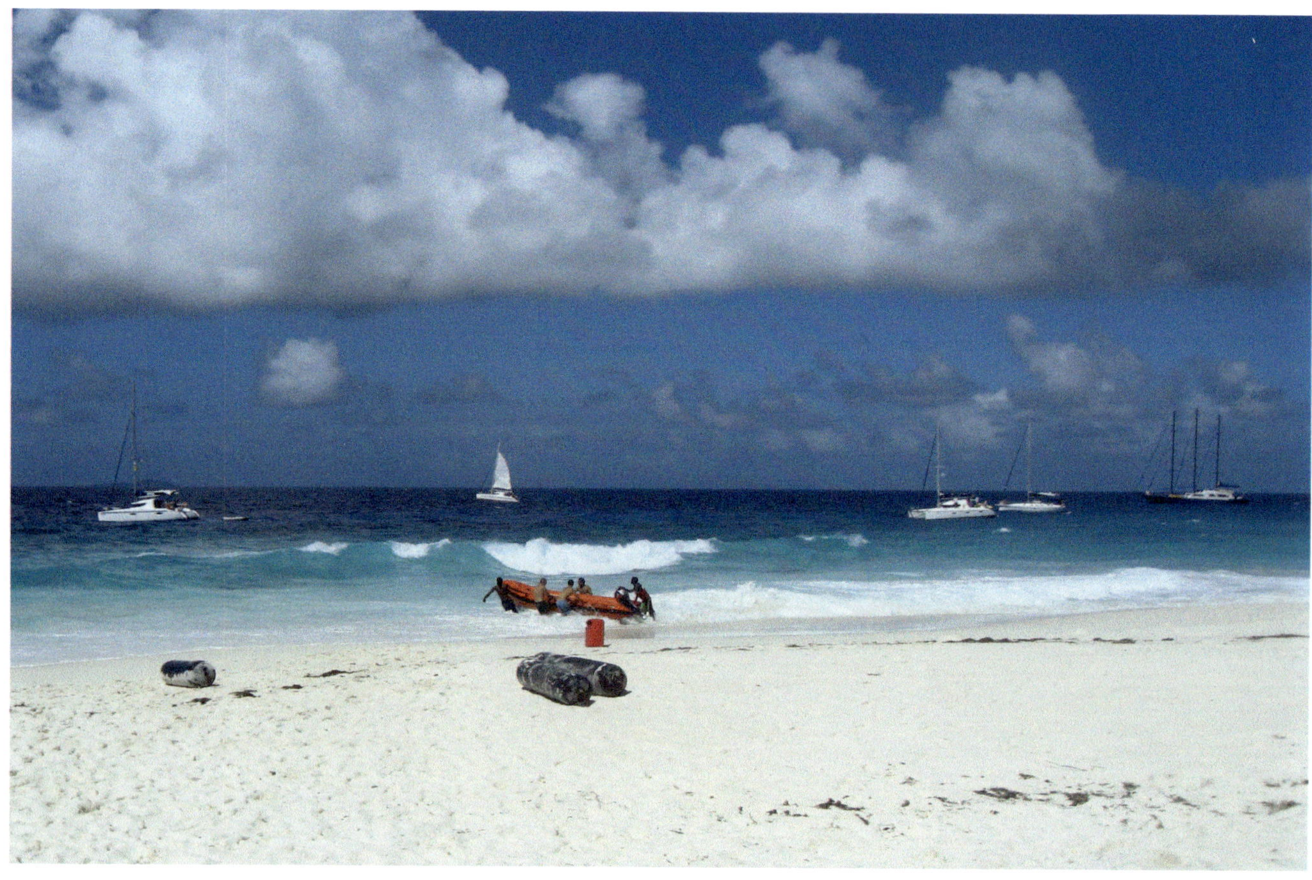

Days like this, when six self-sail boats arrived from Praslin at the same time, looking like a regatta coming across the stretch of water, were particularly memorable. The team gathered on the beach a little apprehensively, but excited for the busy day ahead. It was super to see all those boats heading our way; so often we watched them play safe and not venture out to us.

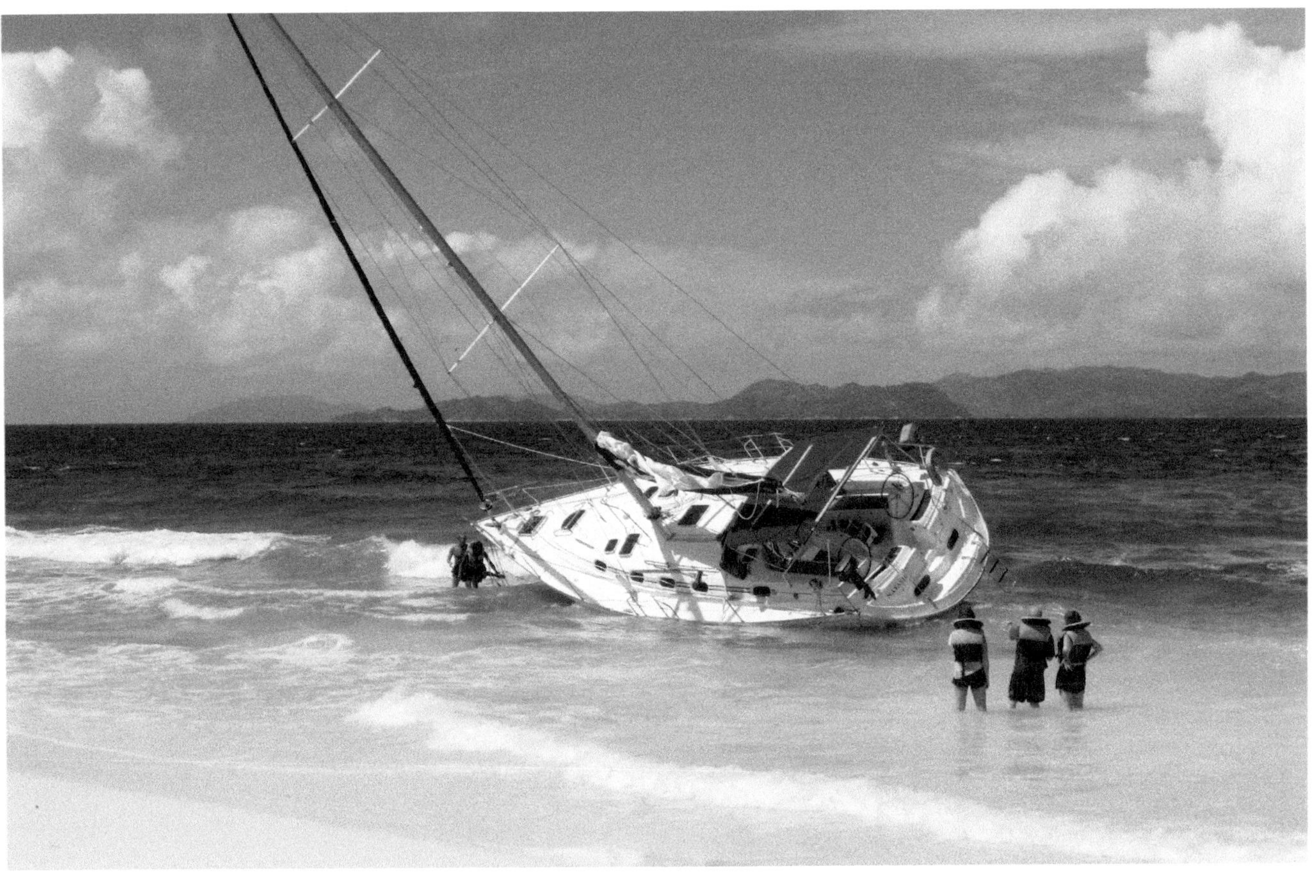

The visitor work also brought its own challenges, and I remember feeling physically sick when I ran out to the beach crest and saw that this yacht had come loose and was on the reef about 10m off the shore. I rushed to the office and immediately made a call to the boat hire company, worrying that all the effort we had put into building a relationship with them had probably been dashed.

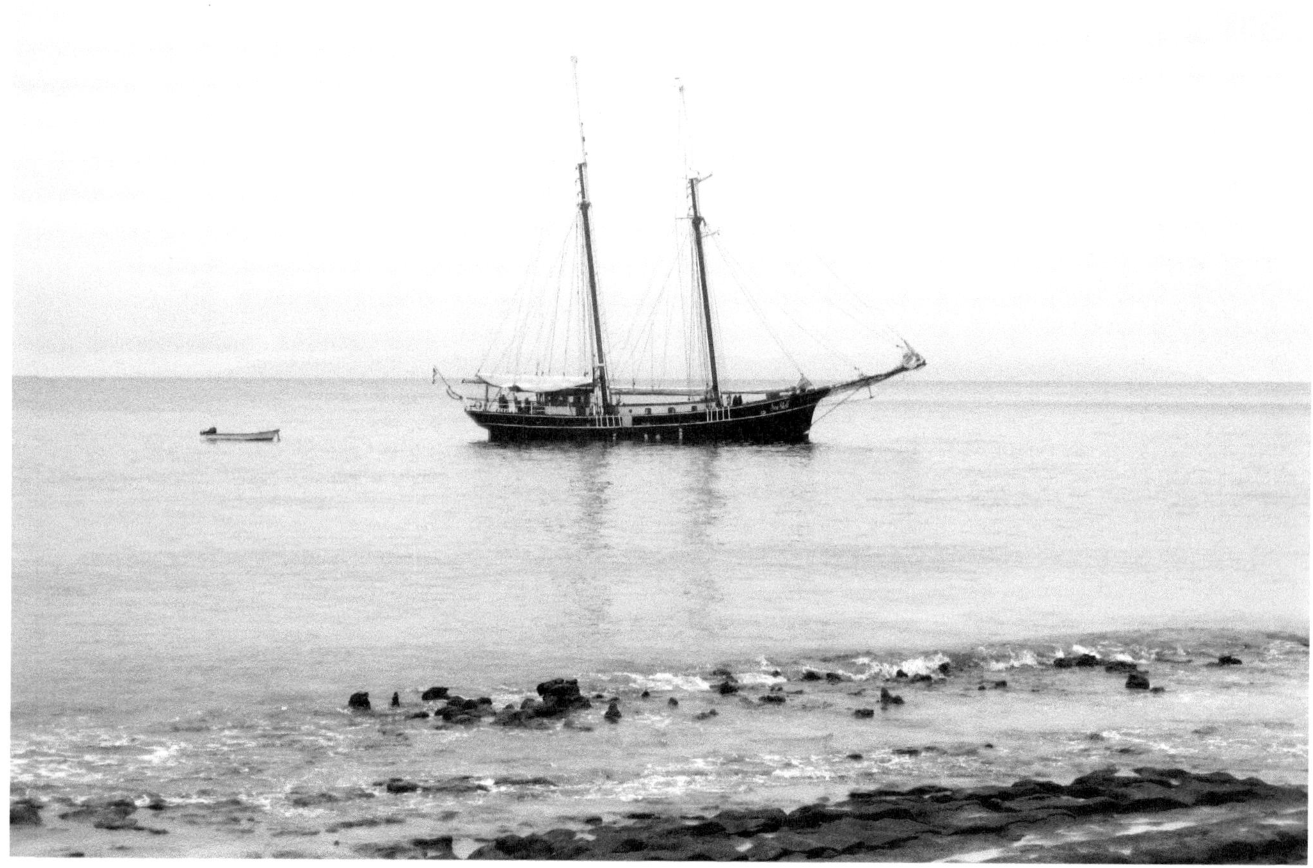

We met a huge range of nationalities: Americans, Russians, Slovakians, and those closer to home: Bulgarians, French, Dutch, Germans and good old Brits, and we always used their visits to catch up on local and international news. On one such visit, by *Silhouette Cruises*, who ran a small fleet of traditional schooners and modern yachts, we learnt that there had been several recent incidents with pirates just beyond Denis Island, which was only a couple of hours north by boat from Aride.

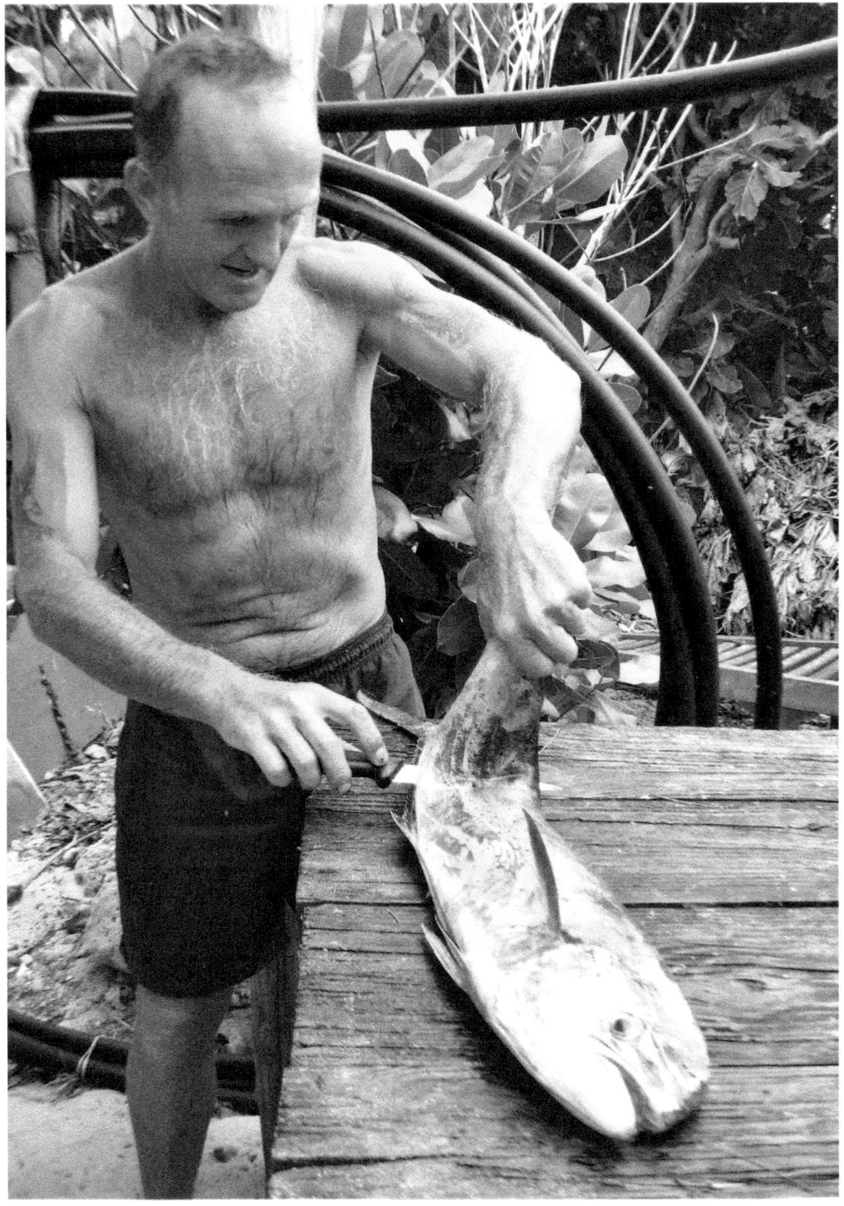

Whilst the meeting and greeting of guests was the main social mixing we did, mealtimes were an excellent time to get together as a team to chat and relax. Evenings were short, but they were the one opportunity we had to learn a bit more about each other. It felt quite odd that there were so few of us on the island and yet we hardly knew one another. After a fruitful fishing trip, supplemented by a dish from each household, we always ended up with an excellent spread.

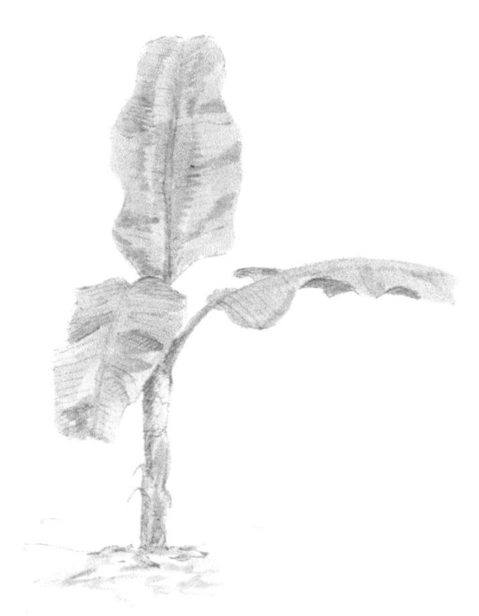

Banana tree

# Chapter 5

## Slimming in the Sun – The Seychelles' Diet

'After enjoying delicious curries in Mahé and fantastic fish in Praslin, arriving on Aride was a bit of a shock,' Melv recalled in one of our blog posts. 'It's absolutely undeniable that the island is paradise — the wildlife, the plants, the sea, the beach, are all second to none — but there was no food. Before we got to the island, we were told to buy supplies from Praslin, enough to last at least a week, which would have been great if we could find a shop that sold things other than rice… As a consequence, our first week, it has to be said, was poor for food. But thankfully, things got better.'

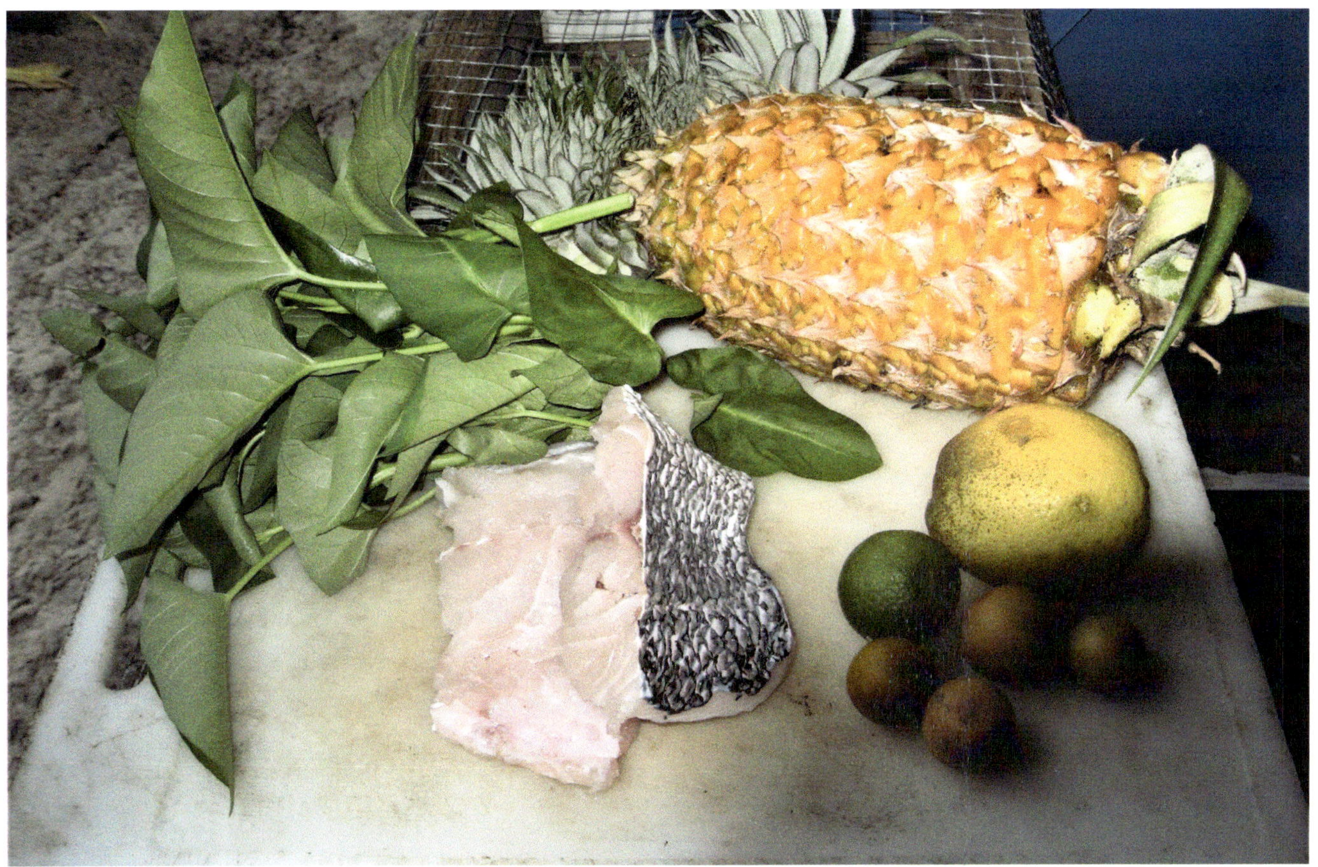

We soon learnt that trying to eat the equivalent of western foods was not the way forward, and to my stomach's relief, before too long we took on the ways of the Seychellois as Melv learnt to prepare local food. This was one of the many cultural shifts we needed to make, but we were expected to do so with very little to no guidance or advice. Through Melv's determination, we slowly managed to move from opening tins and packets to weighing out raw ingredients and harvesting fresh produce.

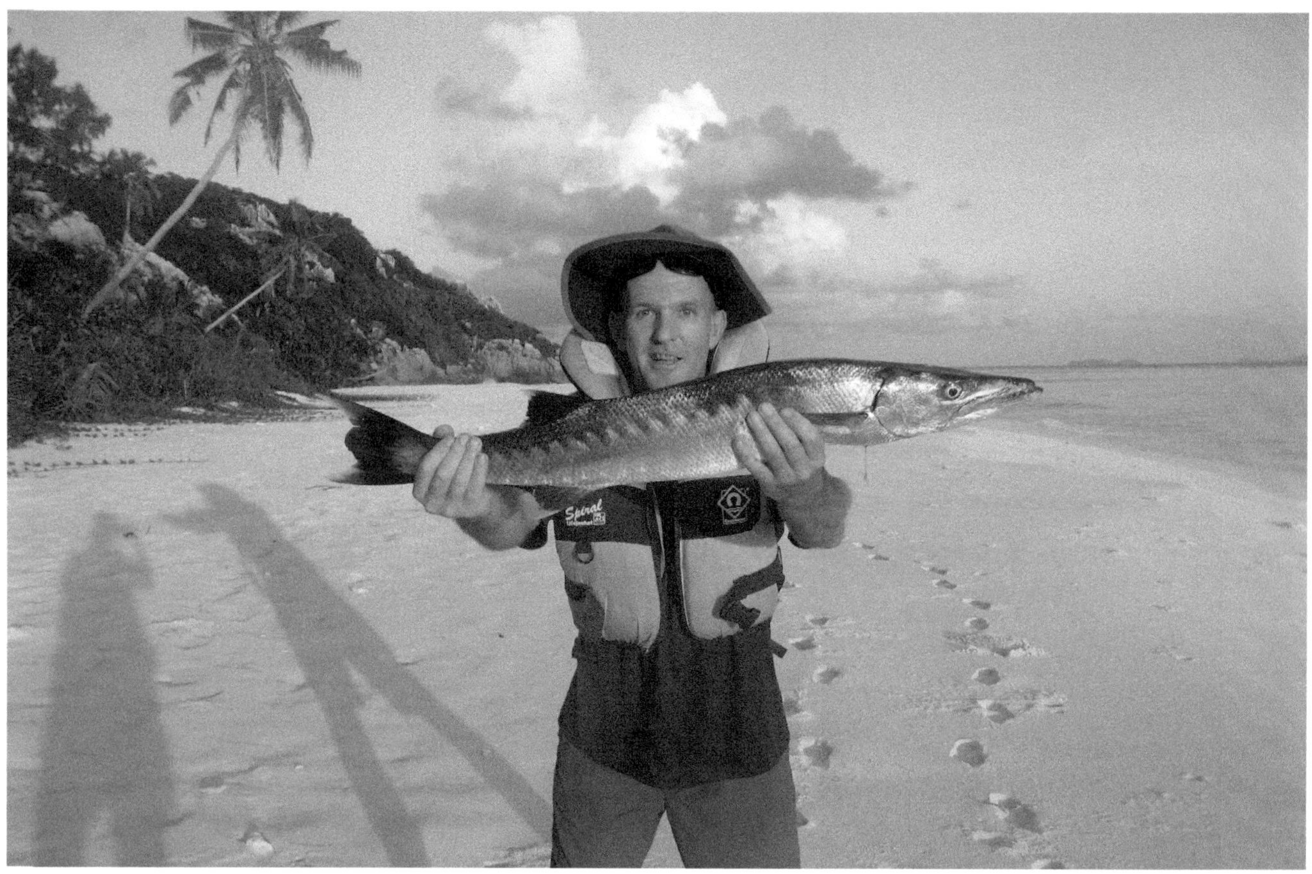

In our first few months, and with the realisation that we needed to change the way in which we looked at food, we found it hard to understand why fishing wasn't undertaken more often, and it soon seemed obvious to us that not only was fishing an essential part of providing fresh food, but it was also a very magical and rewarding pastime. Melv was in his element; he loved his fishing, and boat trips in Seychelles were very special.

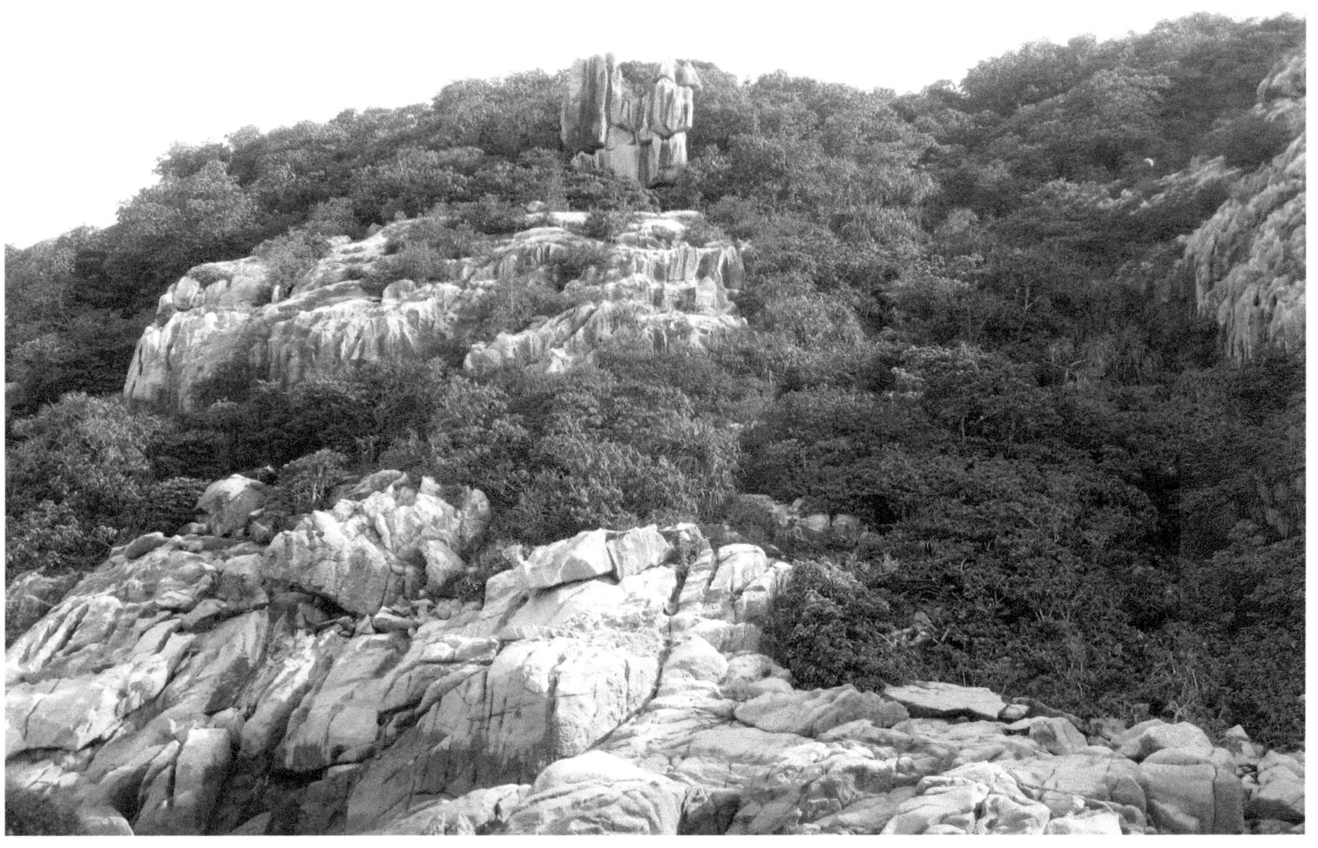

The northern aspect of Aride was not a side we got to see very often. It was beautiful; apart from the small beach, Ti L'Anse, at its eastern end, the interface was mostly sheer rocks that dropped steeply into the water. With very little substrate, the sparsely positioned trees and vegetated areas appeared to cling on to bare rock. Some of the rocky outcrops looked as though they had been sculpted, with rounded corners, deep overhangs and precariously placed boulders.

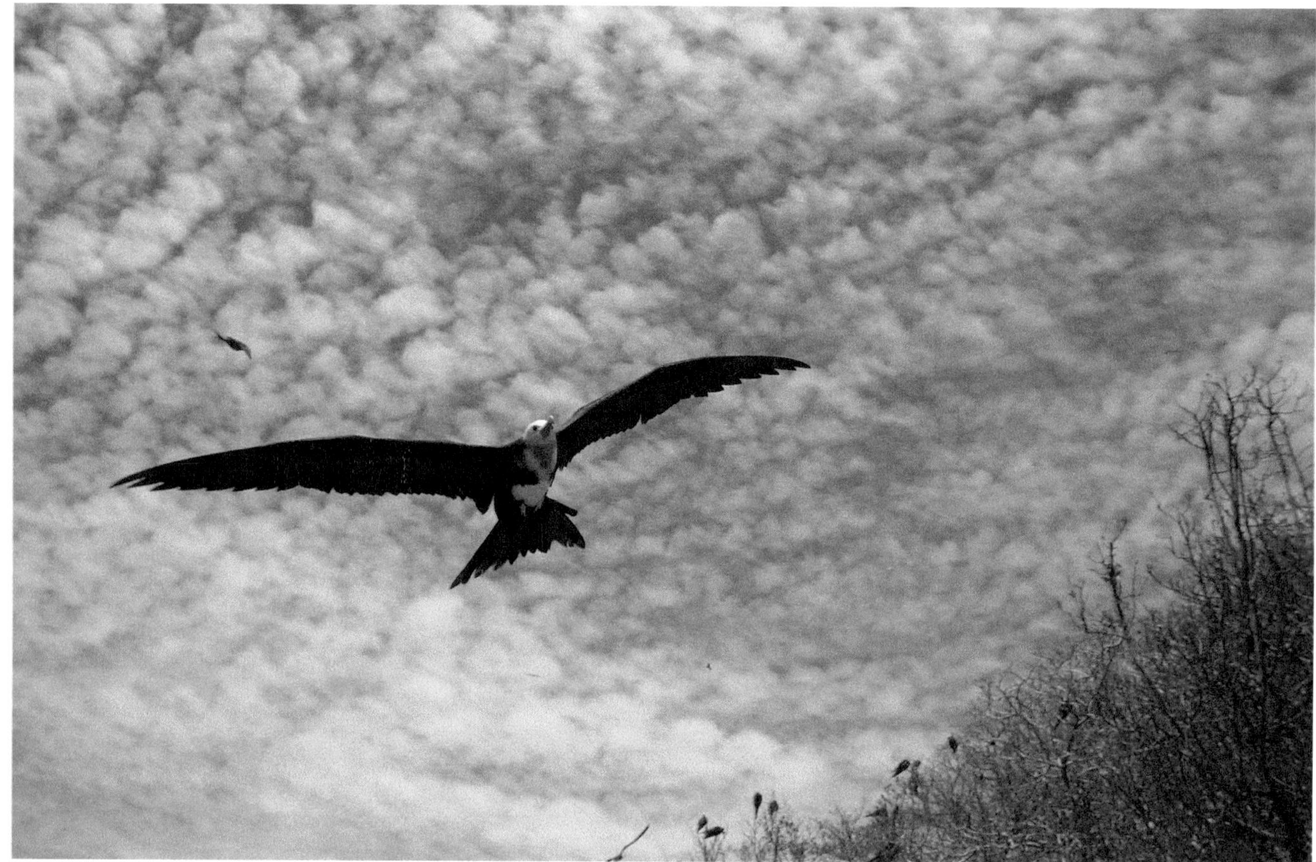

© *Chloe Prehn-Arnold*

The north face of Aride was home to some very important visitors, the great and lesser frigate birds. Although awkward on land, their large dinosaur-like profiles took to the thermals and hung there effortlessly. They were known as the pirates of the sky as their agility on the wing meant that there was never any let up for other feeding birds, from shearwaters to noddies, they weren't fussy, chasing and terrorising them until they dropped their prey.

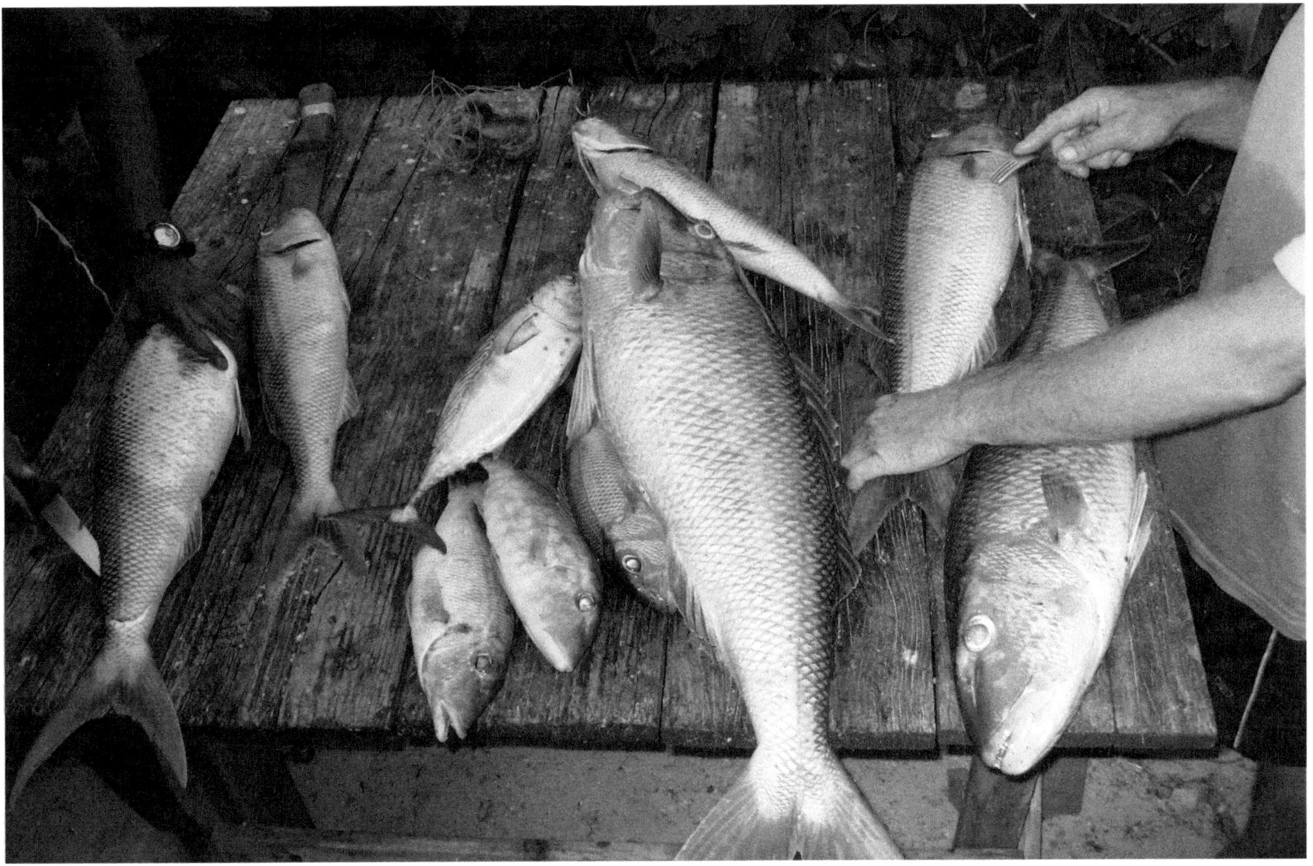

Even in the light winds of the northwest monsoon, the large expanse of uninterrupted Indian Ocean often seemed to make the sea a little rougher on the northern side of the island, especially towards the western end. Typically though, this made for good fishing, and on this occasion we had brought in a great haul, with a 6lb jobfish, more than enough to provide several meals for the whole island.

*A l0lb red snapper caught on 'Red Snapper Day'*

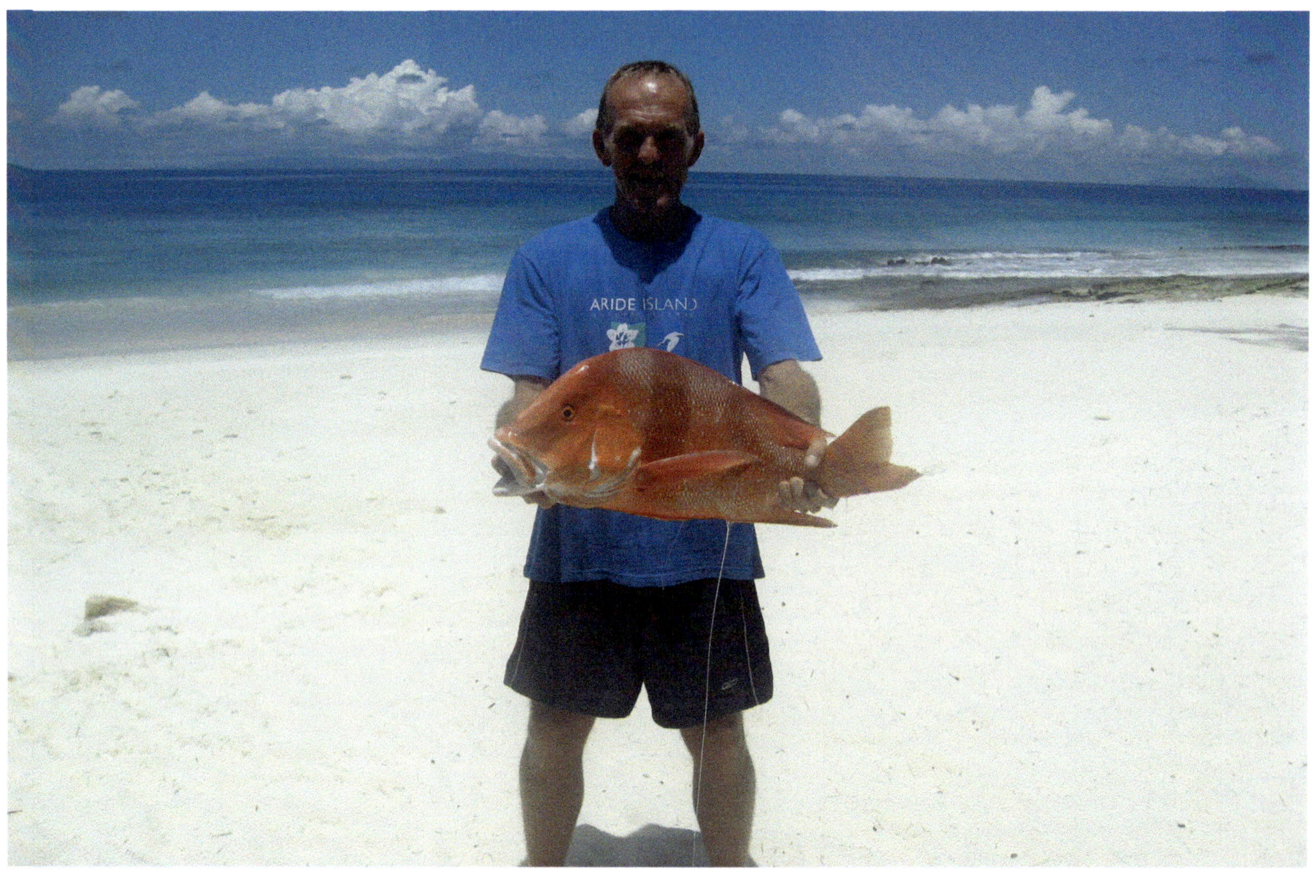

Surrounded by the Indian Ocean, our diets became filled with fresh fish in such variety that any fishmonger would have been proud of, and we ultimately returned home to the UK with a lifetime's worth of fisherman's tales. I recall what we now look back on as 'Red Snapper Day', when Melv's rod bent in two to reveal a whopping great snapper on the other end. What a catch!

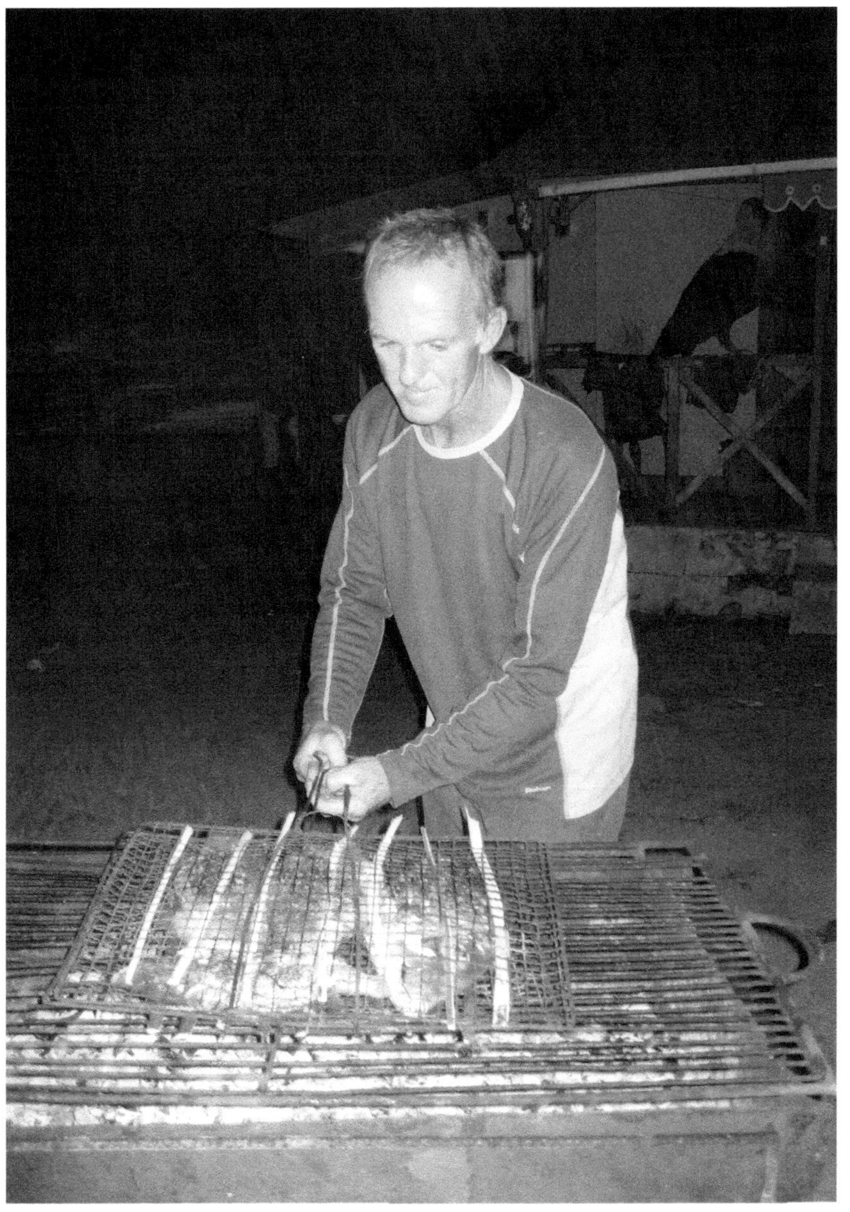

It was satisfying when everyone worked together to prepare food; it was one of the simple pleasures that we all enjoyed and made the island feel homely. Being hungry was a common denominator between all who lived on Aride, which meant that we all valued the simple gratification of food provision. Communal BBQs and eating together were always special and appreciated by all.

## *Fresh pineapple all year round*

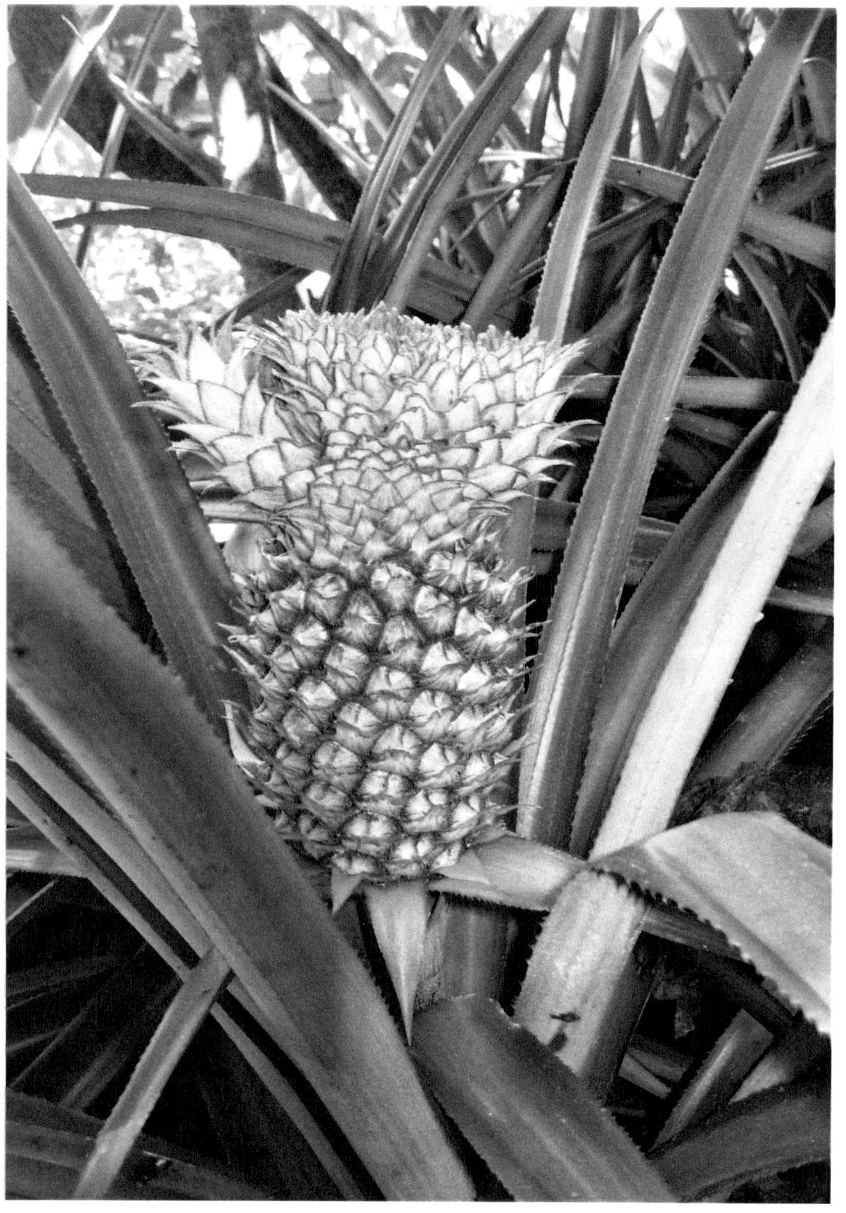

It was a real bonus to have a fresh selection of pineapples, papayas, guavas, oranges, grapefruits and limes on the island. The pineapples grew all year and, thanks to predictable sunny days, they soon ripened. Until I lived on Aride, I never knew they grew on a central flower stalk from a small, bushy plant, almost cactus-like, with long, pointed, half succulent leaves.

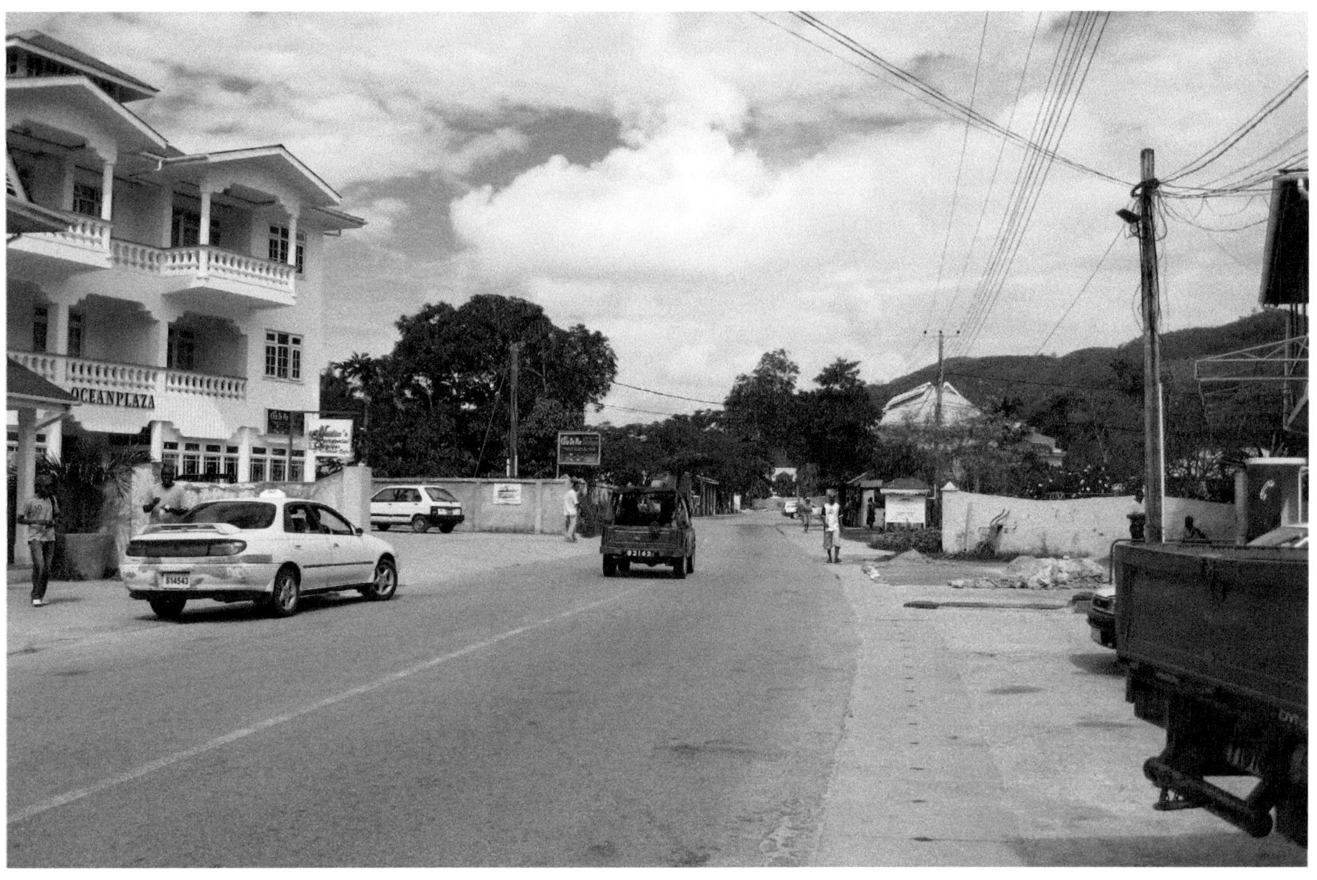

For those of us living on Aride, Praslin was the closest island that had the essentials, although not a lot of variety. It was split into three main areas: Grand Anse, Baie Ste Anne and Cote D'or. Grand Anse was the most convenient, and where we typically visited; Baie Ste Anne involved a longer boat trip a little further round the coast, but did have the main bank and several useful shops and offices, and Cote D'or was the main tourist resort of Praslin, so whilst it was the closest to Aride, it had only a few shops and not many facilities.

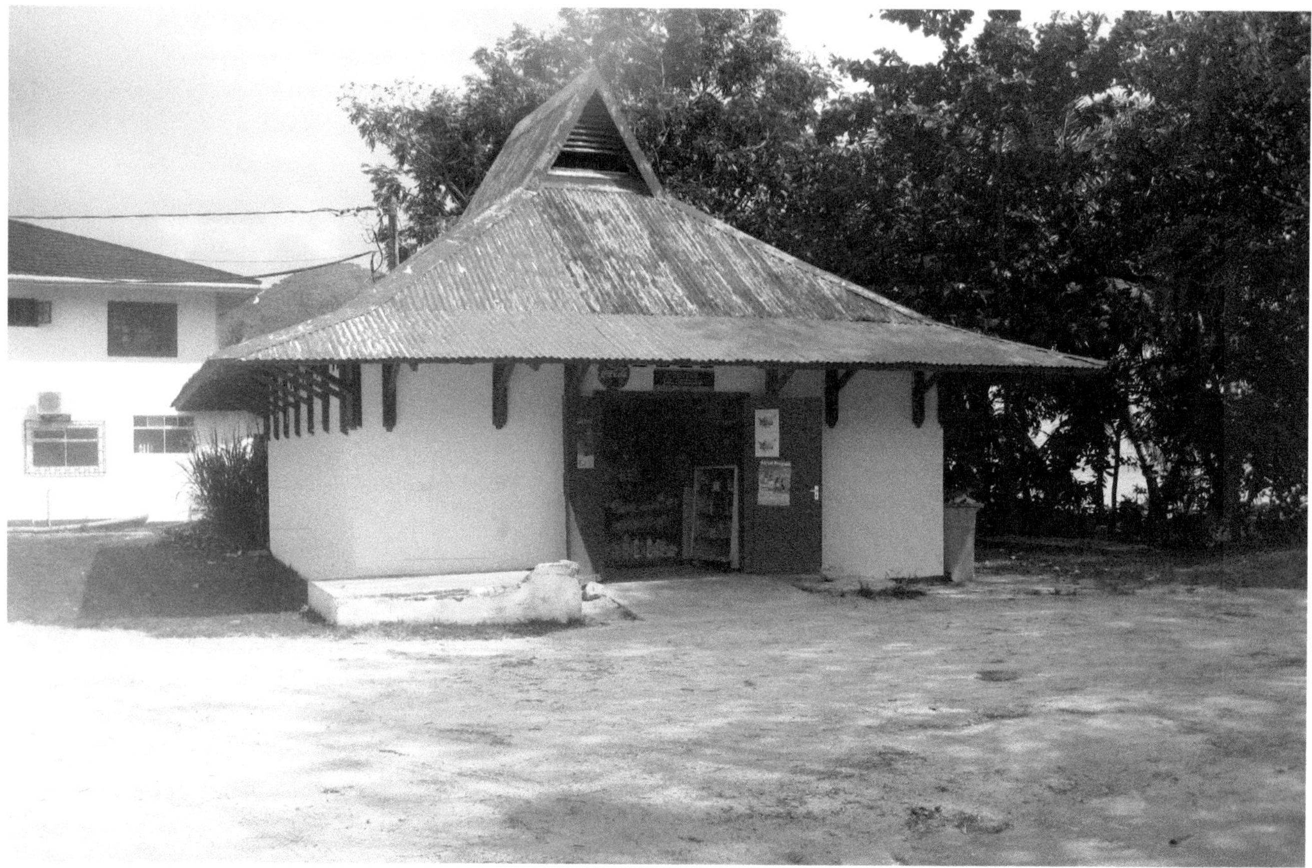

All three towns were rather one dimensional; any shops and facilities were situated along the main street, many a little run down and with a bit of a shanty town façade. Mr Sentile's shop, adjacent to the jetty, was not a shop as you would imagine back in the UK. You didn't walk around; it was more like a stall, where you stood at the counter and looked in.

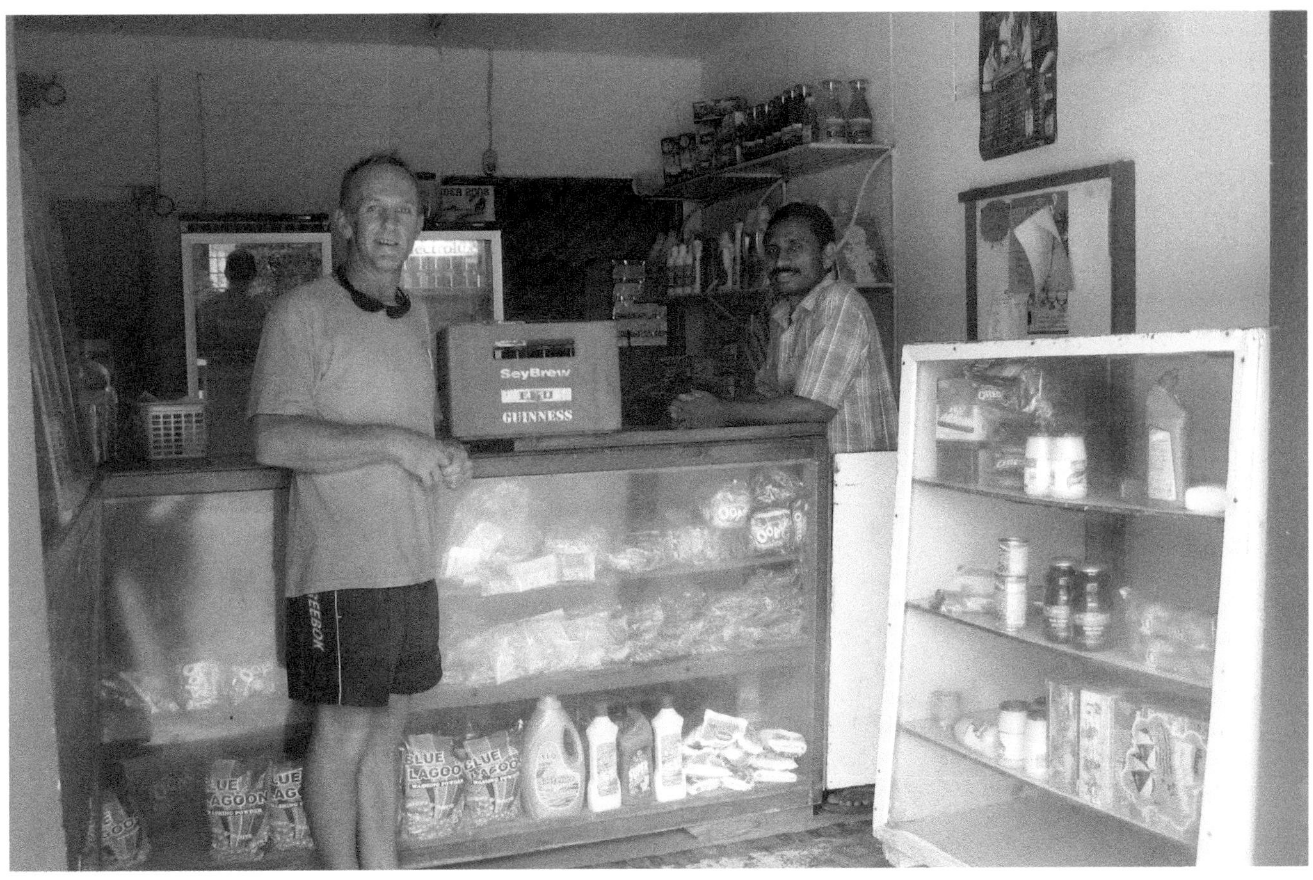

Only if Mr Sentile thought it was going to be a big shop would he invite you in, giving you the chance to delve into the freezer and look at his prize chicken thighs. There were shelves on each side wall for tins and packets, with a couple of chest freezers below for a very limited selection of meat. The vegetables were on the back wall, leaving room for a large refrigerator to keep beer, juices and water cold.

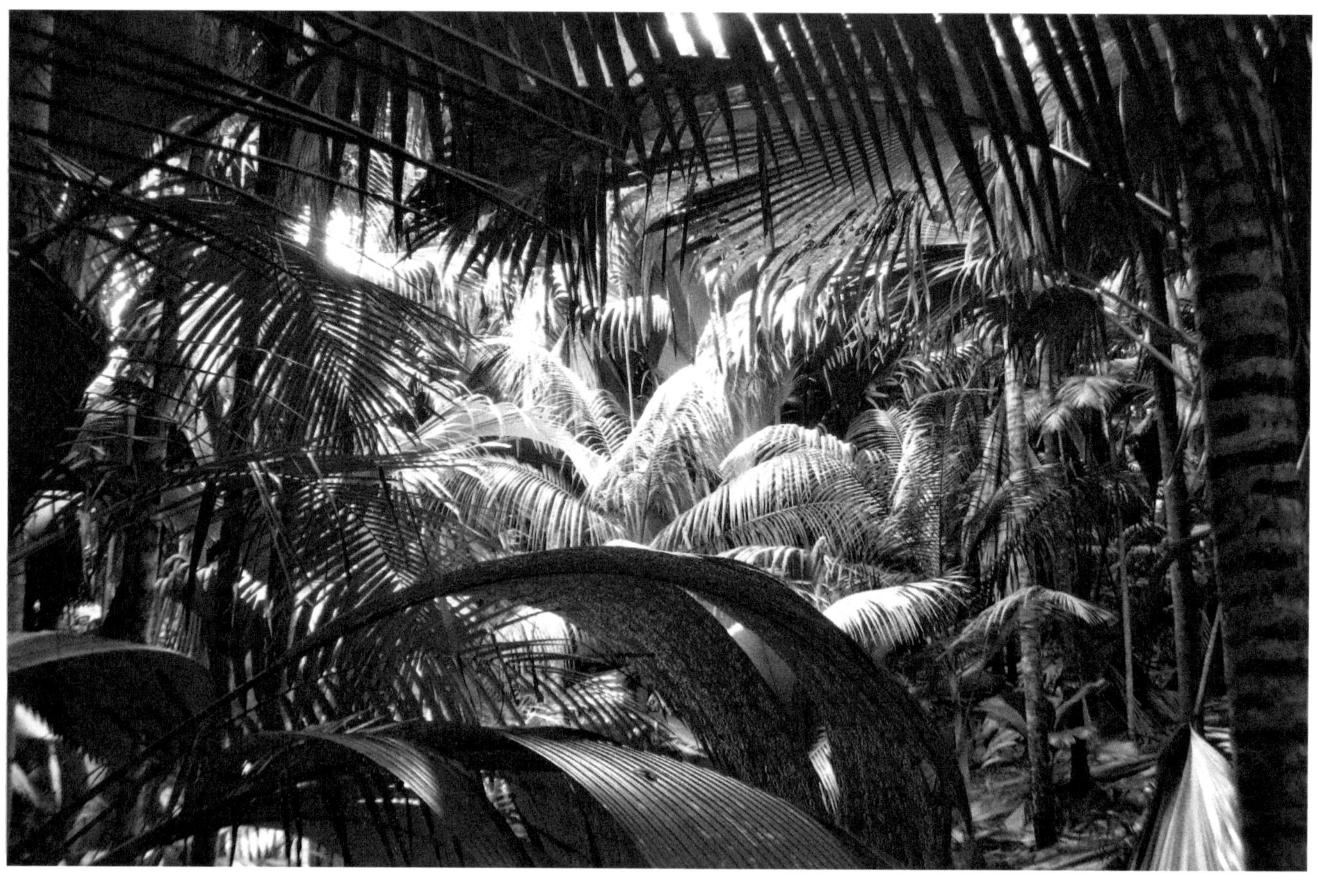

A visit to Praslin brought with it different sights, sounds and smells. The Vallée de Mai Reserve, a palm forest, was in the middle of the island. The forest was a rare remnant of when Seychelles' granitic islands were still part of Gondwanaland, the huge land mass which included Africa, Madagascar and India. Millions of years of isolation enabled a unique community of plants and animals to develop and some of these species are found nowhere else.

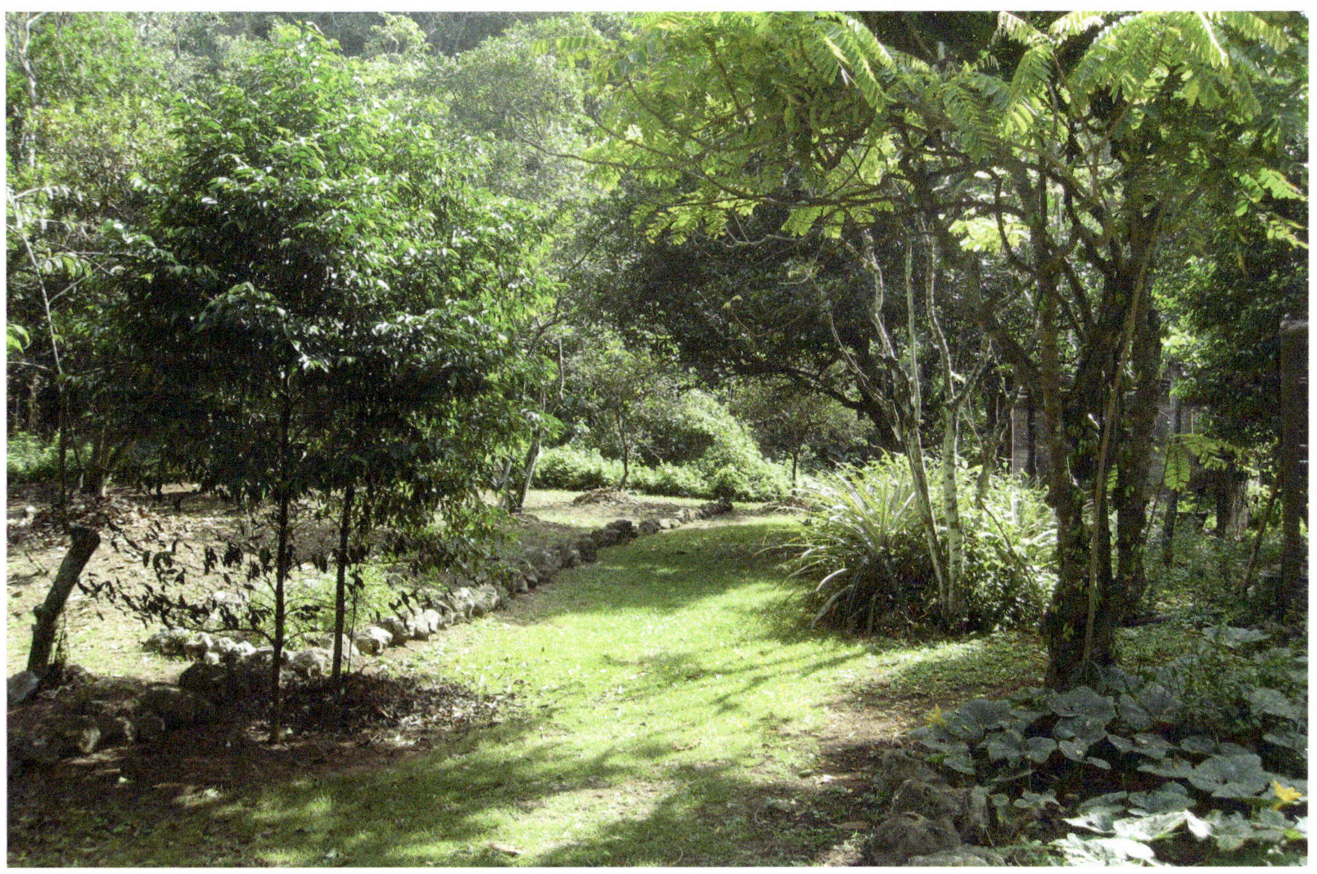

With our shopping trips limited by rough seas and the lack of fresh produce on Praslin, there were often lean times for food, when the larder looked empty and food stocks were low. Alongside the sea, the Aride garden filled a huge gap, providing produce that would otherwise not be available. It was the biggest flat open space aside from the village and was full of greenery.

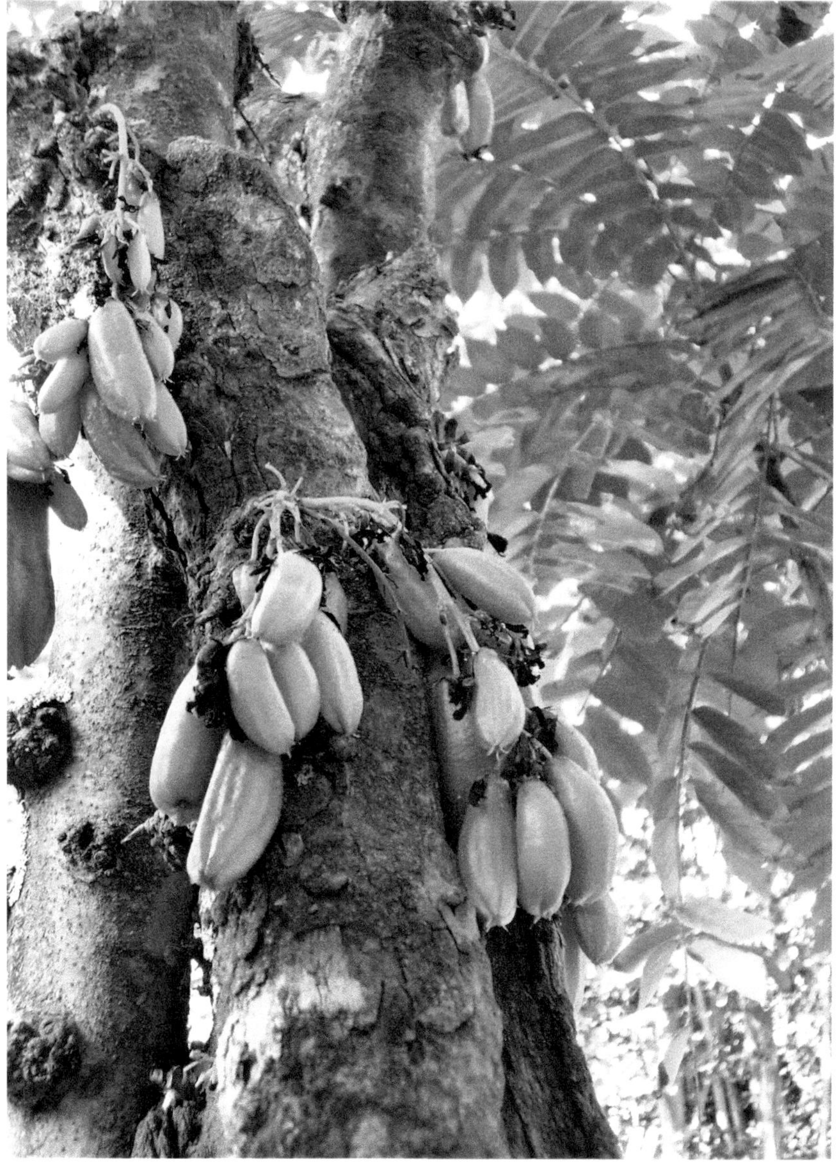

© Chloe Prehn-Arnold

The fruit trees overhung the paths, the papayas lined the back edge, and the bananas were dotted amongst the open grassland areas. The garden was a very important source of fresh vegetables; in the UK it was a novelty to have home-grown, but on Aride it was a necessity.

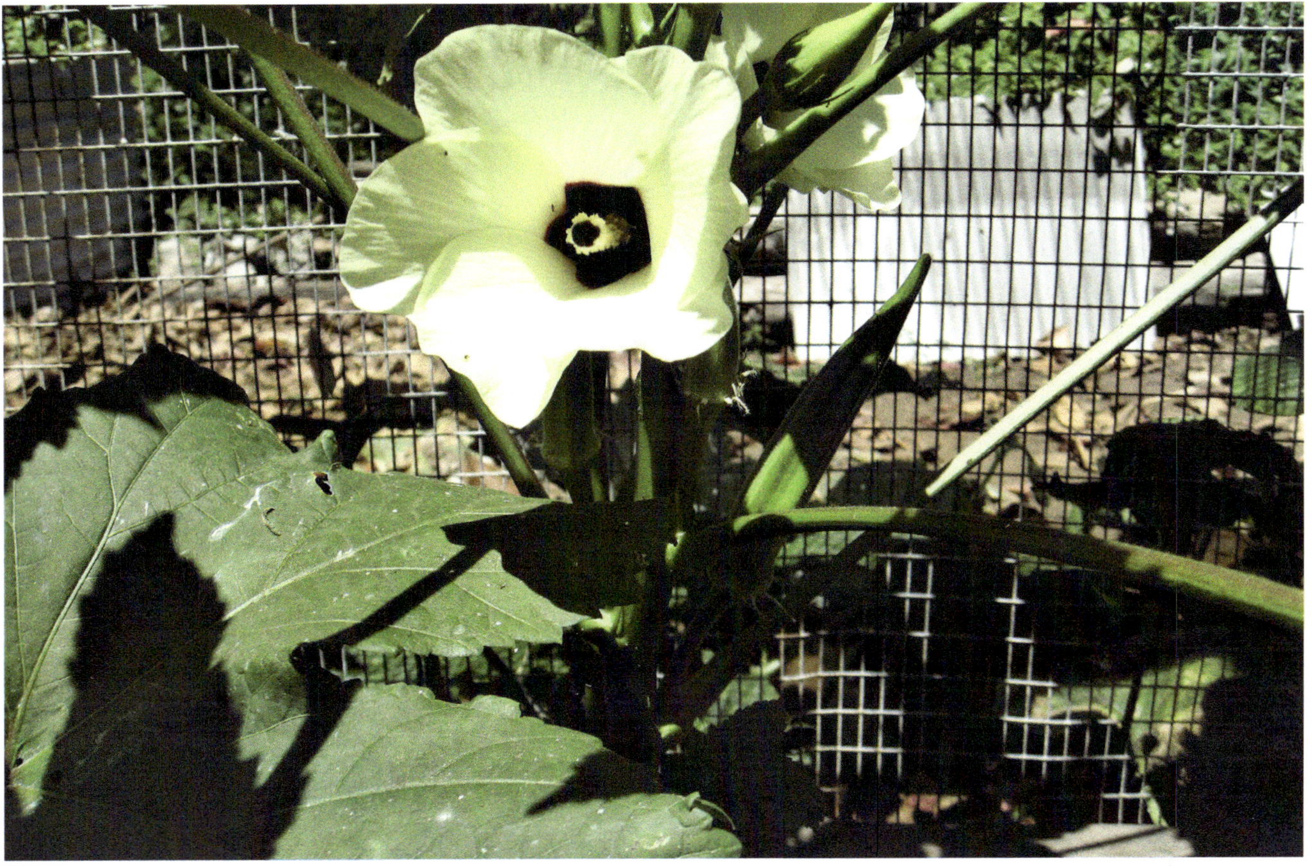

One of my favourite jobs was harvesting the produce we needed for tea, and I distinctly recall picking the first okra. They grew on a large-leaved shrub with very delicate hibiscus type flowers that were a gorgeous sherbet-lemon colour with a deep purple centre.

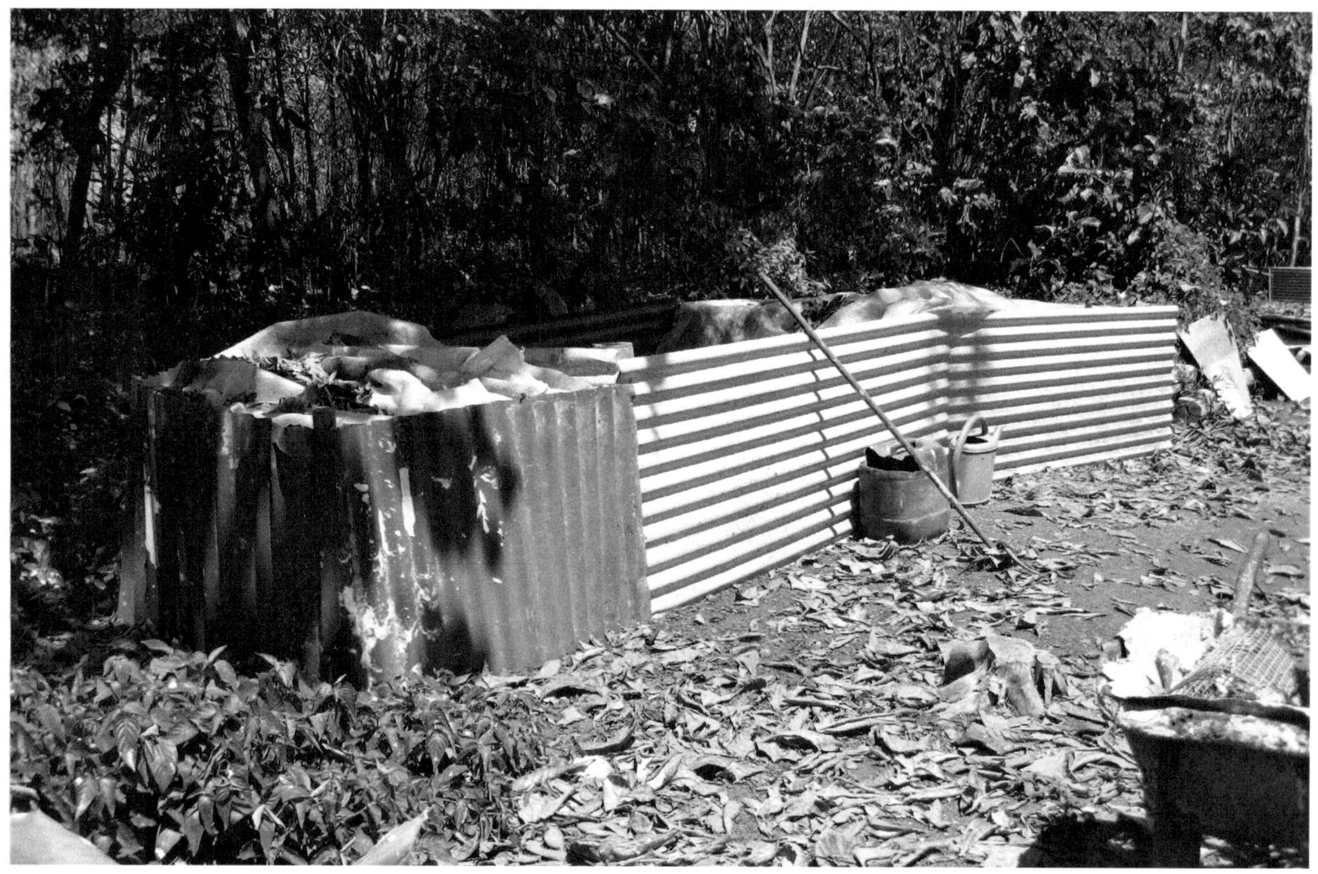

Although a difficult, hot and humid climate for physical work, time spent in the garden was always very rewarding, whether we were clearing areas, harvesting bamboo to make supporting frames or creating a compost heap. Not only did we benefit from fresh, home-grown produce but for me, and I am sure many others, time spent in the garden was very uncomplicated and therapeutic – it was a place for complete escapism.

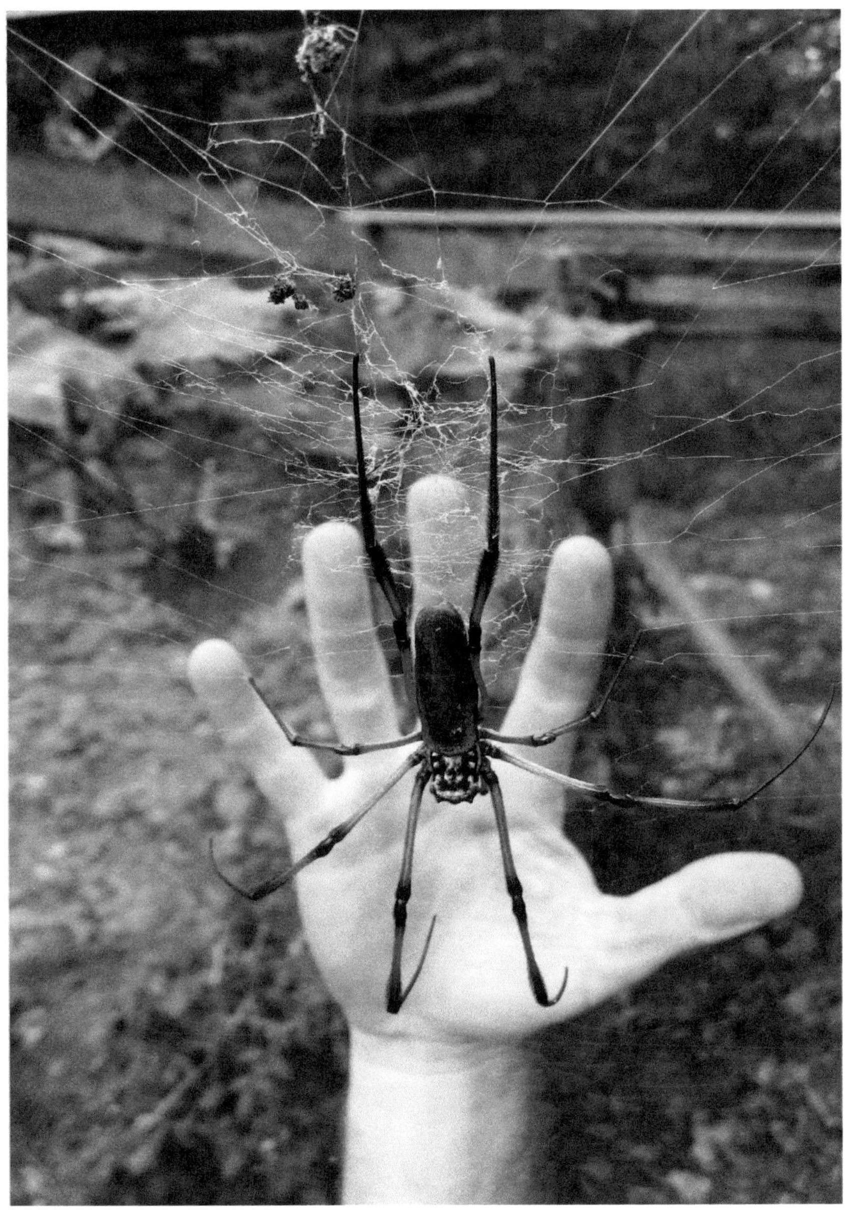

There were two shade houses in the garden, often frequented by golden orb-weaver spiders. The shade was essential for the plants to withstand the extreme heat of the northwest monsoon. Without adequate cover, the plants and produce would cook.

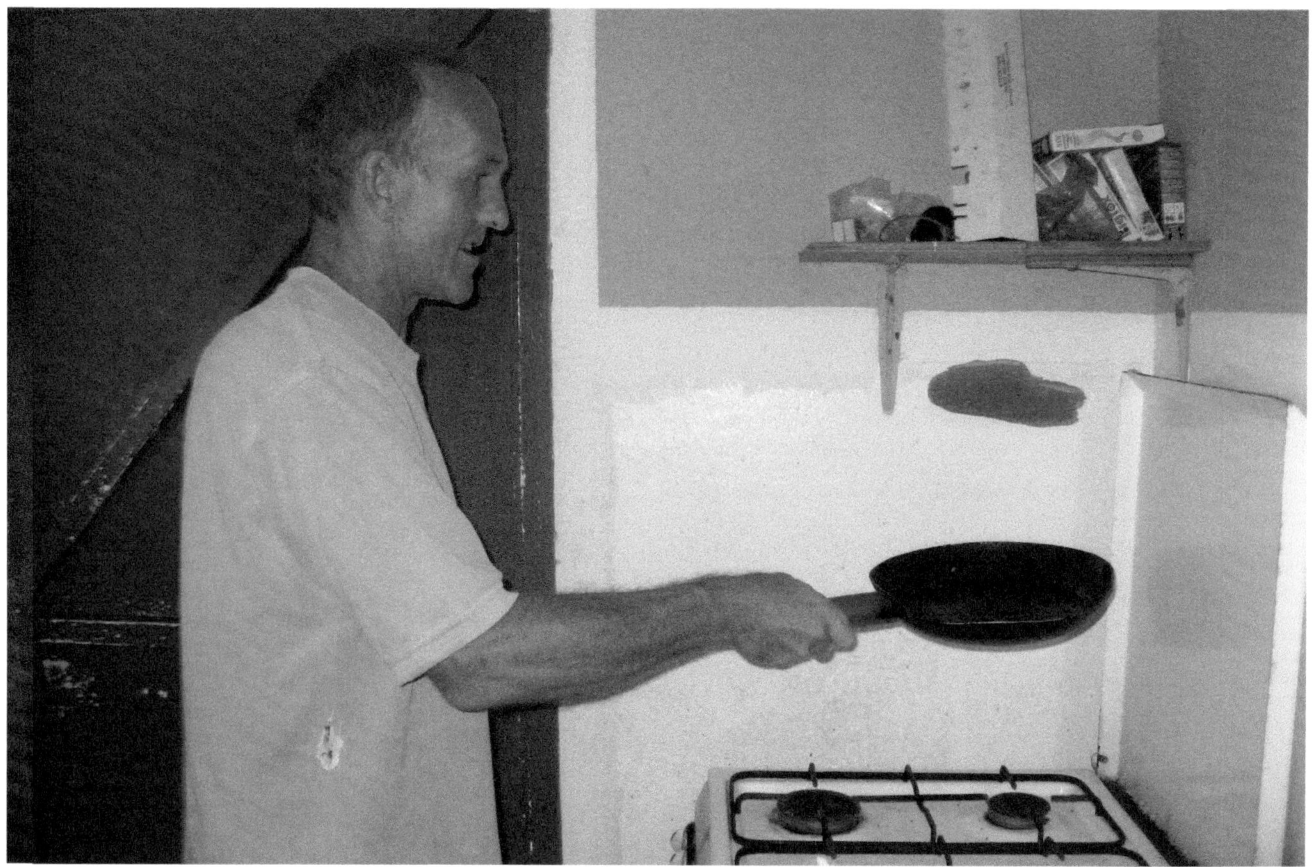

Making do with what we had and getting the most from it was all part of the challenge of both living and working on Aride. At times it would get us down, particularly on the food front. Everything had to be cooked from scratch – if we wanted a sandwich, Melv had to make the bread. There wasn't any fast food, no grabbing a snack out of the fridge when you felt hungry; they just weren't available.

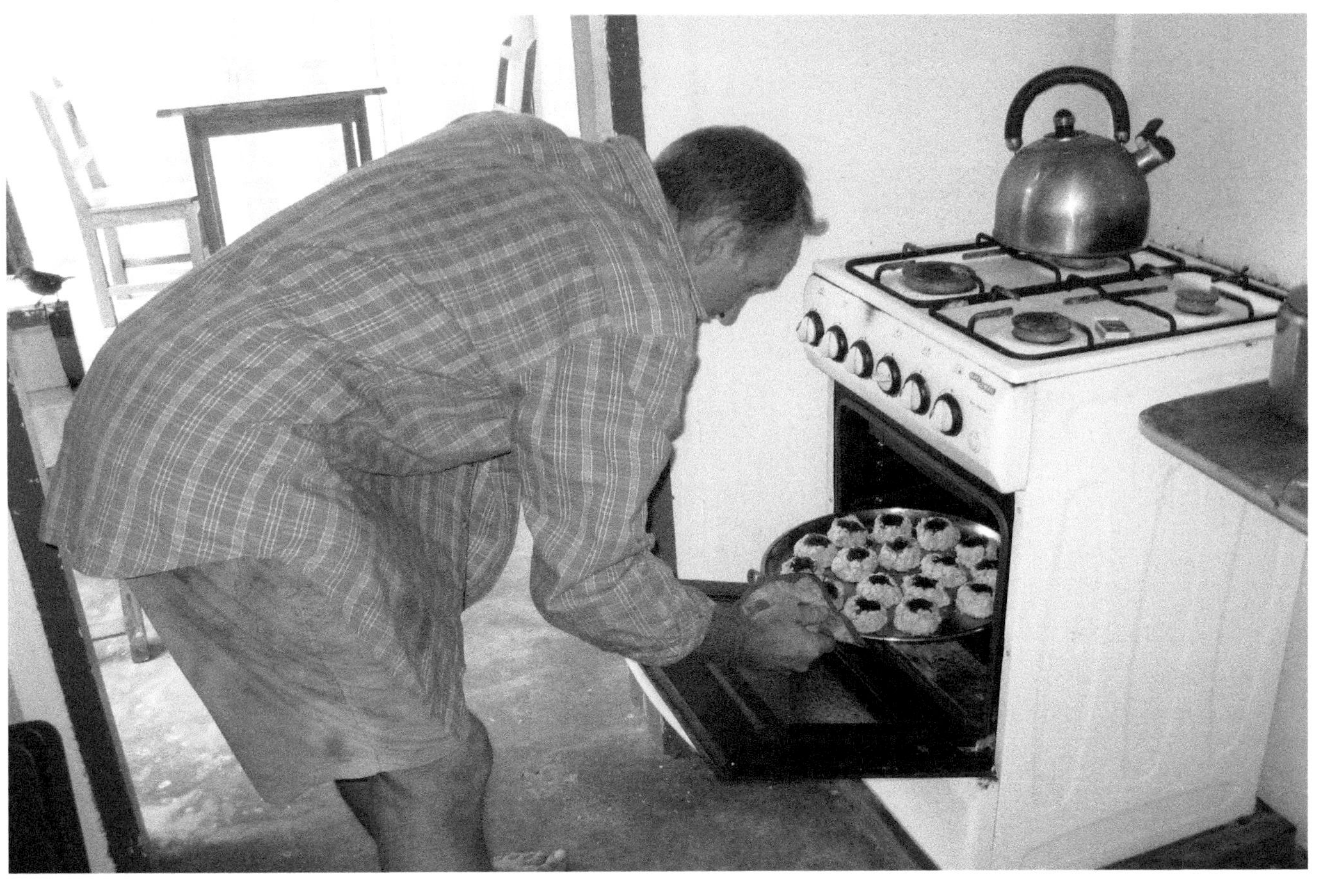

As we adjusted to a Seychellois diet and stopped eating processed food, sauces, biscuits and snacks, our bodies hankered for sweet stuff and the craving was hard to satisfy. However, that all changed when Lara taught Melv how to bake our own cakes and biscuits from the limited ingredients available to us.

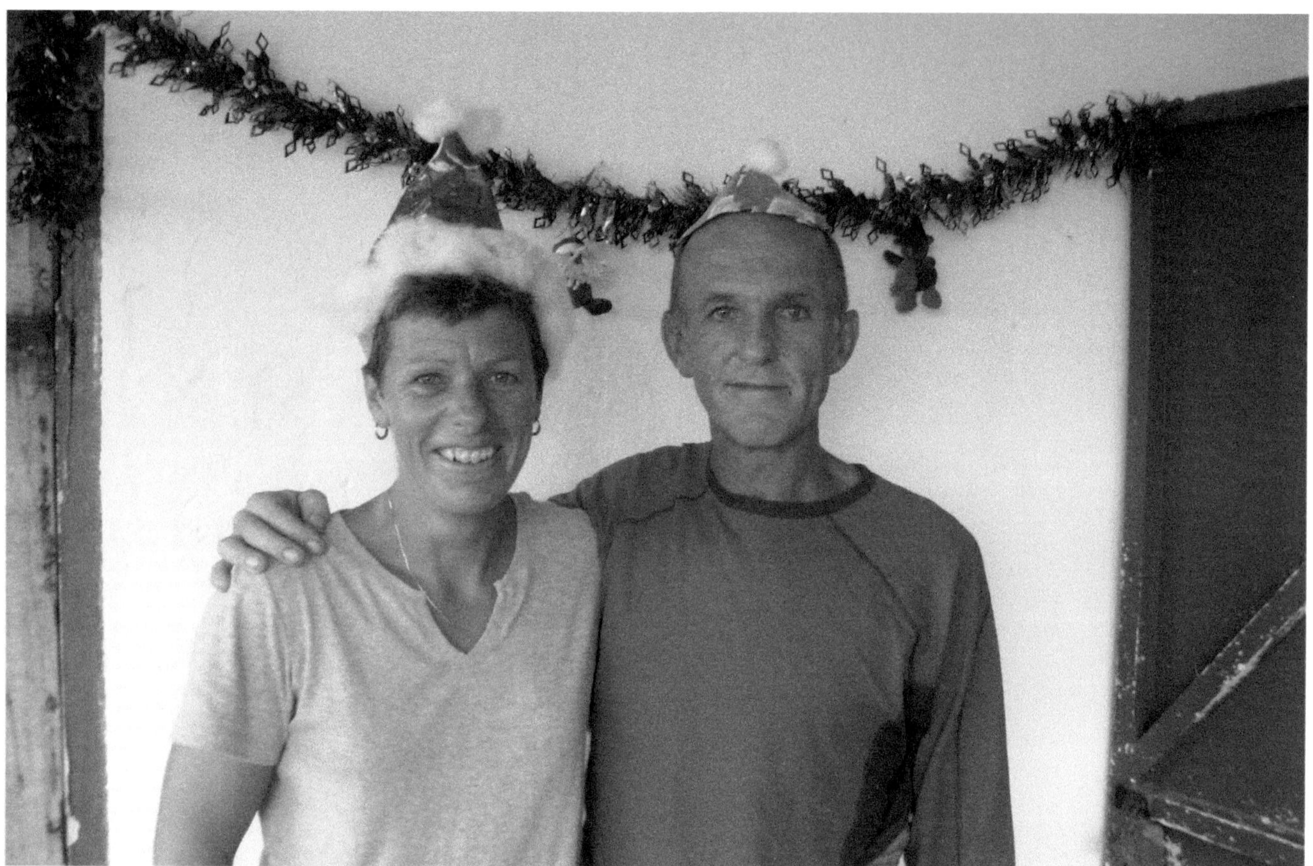

© *Chloe Prehn-Arnold*

In the UK, special days were always dominated by food, but on Aride that tradition became more of a challenge. For Christmas, we rose to it, the island spirit taking over; everyone prepared a dish and we all ate together. Dinner was sorted with a big piece of pork, two large bottles of wine and all the trimmings we could gather between us; from chutneys and sauces to upside down cakes, we utilised the ingredients we had to form the most memorable meal.

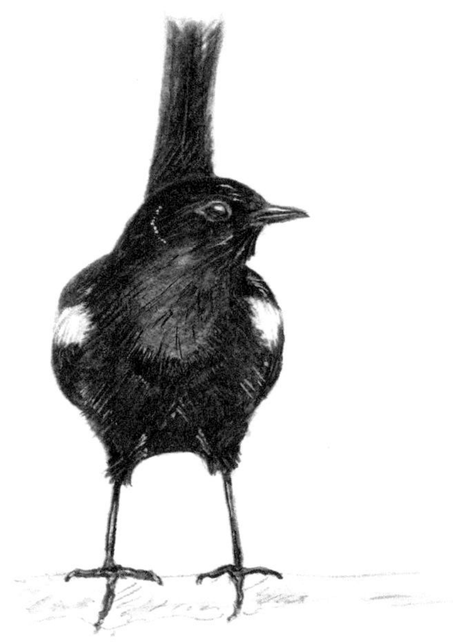

*Seychelles magpie robin*

# Chapter 6

# Man's Best Friend

Living on Aride gave us the rare and fantastic opportunity to get to know birds and other wildlife intimately and individually. With the magpie robins that was made even easier, as each bird had a different ring colour combination on their left leg to allow us to track the population, so we always knew who was who and who was doing what with (or to) whom.

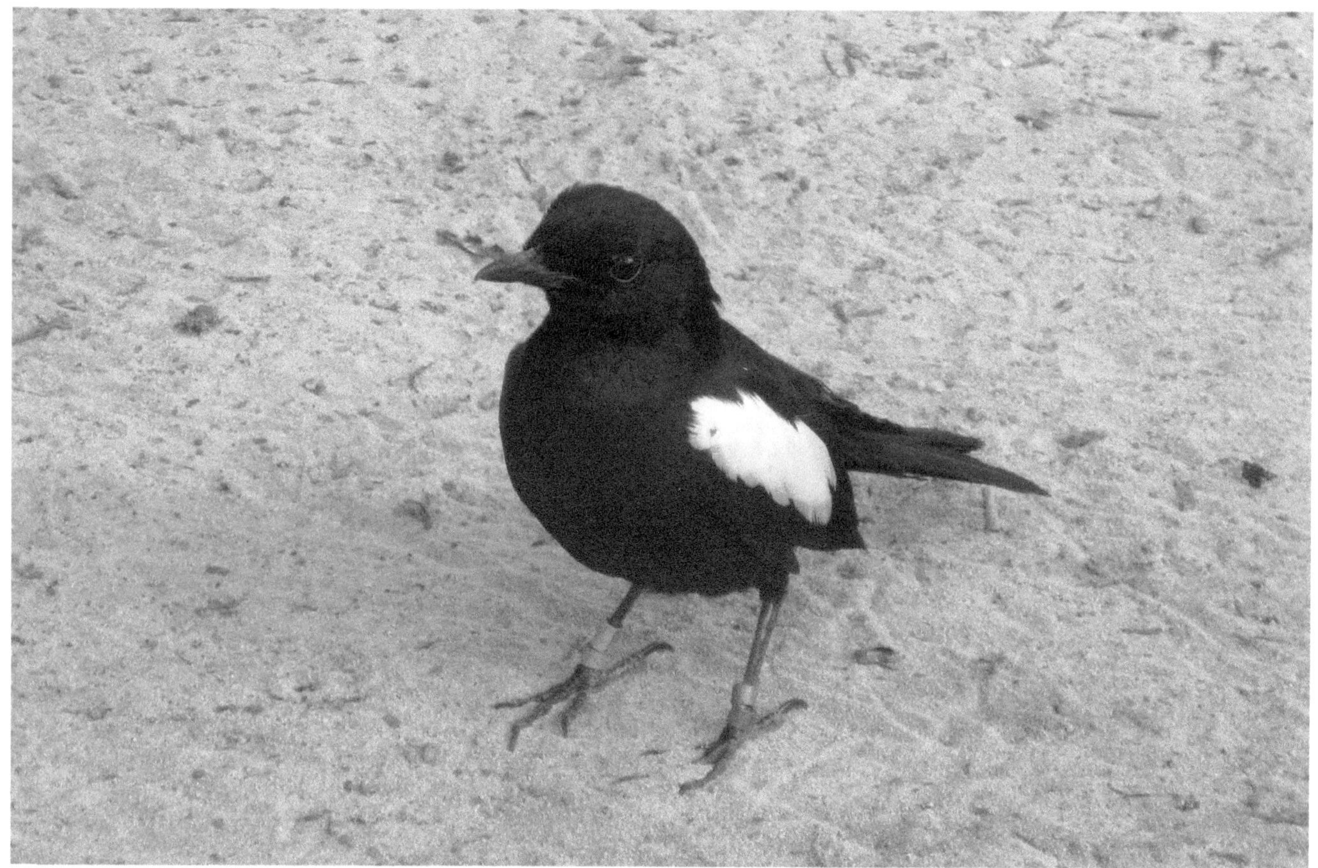

Magpie robins became part of our everyday life; as suggested by their name, they are a cross between a large robin and a small magpie. They have the behaviour, stance and movement of a robin, and the colours, cheekiness and brains of a magpie. Similar to the size of a UK blackbird and with shared behavioural traits, these small, attractive, black and white birds played a huge role in our lives.

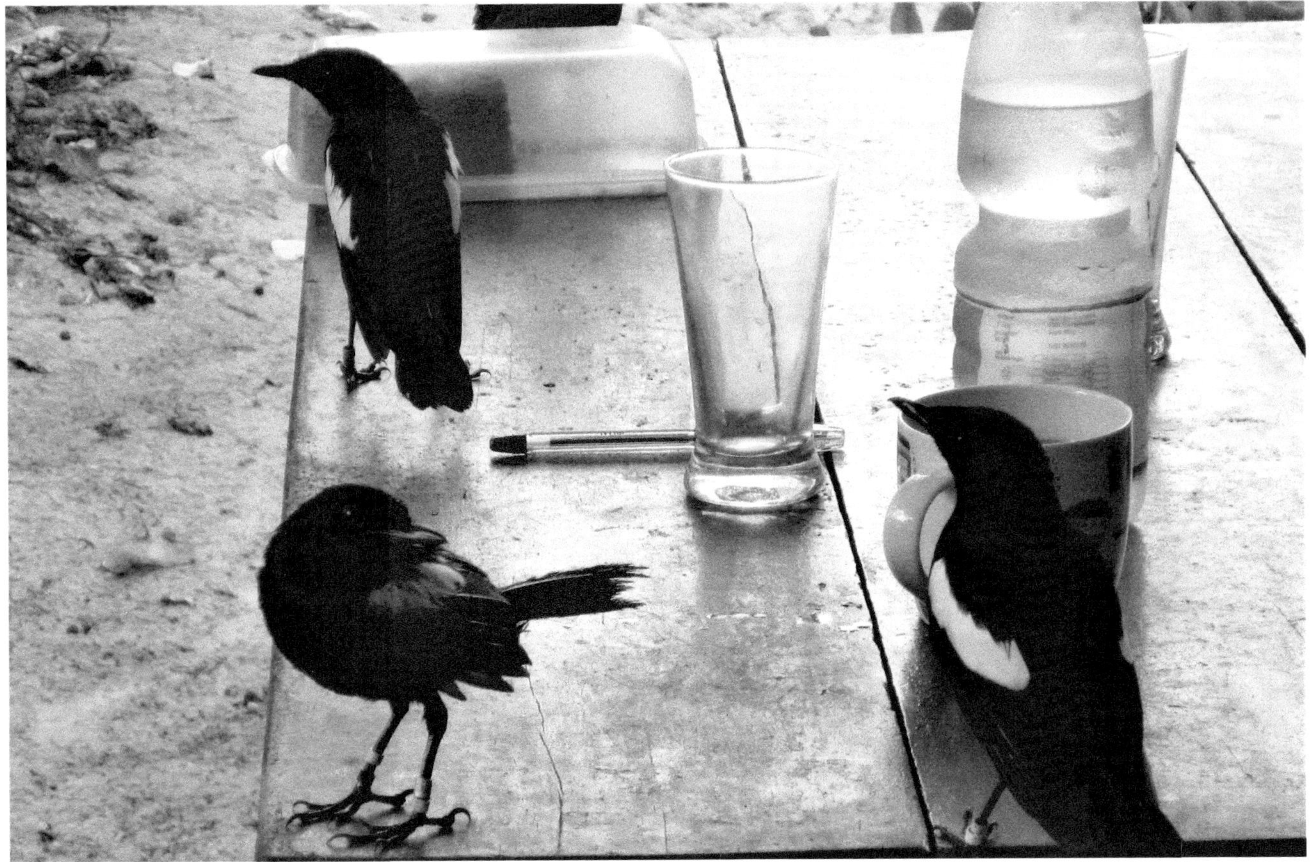

Magpie robins quickly became part of the fixtures and fittings of our home and there was hardly a time in daylight hours when there wasn't one hopping round the veranda or kitchen behind us. This association with humans and opportunistic behaviour may seem like a weakness, but no: they are incredibly smart little birds.

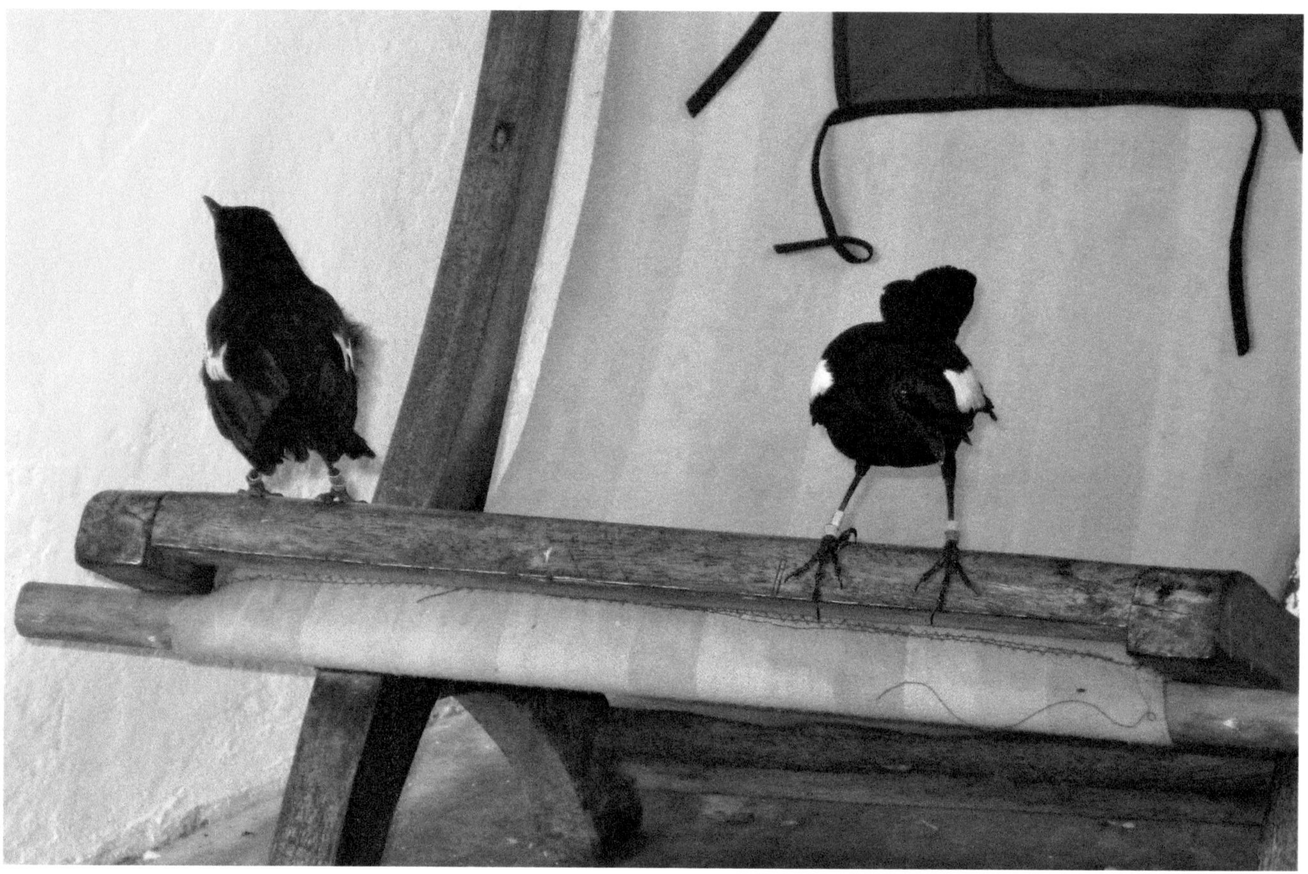

One slight downside to having robins around the house was that they pooed everywhere, but that said, so did everything else. Ziarrah was particularly good at strategic pooing. I wasn't sure if it was out of excitement, or appreciation, but she would always leave a little message in a number of places: chairs, tables, worktops, the water filter… she wasn't fussy.

*Young Seychelles magpie robin, sky-blue/blue*

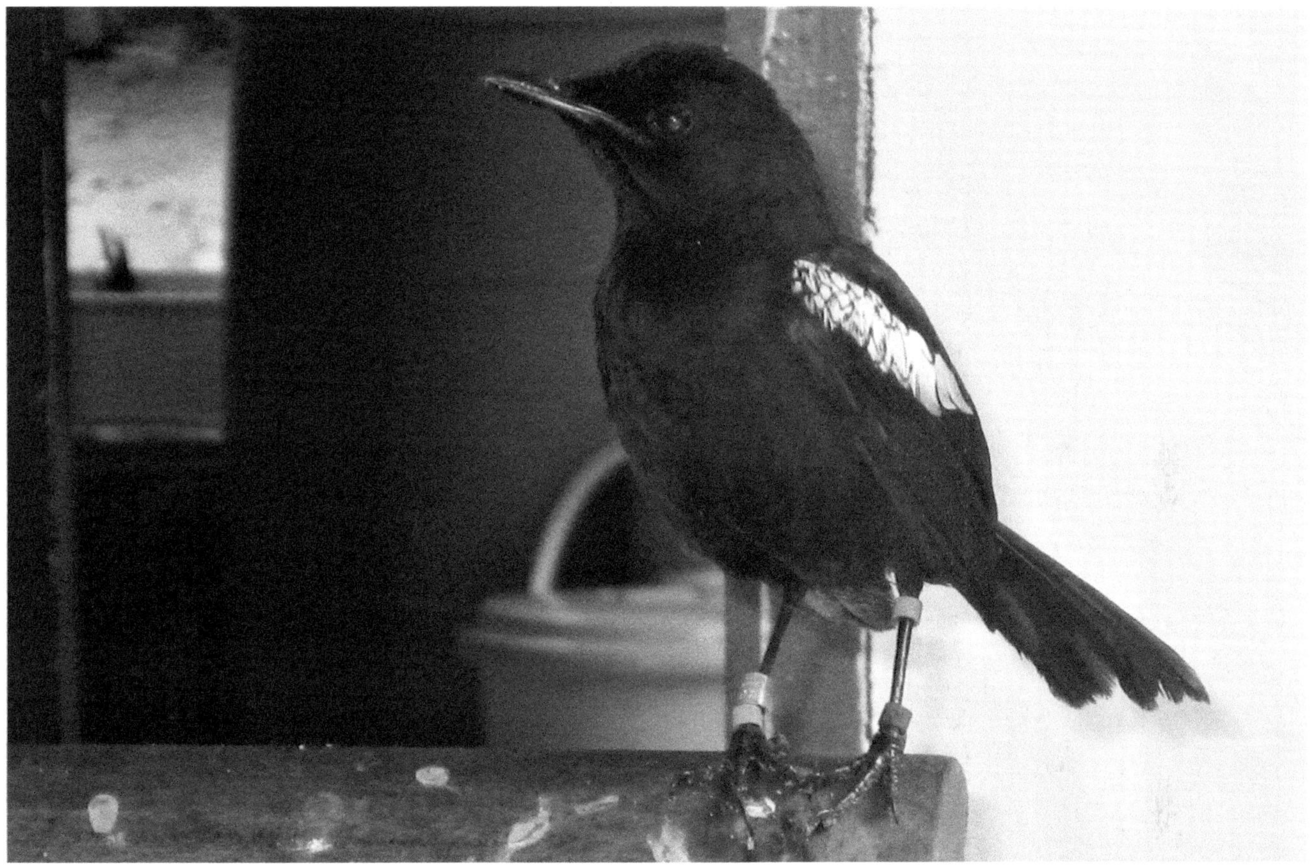

During our time on the island, we were privileged to see robins grow up and mature. When we first arrived sky-blue/blue was a young bird, indicated by her plumage; her white feathers were tinged with brown and the 'robin' black sheen slightly tinted with ginger.

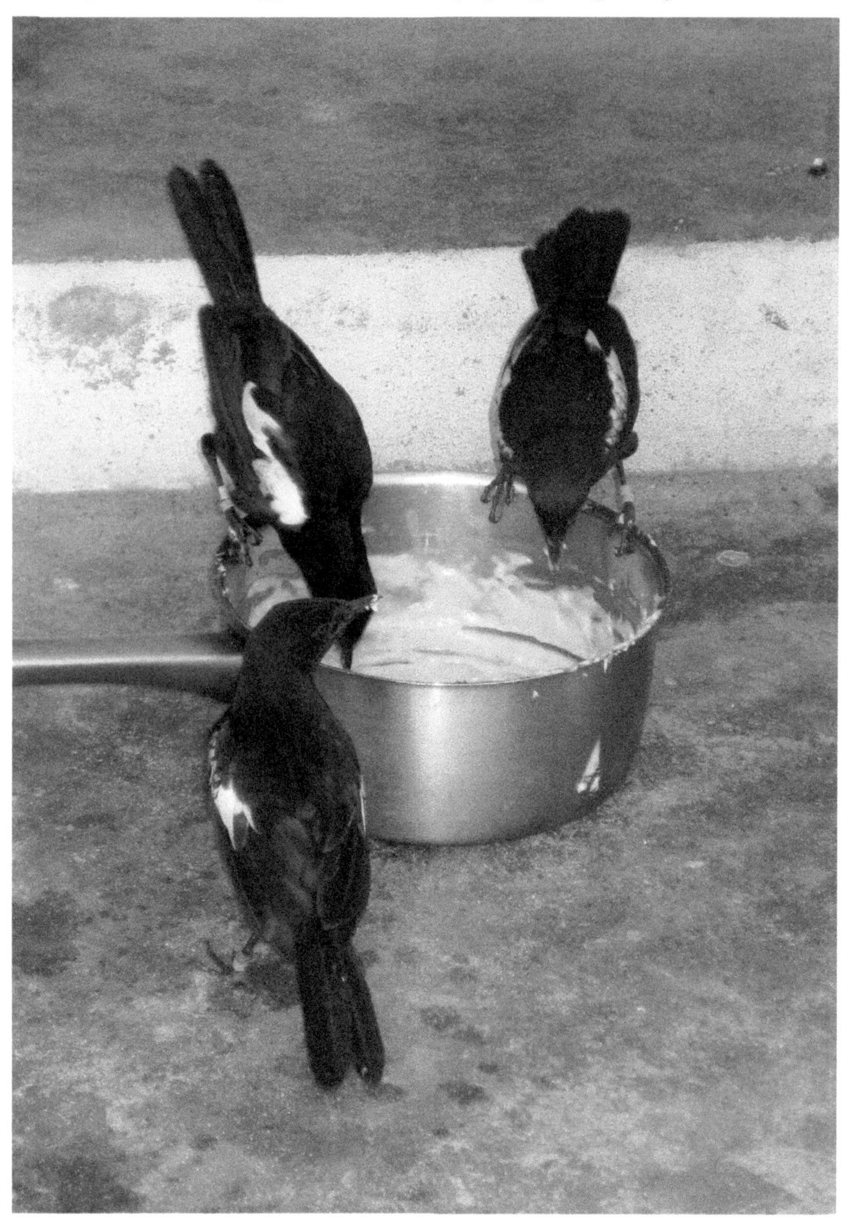

When in a hurry, instead of hopping or running, magpie robins move a little like Labrador dogs, with a sideways gait; they have a bit of a limp and one leading leg. The concrete floors in the houses posed a challenge for them and many a robin learnt to do the splits on our veranda in their rush to devour a piece of cheese. On the subject of food, they will eat anything, from spicy pumpkin soup to rice pudding and, if we weren't careful, they would have a good go before we did.

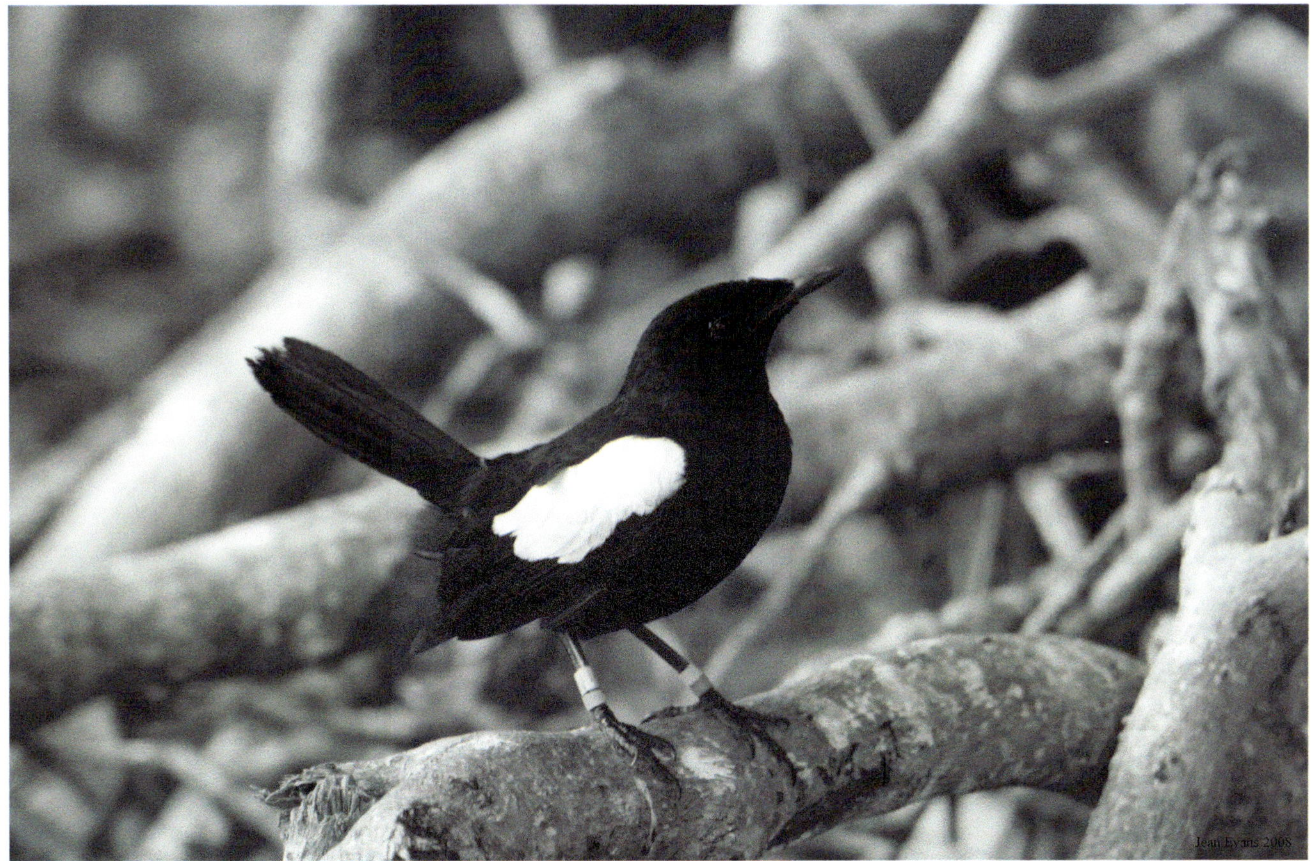

© *Jean Cheadle*

Despite the challenges of ensuring their welfare and coaxing the population to grow, the constant presence of magpie robins provided us with a sense of reliability and certainty, which lifted our spirits. It was odd; despite living in a place where there were so few of us, other people's lives could dominate our world, and the mood of any one of us could significantly affect the way the island felt - the wildlife provided an important antidote.

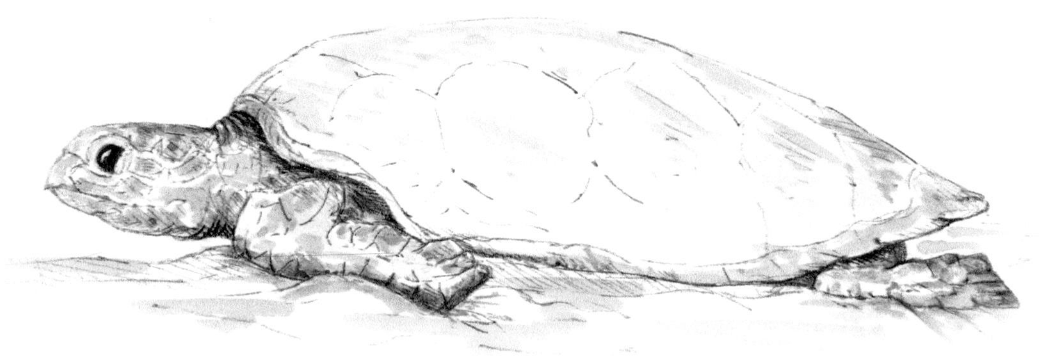

*Hawksbill turtle*

# Chapter 7

# Bulldozers on the Beach

There are two types of turtle that nest on Aride: the hawksbill — smaller with a hooked beak, as its name suggests, and the green – much larger, nowhere near as common and more of a night-time visitor. Both are critically endangered.

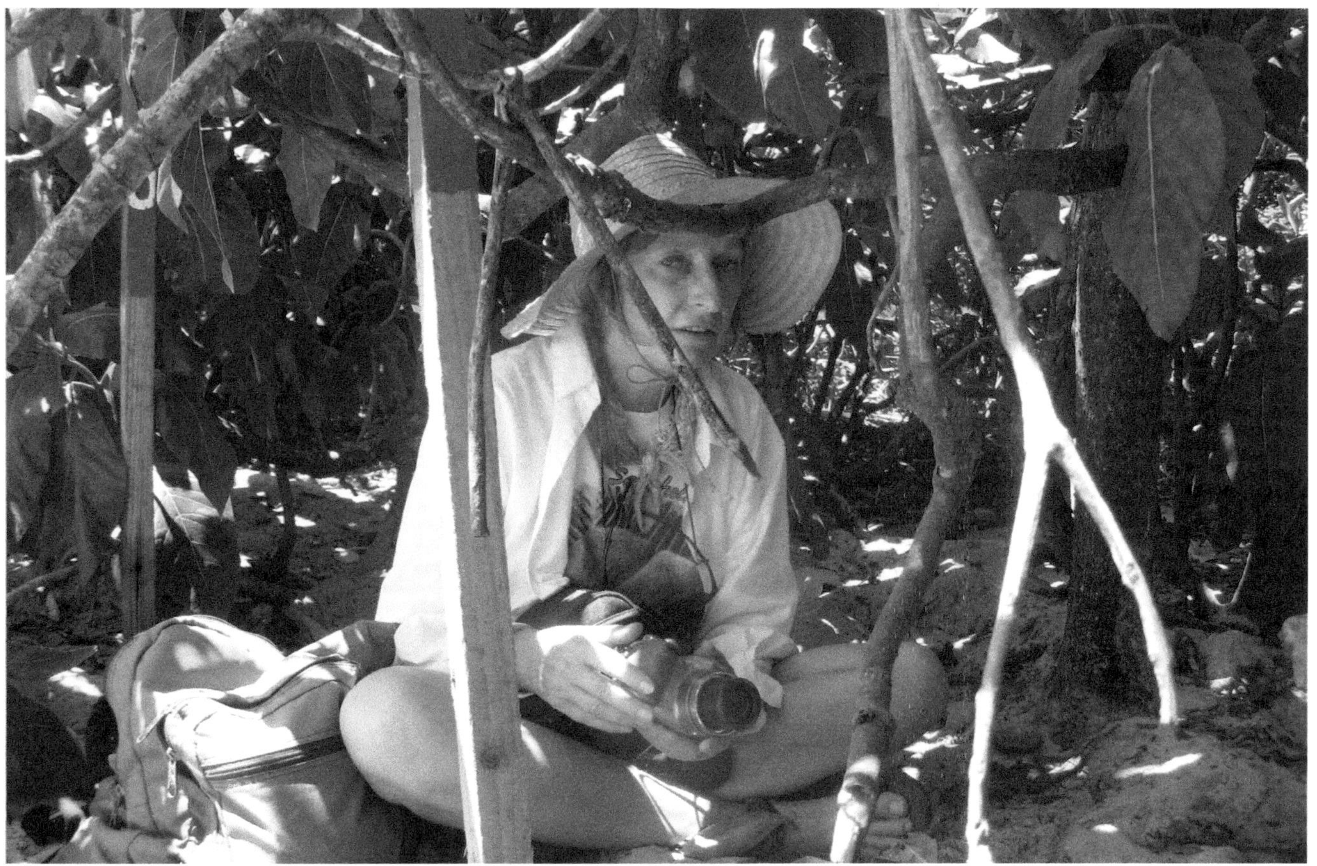

After a frantic, day-long induction from a brilliant, inspiring, eccentric American turtle professor, Jeanne, we were thrown into the deep end with live turtle specimens. What Jeanne didn't know about turtles wasn't worth knowing. Her knowledge was vast and her enthusiasm was infectious. With no experience, but as keen as mustard, we soaked up as much about turtles as our heads would allow.

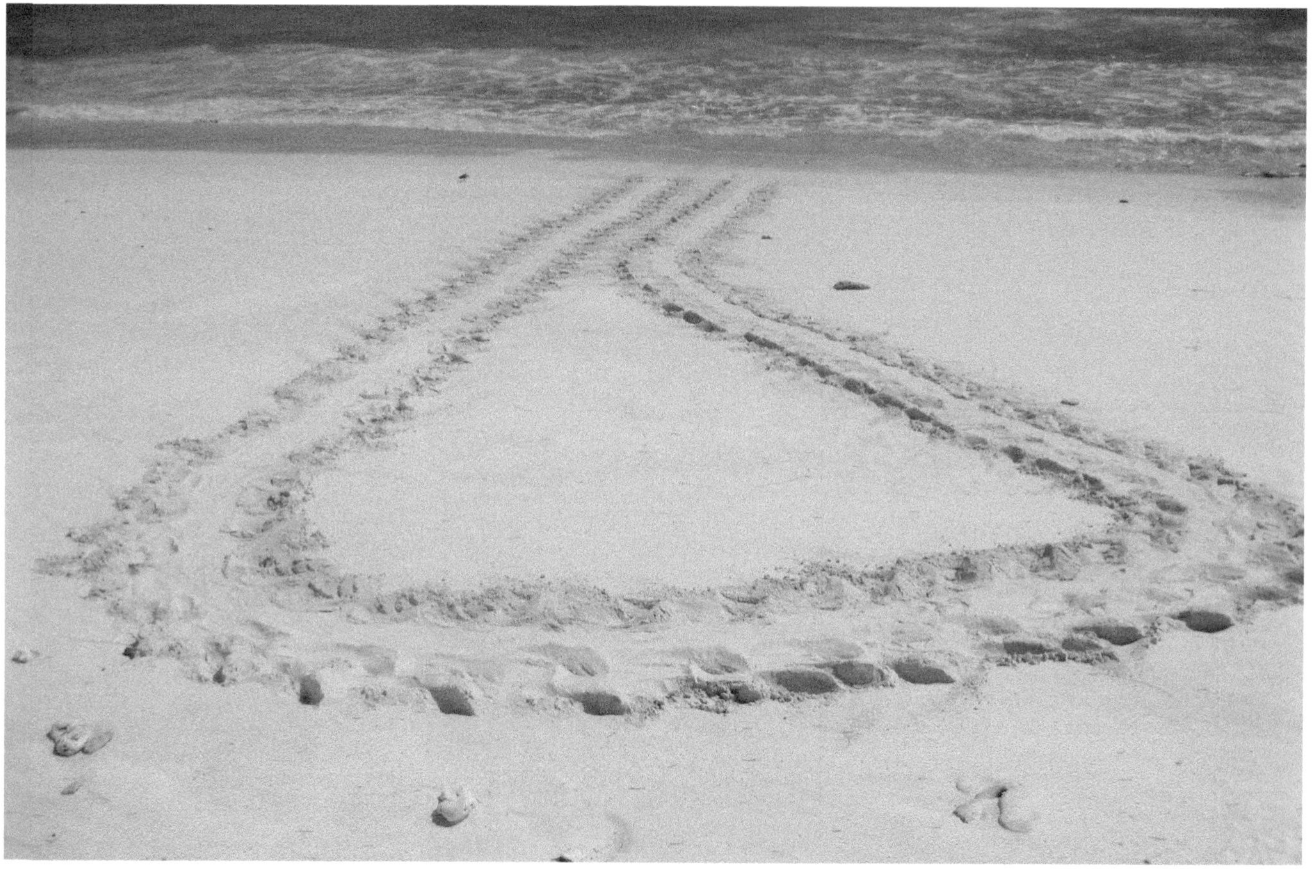

Hawksbill turtles generally nest during the northwest monsoon, though there can be activity either side of this, whereas green turtles have been recorded nesting up until and even during the southeast monsoon. You would be forgiven for thinking that the prospect of walking the beach five times a day to record activity over such a length of time might seem quite a laborious task. On the contrary, shared between the wardens, rangers and the volunteers, it was a real pleasure and what any nature lover would jump at the chance to do.

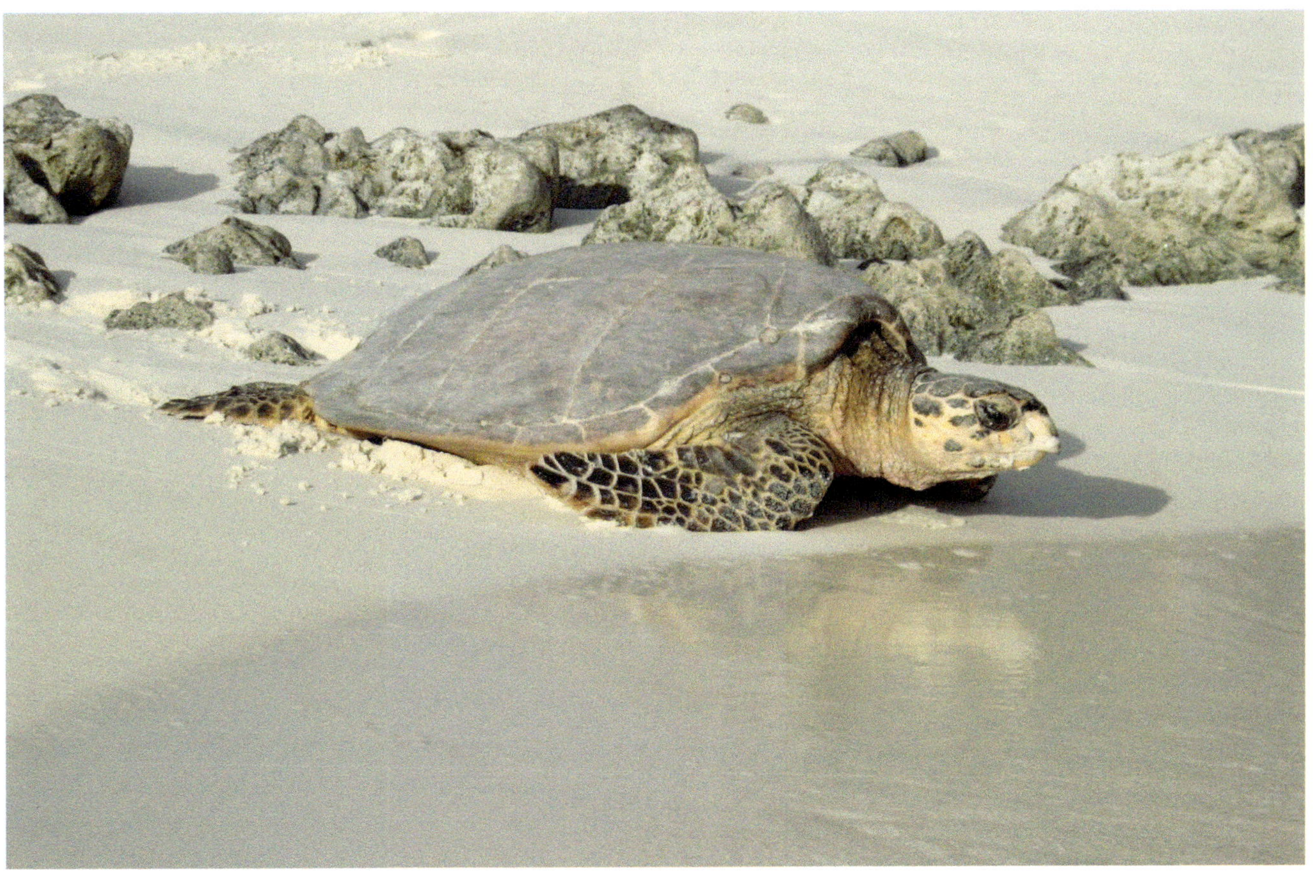

© Chloe Prehn-Arnold

The hawksbill is one of the smaller sea turtles; growing to an average length of 80cm and weighing up to 150lbs, they have a narrow head and jaws shaped like a 'beak' to allow them to get food from crevices in coral reefs. Their bony shell (carapace) is yellowy brown with an orange tinge, elliptical in shape and perfectly streamlined.

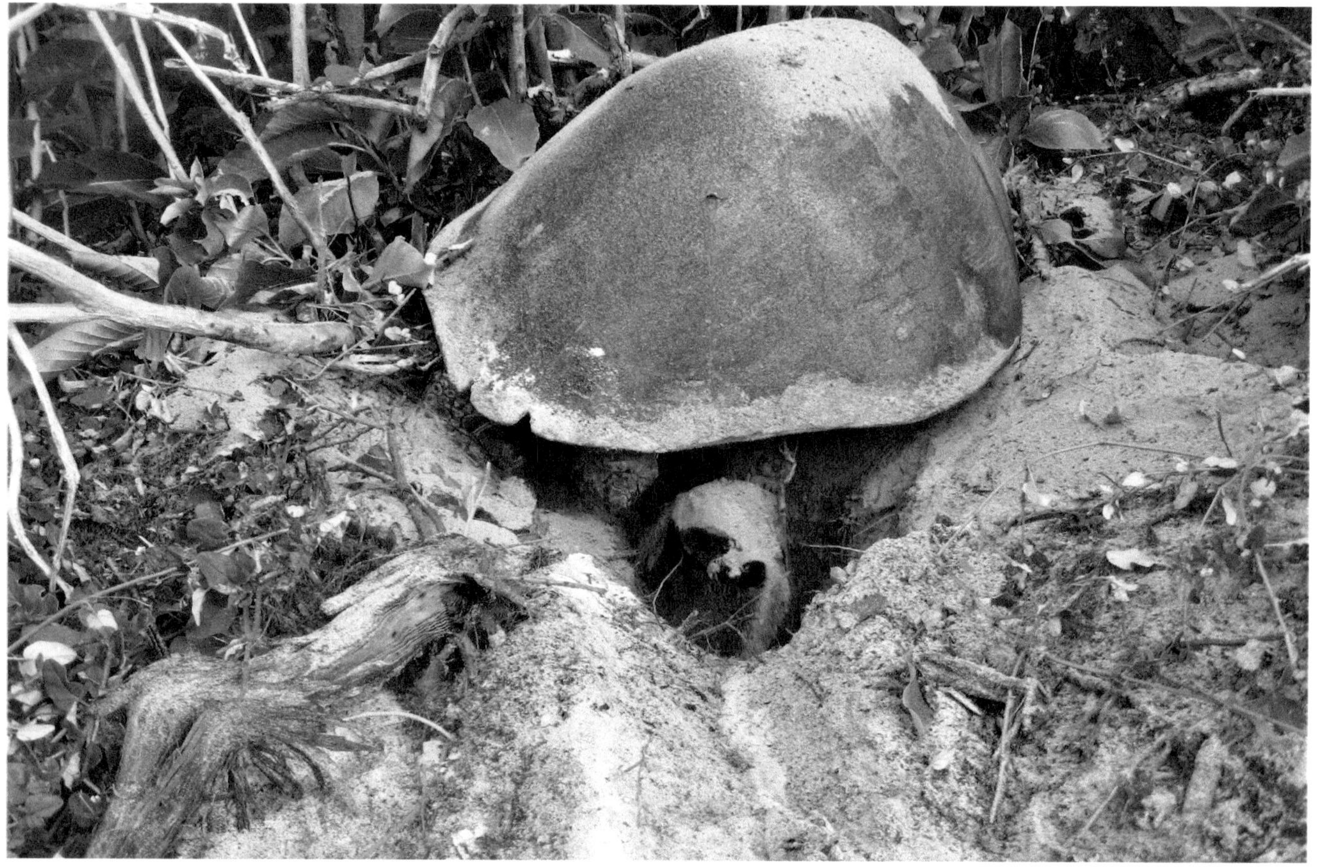

Hawksbills will often come up the beach during the day, unlike their green counterparts, who always use the cover of darkness to lay their eggs. Once this female hawksbill had finished laying, we watched her fill in the pit. Her back flippers worked blind, like small articulated paddles lifting sand on top of the nest.

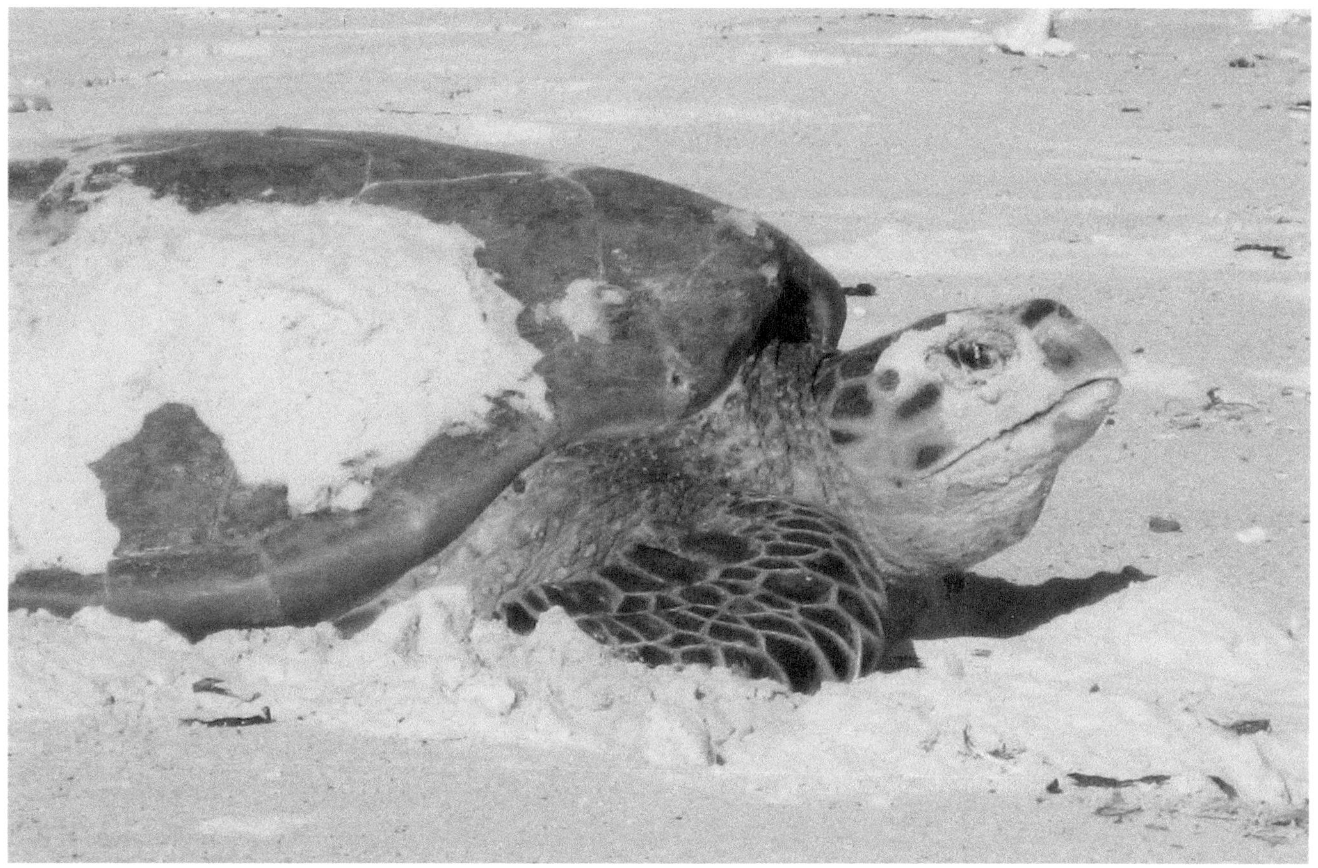

We always felt so privileged to have the chance to get a glimpse of such a splendid animal in broad daylight. With her task and mission accomplished, we moved in to take the tag readings and the carapace measurement. All measurements taken, we released our hold and she employed her front flippers to gather momentum over the hot sand and proceeded with a quickened gait to the water. As we backed away, she relaxed her pace and paused intermittently to lift her sand-covered head to get her breath back.

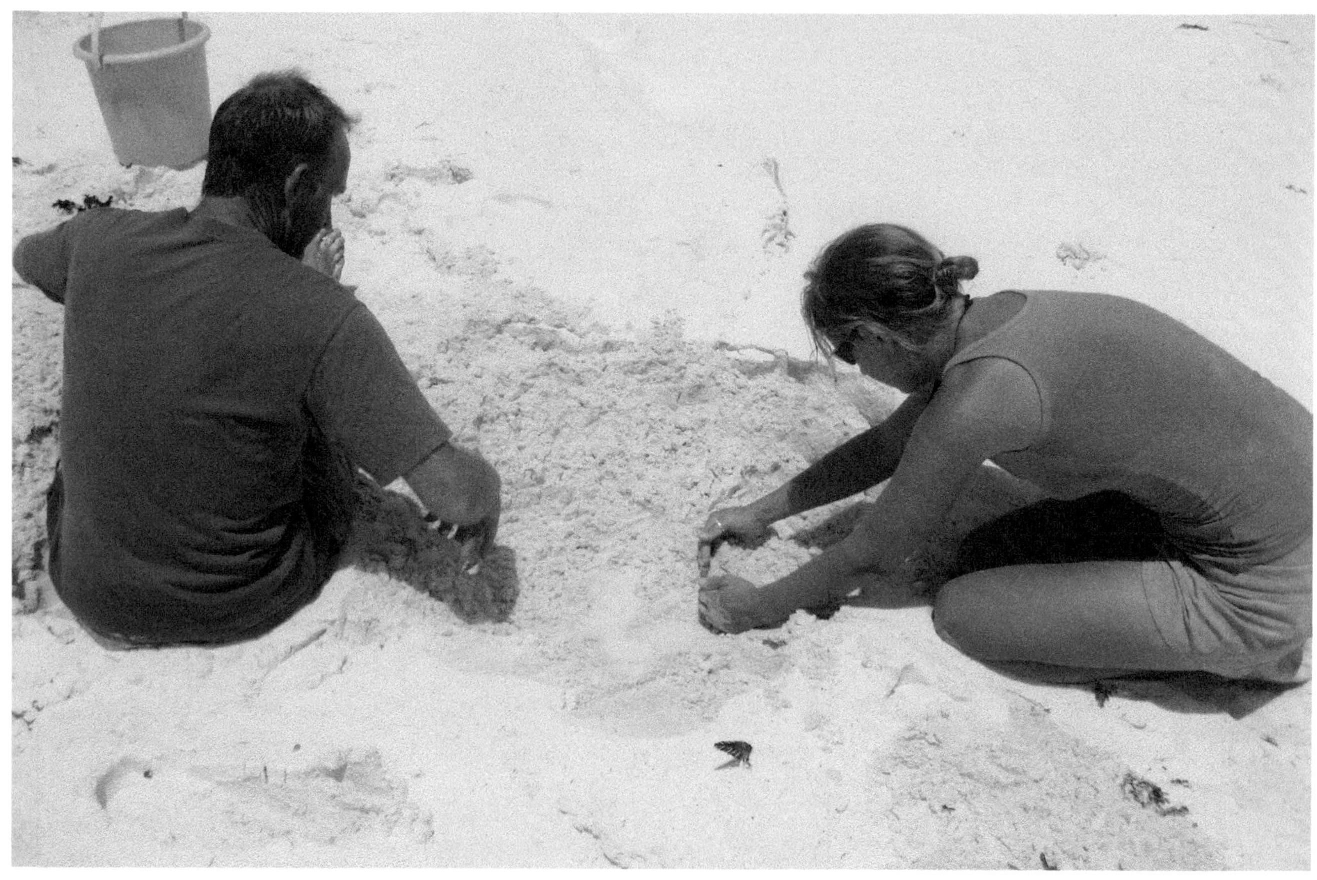

Unfortunately, some of the big old girls seemed to run out of steam, as if the effort of finding the beach and hauling themselves out of the water was too much. Some of them couldn't make it to the crest, and had to settle for laying mid beach. We knew these nests had to be moved to stand any chance of survival, so once excavated, we would relocate to the beach crest, being careful not to contaminate the surrounding ground, to prevent crabs from tracing them. But first, we had to find them.

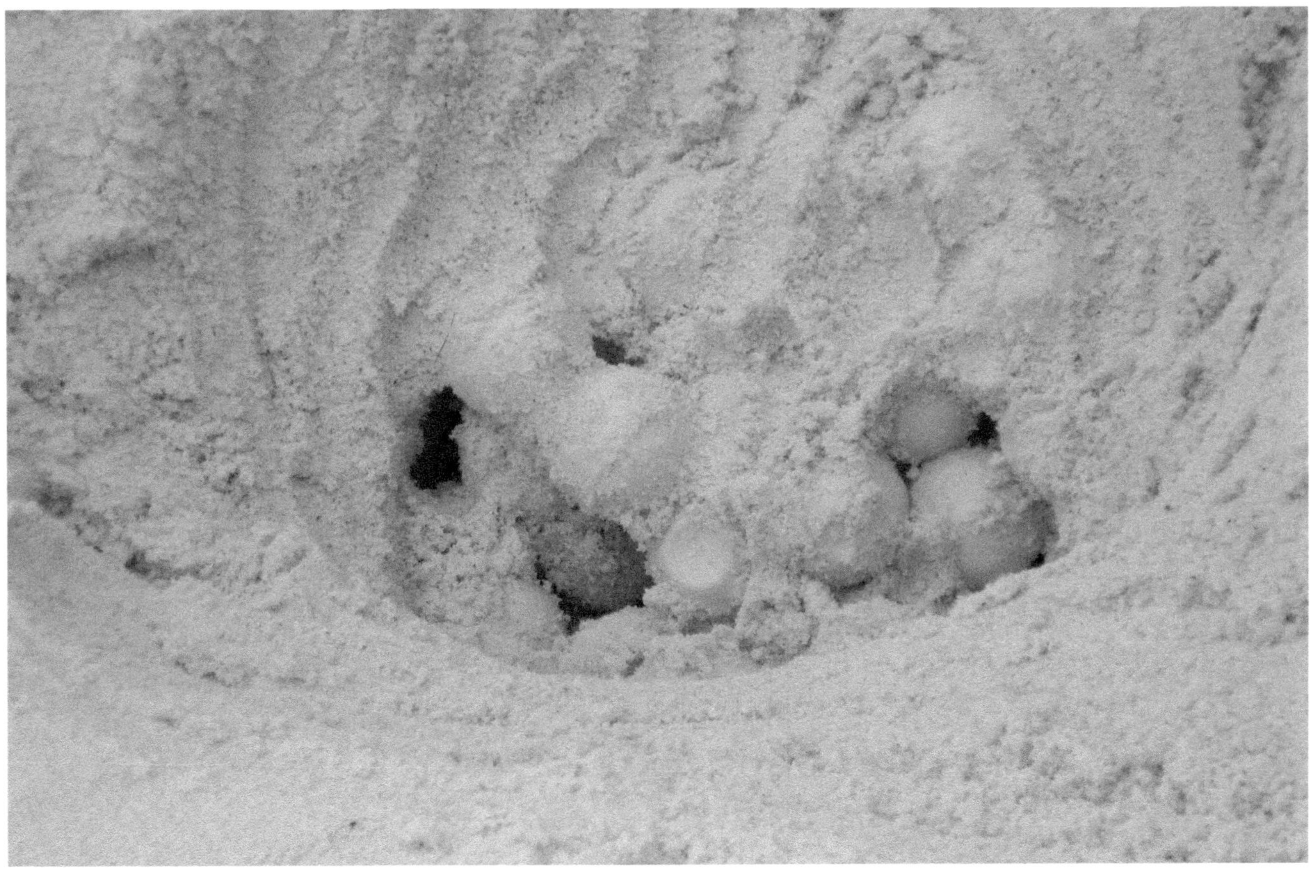

Hawksbills usually bury their eggs a little short of 50cm down. About the size of ping pong balls, the eggs don't feel like shell, but a more pliable material; so soft to the touch and easily dented, we always had to be exceptionally careful when excavating and moving nests.

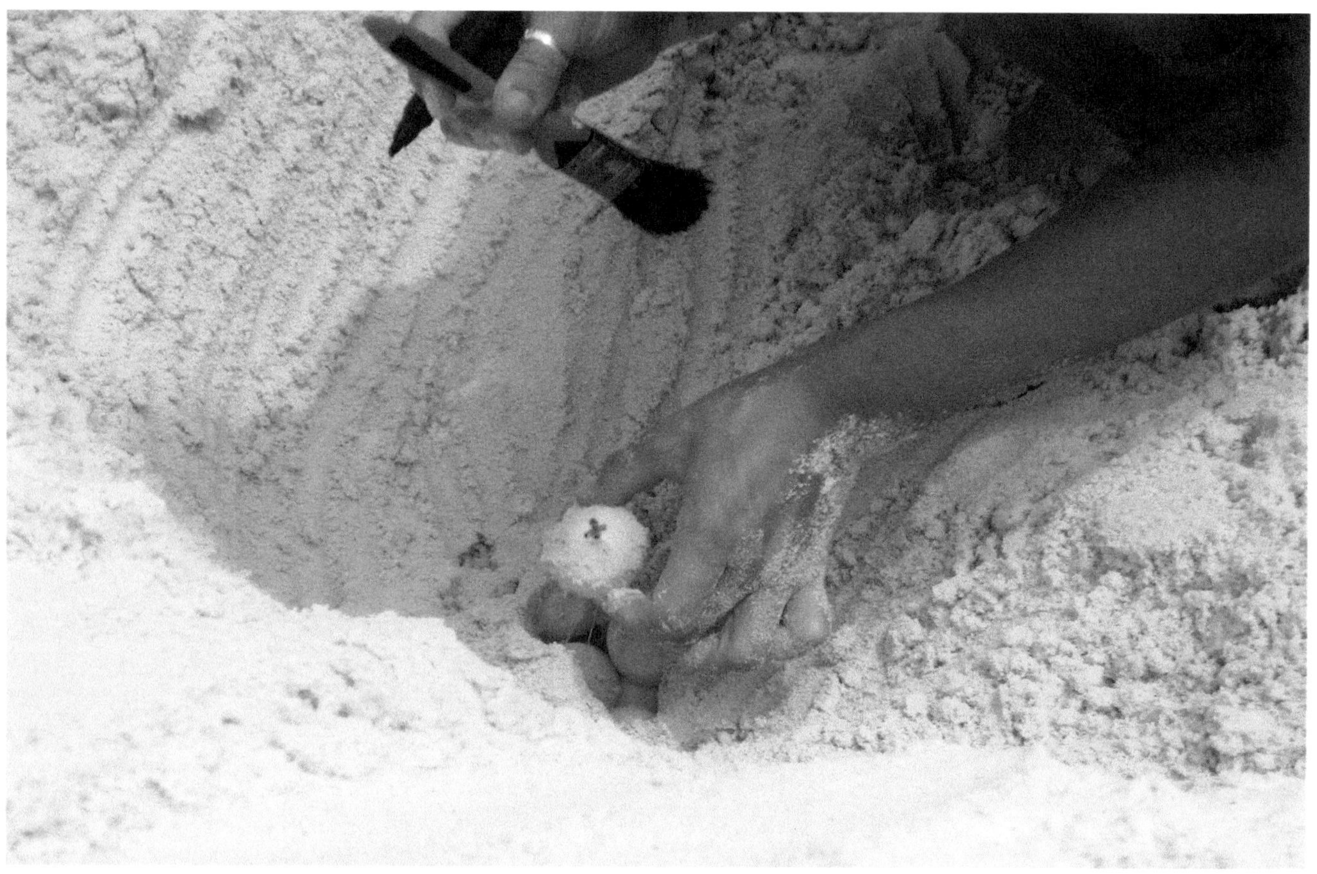

We had to mark every egg to make sure it stayed in the same alignment as it was laid. When a turtle embryo begins to develop, it attaches to the top of the eggshell, where the air in the egg is stored, providing the growing turtle with precious oxygen. Keeping the eggs upright while we moved them was critical to ensure the air bubble remained undisturbed so the embryo didn't detach itself.

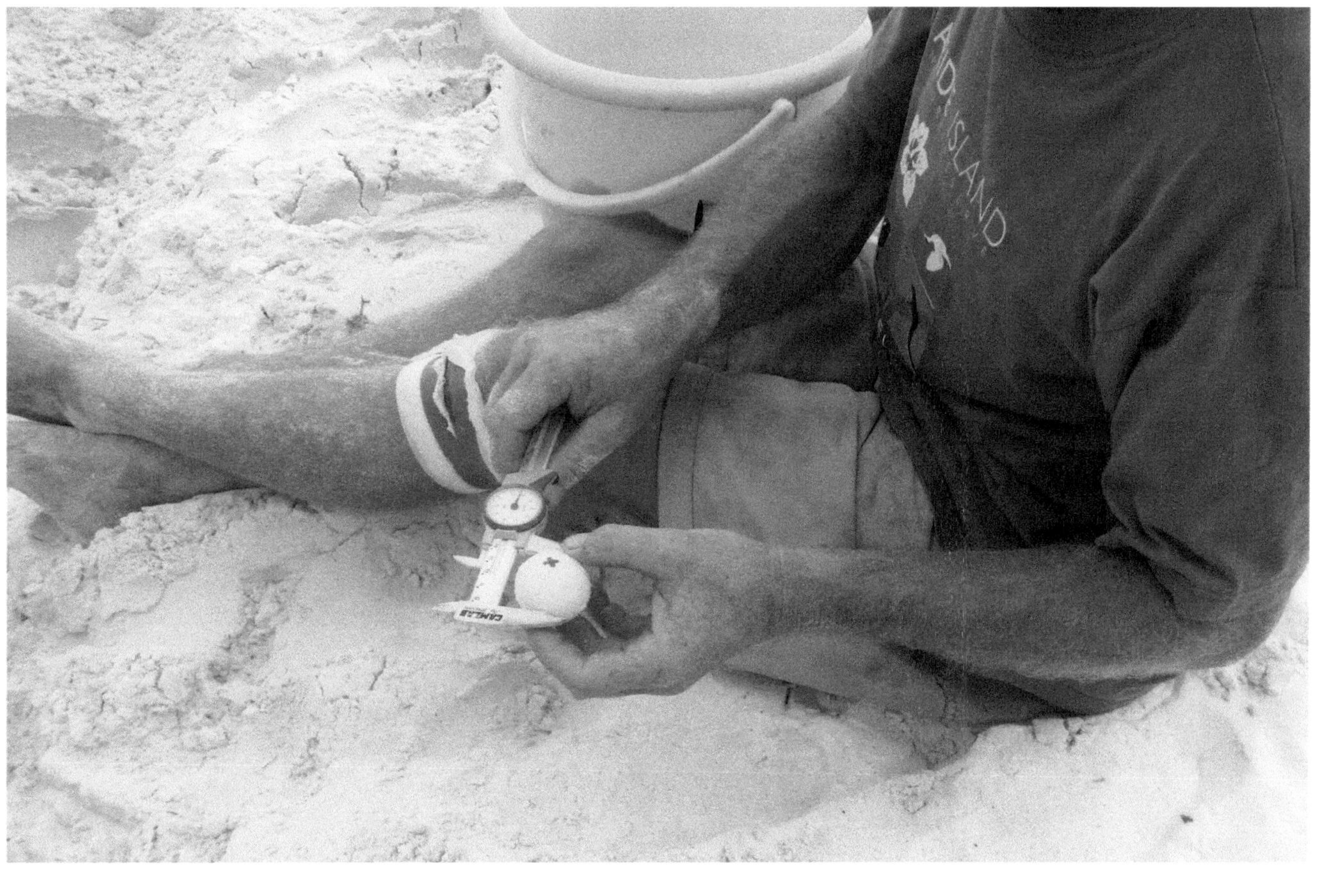

Whenever we moved a nest, Jeanne asked us to take measurements and record as many details as possible. It was always special to mark and lift the eggs out of the nests, ready to relocate, the right way up, to a safer place.

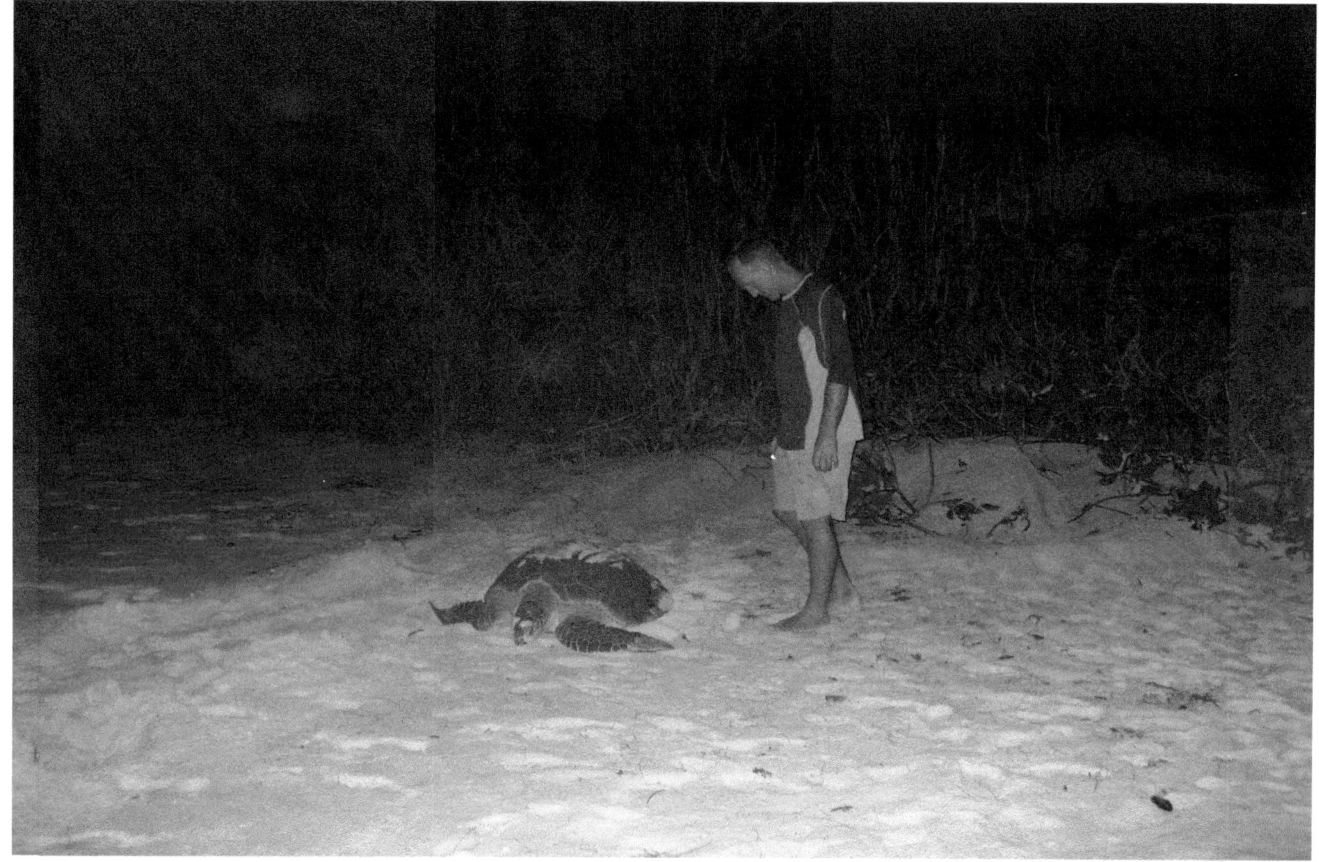

In comparison to hawksbills, green turtles are much bigger, reaching sizes of up to 1.2m and weighing over 440lbs. They have a small head, with a blunt face, and their shells are flat and heart-shaped, with a green sheen, which is also replicated in the colour of their skin.

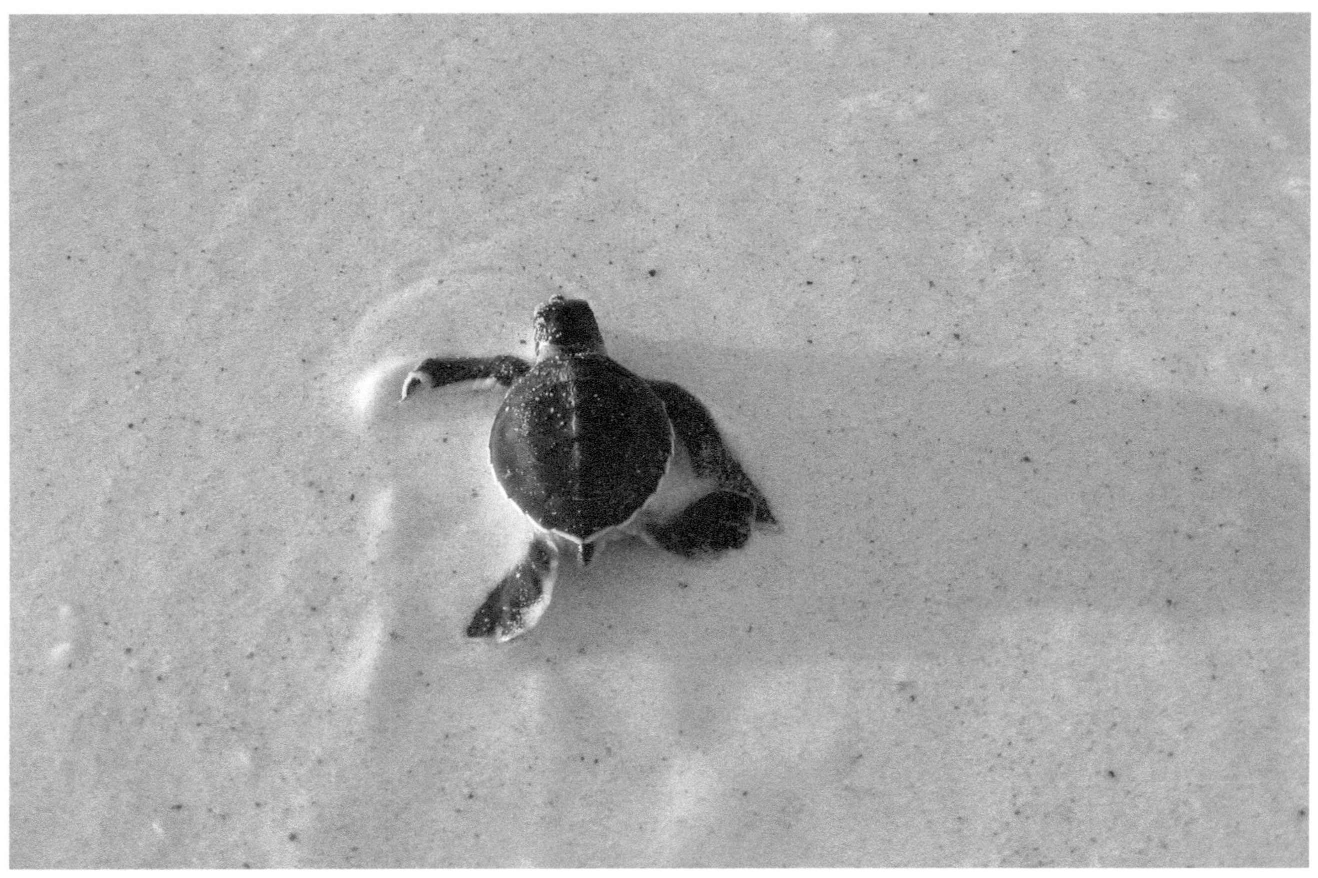

The hatchlings were strong little fellas with big necks and black shells, trimmed with white; they looked like perfect miniature turtles. Their flippers were continually on the go, whirring frantically as they tried to propel themselves as quickly as they could towards the safety of the sea.

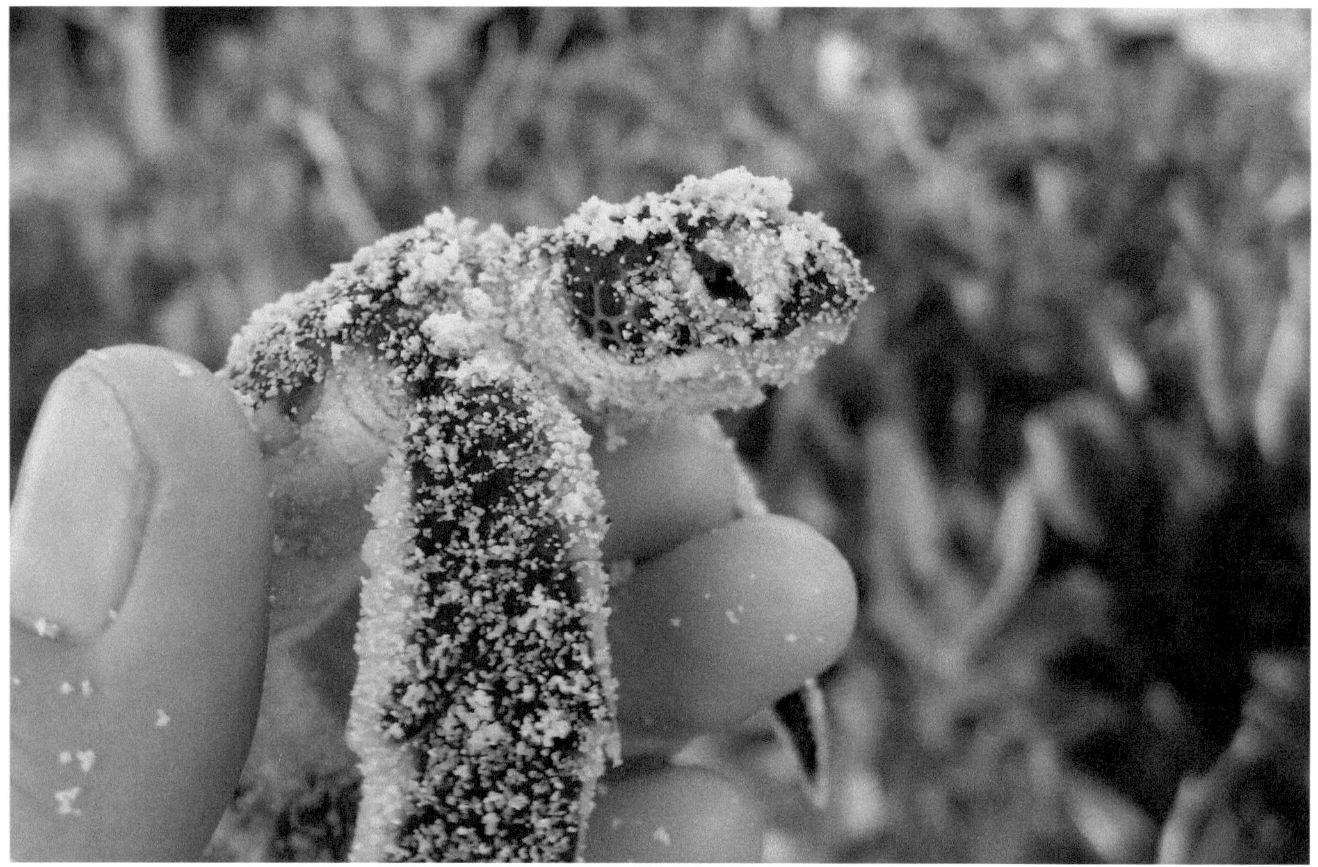

I vividly remember rescuing this tiny hatchling. Its body was just a little bigger than a 50p piece yet it felt so strong; its large front flippers resisted my fingers as it tried to 'swim' away. It had only just opened its eyes, which were like small slits, and its shell was so perfectly formed, just so perfect and smart, not in the slightest bit ugly like the newly hatched hawksbills.

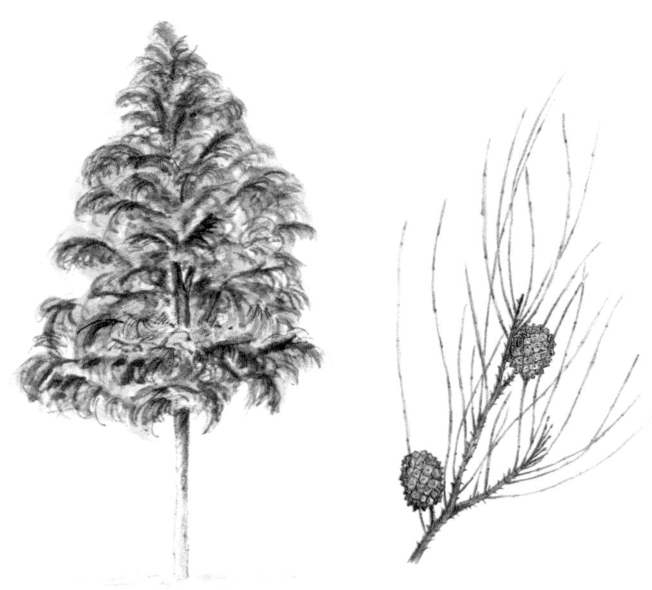

*Casuarina tree with needles and cones*

# Chapter 8

## Keeping the Status Quo

There was no middle ground when it came to life on Aride; it was always extreme. I found it amazing that, for an island only sixty-eight hectares in size, there was never a dull moment – how wrong I had been when I thought I was moving there for a quiet life!

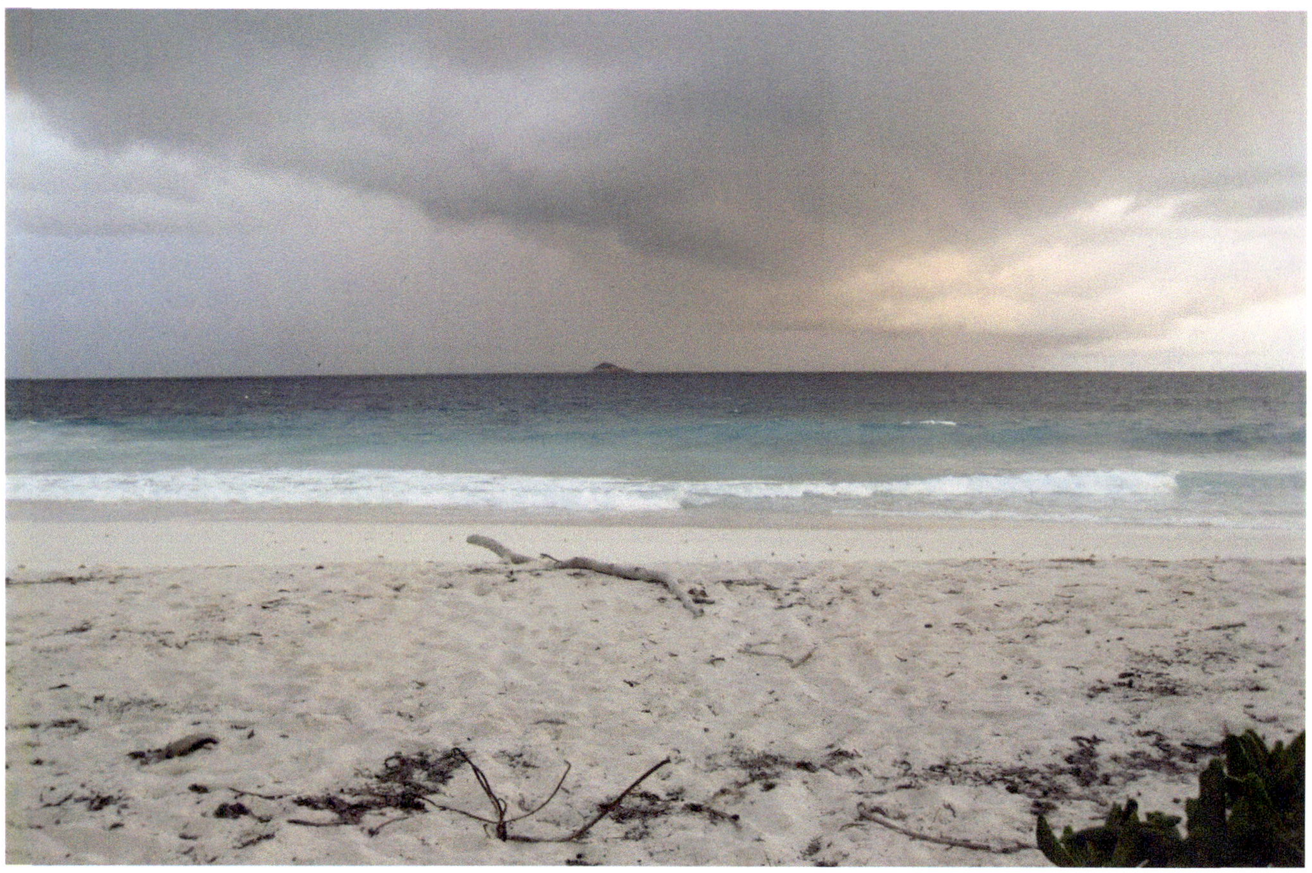

A walk on the beach was always an excellent antidote for emotionally challenging times; the panorama constantly changing provided a refreshing distraction. The colours of the ocean were amazing; the stormy sky and softened light made the water an intense turquoise. As the fresh breeze brought inland by the rain blew through the casuarina trees, it rattled their cones and made their long, slender needles sing and whistle.

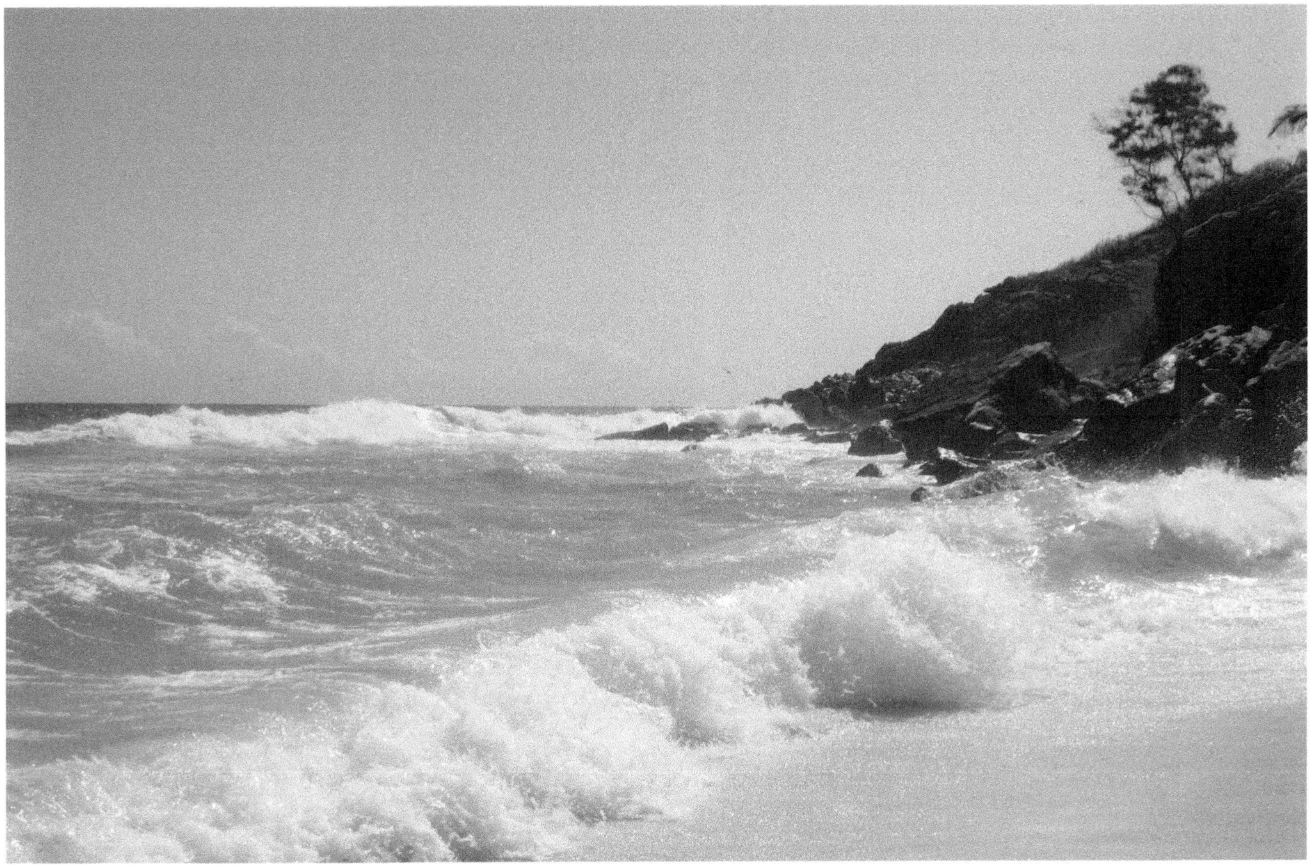

After an extraordinarily difficult day, involving a major heated dispute with one of the rangers about landing the boat, I wanted to be on my own for a while. I walked towards the western end of the island and went as far as the sand would take me, sat on the rocks, and watched the tide wash over the top.

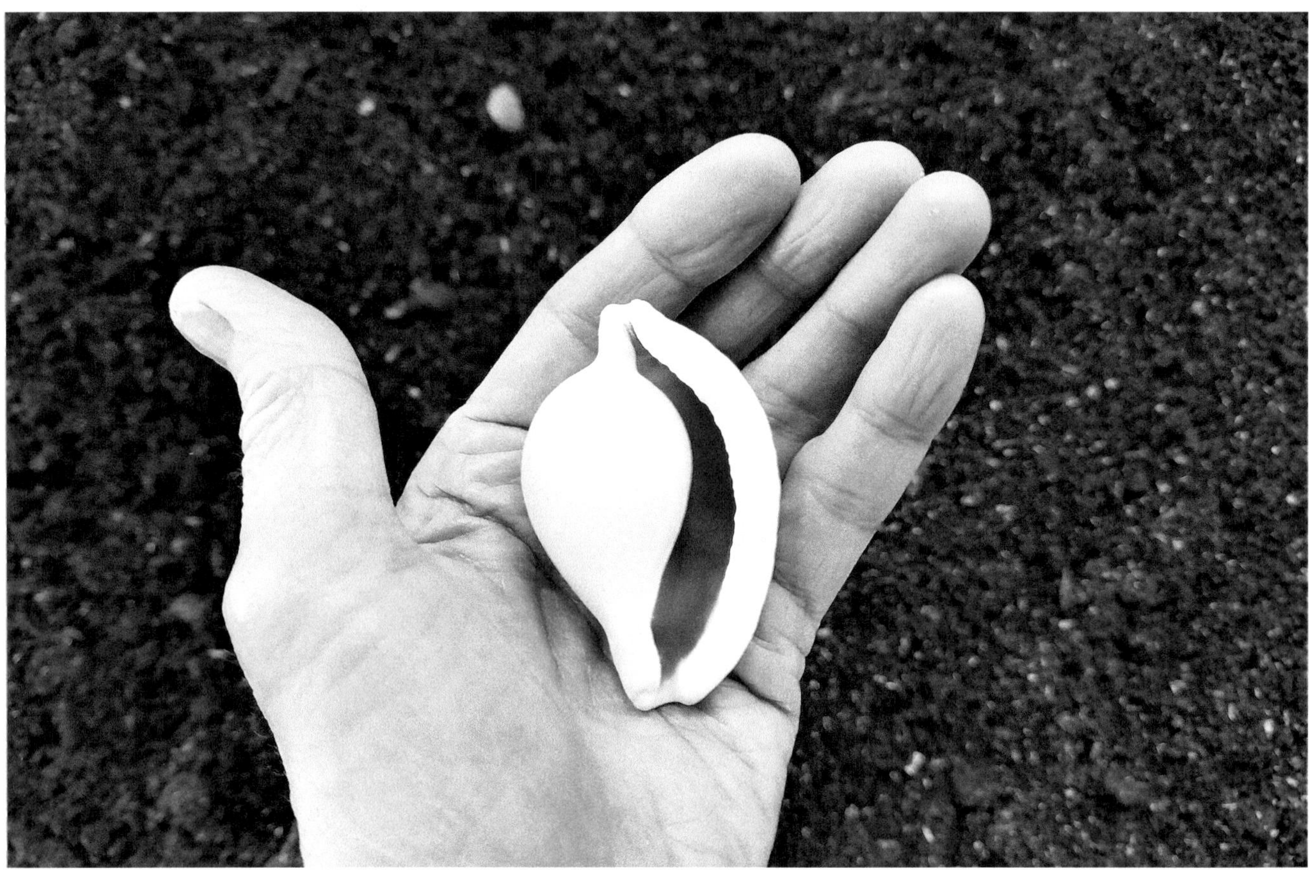

It is a misconception that the Seychelles have beaches littered with shells, and they were certainly not common on Aride. So when I found this perfectly white conch shell, smooth and unblemished, about the size of a large plum, I was drawn to its serene appearance. Its spherical form felt calming in my hand, I clutched it tightly, for it felt uncomplicated and comforting, its natural white shape unchallenging and begging to be held.

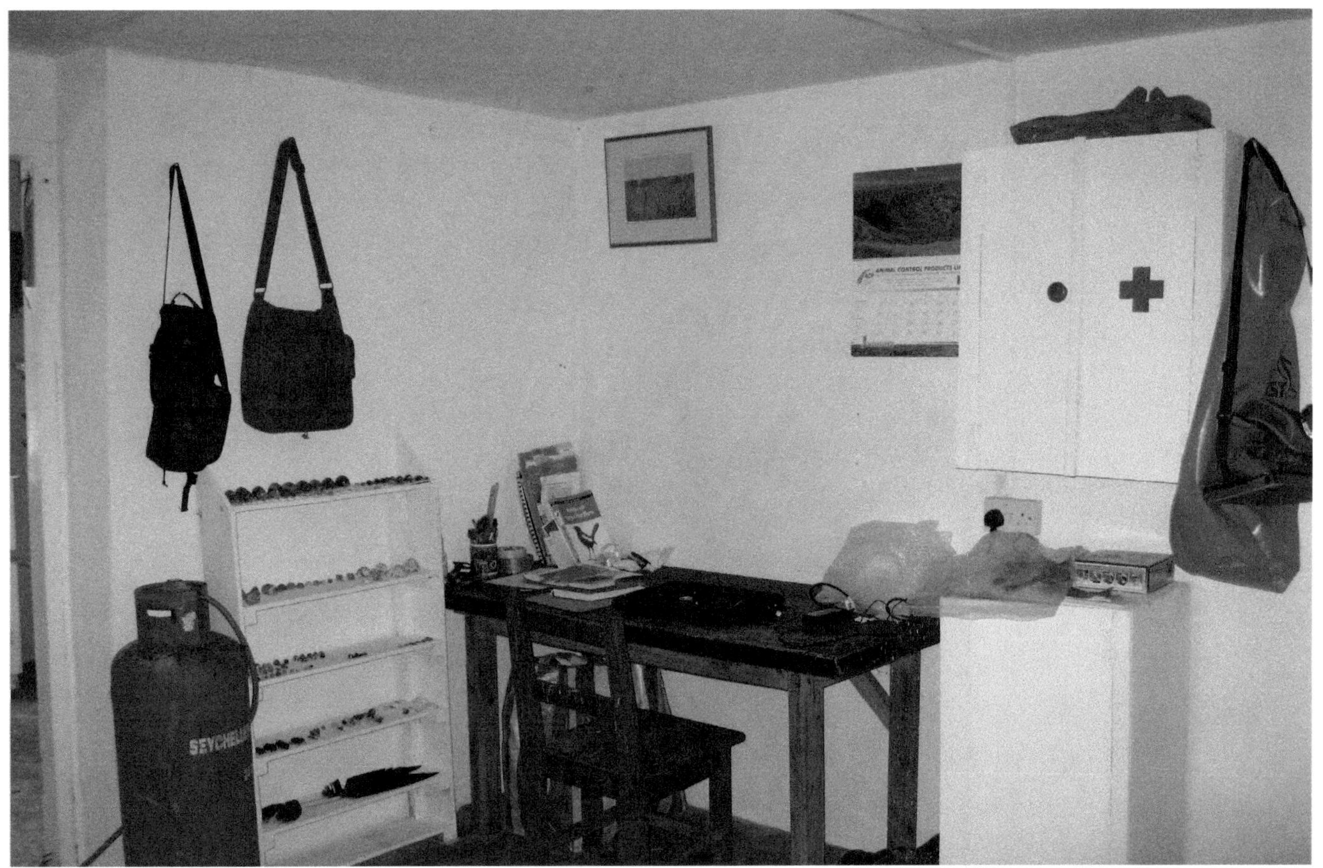

The white conch shell lived on my desk for the rest of our time on Aride, and became something of a natural symbol representing my carefully guarded human emotions, their vulnerability typically hidden by an outer strength, unless pushed to the limit and then exposed.

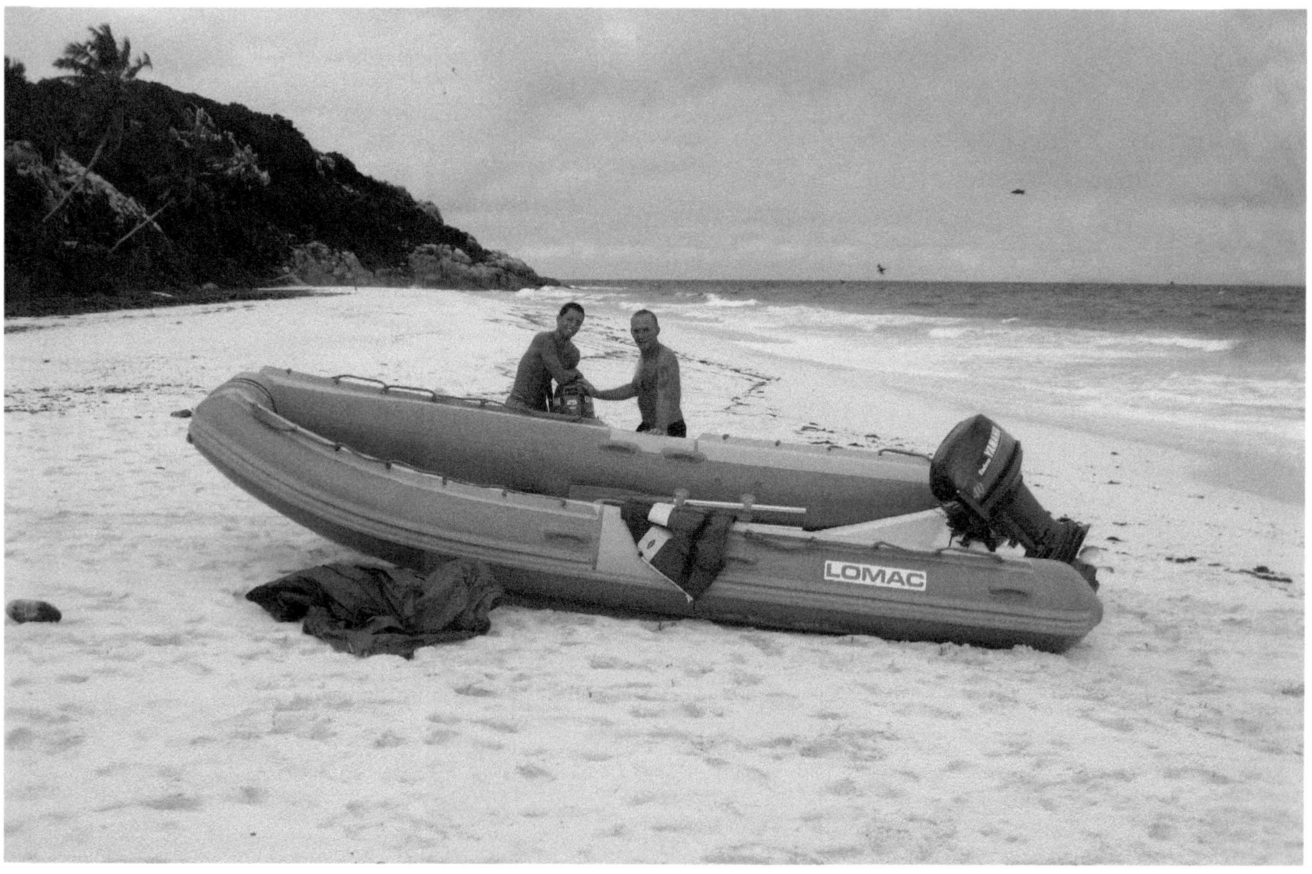


Keeping the boats in good working order was another regular battle. The intensity of UV and heat ultimately melted the glue on the inflatable tubes of the ribs, and on one occasion, with a hole forming in the Tornado, we ended up entirely reliant on one boat. Fortunately, this situation was quickly remedied in the form of a very timely present from the mainland… a new boat! Seychelles was a little like that, nothing was ever planned for, but somehow, things just seemed to work out and we just had to learn to go with it.

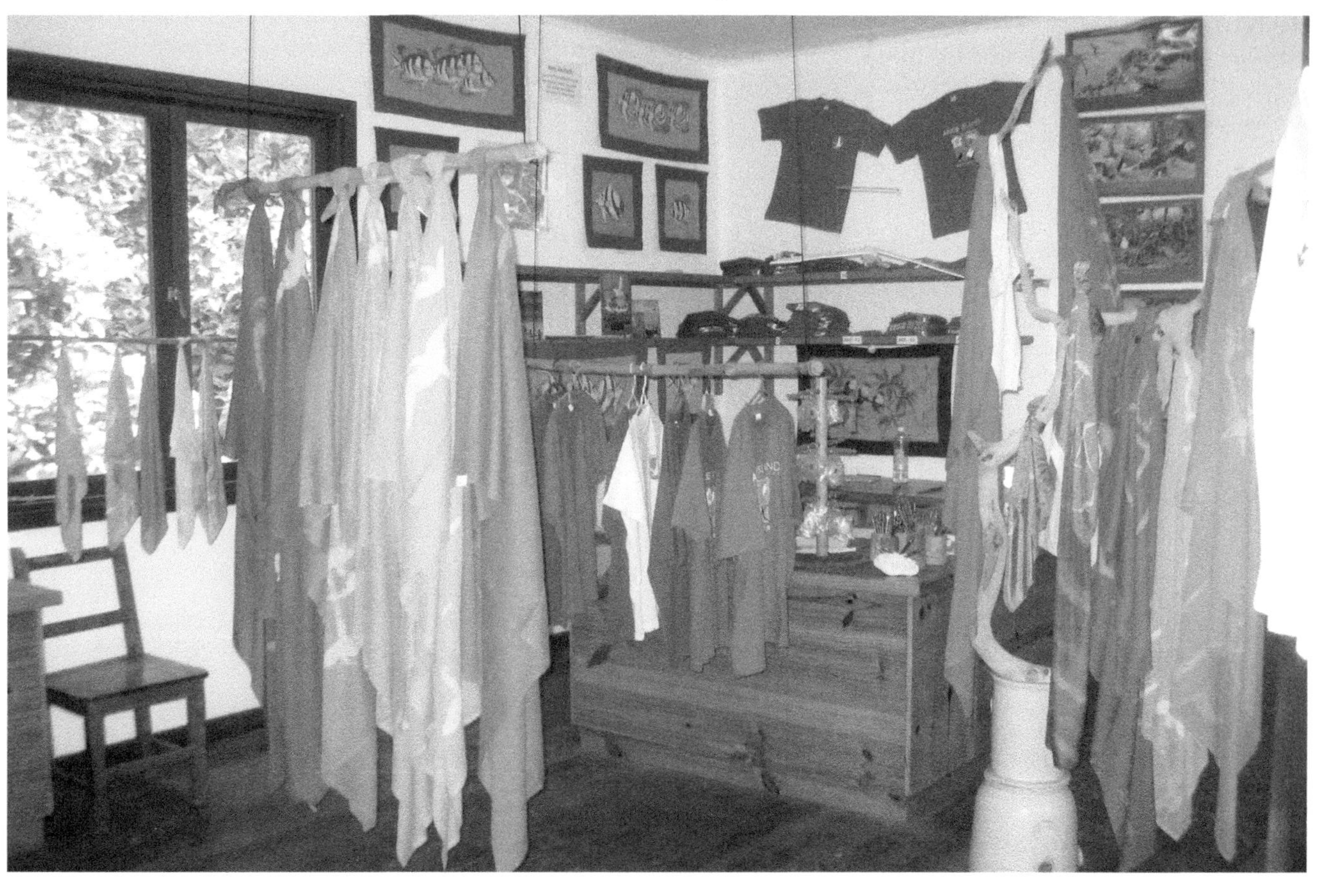

Juggling guests, guides and roles was also a challenge, and crucially relied on the team all pulling together. For the most part, all visitors went away extremely happy, and the results of one particular day seemed to reflect those feelings: the Americans were full of praise and spent nearly €850 in the shop! Teamwork had come to the fore and there was little we could have done to improve their visit with the staff resource we had.

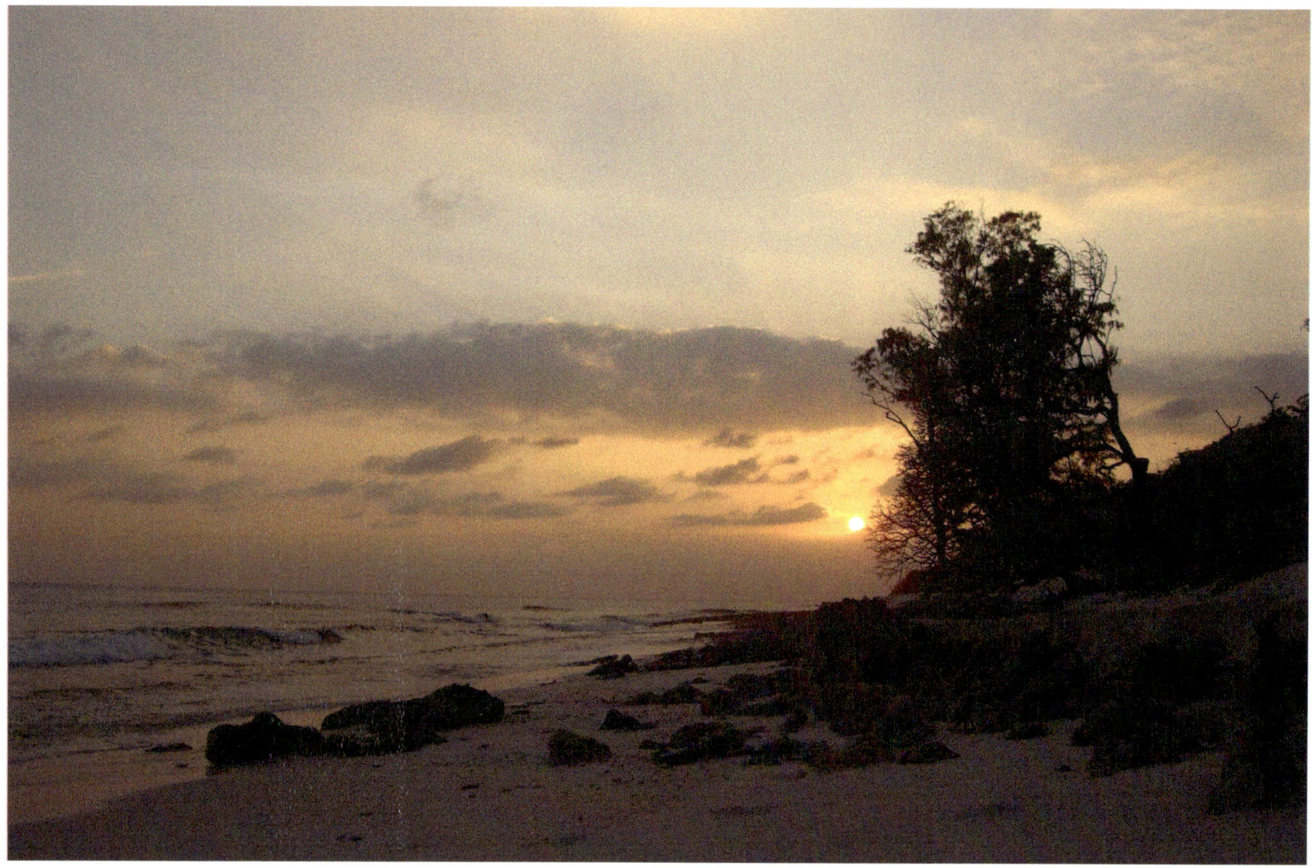

*© Chloe Prehn-Arnold*

With the arrival of new volunteers and rangers came the injection of new personalities and a bigger team; this meant we were not so reliant on just a few individuals, making us less vulnerable to unreliability. I remember feeling like this was a turning point; that just maybe we were starting to see our endeavours regarding team management come to fruition.

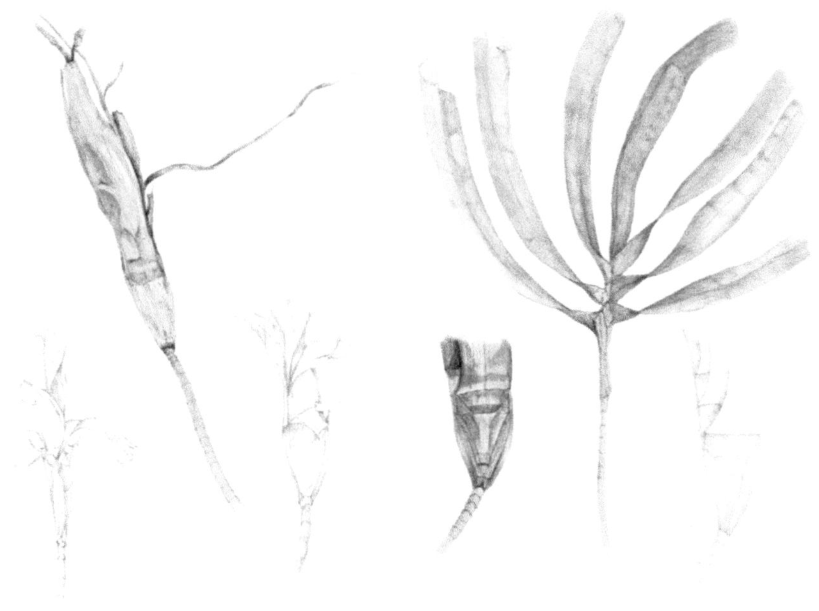

*Seaweed*

# Chapter 9

# White Knuckle Ride

Lying just south of the equator, Seychelles has a tropical climate: warm and humid. Typically, the temperature remains at a consistent 24-32°C and there is a degree of humidity all the time, influenced by the rainfall which is in turn determined by some very distinct seasonal changes.

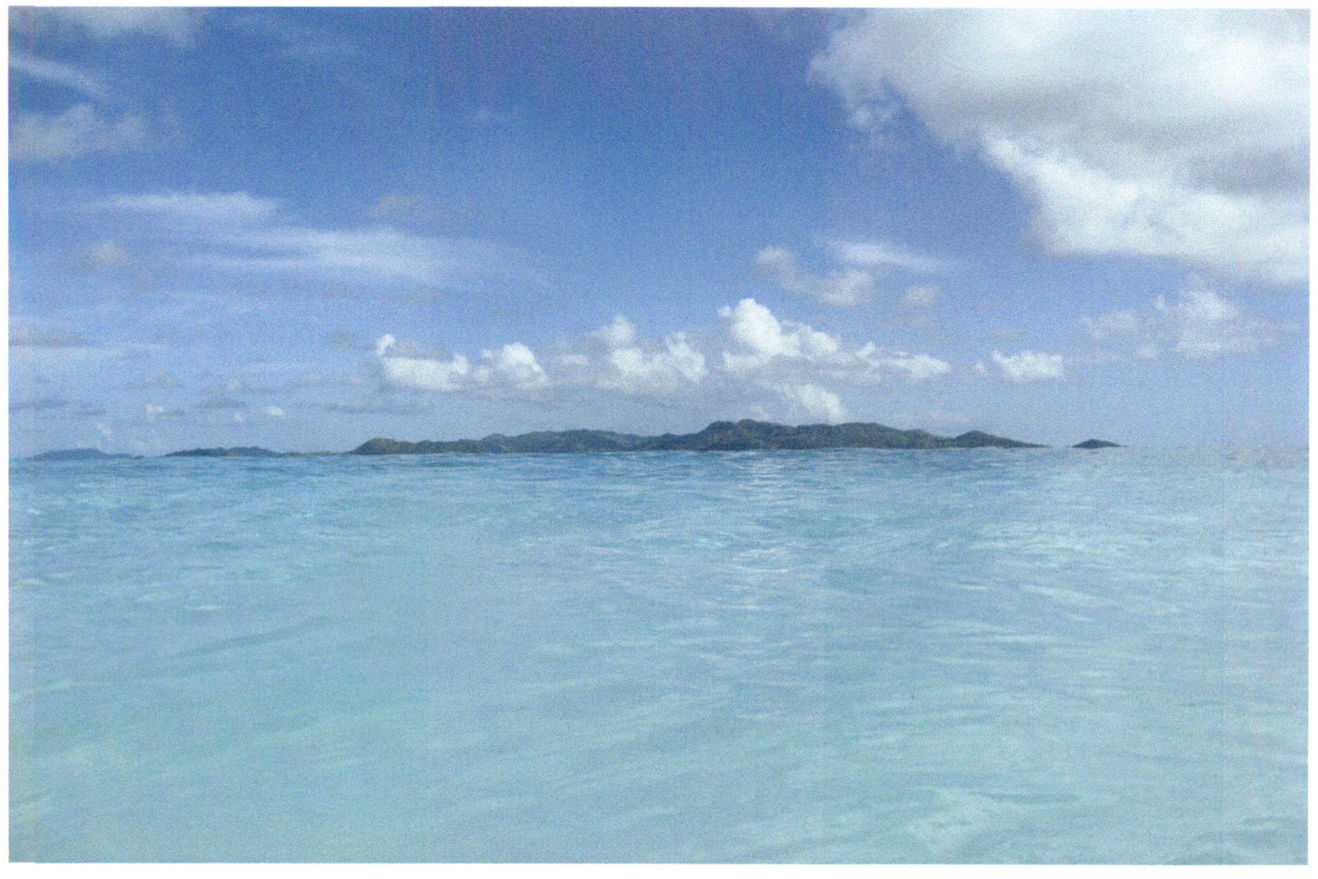

The northwest monsoon lasts from November to March, causing rainy and muggy weather due to the generally light north-westerly winds. The vegetation turns green and lush, and the ground water rises as the rain falls on the hill and rushes down to the lower ground below. The sea is at its calmest at this time of year as the weather is largely settled, and temperatures regularly reach over 30°C in the day and never drop below 28°C at night.

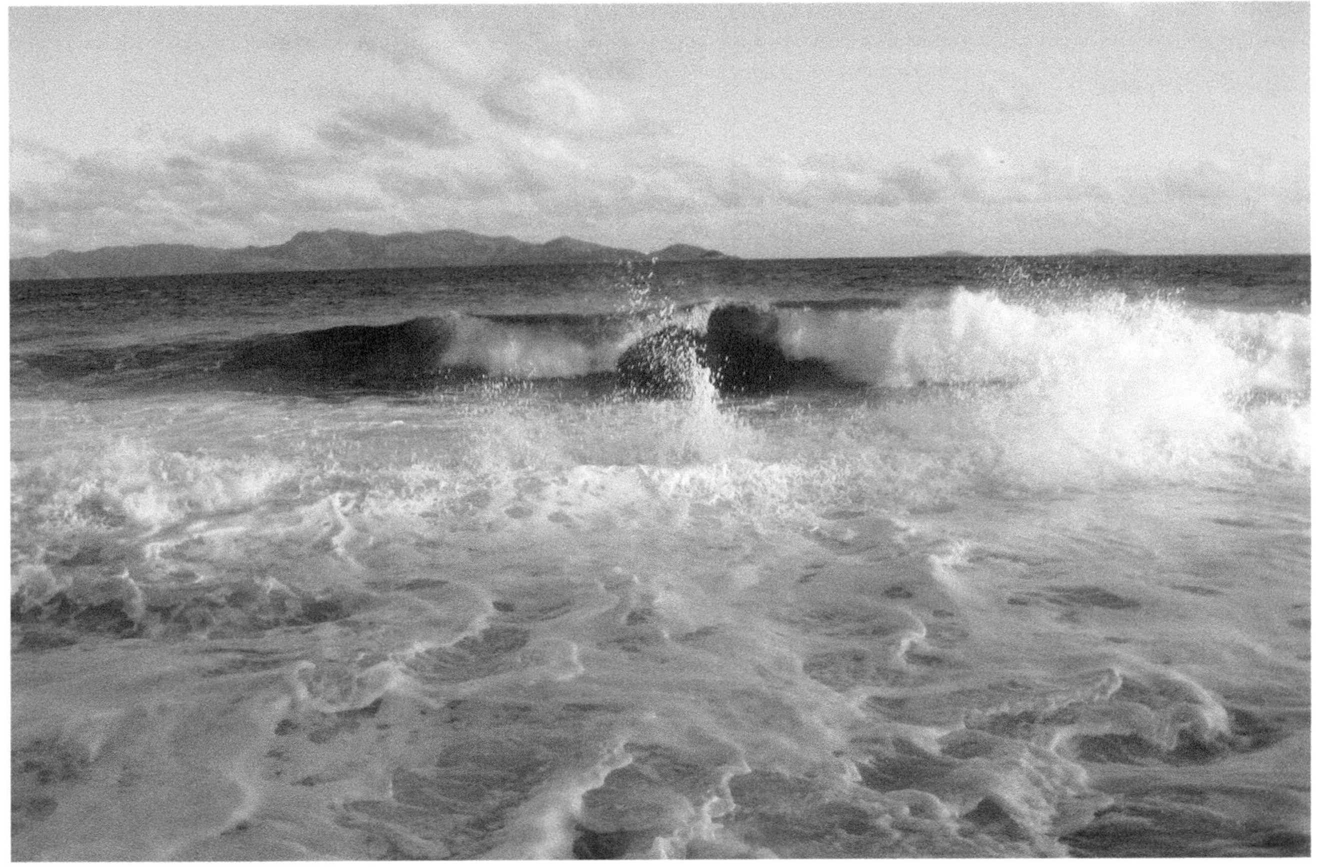

In stark contrast, the southeast monsoon is at the opposite end of the weather spectrum, and had a significant impact on our existence on Aride. This season brings a much drier episode of weather, temperatures are typically a little cooler, and the winds are intense, reaching speeds of 30 to 37mph. Such winds cause rough seas and create dangerous currents, especially around the unsheltered islands which are exposed to the elements on all sides.

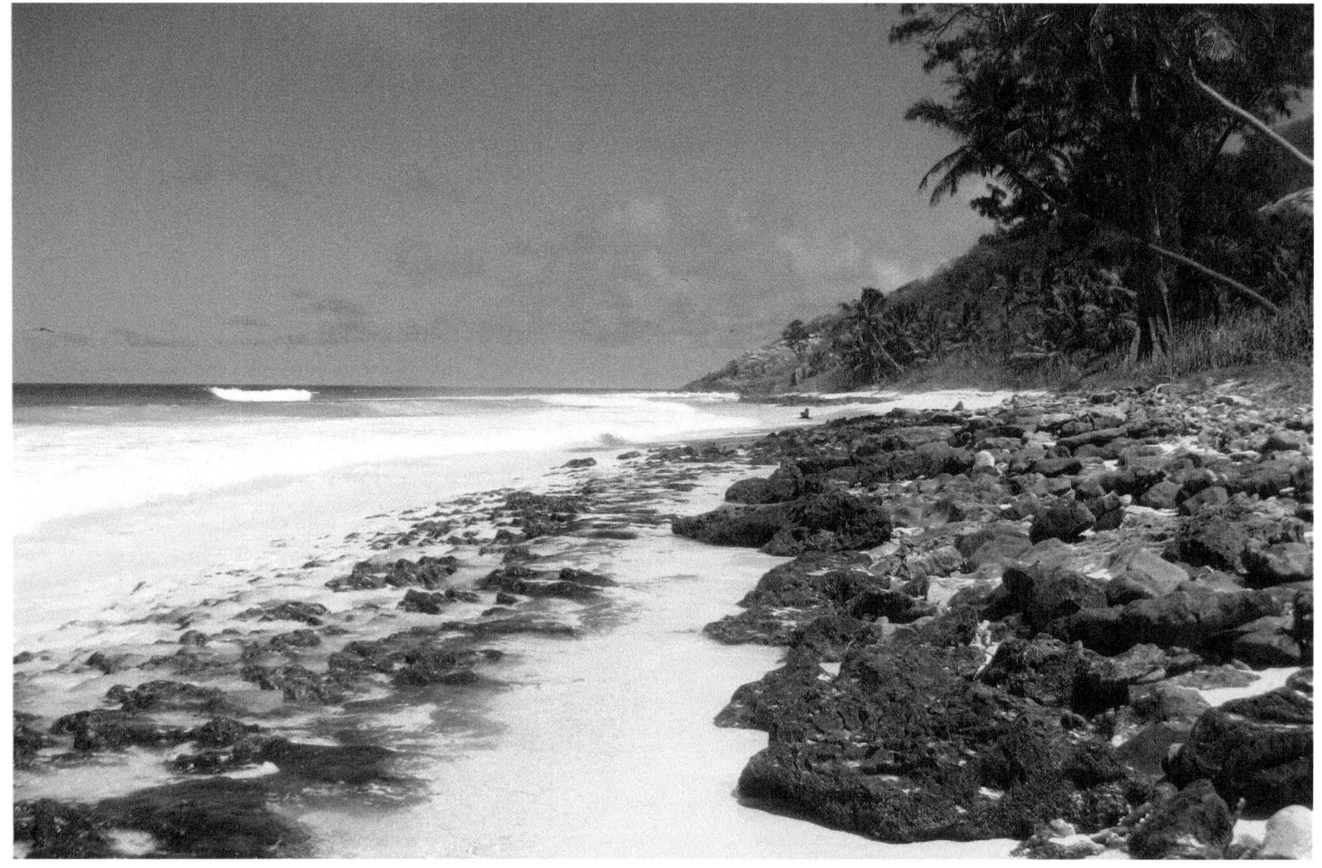

While we were there, the rough seas completely eroded the beach at the house, removing tonnes of sand and leaving just 3m of beach. Further along, the sand was replaced by rocks and broken bits of coral, which made it particularly hard to negotiate safely. Although the sun was bright the sky looked hazy – it was the salt spray in the air, a real telling sign that the change of monsoon was imminent.

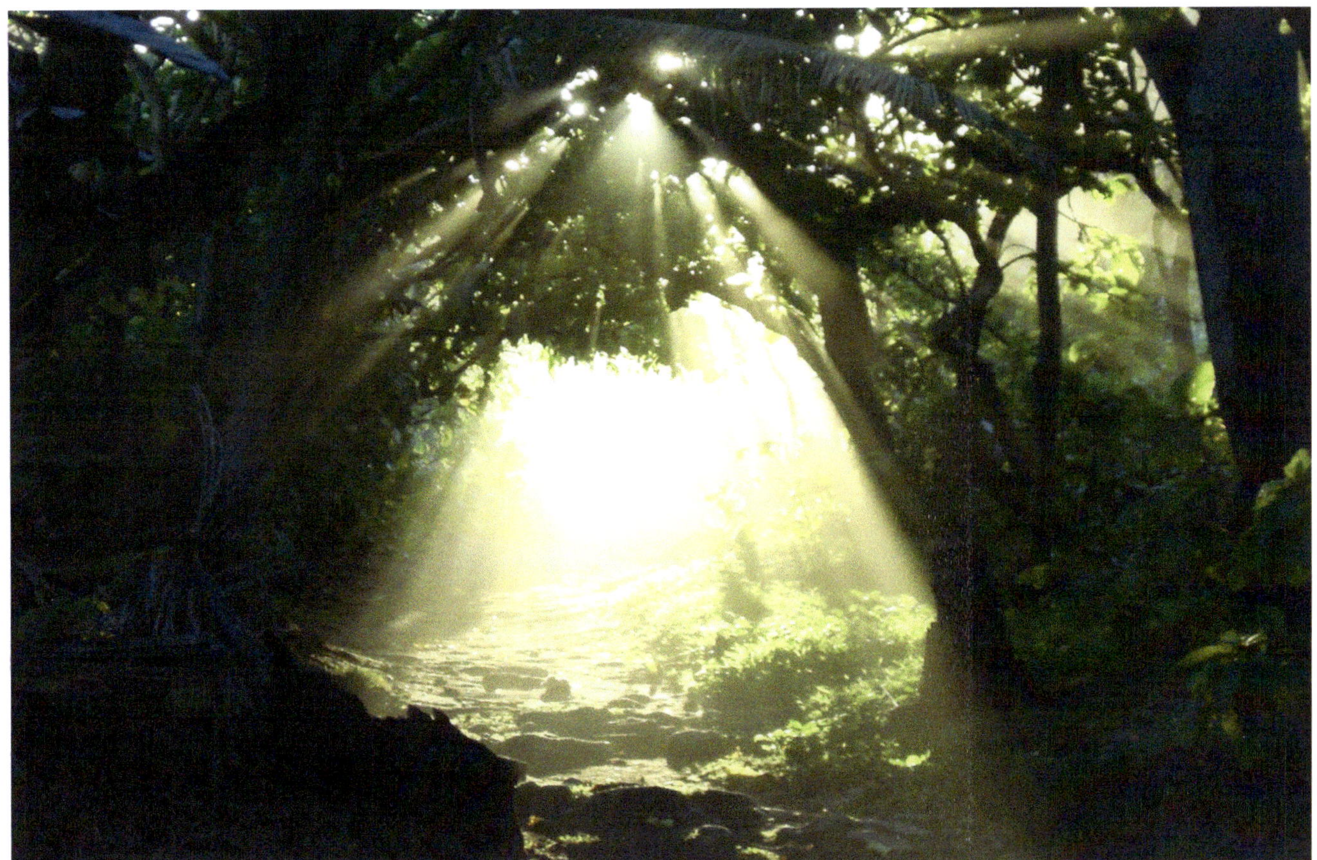

*© Chloe Prehn-Arnold*

Though we were both apprehensive about the arrival of the southeast monsoon and the conditions it brought, the ocean spray made the whole plateau look rather magical as the sun shone through the trees and the salt particles glistened. The effect of the spray in the house was less pleasant: all surfaces and objects were coated in a greasy film and I noticed, as I changed the sheets on the bed, that even the mattress felt wet.

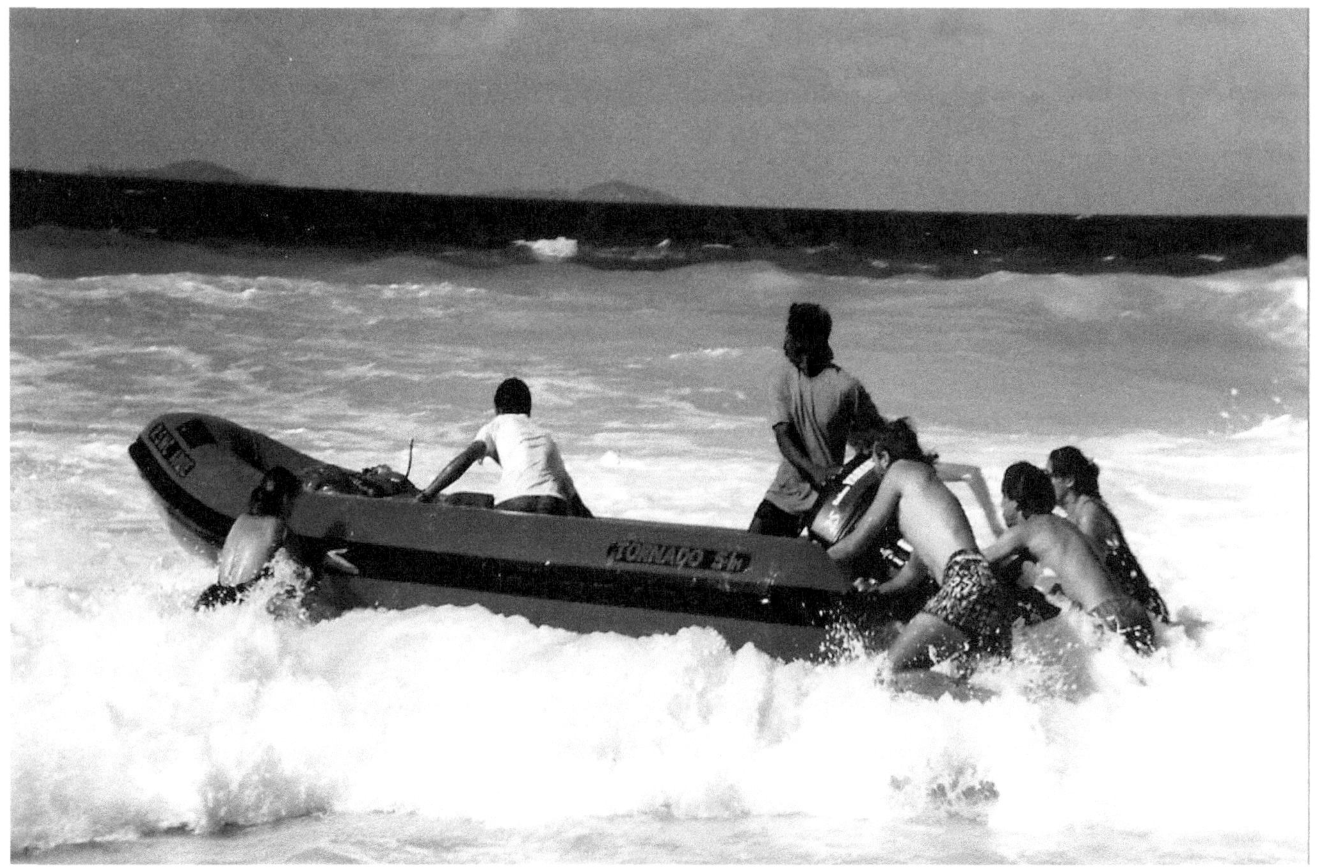

*© Colin Taylor*

Launching the boat was no easy task during the southeast monsoon. The waves continued to break angrily one after the other, and the boat would make it past the shallows only to have to negotiate a wave that would violently lift the front vertically. Within minutes the 3m waves would grow to 9m, and the sea would open up into a giant hole big enough to put a football pitch in. Melv told me it was the closest he had ever felt to not knowing how he was going to get out… alive.

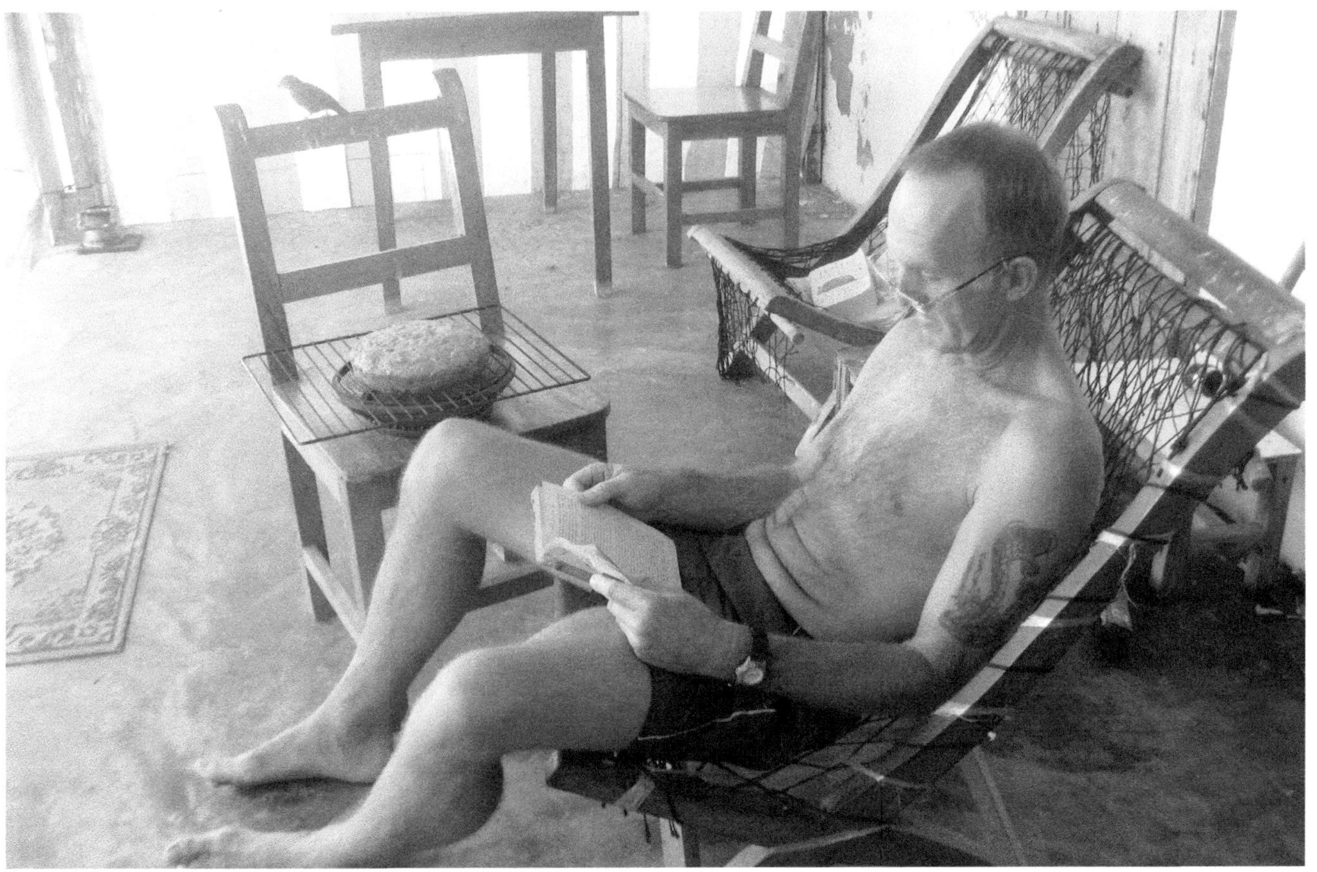

*Melv enjoying his newly refurbished deck chair*

With the southeast monsoon came debris washed up on the beach, from seaweed to seeds and shells. We both loved the simple pleasure brought by beach combing, and on one occasion Melv retrieved a piece of fish netting that had come off a tuna float, ideal to fence off the new garden plots and great as a chair cover that didn't hold the damp. It also served to lighten the mood as it produced a lovely fishnet stocking imprint on Melv's back when he wasn't wearing a shirt.

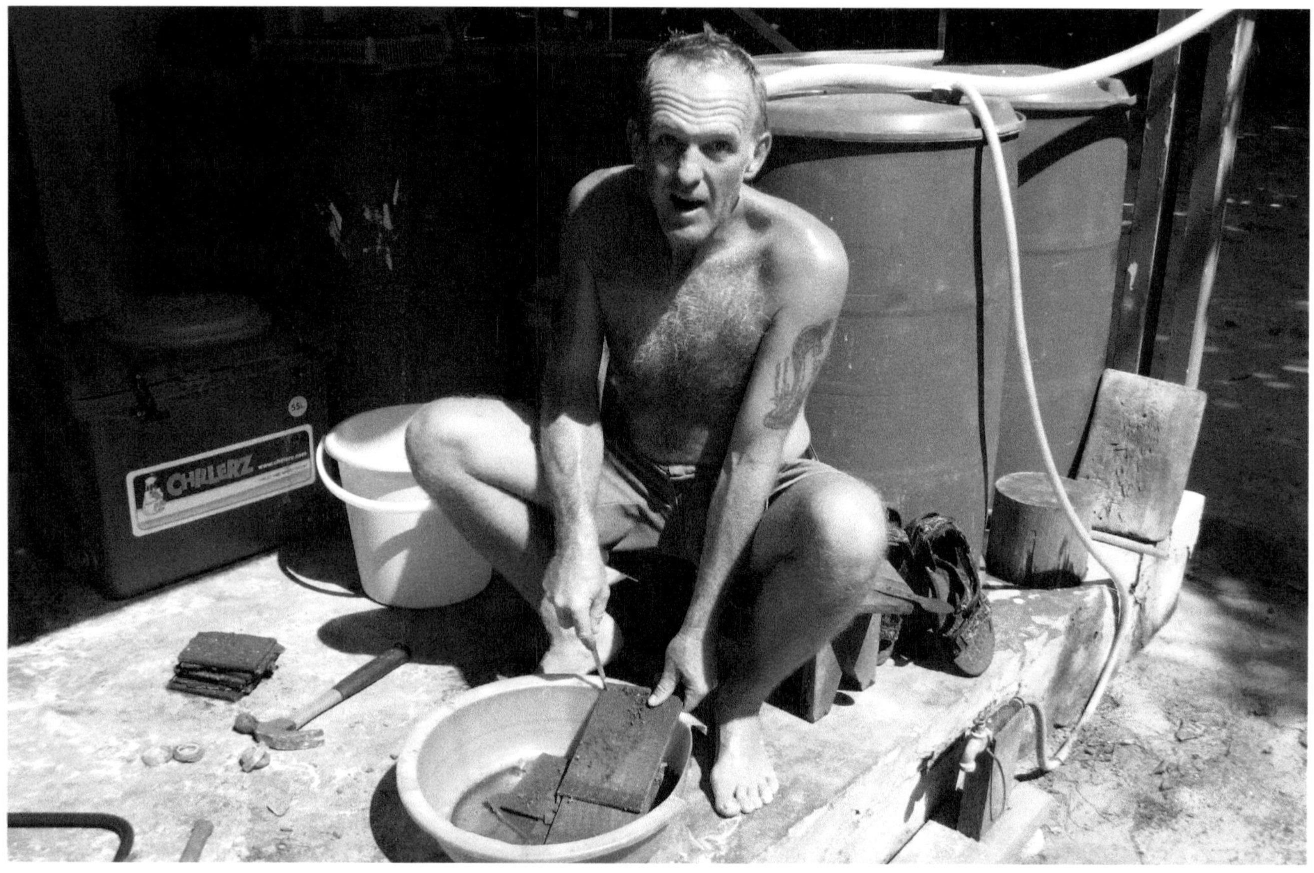

One aspect of life on Aride that I particularly enjoyed was that nothing was wasted and a use was found for most things.

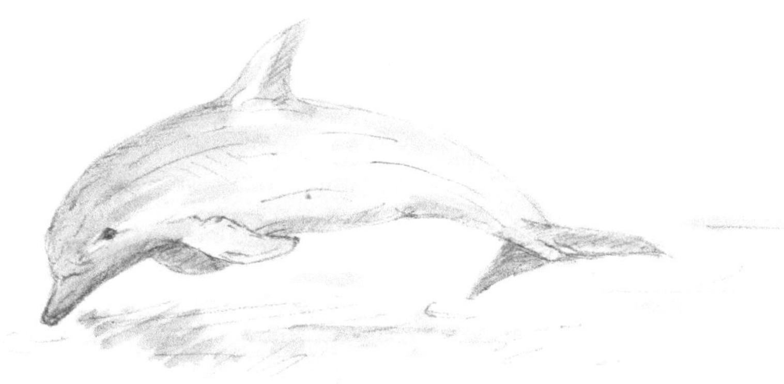



# Chapter 10

## Classrooms to Courtrooms

During our time in Seychelles, Melv and I were keen to try to build good relations with groups of people and organisations over there to help ease the way for future projects. One of the missing links I was particularly interested in was developing a relationship with the local schools. Much like in Somerset, where we had worked with local children about the cessation of peat extraction and they had helped with the creation of a nature reserve, in Seychelles we wanted to teach children about poaching and reserve protection.

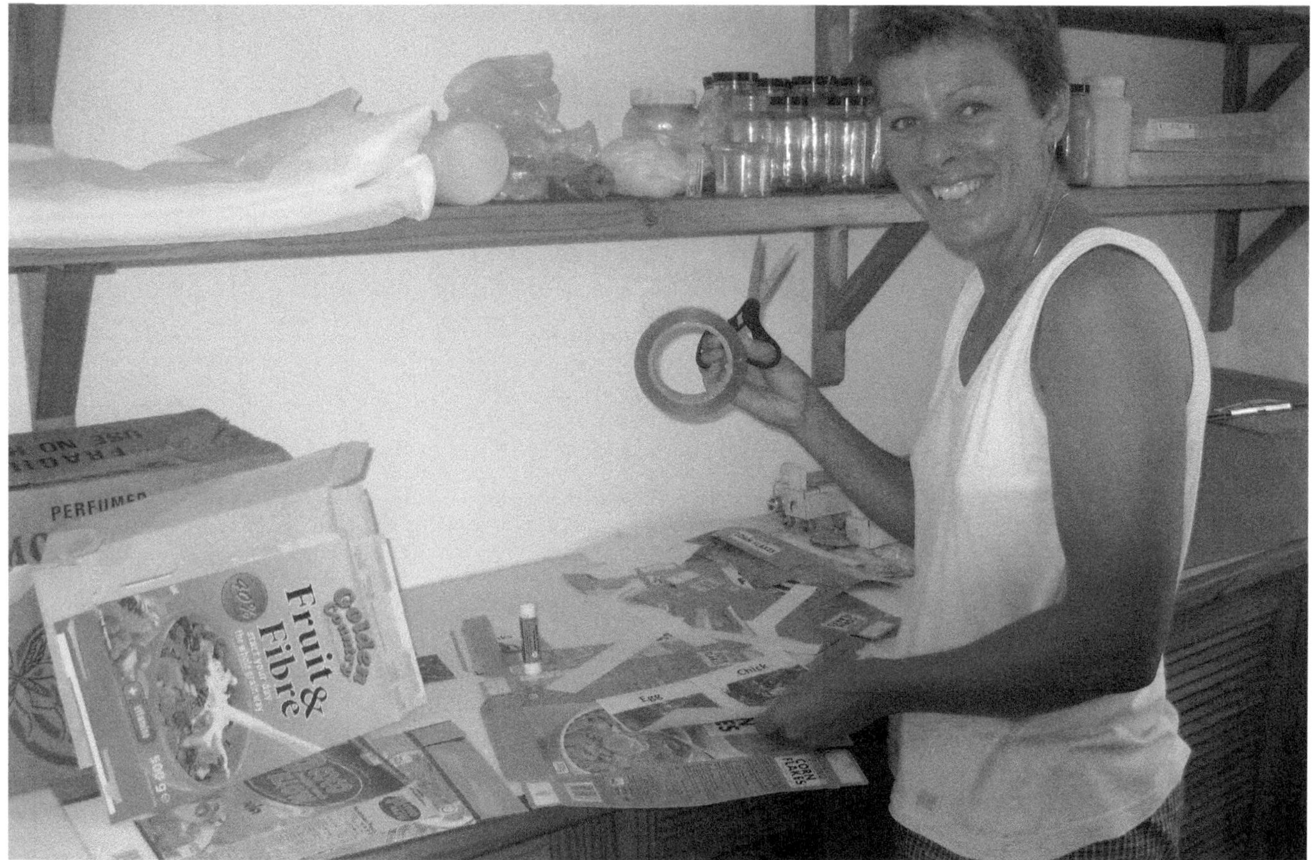


© *Melvyn Yeandle*

I had thought my days of making educational resources out of cornflake packets and pieces of string were long over, but to my delight, they weren't! My first visit to Grand Anse Primary School was the start of an inspiring journey for me, opening up new learning opportunities for the children and providing me with a different perspective together with an important link to the mainland world.

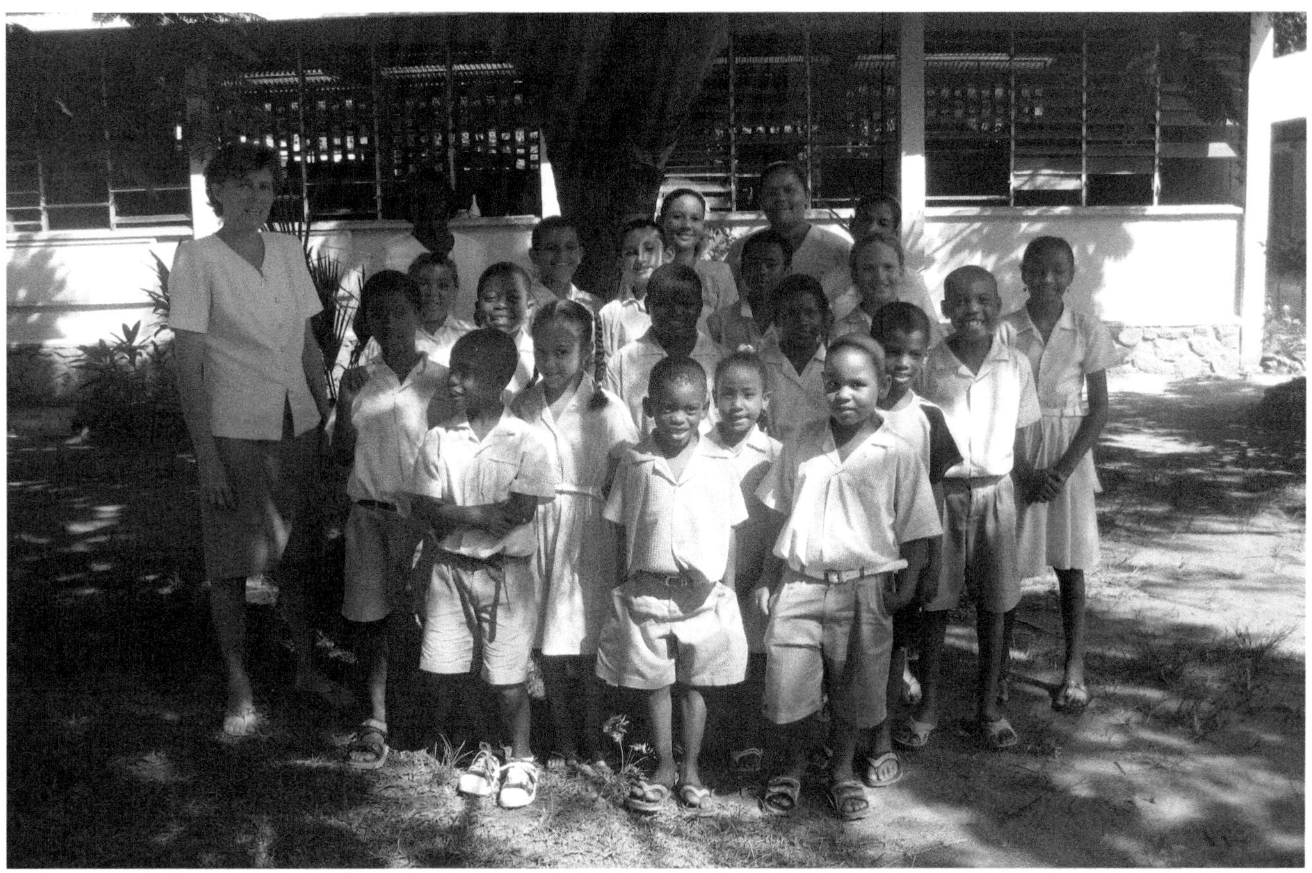

We undertook some excellent projects, and Miss Veronica, the teacher became a reliable friend. We formed the EcoAride Club, an after-school club for children keen on the environment. I helped with the organisation of it as distance allowed and linked the meet day with shopping trips. We connected with Meare Primary School back in Somerset and communicated via our blog, through which differences about culture and country were exchanged.

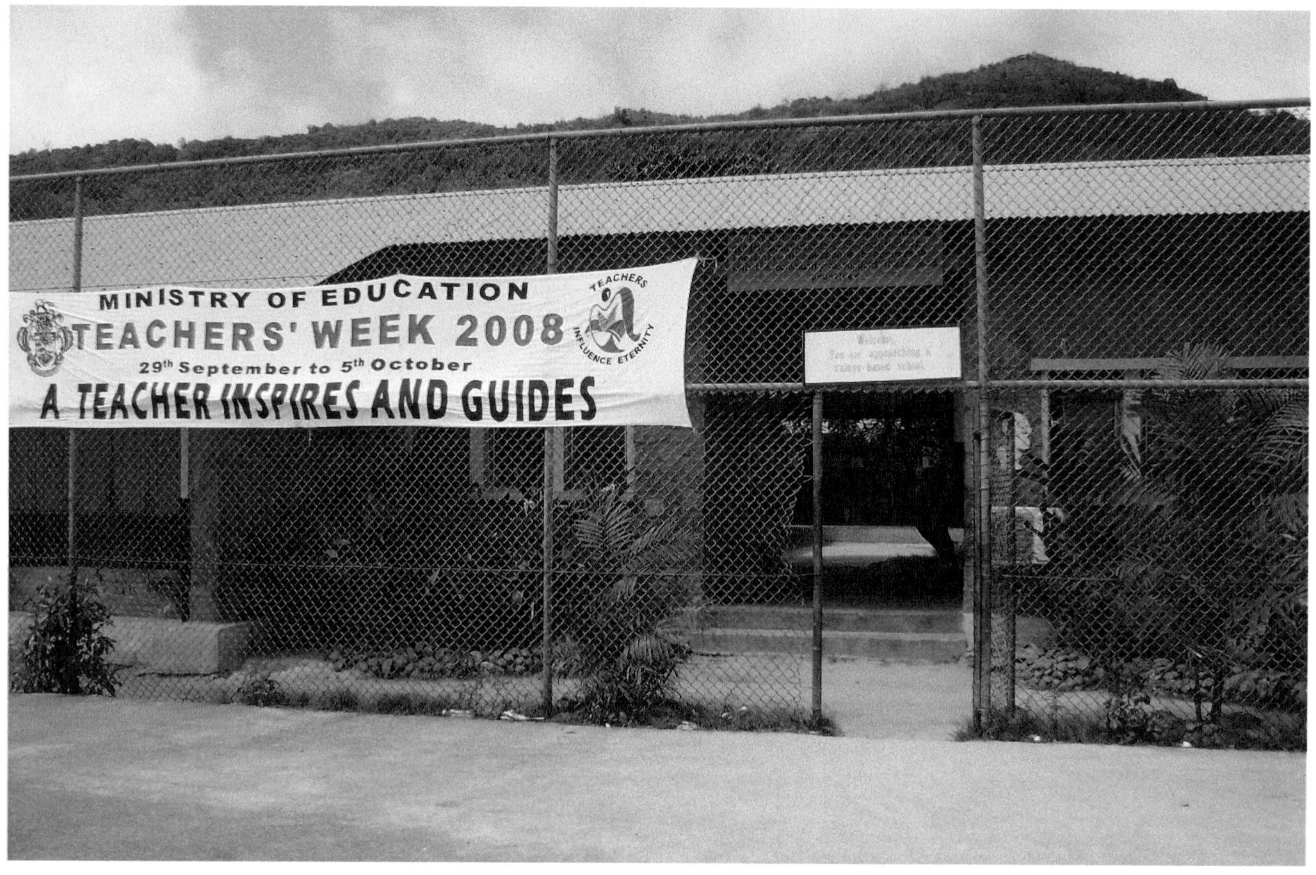


The school was a clean and tidy place but a little barren in appearance. Constructed of concrete lined blocks with a concrete floor and corrugated tin roof, the black holes for windows made it look a little dark. Each classroom was spartanly furnished: traditional wooden desks and a blackboard, with no soft furnishings and only shutters hanging on the walls, which served to block out the elements.

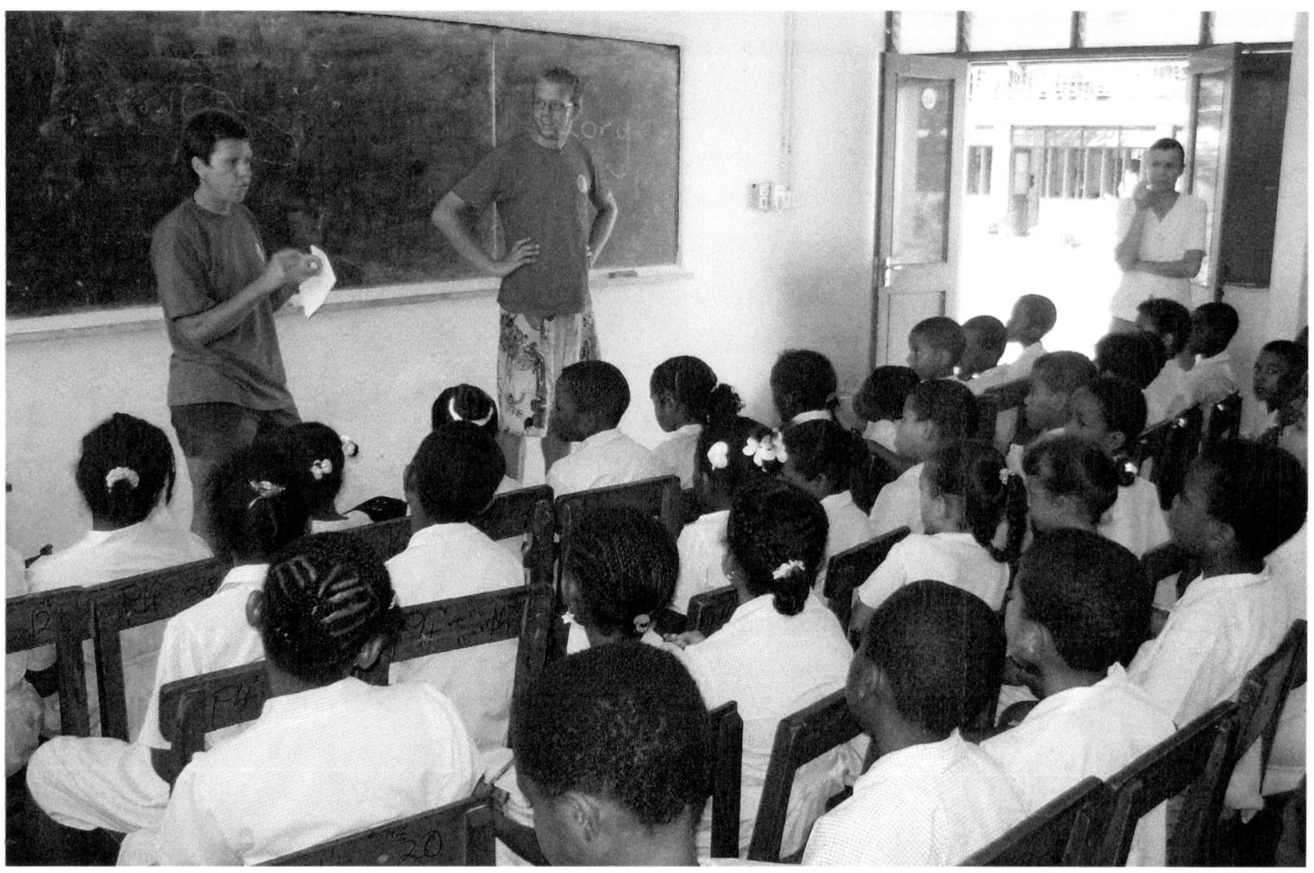

Even when you know your subject, eighty minutes with primary school children is a long time, and a suggestion from Lara that Finn (one of our volunteers), with the help of his ukulele, should write a song about birds and adaptation, was inspired. We were greeted that day by sixty-six eager faces: this wasn't going to be any old lesson and they knew it.

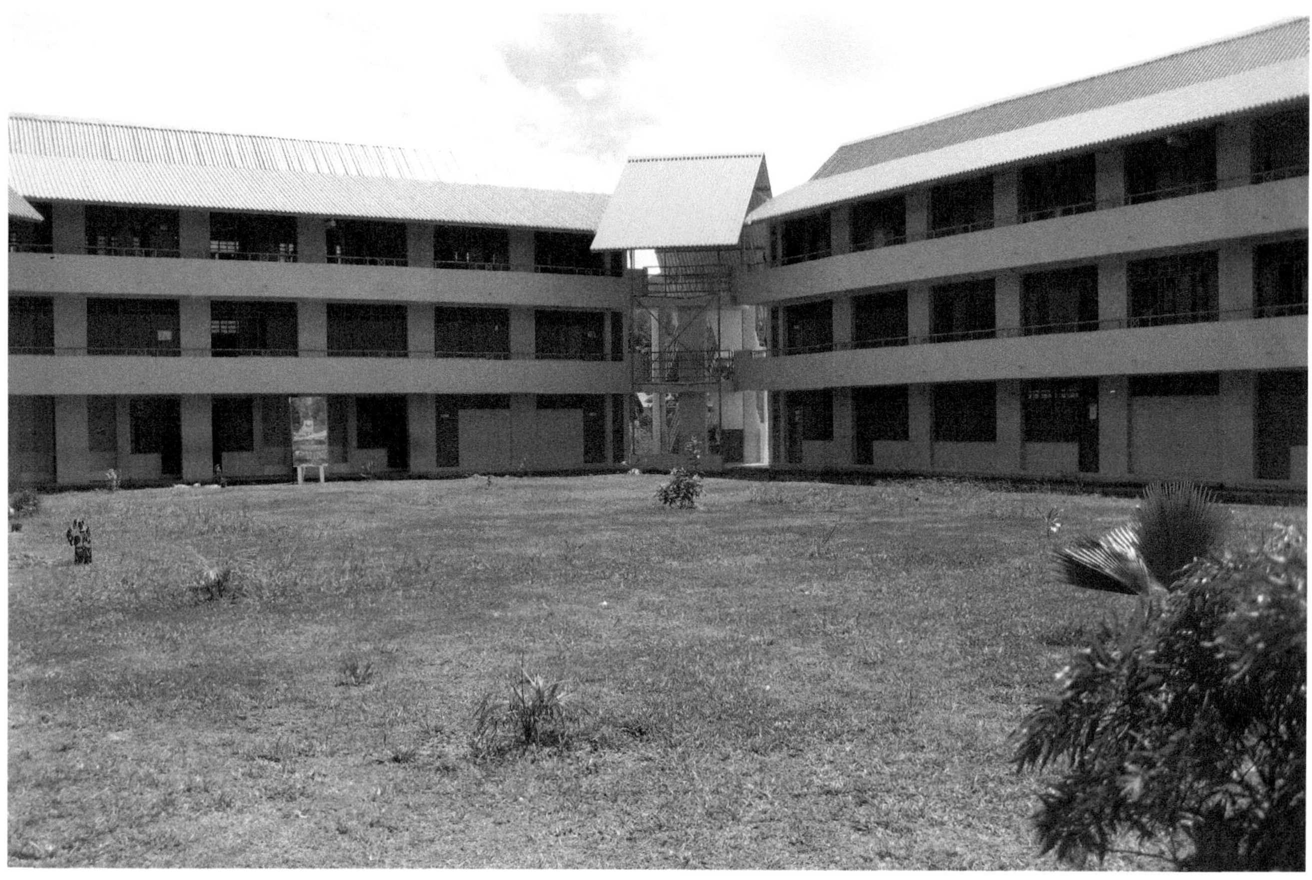

On Mondays, after shopping and bank duties, I took the opportunity to grab a bus across the island through the Vallée de Mai and over to Baie Ste Anne, to attend the after-school club at the primary school. The  school was larger than Grand Anse, with a total of three floors built around a central courtyard. There were open-air staircases and corridors along each floor leading to the classrooms and standing in any of the corridors enabled you to see the whole building.

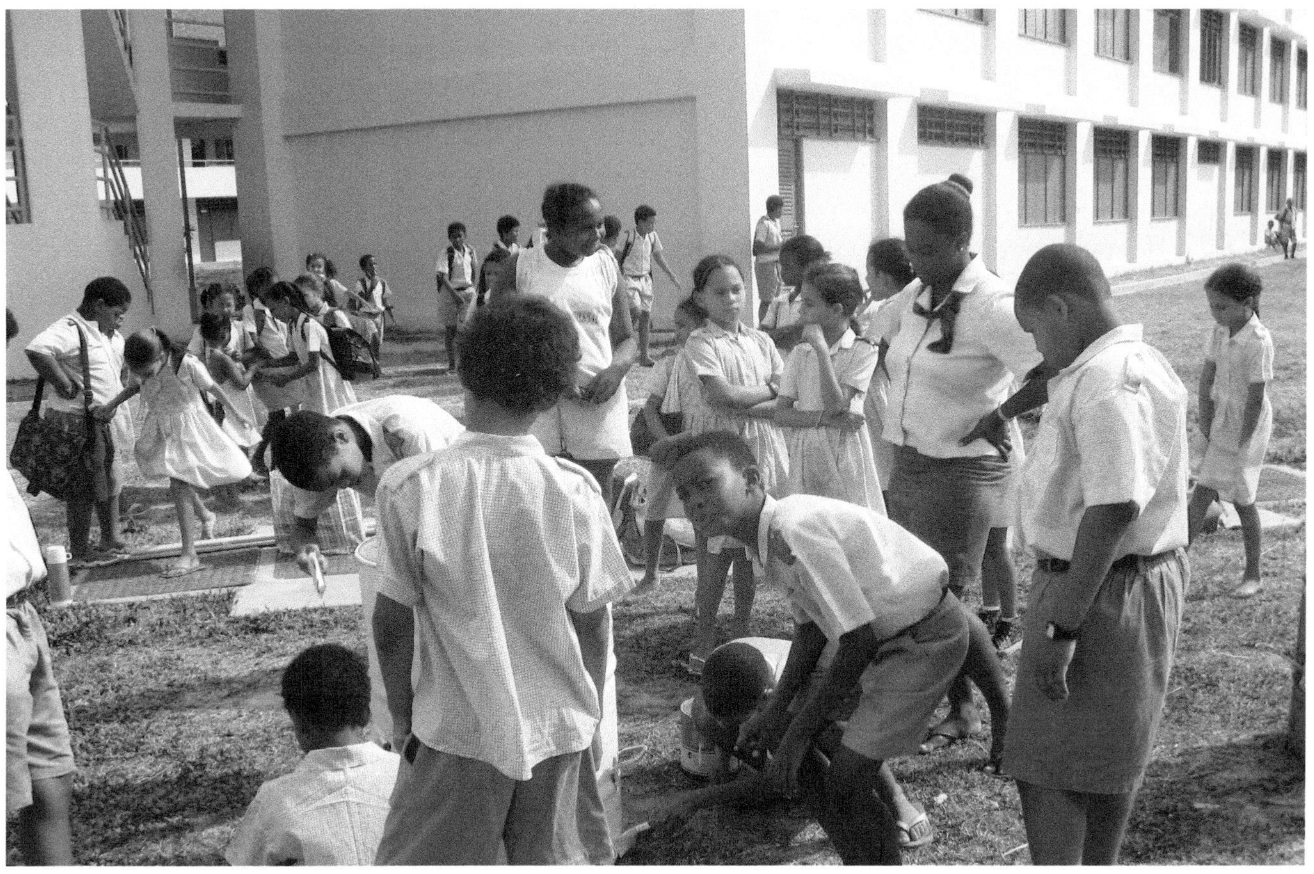

Baie Ste Anne Primary School was a friendly and welcoming place, and I was always greeted with smiles by both teachers and pupils, who recognised me as the Aride lady. The children were keen and on this occasion we were painting barrels as rubbish bins, and they didn't seem to mind that there was only one tub of paint and three paint brushes among fifteen of them. They just all took it in turns to paint a bit then pass the brush on.

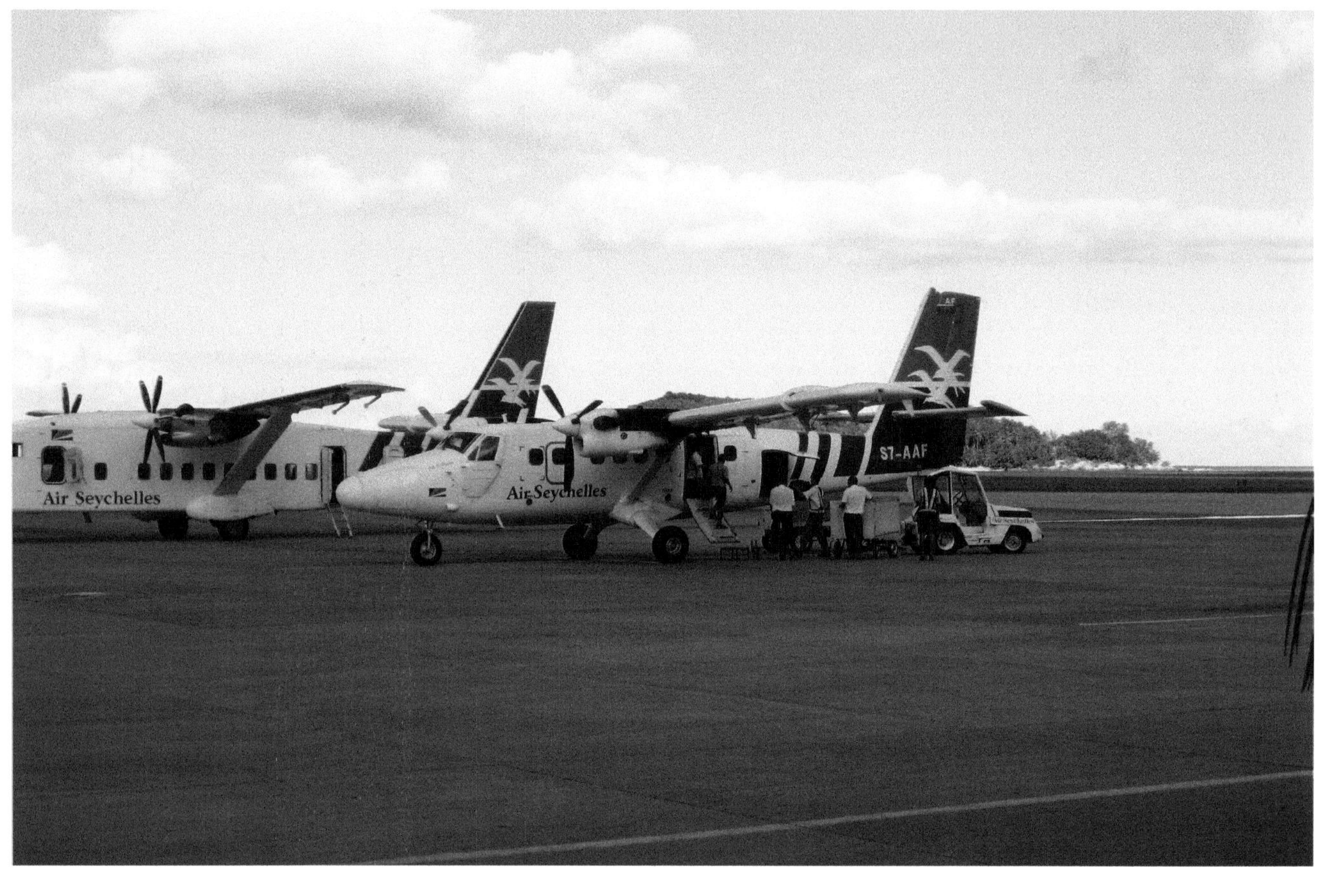

I certainly never imagined that I would have to go to court during my time in Seychelles, but when one of our former rangers accused me of 'unfair dismissal' I found myself travelling to Mahé. I remember staring out of the window on the plane, thinking about what I was going to say. I felt for my symbol of strength, the uncomplicated little white conch shell that was nestled in my pocket.

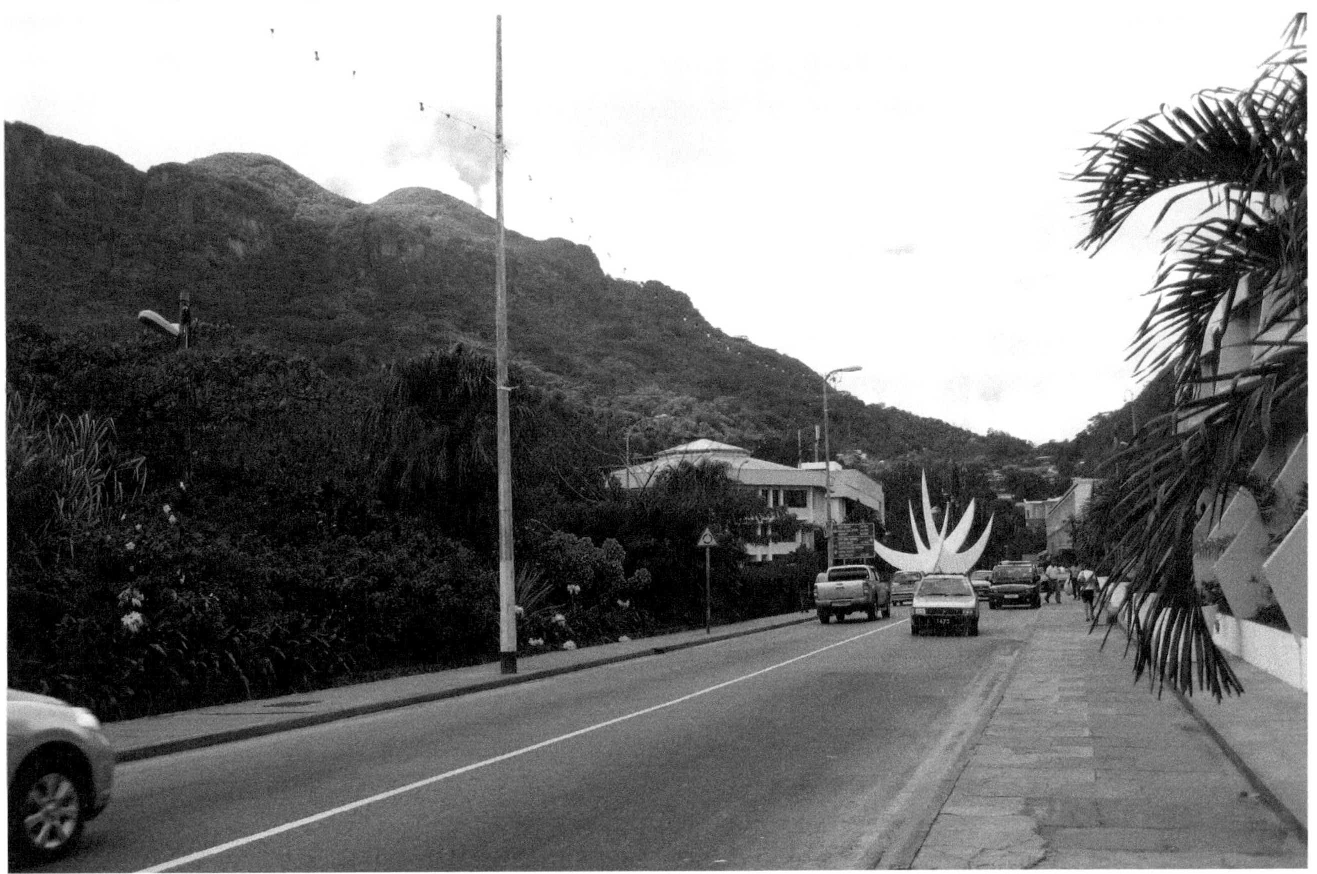

All travel went to plan, and I was very relieved when the taxi pulled up outside Independence House, the home of Seychelles' court rooms, with half an hour to spare. We proceeded to the waiting room, which was dark, narrow and claustrophobic, with no windows or natural light, a stark contrast to the bright sunshine we had left outside.

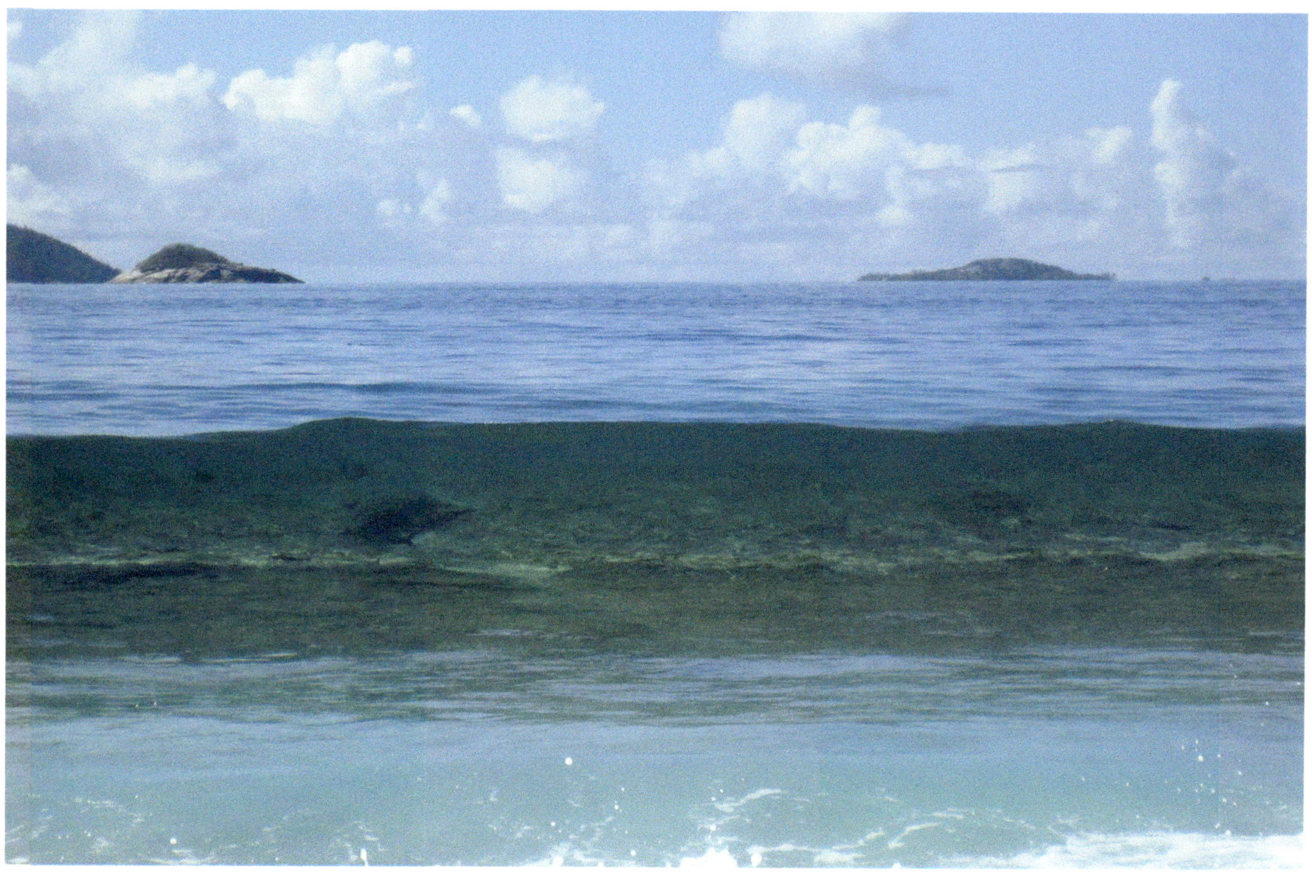

When we heard the news that the court case was settled, the relief was huge; it had been a long haul since the day of the dismissal. With such good news, nothing seemed a problem for the rest of the day, and over a late breakfast we sat and looked out to sea, watching the dolphins rising, breaking the water's surface, and the eagle rays surfing the waves.

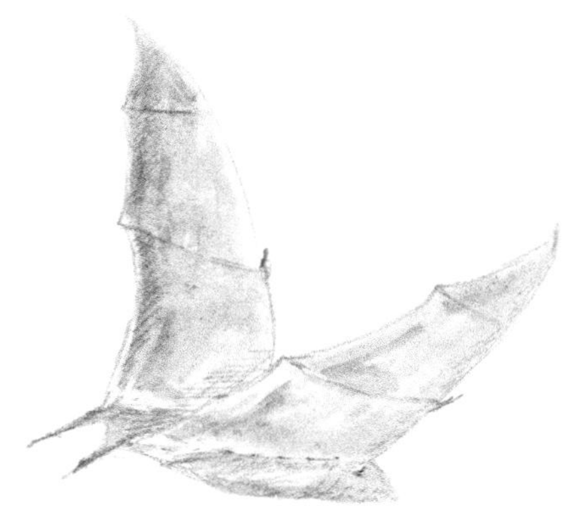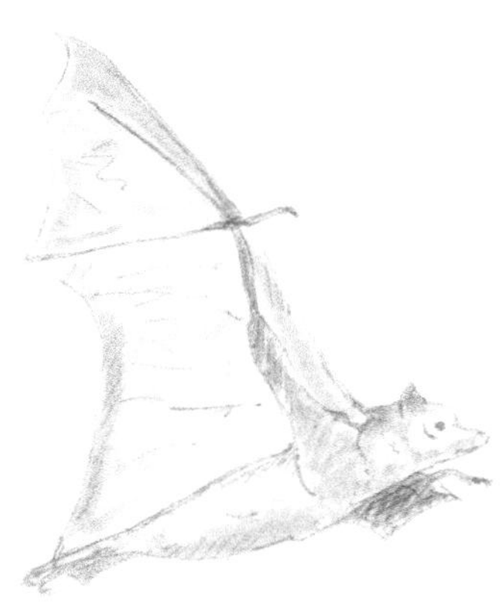

Fruit bats

# Chapter 11

## Living with Skinks

It was no secret that one of the main reasons we moved to Aride was for the wildlife, but every so often, its sheer abundance hit home, like when I showed a group of local school children round. The kids were able to stand less than a metre from white-tailed tropicbirds, see magpie robins feeding right in front of them and watch geckos protect their eggs in our spectacular Banyan tree.

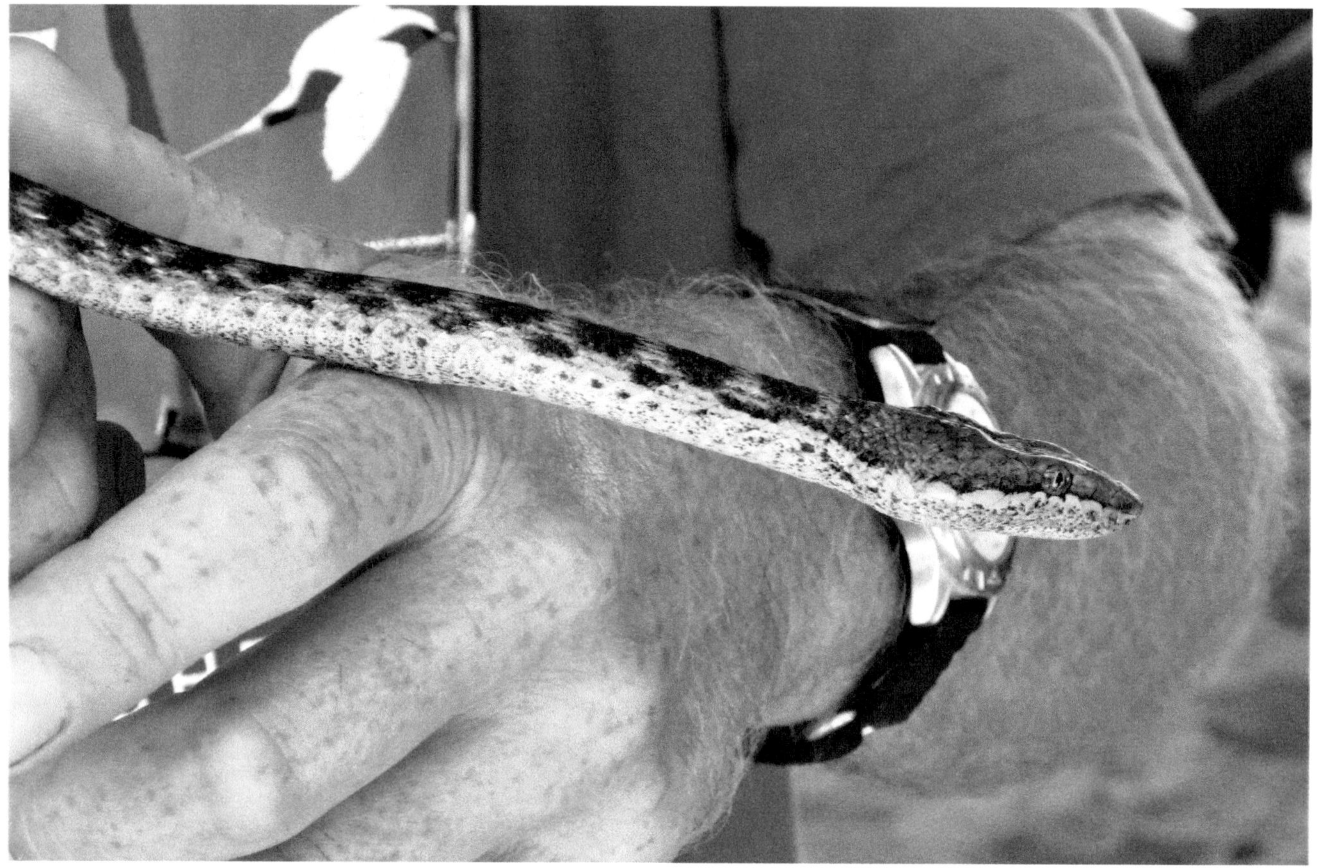

Aride inspires many people, adults and children alike, and I still feel privileged that part of my job was to facilitate this, to open up this wonderful island for visitors, and let them, too, enjoy the wealth of wildlife it supports.

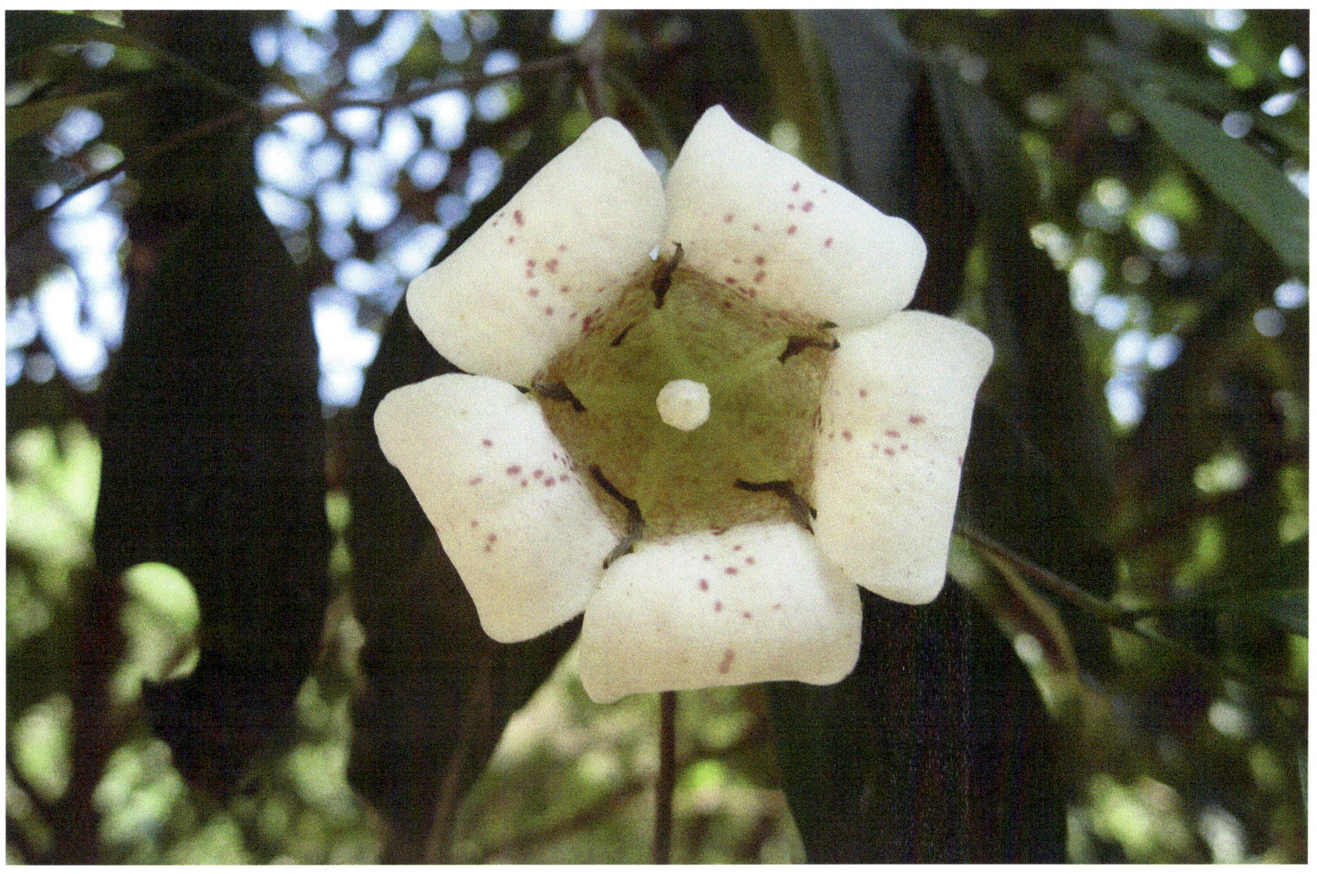

The Wright's gardenia is exquisite, often flowering after rain; the distinctive, sweet aroma would drift across the island. The beautiful pink and white flowers of this rare and native shrub adorned both the hill and the plateau periodically, supported by the deep green, leathery leaves and bulbous fruits. Identified by the Irish scientist, Percival Wright, in 1868, Aride is the only place where Wright's gardenia occurs naturally, and it has remained one of the island's unique attractions since.

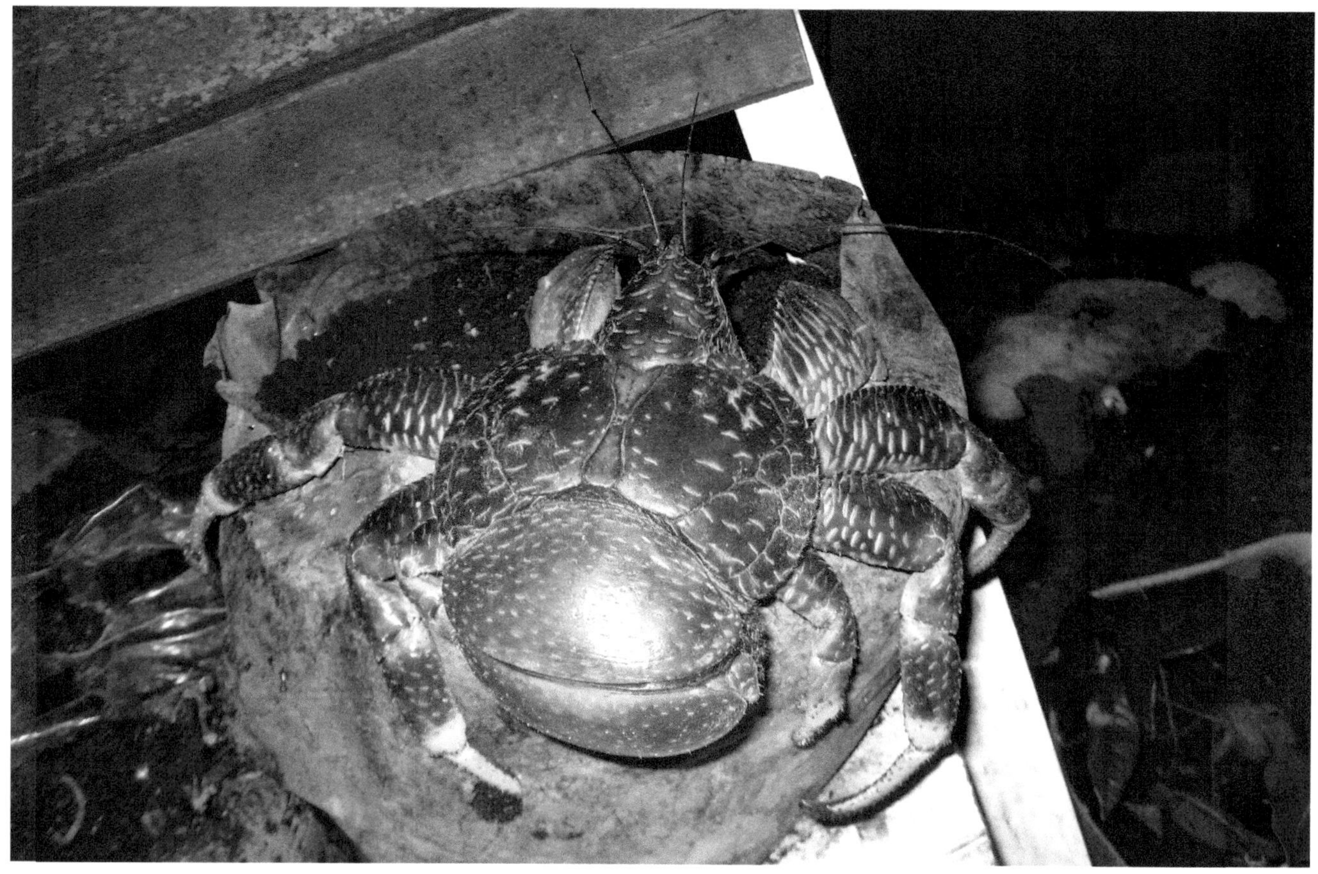

A cross between a purple hermit and a lobster in appearance, the distinctive robber crab's shell is the size of a tea plate, and sits like a shield on its back. Its front pincers can open to a metre wide or more and six articulated legs make it very agile. They are not common on Aride, and had only been sighted three times in the year before we arrived: once at the volunteers' house and twice in the wardens' bedroom!

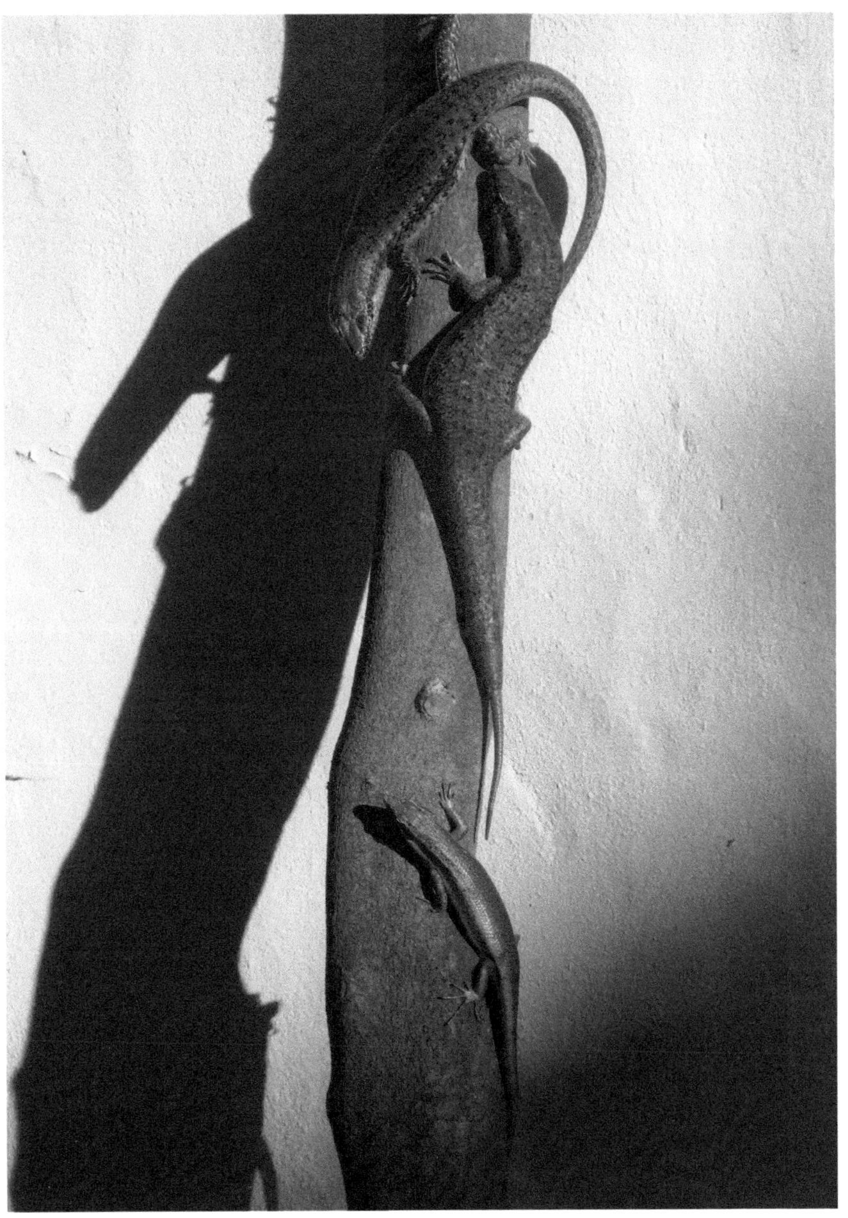

We shared our home with many wildlife species, but aside from the ants, the skinks – a type of lizard – were the most common. All the literature written on Aride claims that it has the highest density of skinks in the world, with one per every square metre of island. I found this hard to believe before we arrived, but once we were there it was clear - the literature was right!

**Sally sitting amongst Aride's spectacular Banyan tree**

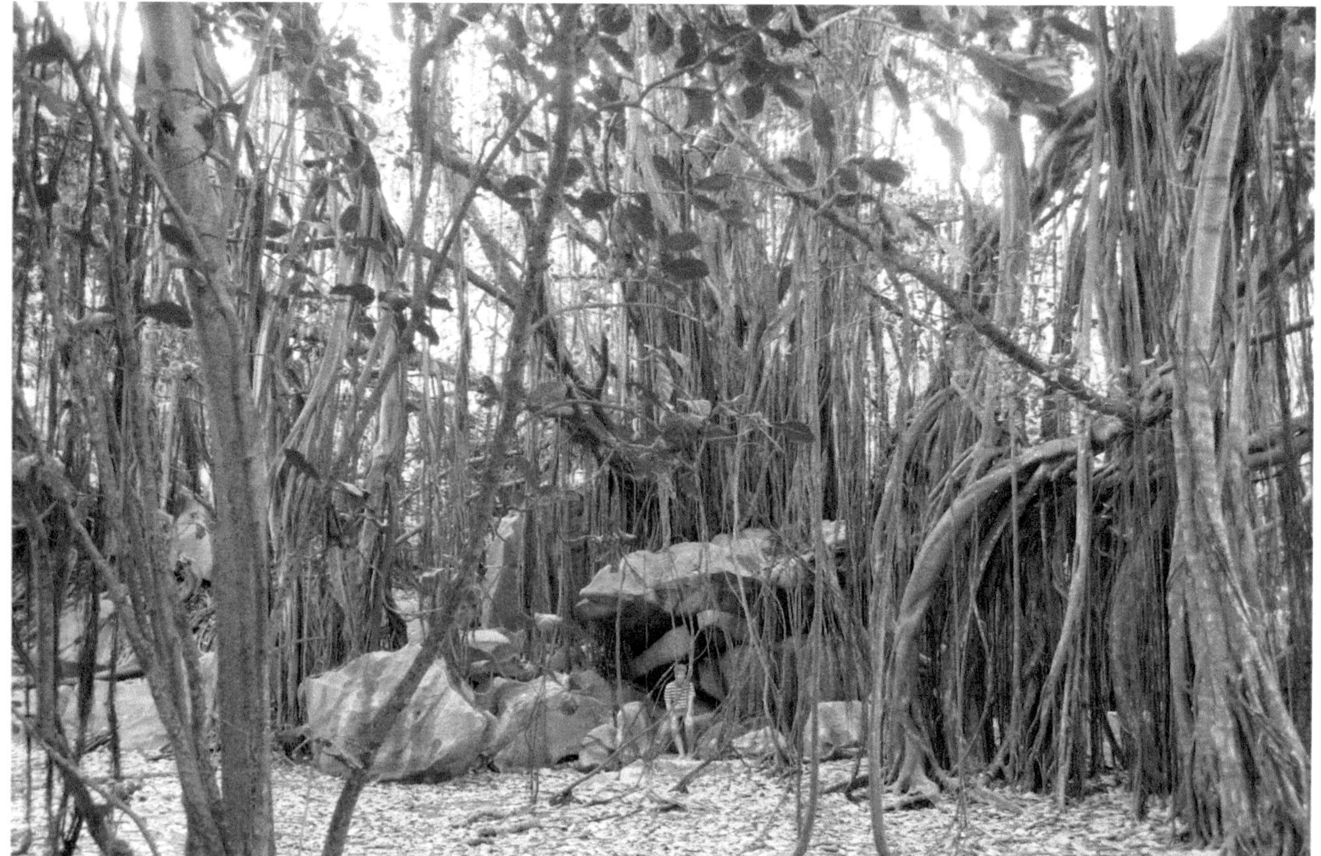

© Melvyn Yeandle

There was only one Banyan tree on Aride, and it provided refuge for a huge variety of wildlife, from birds to bats to geckos. The national tree of India, Banyans are some of the world's biggest trees and were introduced to Seychelles and Aride to provide shade. Even the Aride Banyan marched impressively across the plateau, covering a ground area of at least 200m².

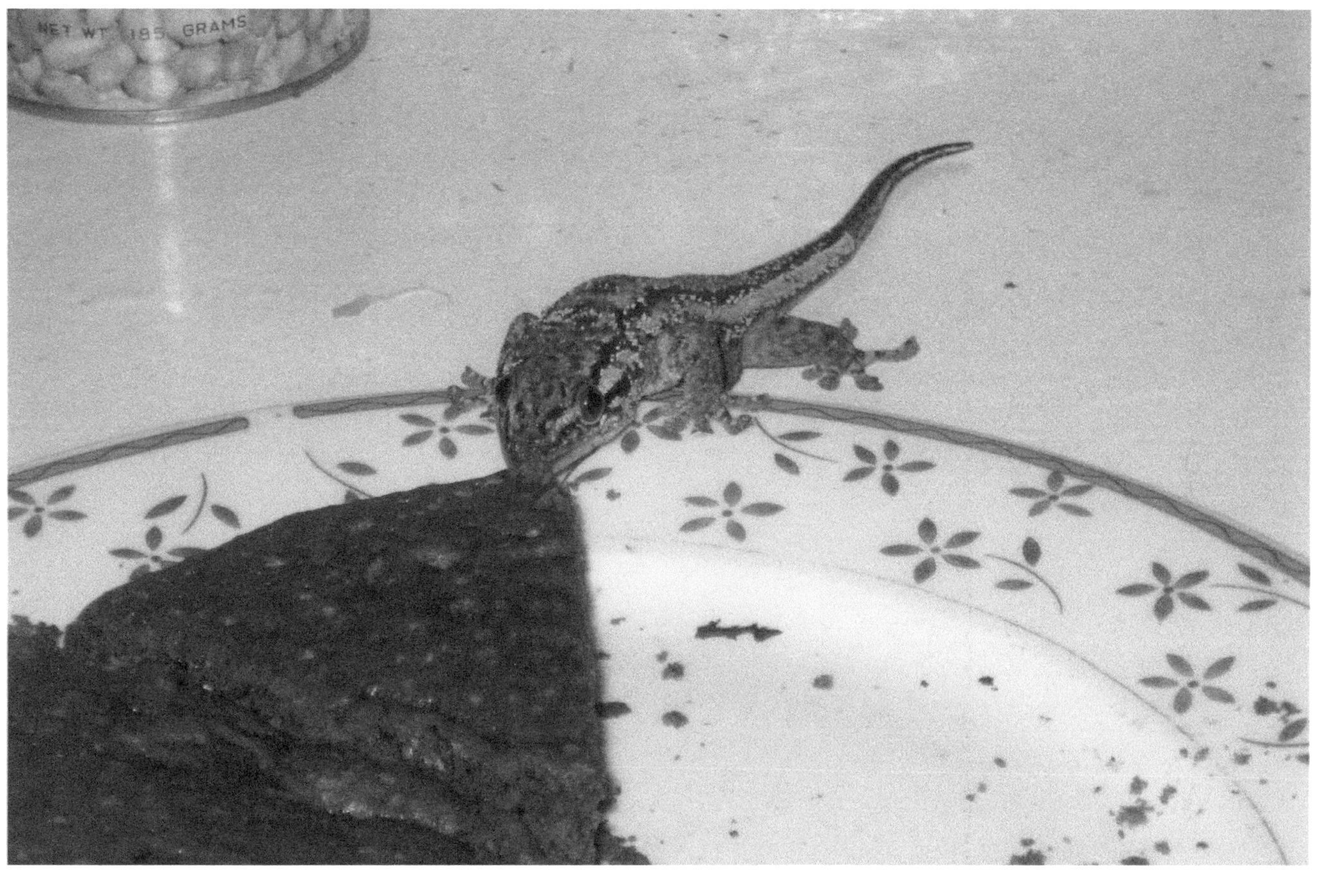

One particular bronze-eyed gecko, which took up residence in our kitchen, often lingered by the kitchen window to spy on the food that was being prepared. It was only interested in sweet stuff and developed a nose for it, slinking down the wall before advancing on chocolate, custard, cake or even a bit of pastry.

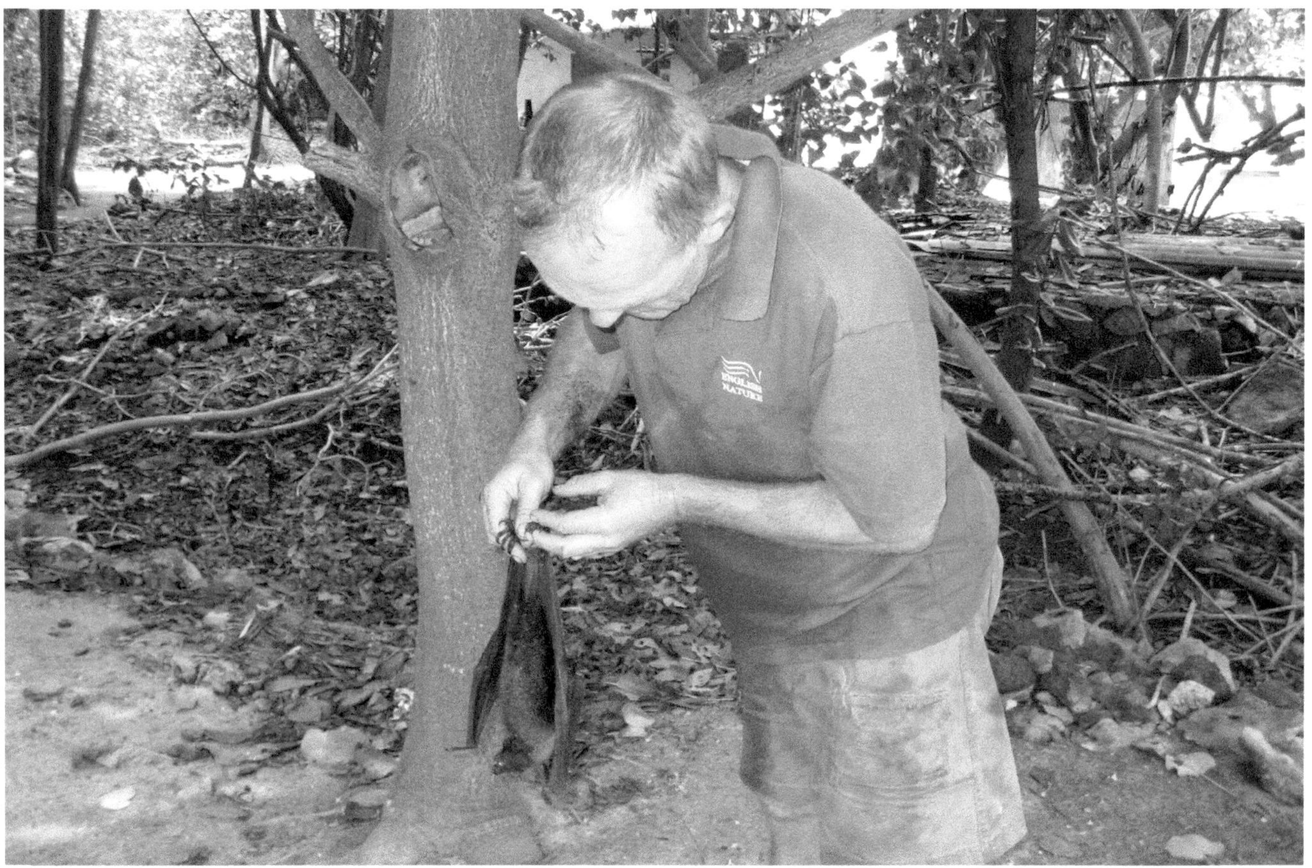

A lot of the wildlife had unusual, opportunistic habits, particularly the fruit bats and blue pigeons, which gorged themselves on fermented fruits and ended up looking like many of us have done after a heavy night out. Melv rescued such a bat from the garden and brought it back to the house and the safety of a cardboard box, to give it a chance to sleep off its hangover for a while. Come the evening it was looking much livelier, and was soon flying around with the other fruit bats, chattering as if boasting about its drunken antics.

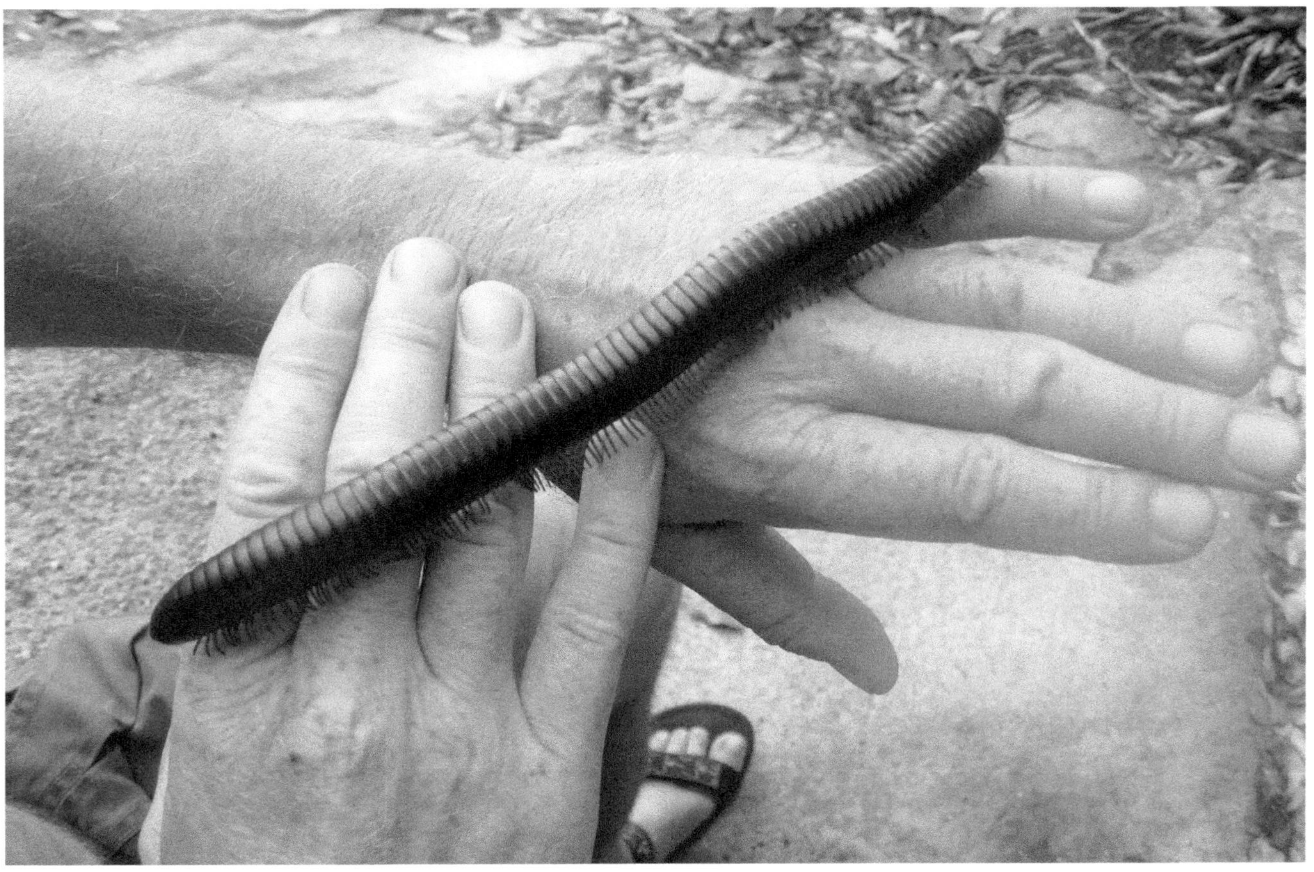

At night, a walk up the hill on Aride was a full sensory overload of a special kind; the sights, sounds and smells were like nothing I had ever experienced. Every step had to be taken with caution, for the ground was littered with 15cm long millipedes, like props from a science fiction movie; everywhere you looked they glistened in the torchlight as their many legs scaled the trees and rocks and carried them slowly along the paths.

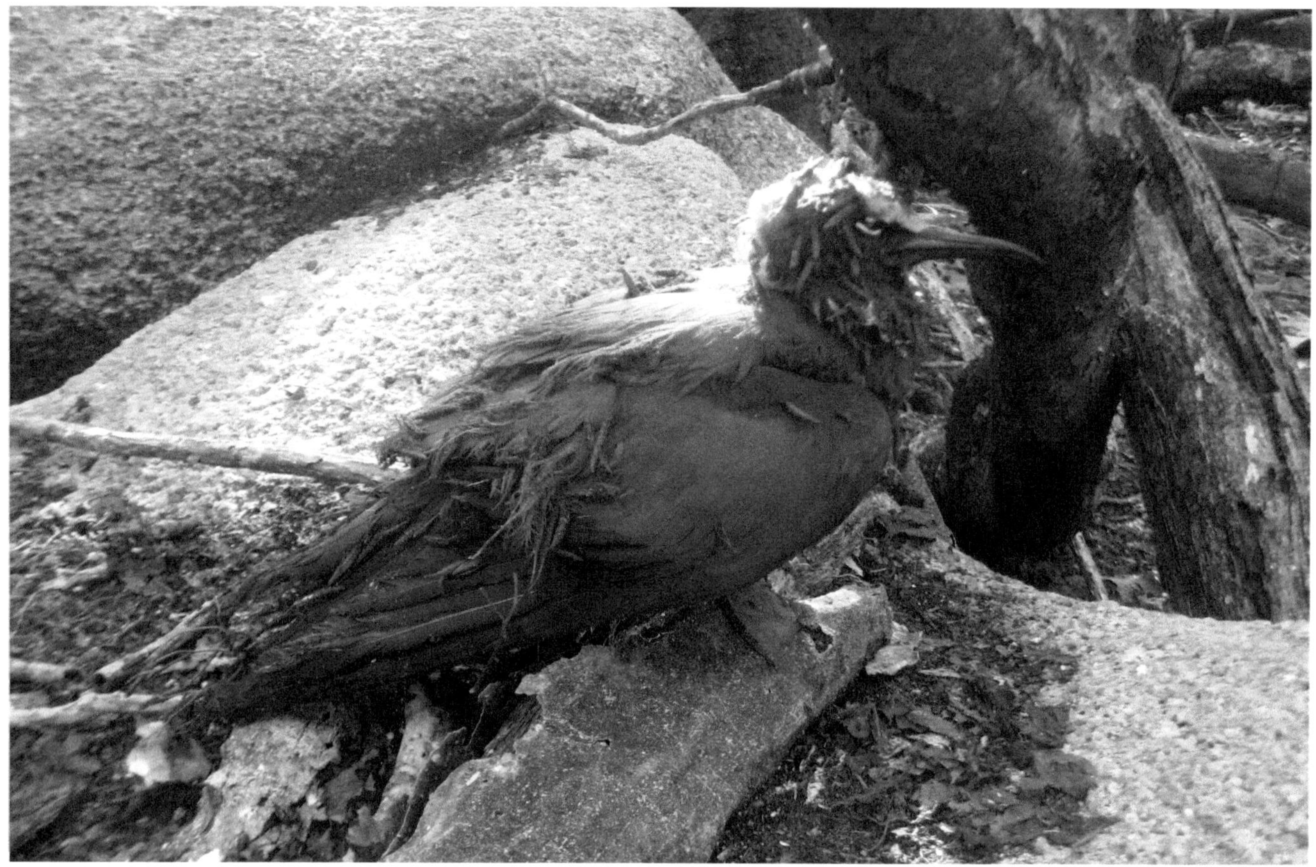

Our life on Aride provided some unforgettable wildlife highs, so much so that I'd almost been waiting for the lows. But I could never have been prepared for the low resulting from the effect of pisonia, the pioneering species of tree that had colonised the island after the coconut plantation was removed. Pisonia is a very clever species but has a rather evil side, spreading via seeds that are so sticky they adhere to almost everything.

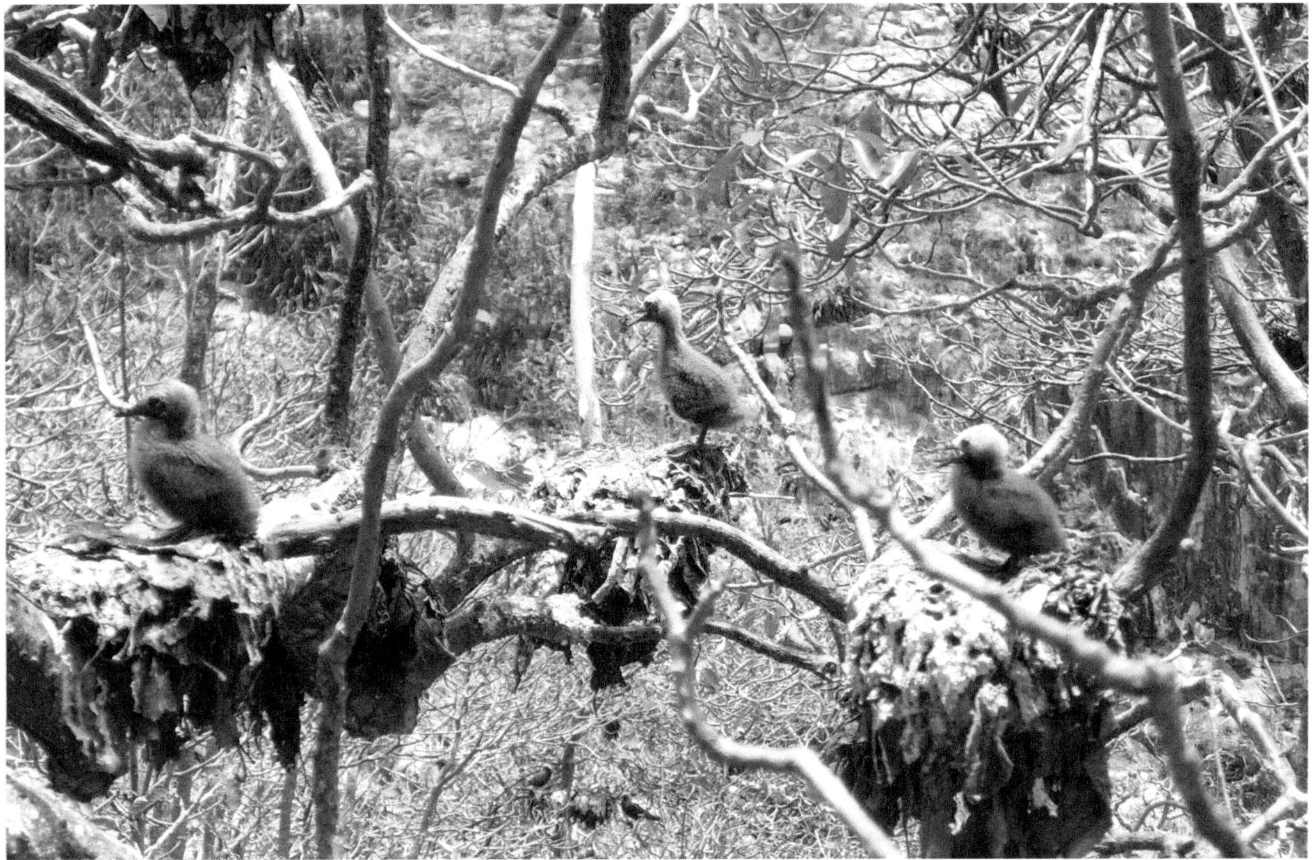

© *Chloe Prehn-Arnold*

One of the arguments for why we couldn't intervene and remove the pisonia woodland was that Aride holds the world's largest colony of lesser noddies, birds that rely on pisonia trees and their leaves for nesting. But we were concerned that at a certain point the number of deaths caused by pisonia seeds would outweigh their value.

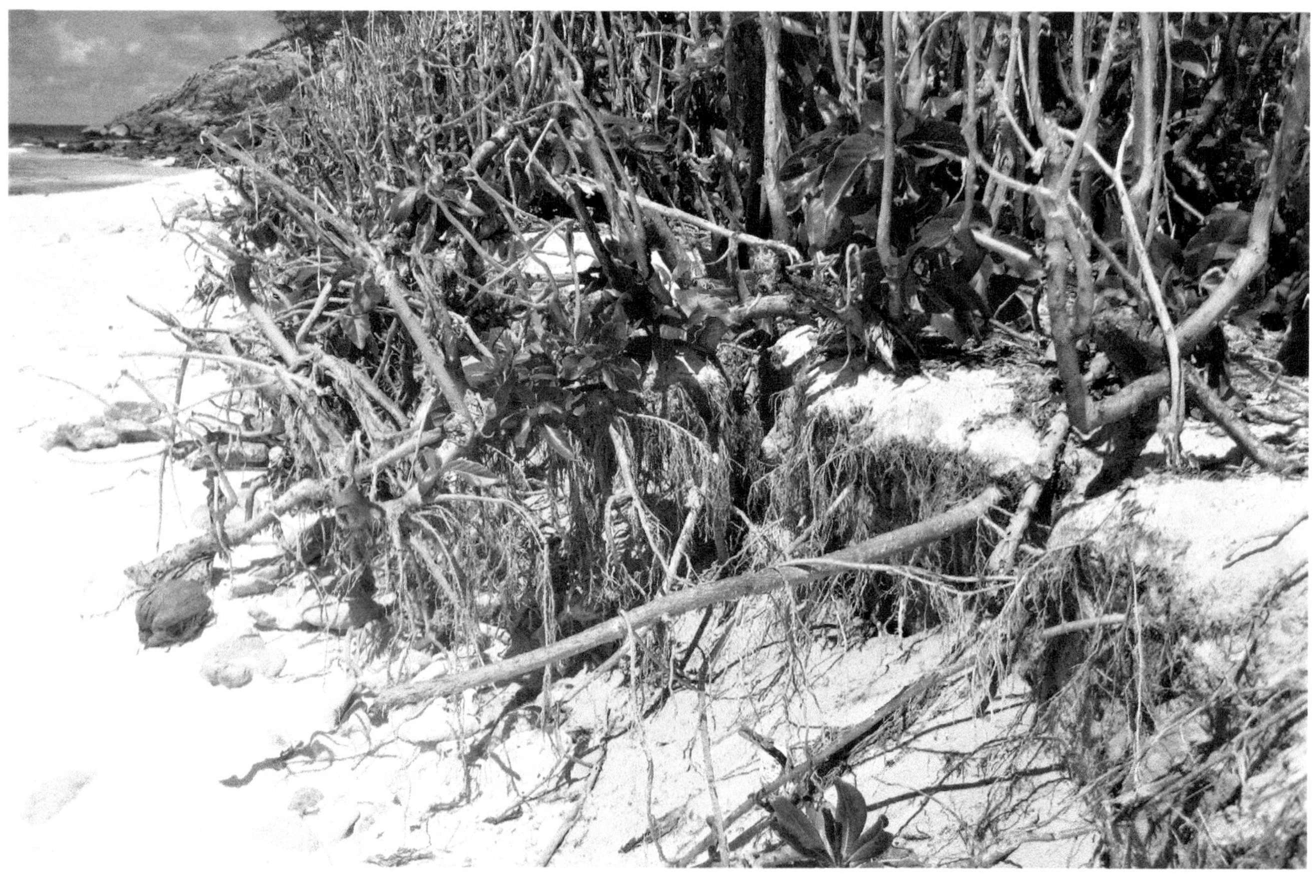

After contacting the Island Conservation Society Mahé office about the pisonia issue, they agreed to come over to see the level of devastation for themselves. After a healthy debate, I am relieved to say that we got the result we wanted, and we were able to move forward with our plans; to change the habitat makeup of Aride.

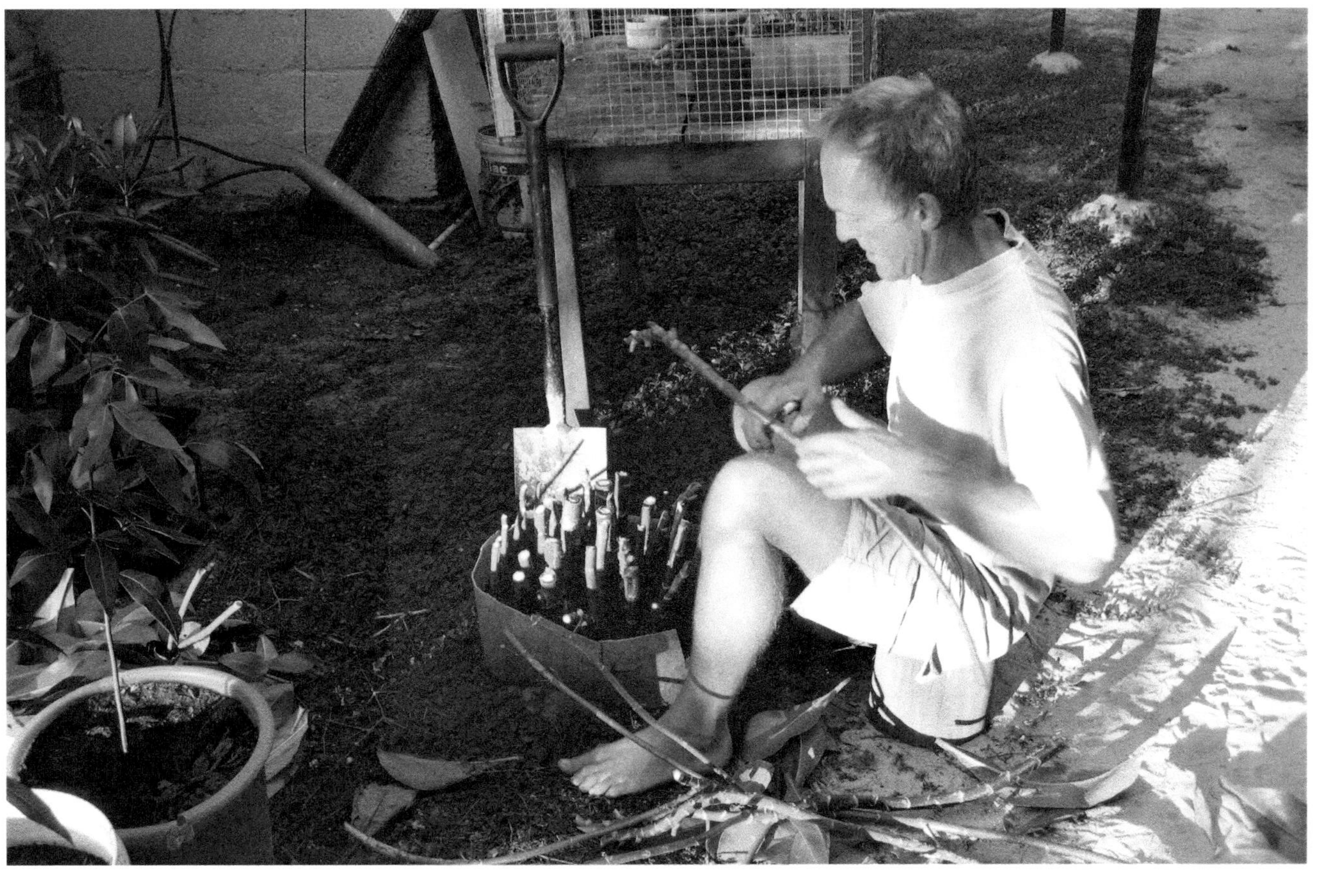

The agreement was that we would work on the beach crest to replace the pisonia with salt tolerant vegetation, and remove all pisonia on the plateau to allow other species to come up through. For the hill, the plan was to target the stands of mixed vegetation and remove the pisonia trees.

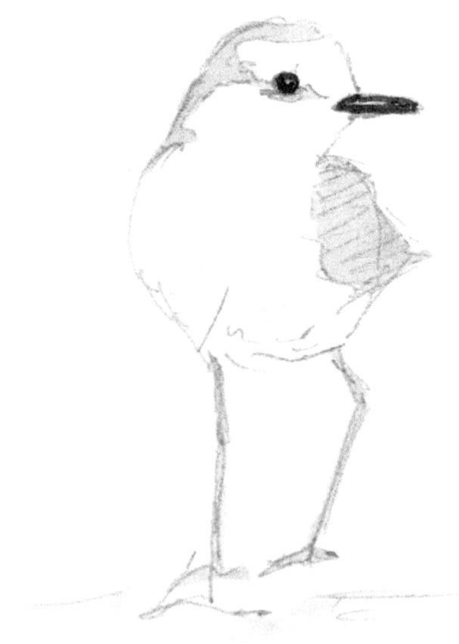

**Chapter 12**

**Wailing Wedgetails and Nodding Noddies**

When we first arrived, it felt like the birds and other wildlife on Aride made up their own rules — every available space on the island is utilised; there are turnstones in the woods and moorhens on the beach, and the roseate tern colony, made up of over five hundred pairs, is the world's only woodland nesting colony, and one of the largest in the Indian Ocean. The fairy tern population is the largest in Seychelles, with over four thousand pairs. They lay just one egg on the nub of a branch; it is very bizarre to see a tern incubating an egg on a branch, knowing they too normally prefer a scrape on the ground.

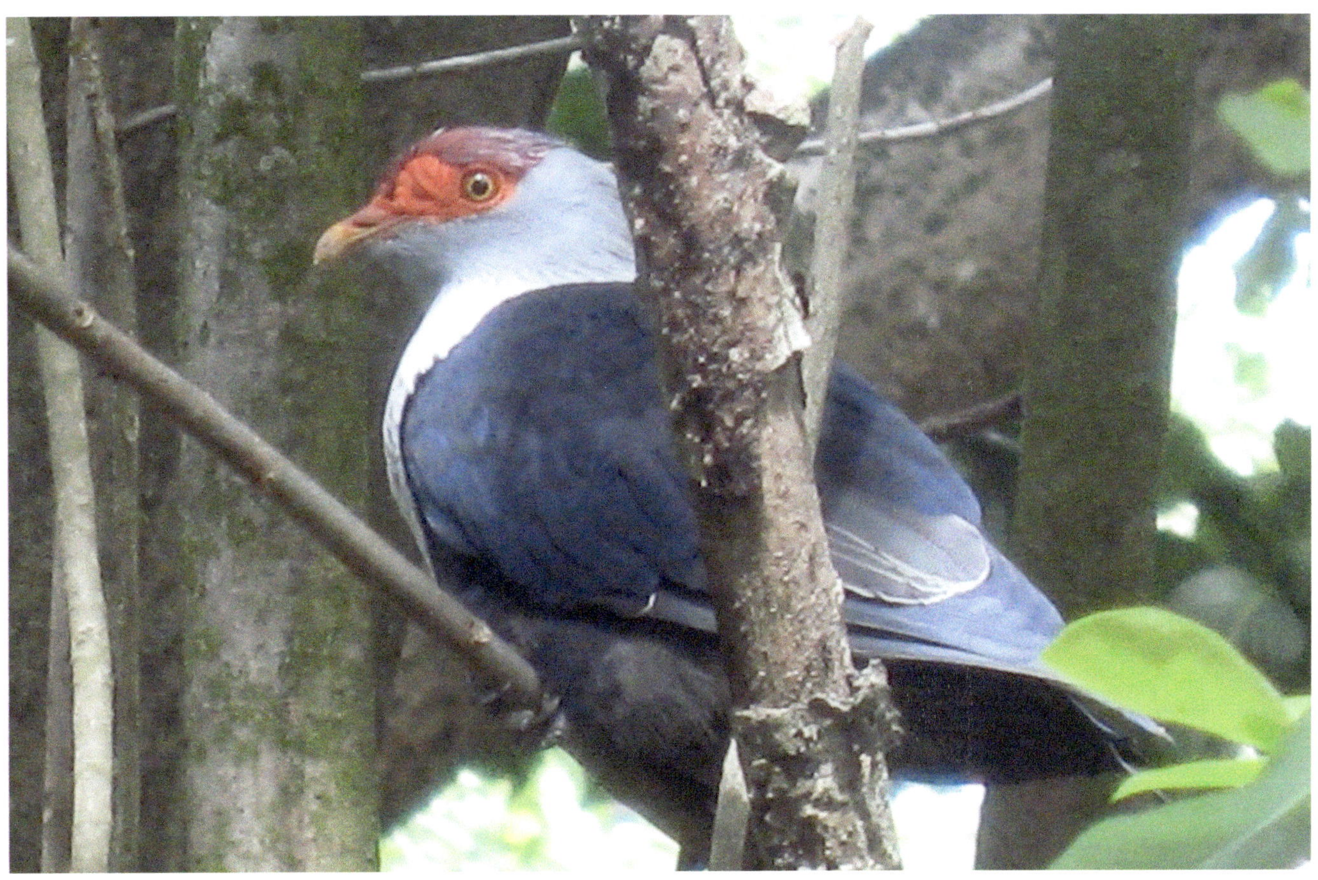

After a long and busy day, I often grabbed the remaining daylight and spent it in the garden, a perfect spot to sit quietly with my sketchbook. Not that I ever needed to look for inspiration on Aride, but it was one of my favourite places. This day brought fantastic views of blue pigeons. They are stunning birds, endemic to Seychelles, and a species that naturally re-colonised Aride in the nineties.

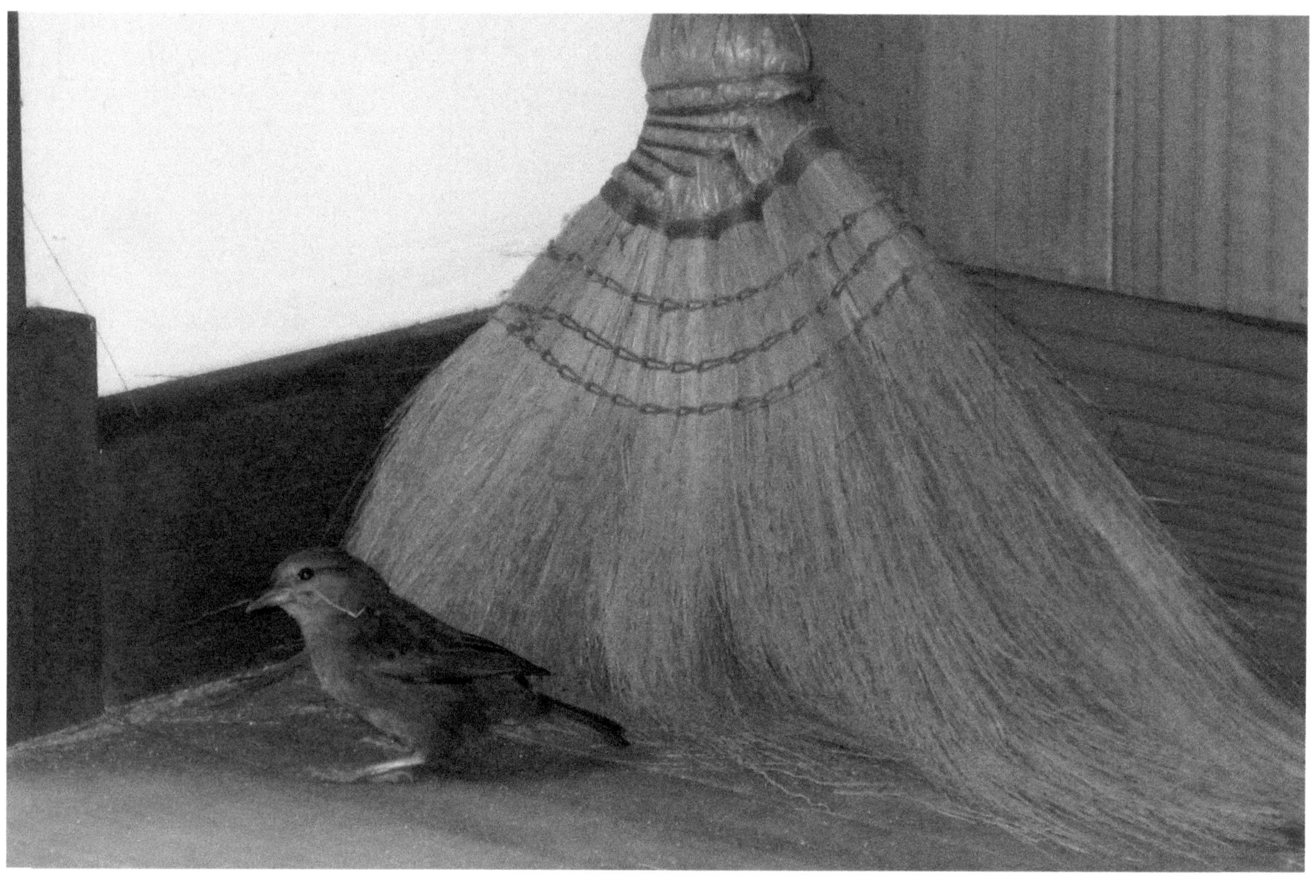

Another bird endemic to Seychelles is the Seychelles fody, known locally as 'tok-toks', cheeky little birds of a similar size and character to the UK house sparrow. They were a very common sight around the houses and buildings and must be Aride's most persistent scavengers; nothing could be left unattended in the kitchen, and their loud piercing song was blasted out when they were scavenging for food or a piece of the office sweeping brush.

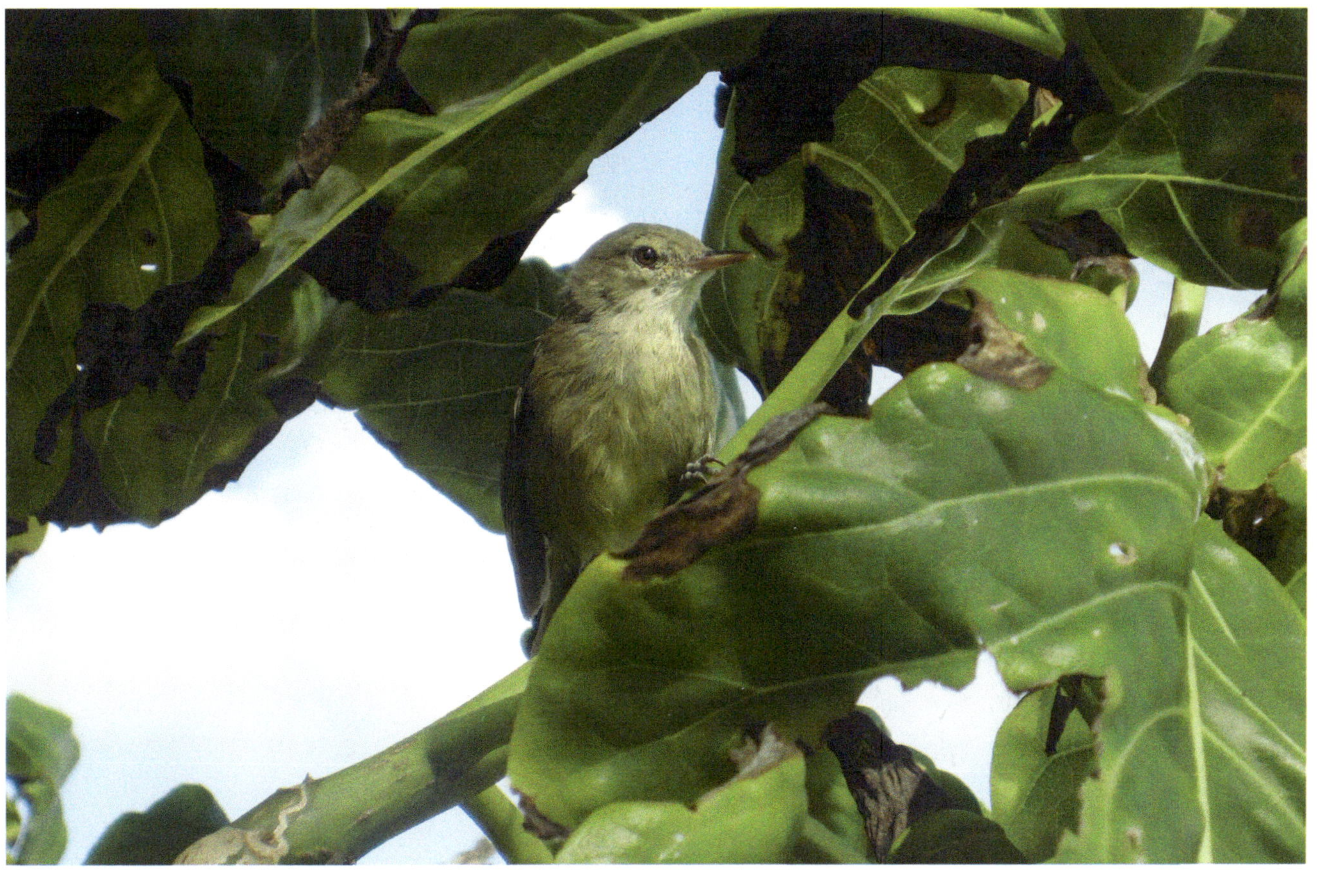

The vegetation around the house often attracted Seychelles warblers. They are smart birds, long legged and bulky, with a typical warbler face, a pointed but thick beak and beautiful olive colouring on their wings and back. One of the best Seychelles' conservation success stories, these birds were reduced to fewer than thirty individuals on one island in 1969, but in the late nineties, twenty-nine birds were brought to Aride and the island now has over two thousand, the largest single population.

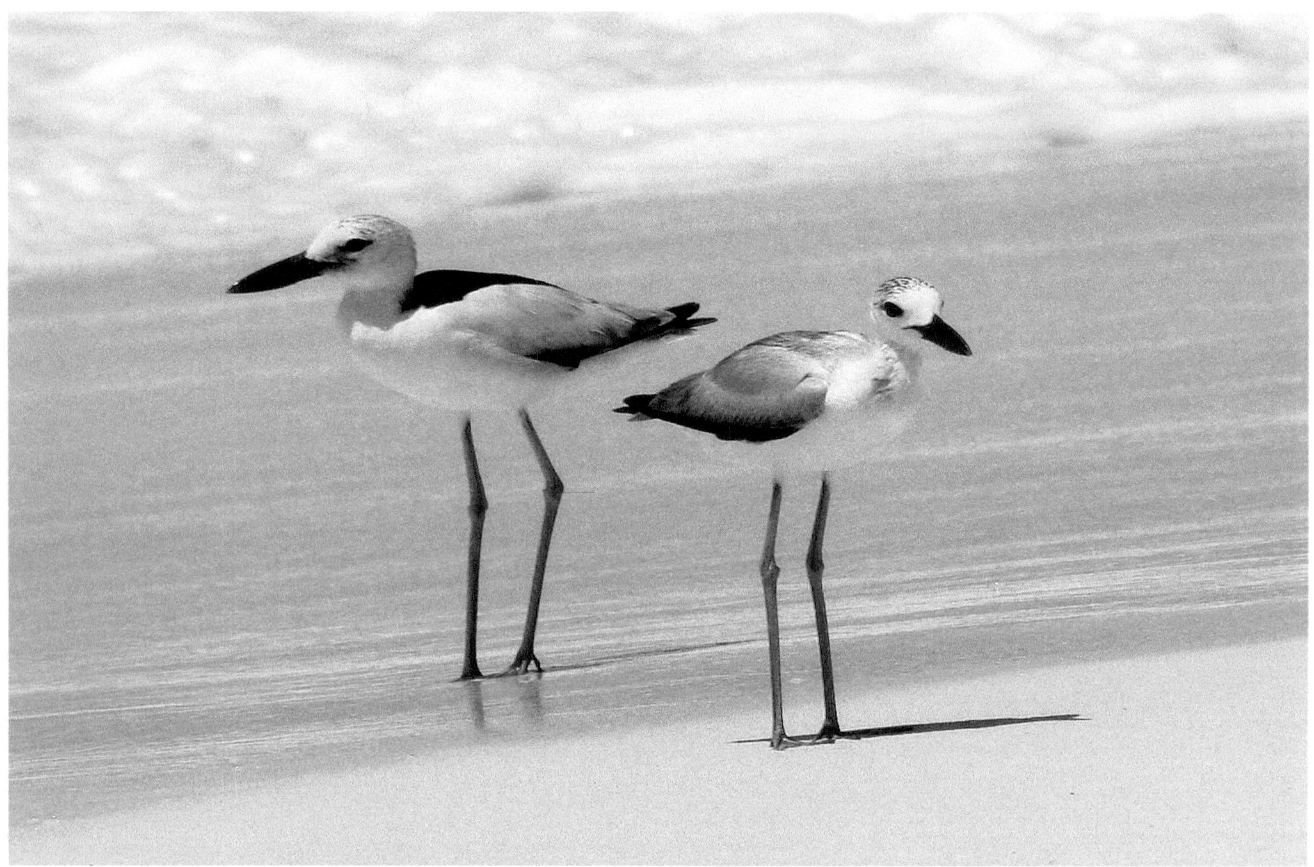

© Jean Cheadle

During the northwest monsoon, the presence of feathered migrants became something of a highlight. The crab plover was one of them, a beautiful, tall, rather leggy bird with a slate grey back, dark nape and wings. They are nimble creatures with a bill like a tomahawk, which is purpose-built to catch crabs, and extremely long legs which give them a stride the length of one of my size seven feet.

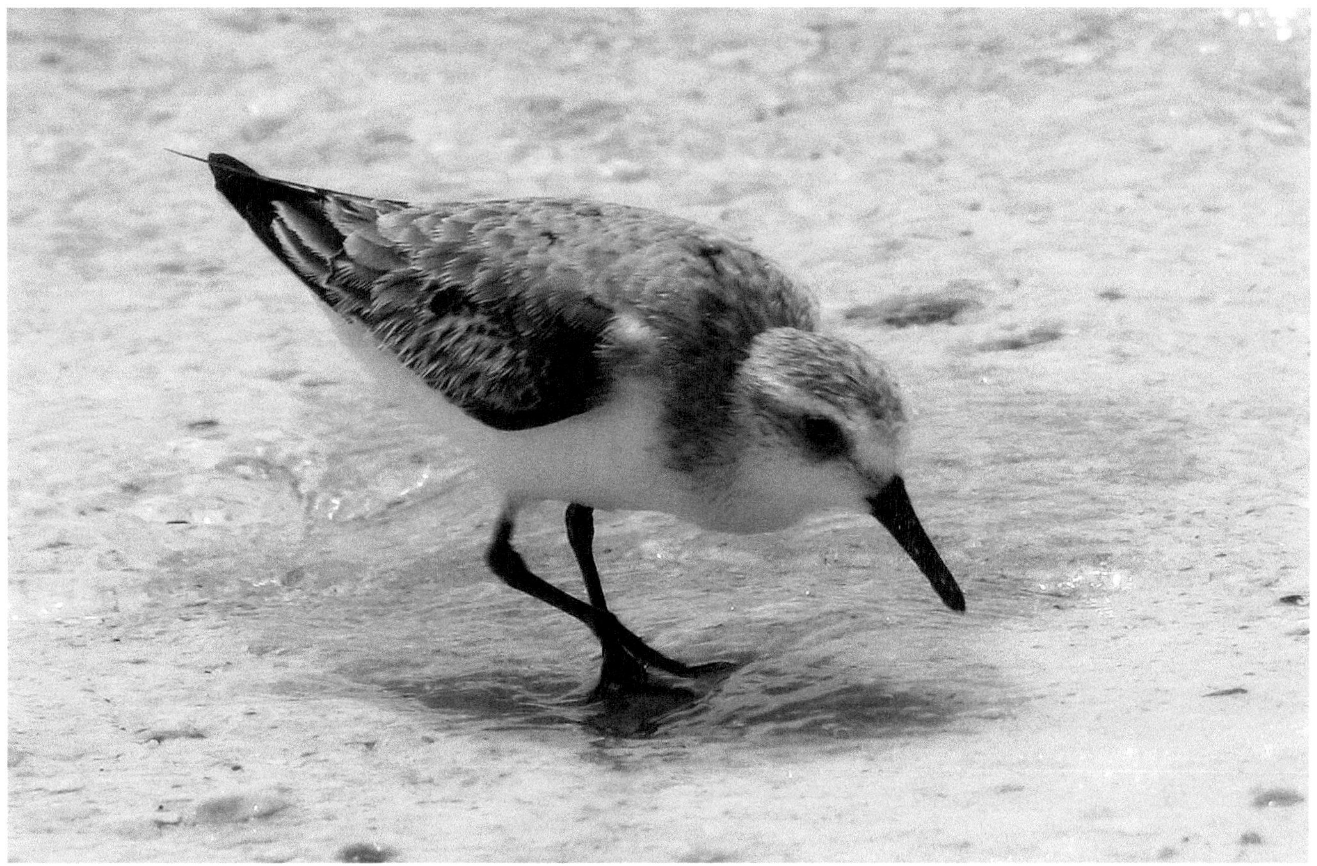

© *Jean Cheadle*

Sanderlings were another visitor, but unlike in the UK, where they come across as rather timid, on Aride they had no fear of humans at all. They would often scurry around our feet as we hauled the boat up the beach and ran up to us as we sat and waited for turtles to do their thing. Of a similar size were the lesser and greater sand plovers, which in summer plumage looked stunning, but by the time they got to Aride were rather dull and brown. Still, not to be knocked, they were welcome additions to the group of turnstones that frequented the beach daily.

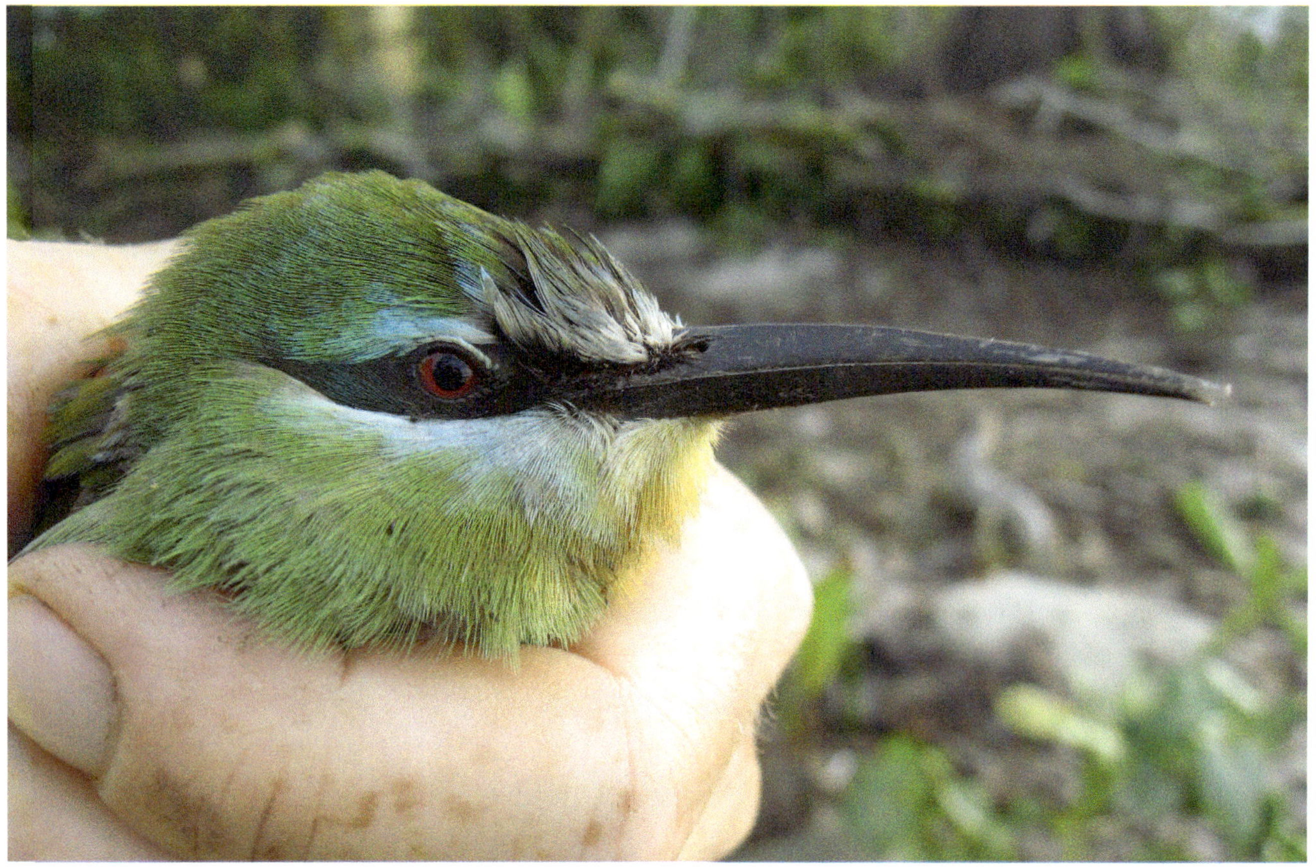

The real star of the migrant show was the blue-cheeked bee-eater. They are magical birds; the adults' blue cheeks, yellow chin patch and rusty throat are vibrant and their wonderful call certainly sat comfortably in the tropics.

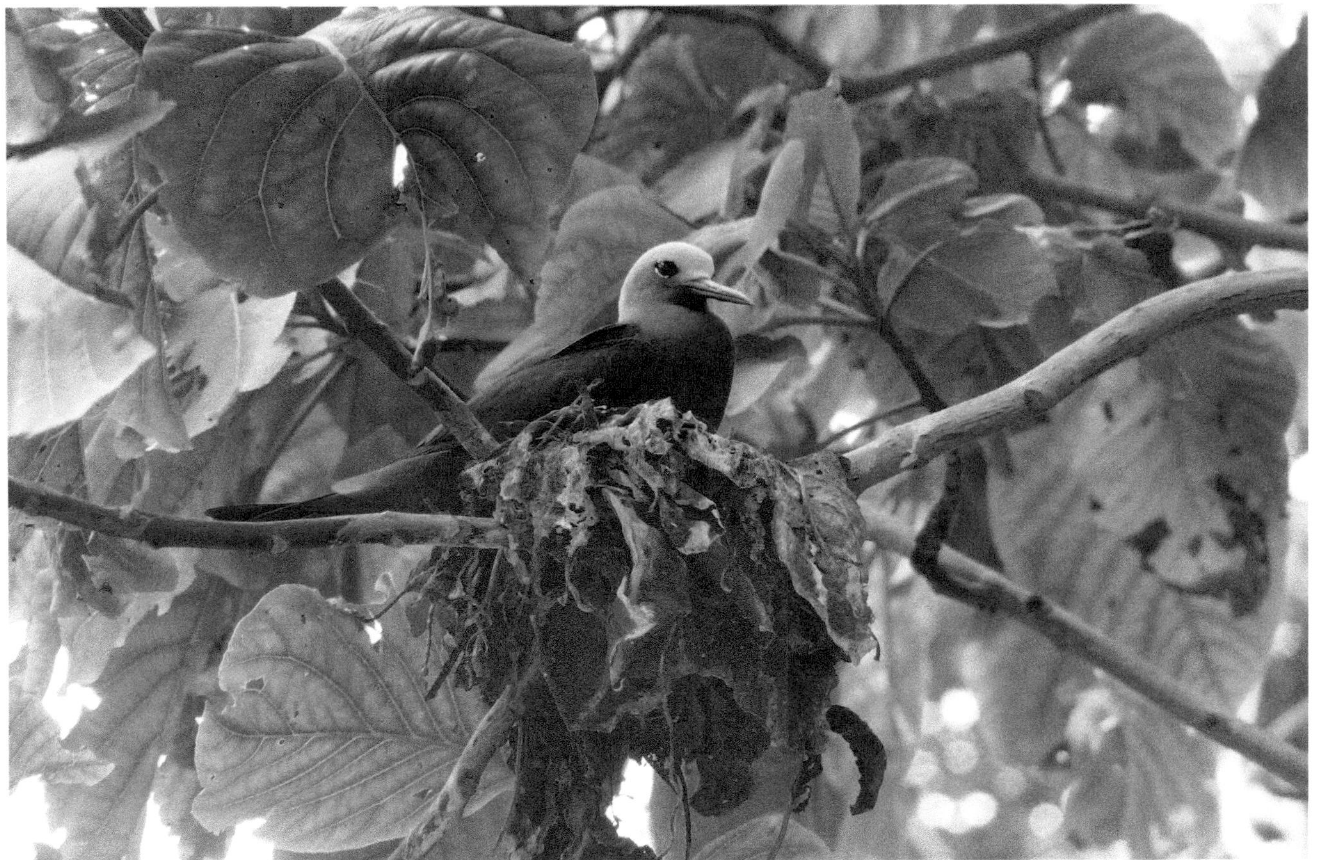

© Chloe Prehn-Arnold

It was great to be given the chance to be immersed in wildlife as part of our everyday lives. We watched the lesser noddies build their nests, forming the wet seaweed and leaves they had collected into small cups precariously balanced in the fragile branches of the pisonia. Regardless of the threat from the sticky seeds, pisonia was their preferred tree and the large leathery leaves seemed to be an excellent building material.

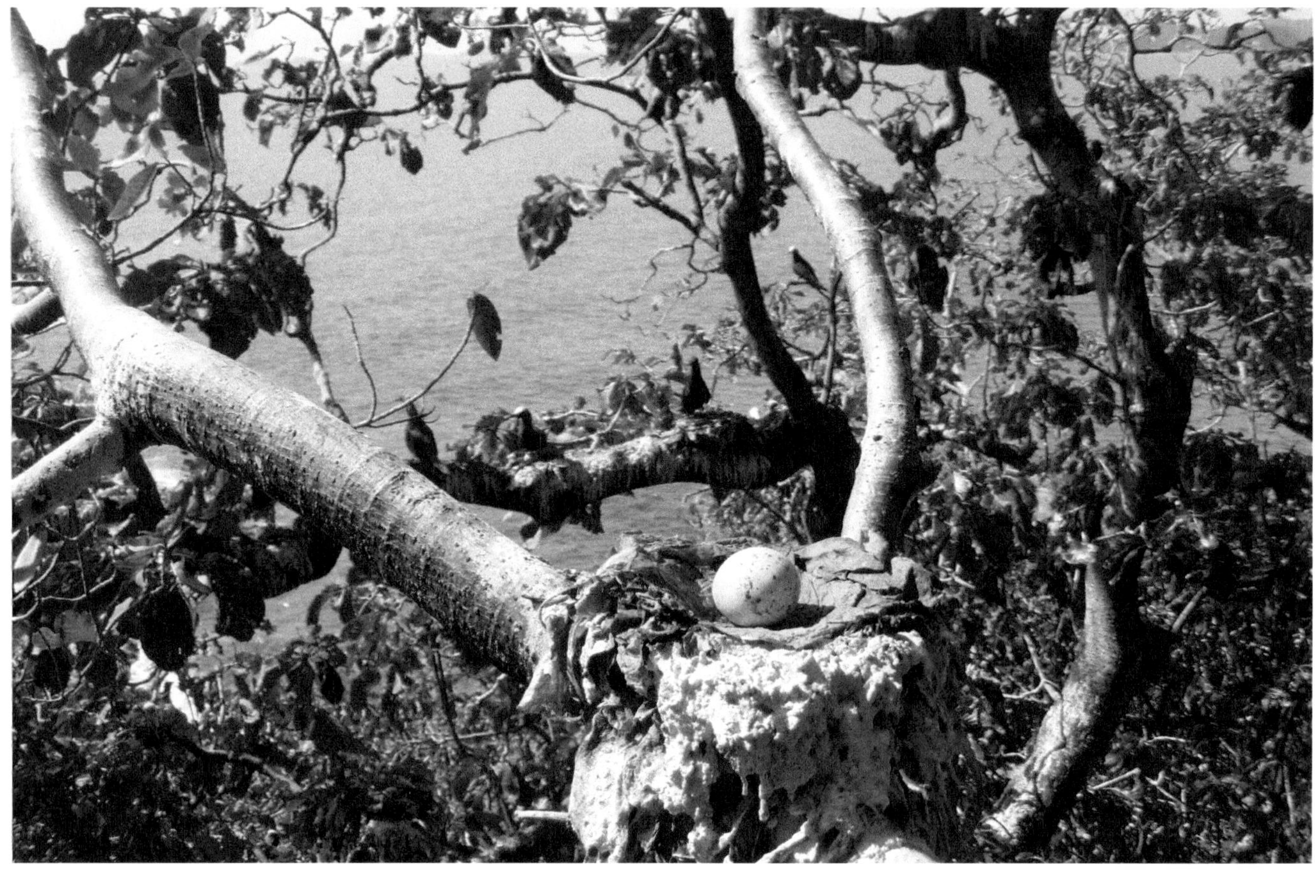

Of very simple construction, lesser noddy nests often appeared in peculiar and precarious places; draped over branches like floppy, wet chamois leathers, they adorned the trees like Christmas decorations.

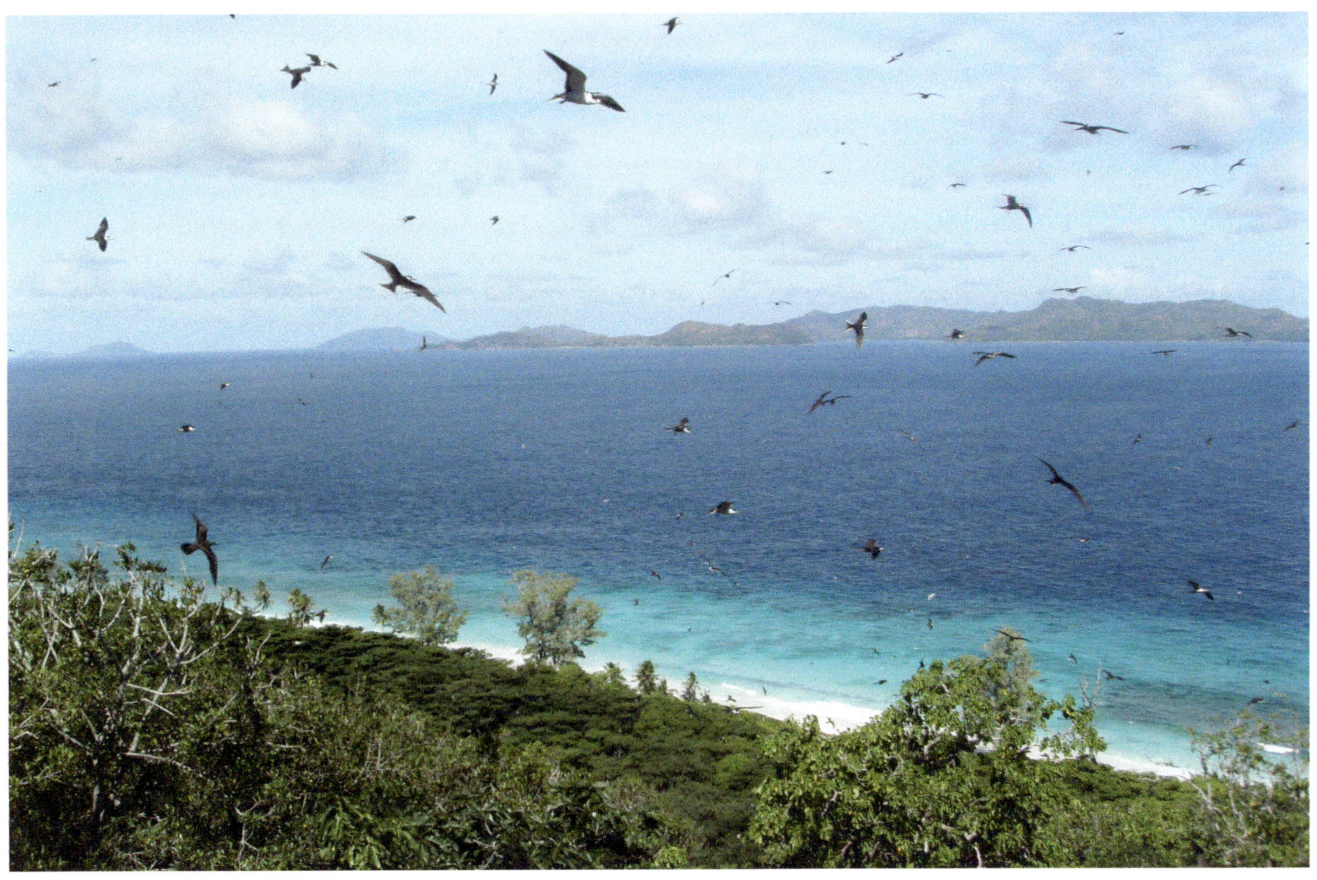



In the southeast monsoon, during the breeding season, the island became alive with birds, and the sooty terns swarmed like bees in their thousands. It reminded me of the midges we used to get above the trees in the wetland areas of the Somerset Levels. The noise was intense and the sight simply out of this world; it was a real sign that the seabird census was about to commence.

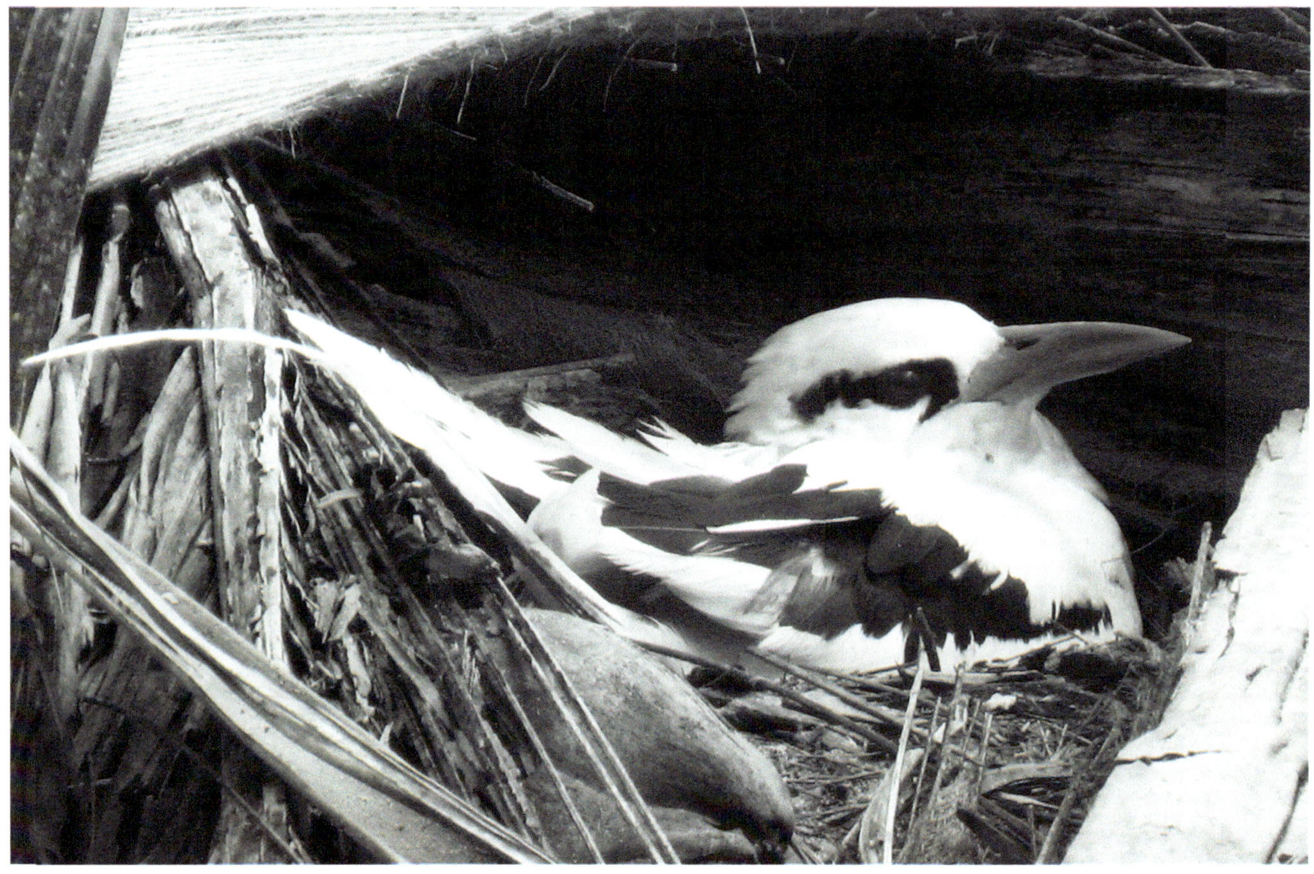

During our annual seabird census, we tried to capture estimates for five key species: brown and lesser noddies, sooty and fairy terns and white-tailed tropicbirds. But accomplishing this at one hundred and forty-five different points, each measuring 300m², whilst traversing rough terrain was no mean feat.

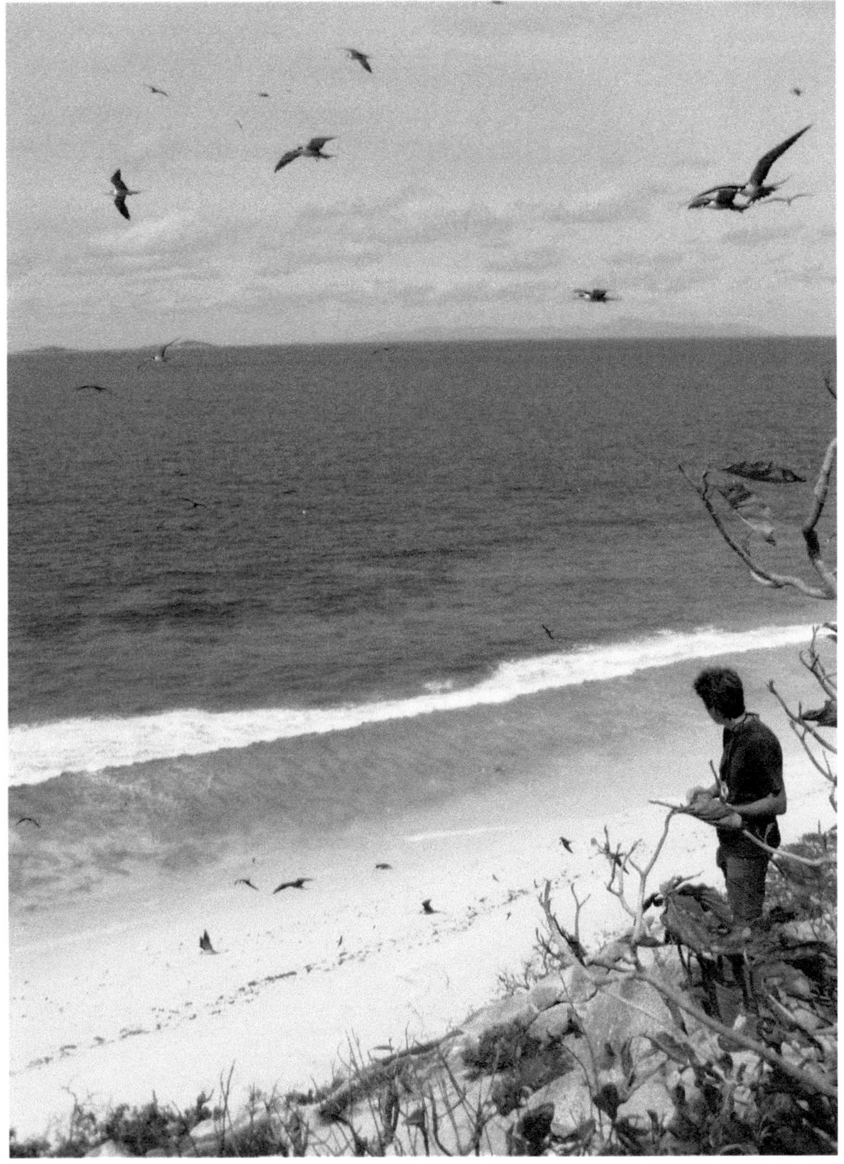

© Chloe Prehn-Arnold

Jude, Cash, Lara and I were the designated surveyors. It was interesting to watch the team together. Cash and Jude continually debated the survey in their aggressive Creole way, and Lara and I just got on with it, quietly looking for reassurance now and again. We must've walked miles and I had never had to climb, traverse, scramble, descend and negotiate such difficult ground.

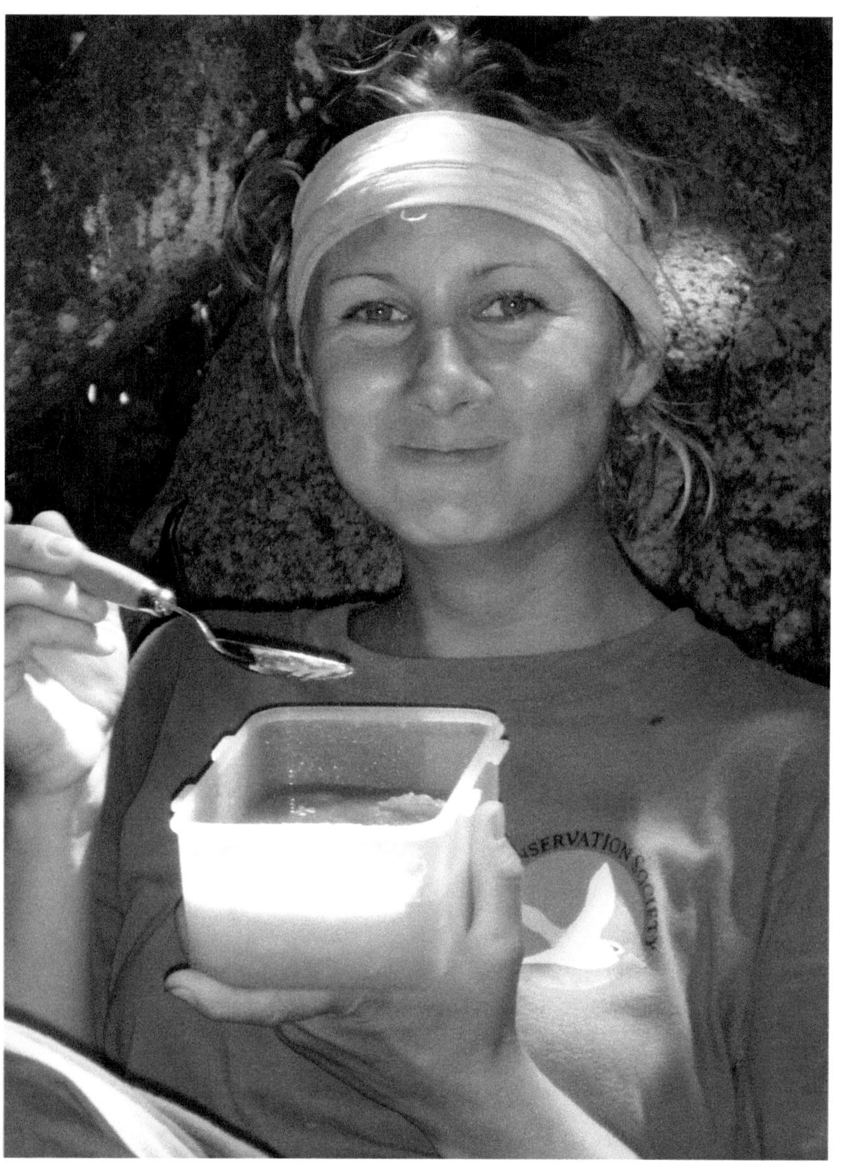

Despite the many challenges, everyone did well and kept going during the census. Lara generously shared a bag of toffees from her grandmother which went down a treat, providing a much-needed injection of sugar which greatly helped to ease the way.

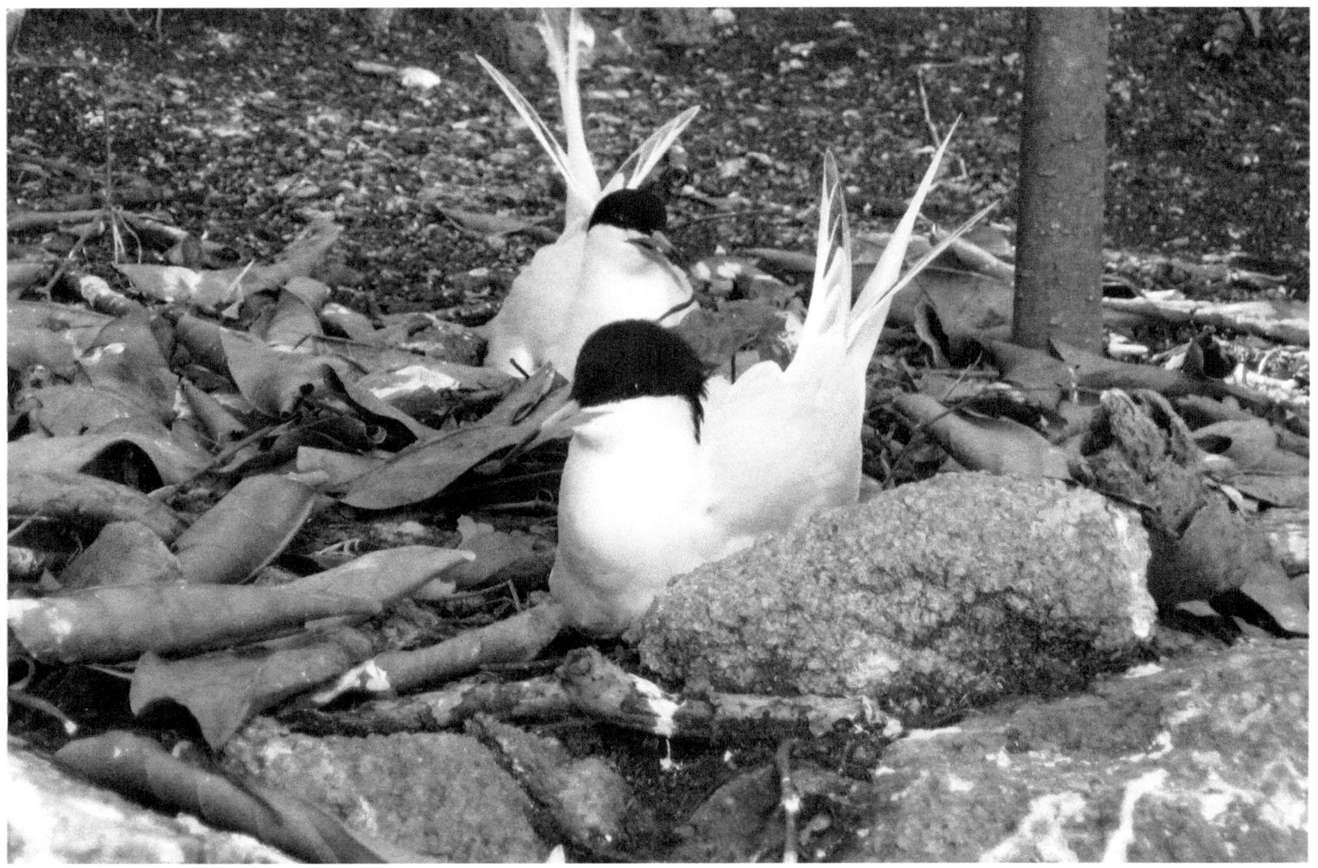

When the time came to survey the roseate tern colony, Lara and I volunteered ourselves. It was not a job either of us had done before and with the birds very prone to disturbance, I was more than a little apprehensive. Purposefully, we were both barefoot to ensure that we were sensitive about where we stepped. Our mission was to record all the nests and the number of eggs in each; once completed, we sat out of sight to watch and listen. Lara did the count up and, to our delight, we had recorded five hundred and twenty-four nests.

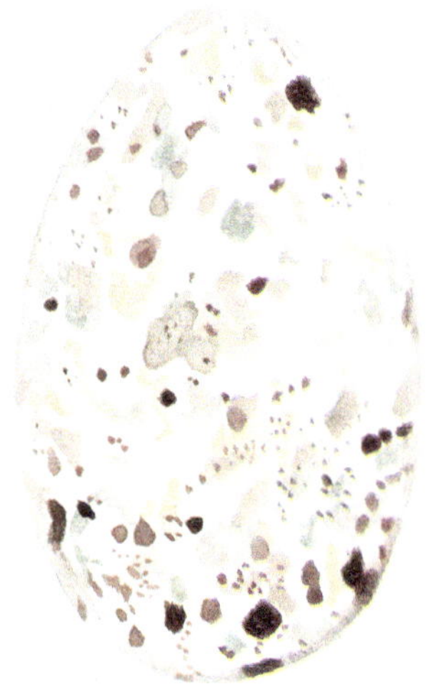 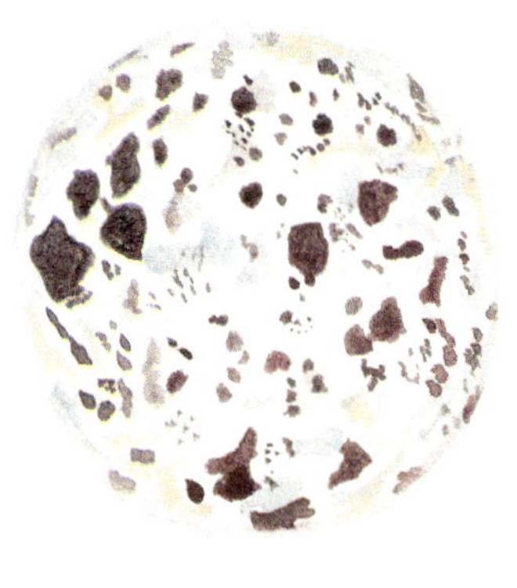

*Sooty tern eggs*

# Chapter 13

## Local Delicacies

We had read in all the past reports that poaching was an ongoing problem. During the main bird breeding season, despite being able to get chicken eggs daily, poachers would take sooty tern eggs to sell for eating. As neither Melv nor I had ever dealt with any poaching episodes or anything similar in the UK, we were both extremely shocked at the scale of the operation.

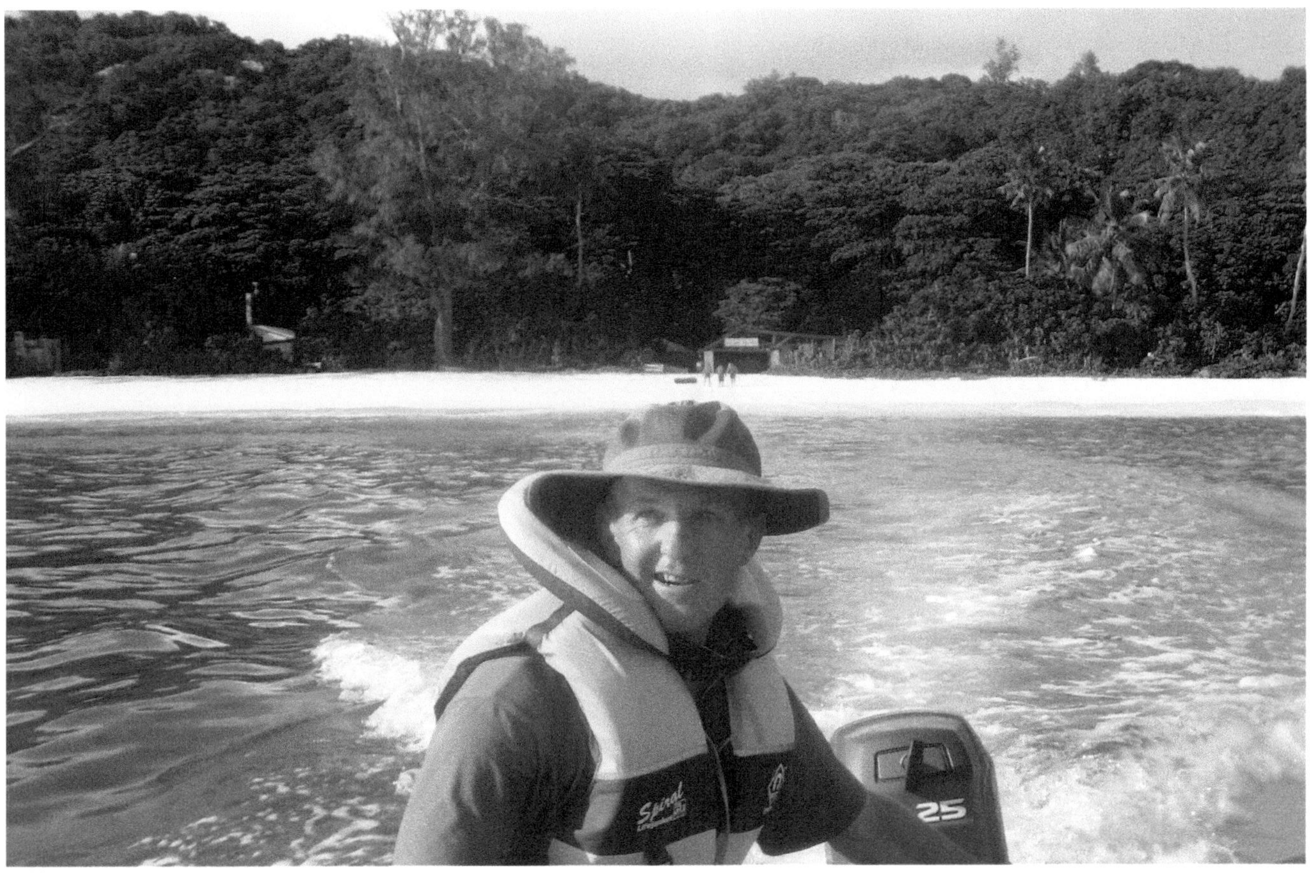

'On one occasion, whilst on a fishing trip, we discovered an octopus boat to the east of the island, 6m from the cliffs,' Melv recalled in a blog post. 'Not a boat shaped like an octopus or a boat driven by an octopus: a boat with people catching octopuses. It should have been 200m off our shore, but what's a couple of hundred metres between friends? So, we confidently took our boat close to theirs and said, in a friendly manner, "You're much too close.".'

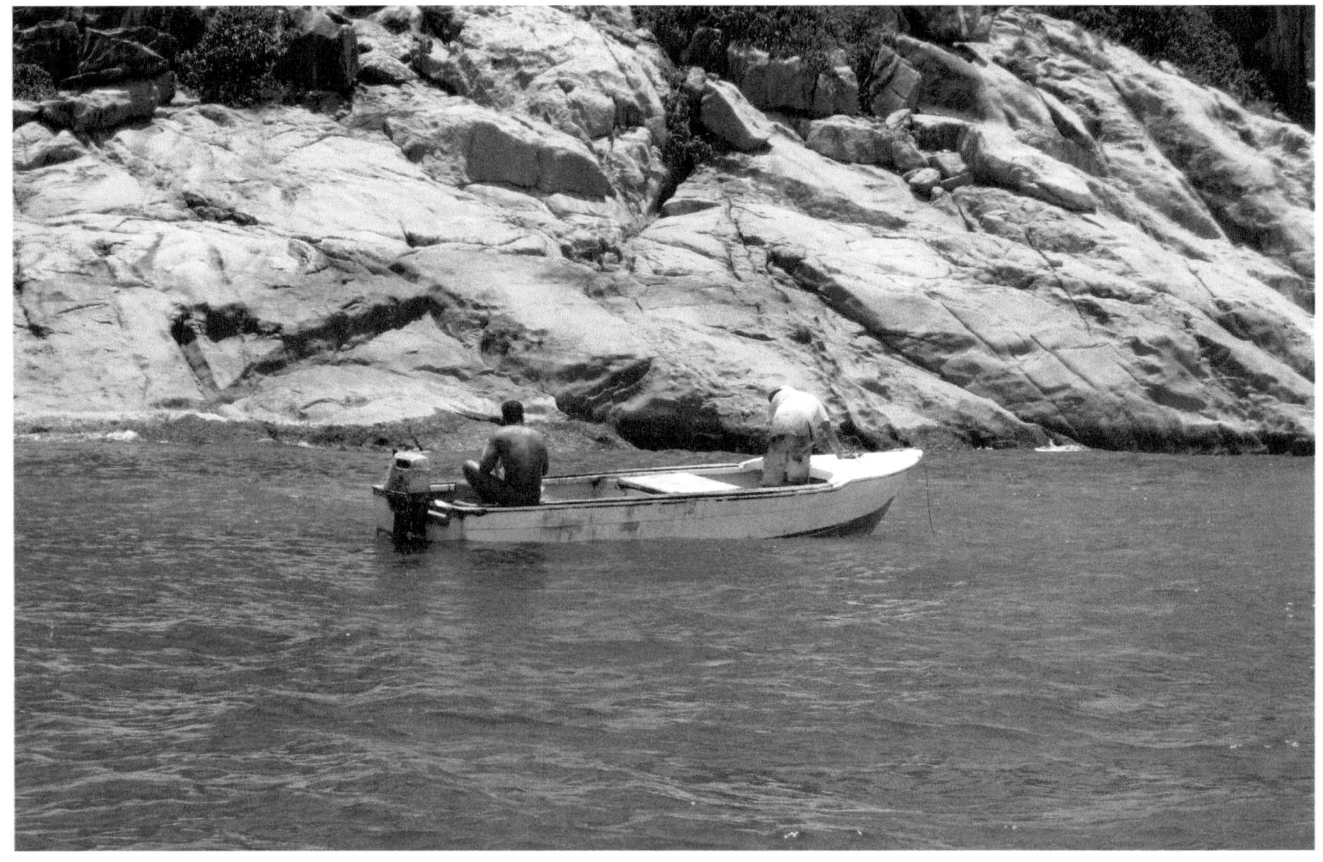

'In response, the octopus hunters just said "huh", looked away from us and carried on fishing. Incensed by their lack of respect for the wardens of Aride, we got out the camera and took their photo. Bad move… they gave chase. Luckily, the rangers saw what was happening and launched our Tornado. Sadly, poaching goes on at all times of year. Whatever the season, there are opportunities for taking something, whether it's shearwaters or octopuses.'

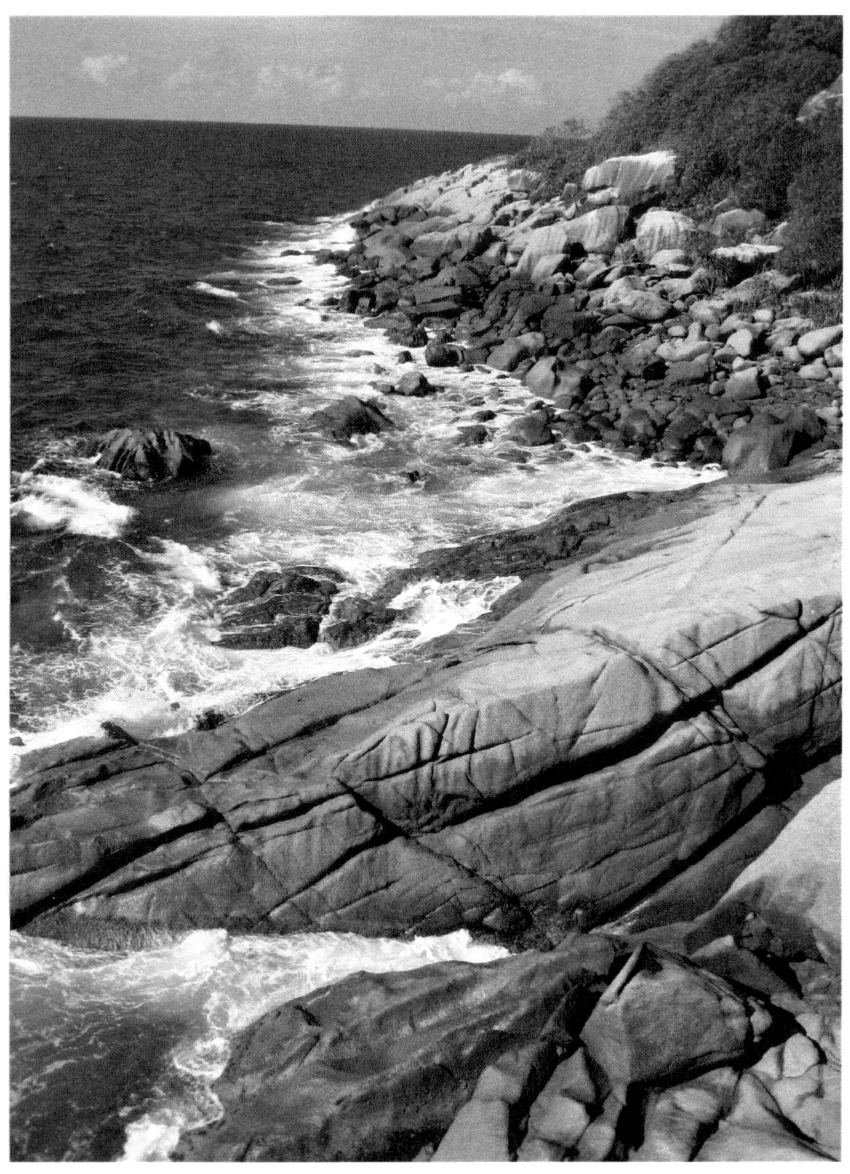

Despite the first records in the 1700s describing Aride as a hostile and difficult place to get to, with no water supply, hence the name 'Arid(e)', sooty tern eggs have been harvested both commercially and by poachers for years. From 1947-67 alone, around two hundred cases of seven hundred and fifty eggs each, a total of one hundred and fifty thousand eggs, were taken annually.

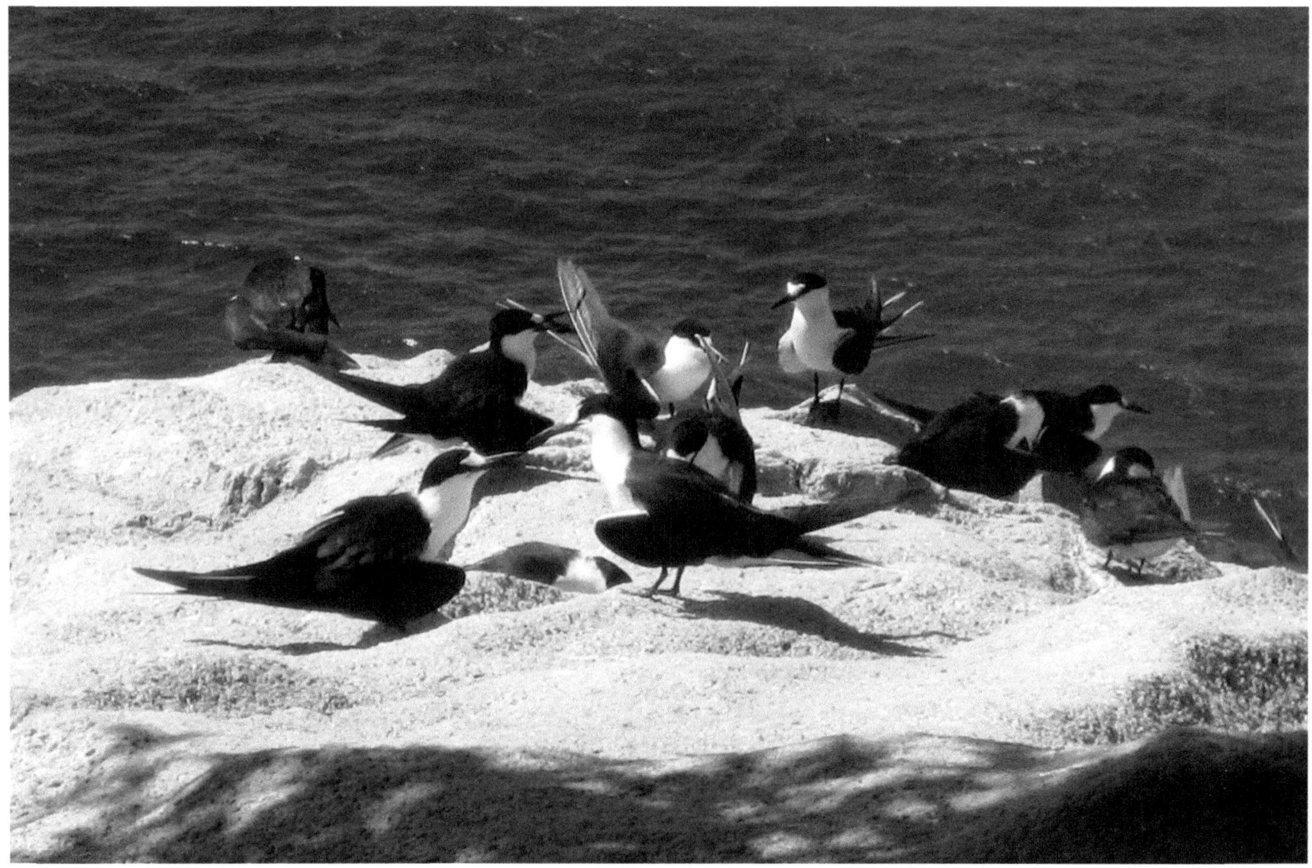

There is no doubt that the size of the bird populations on the Seychelles' islands bring lucrative poaching opportunities. During our time on Aride, there were one hundred and fifteen thousand pairs of sooty terns and they bred across the island, on the rocks, in the woods, on the paths... in fact on any bit of spare ground they could. But despite the best efforts of the wardens, rangers and volunteers, including ourselves, we knew that around 80% of those eggs would be taken by poachers in any one year.

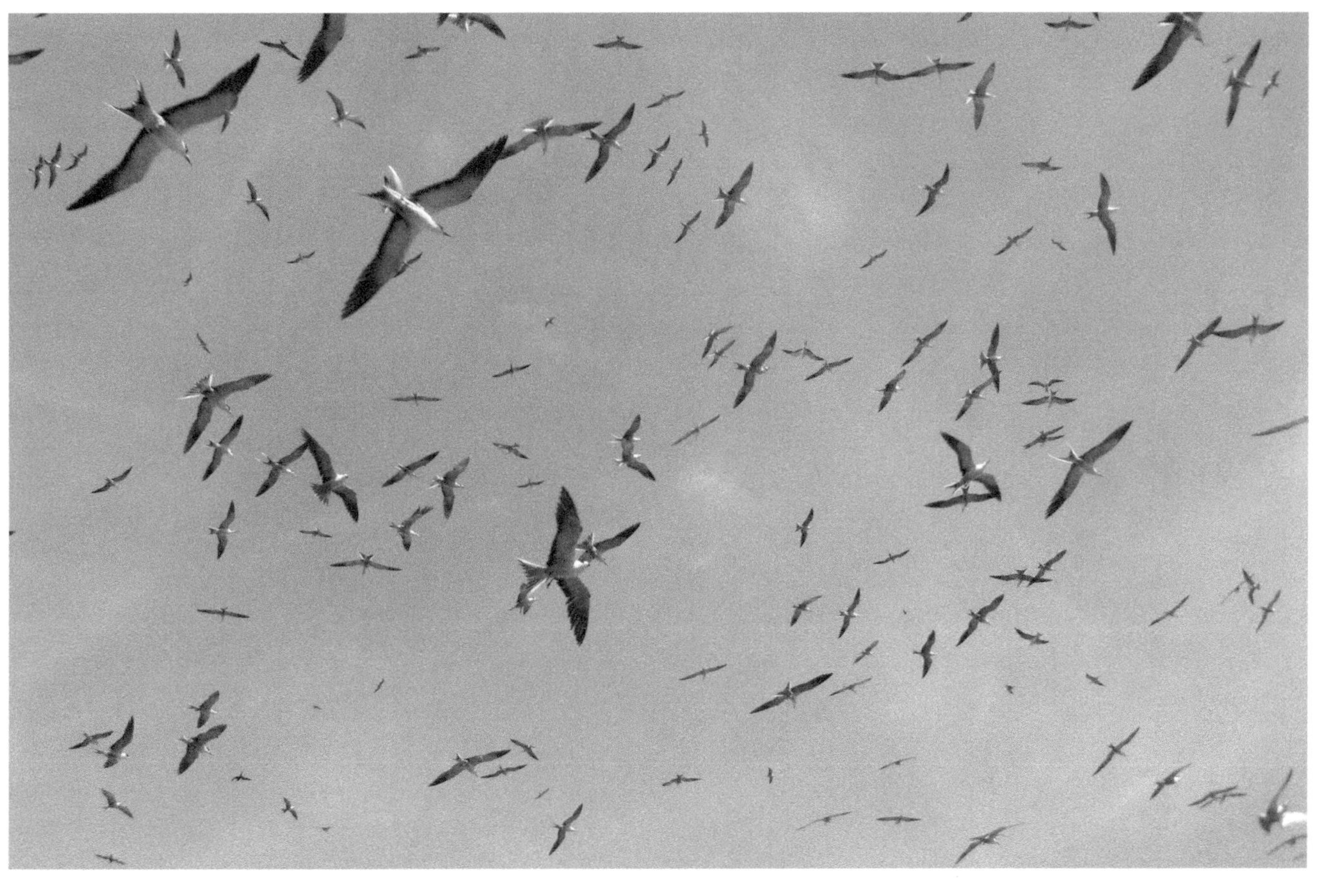

It felt very alien to be going in search of poachers. I distinctly remember when there was a major disturbance on the island around Grolatet, the highest point. There was only one thing it could mean – there were already poachers on the island. The sooty terns were up in swarms, forming a dense cloud over the areas where the poachers were; like bees they massed above the trees. To try to assess the scale of the devastation, we had to carry out patrols at dawn and dusk to record the boats and number of poachers we saw.

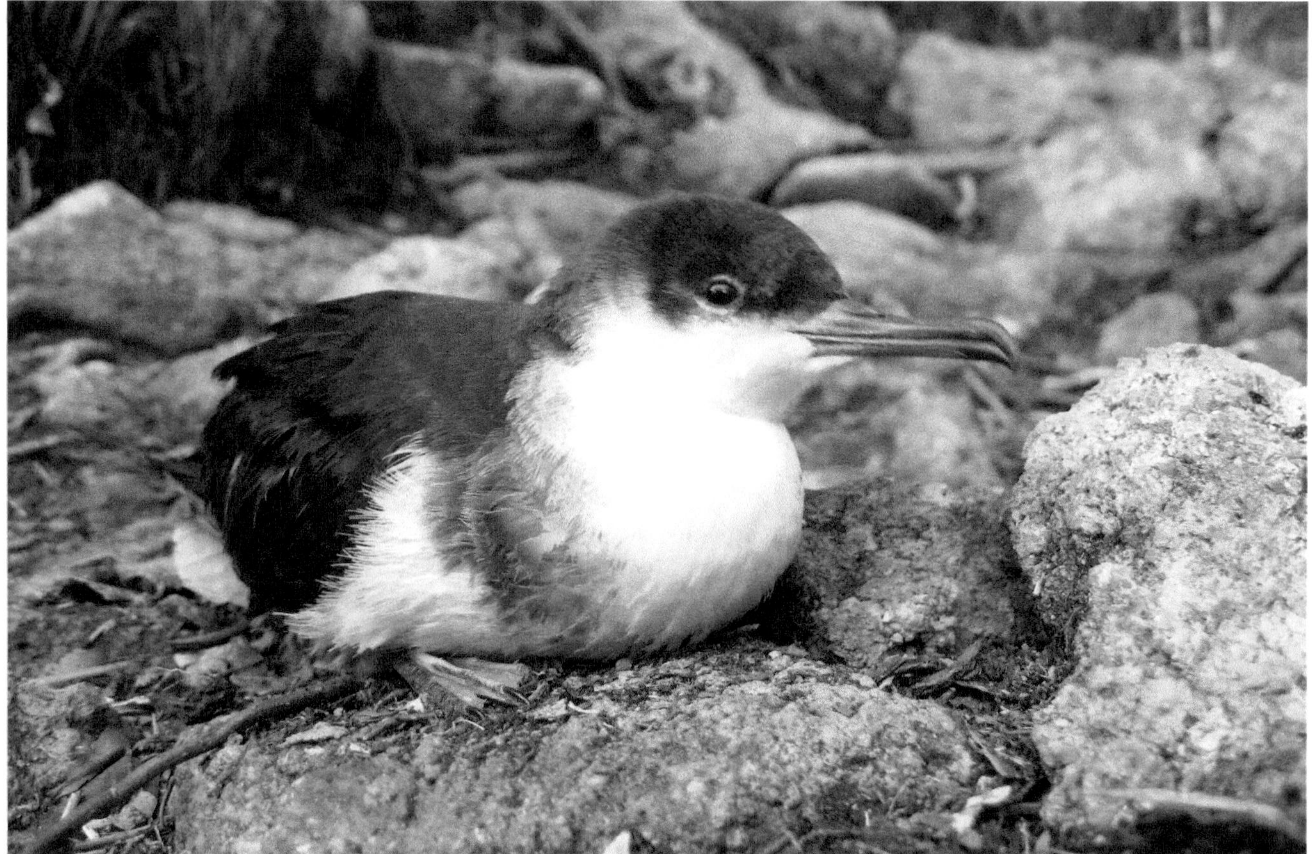

*© Chloe Prehn-Arnold*

Patrolling for poachers on the hill at night felt like exploring a different world; Aride was so alive it was a sensory overload. We would often pass one of my favourite species, the Audubon shearwater, sitting quietly on the paths. These evening searches were to be the routine until the sooty tern chicks had hatched. Melv and I alternated with the rangers and volunteers, and we all worked together when needed.

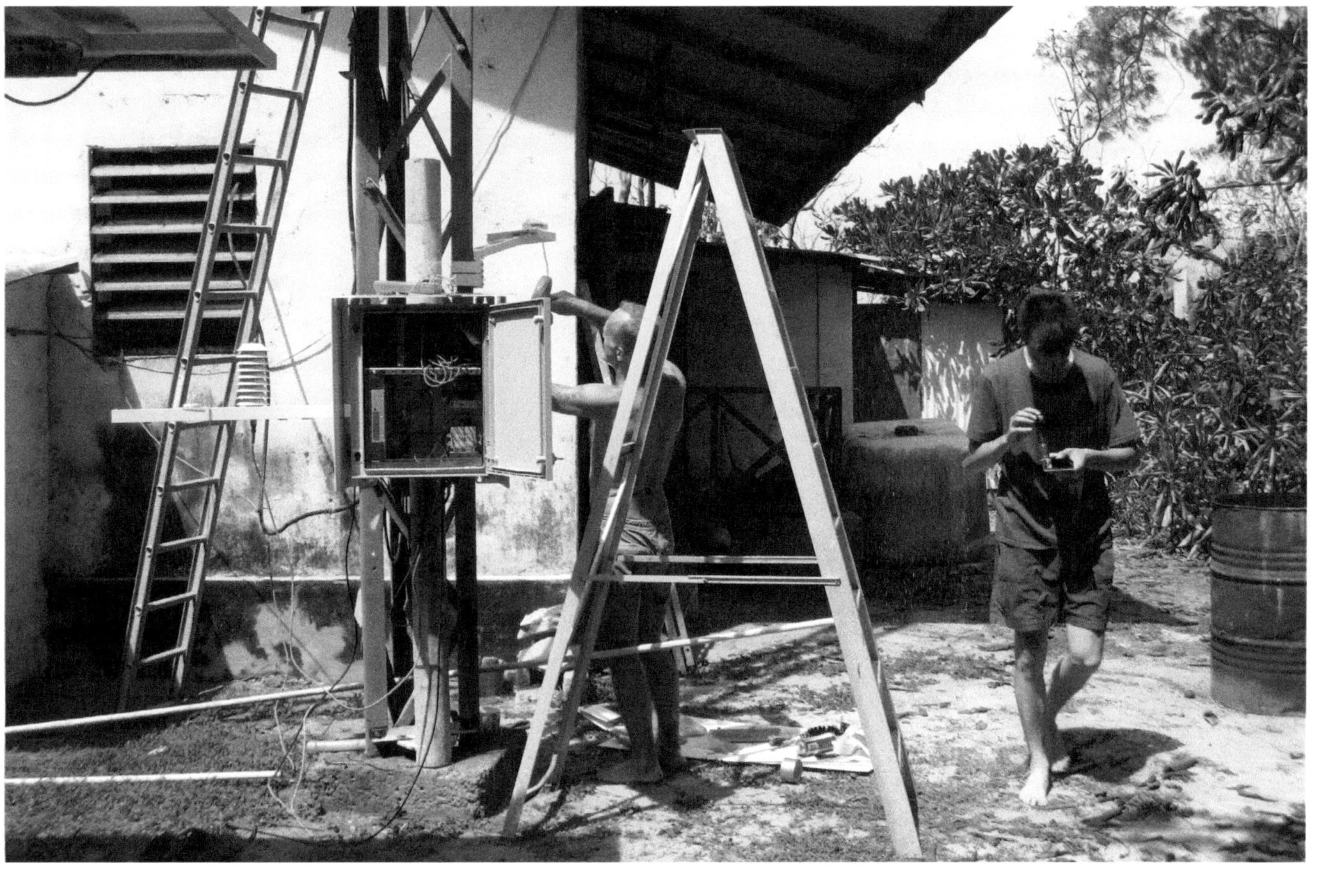

Although the poaching work dominated our lives during the breeding season, other tasks and projects still needed to be undertaken, including replacing the weather station. Marcus, a technical specialist from Finland, arrived on Aride to connect the new system. He was a friendly chap, but very conscientious and intense; we had expected the latter as he had travelled across the world to three islands in Seychelles to set up weather stations – not your run-of-the-mill occupation!

### *Installing the new rain gauge*

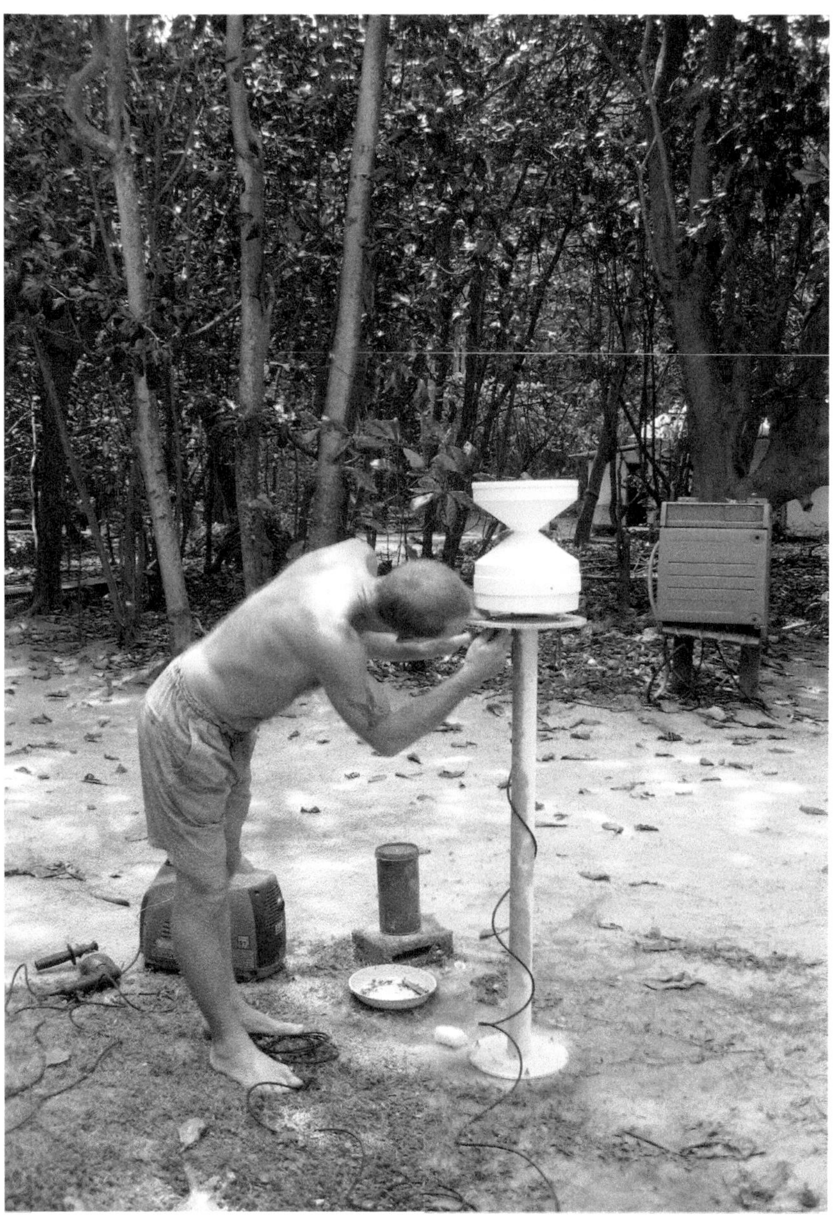

It was a novelty for us to spend the day working with someone new, and we enjoyed chatting to the eccentric Marcus. It had been a good, positive day, despite the upset of the poaching work.

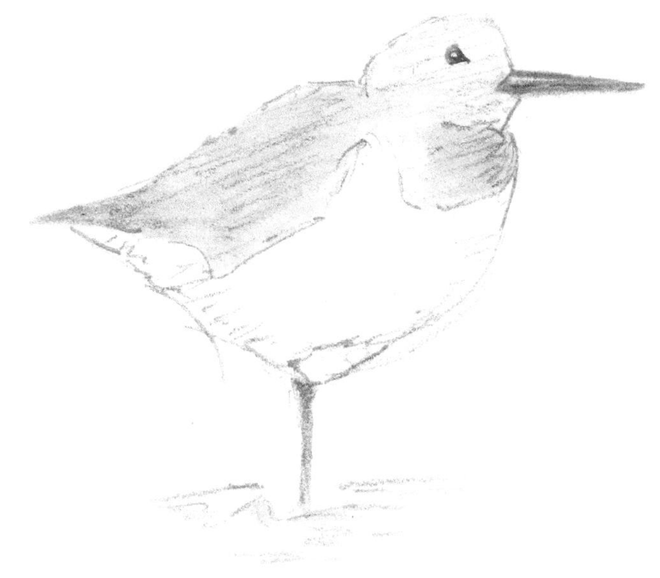



# Chapter 14

## Family, Friends and Free Time

During our two-year contract, we were able to take a month's leave, with a flight back to the UK paid for. It was a challenge to decide when to take this time off, but with the breeding bird census completed and the southeast monsoon almost at an end, Seychelles would be entering into the transition, the period between the two trade winds, a generally quieter time for weather which would make island life easier. With this in mind, we decided it was the perfect time to take a break.

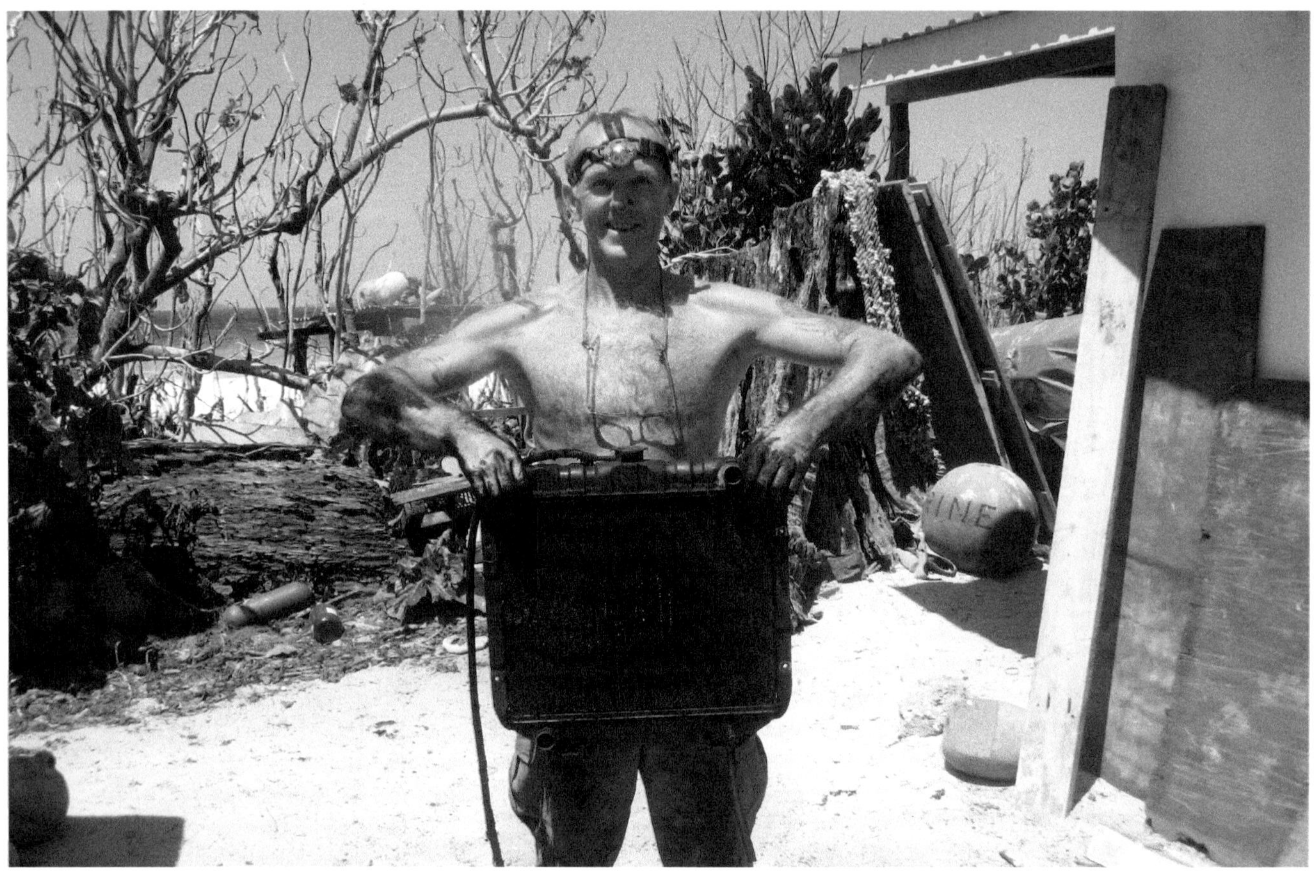

We soon realised that getting time off from the island was not going to be that easy or straightforward. One of the big challenges was finding cover for when we were away, the situation only made worse by the generator failing yet again at 6pm. Unsurprisingly, not having electricity created a great deal of friction, as of course it had a significant impact on peoples' lives. The timing of this failure was appalling.

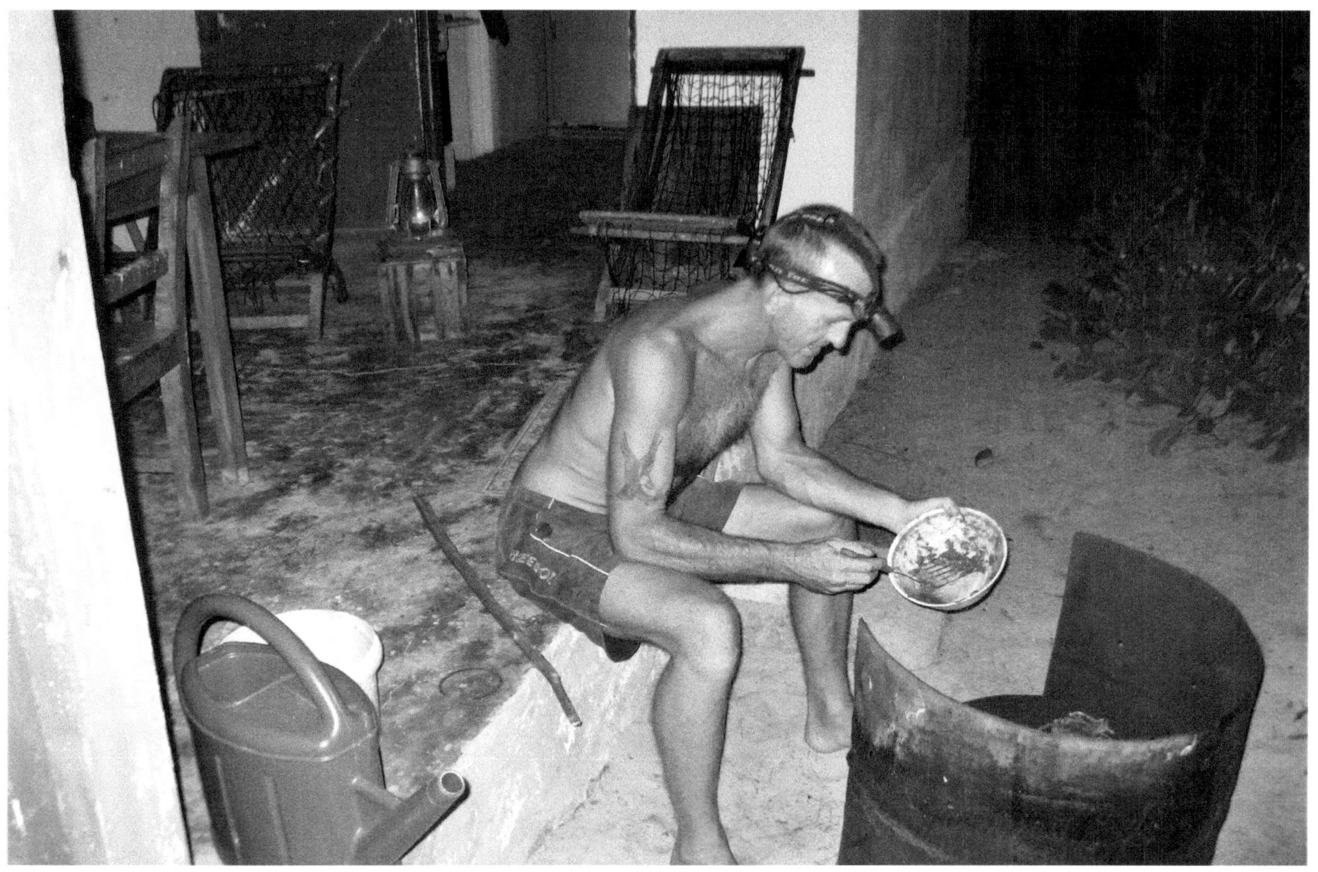

Unable to face trying to fix the generator, and there being little point whilst it was dark, we resigned ourselves to the fact that it was going to be another evening without lights. Melv cooked tea with a head torch, we ate by candlelight and I left the washing up for the crabs.

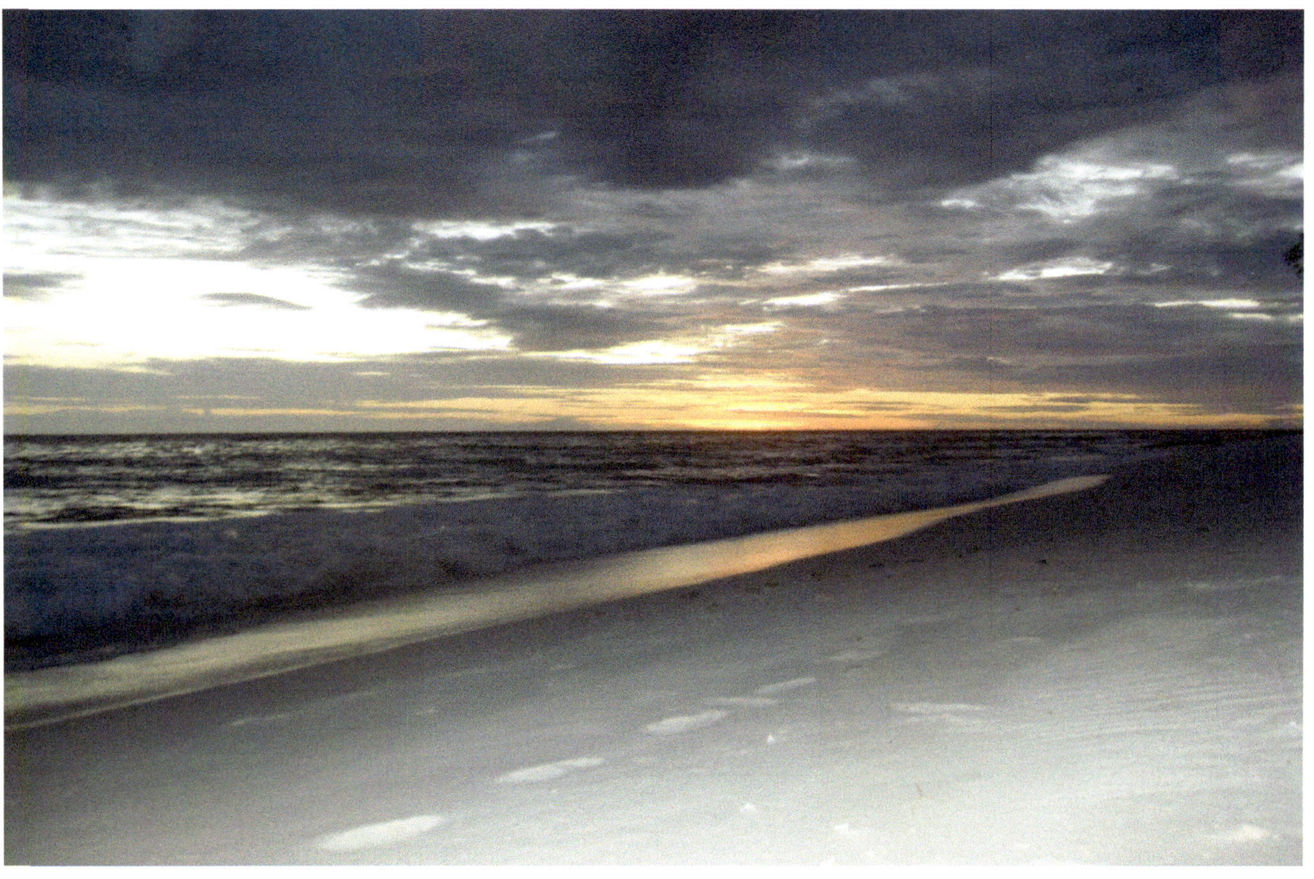

The sun had just set and I took a walk; the moonlight was incredible, breath-taking. The soft sand and calm sea were alight, the moon began to tickle the moving waves and they glistened silver. It all looked surreal and I felt like I couldn't open my eyes wide enough to take it all in.

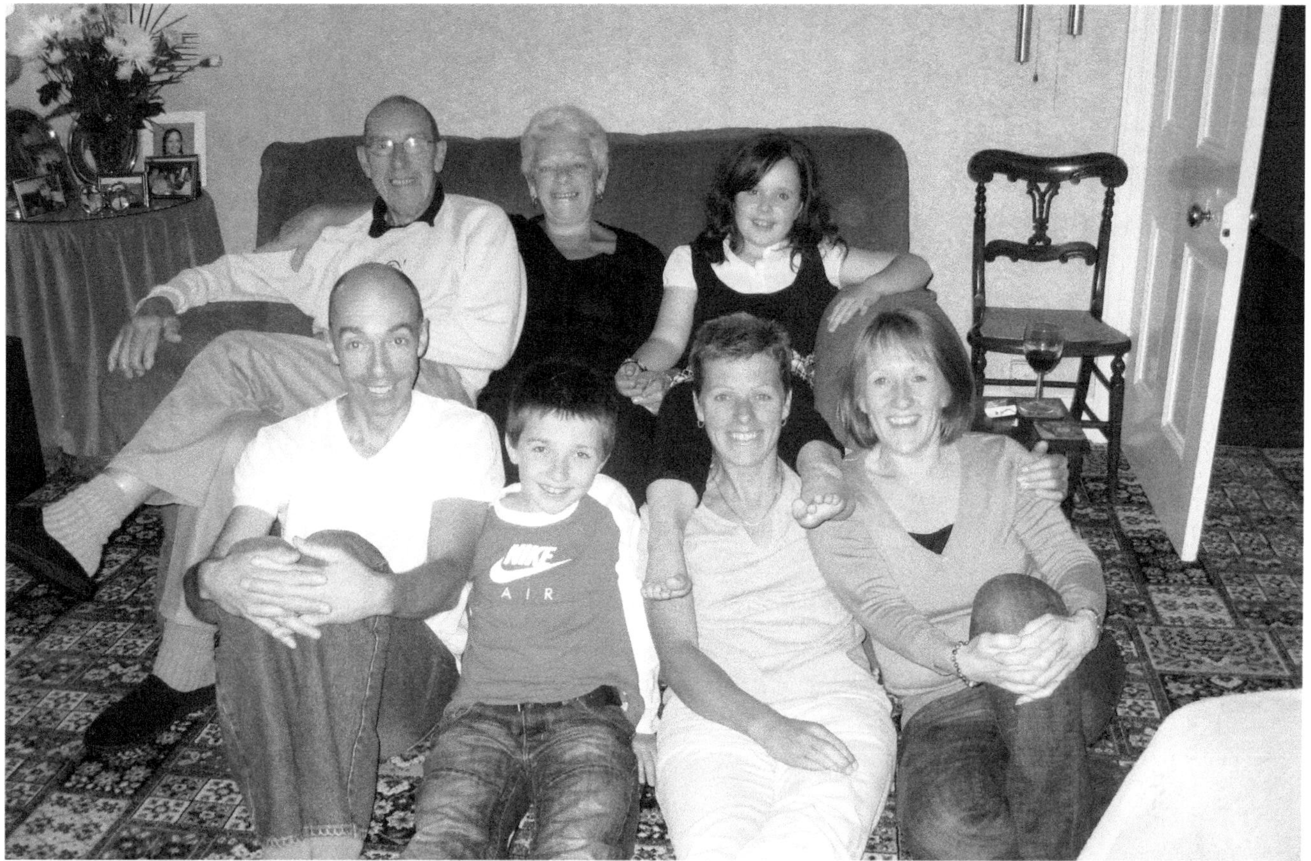

© Melvyn Yeandle

Eventually, our holiday finally began. Time in the UK went very quickly. We savoured the simple pleasures and conveniences of life, like a choice of foodstuffs, running water, clean, tiled showers and soft carpet beneath our feet. We enjoyed the wildlife too; oystercatchers walked along the shore in their smart black and white suits and ringed plovers scurried around the rock pools. It was super to catch up with family and friends and an opportunity to recharge our enthusiasm.

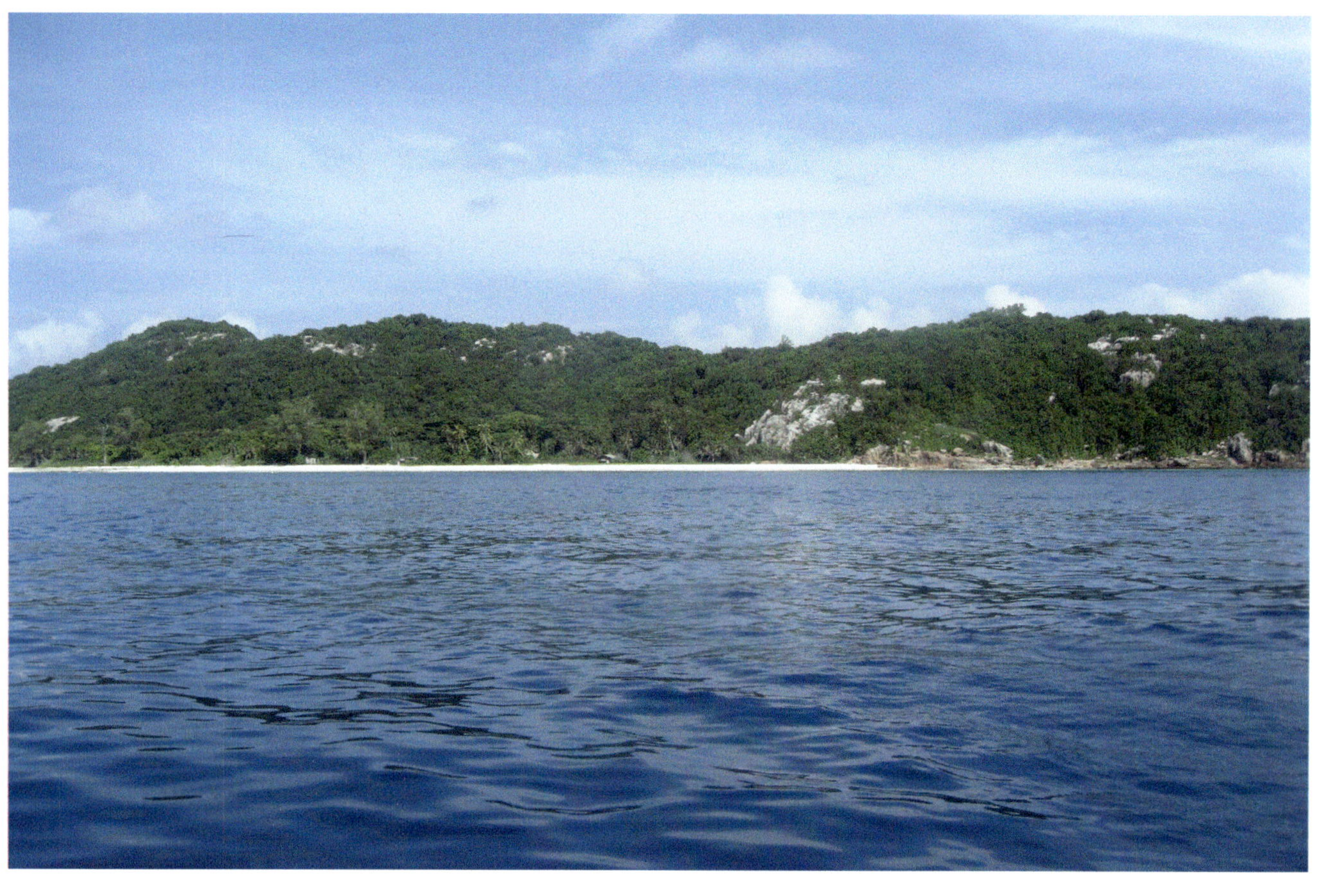

When we returned to Aride, the sea was calm as we zipped across its surface, hardly creating a splash, very different from the day we left, a true sign that we were leaving the southeast monsoon behind and entering the more habitable northwest. The island looked clear and beautiful, and as we drew closer, the long length of sandy beach which edged the southern side glistened magically. I felt goose pimples at the thought of being the lucky one who was allowed to live in this place, who was privileged to have the experience of doing so.

### *Ghost crab*

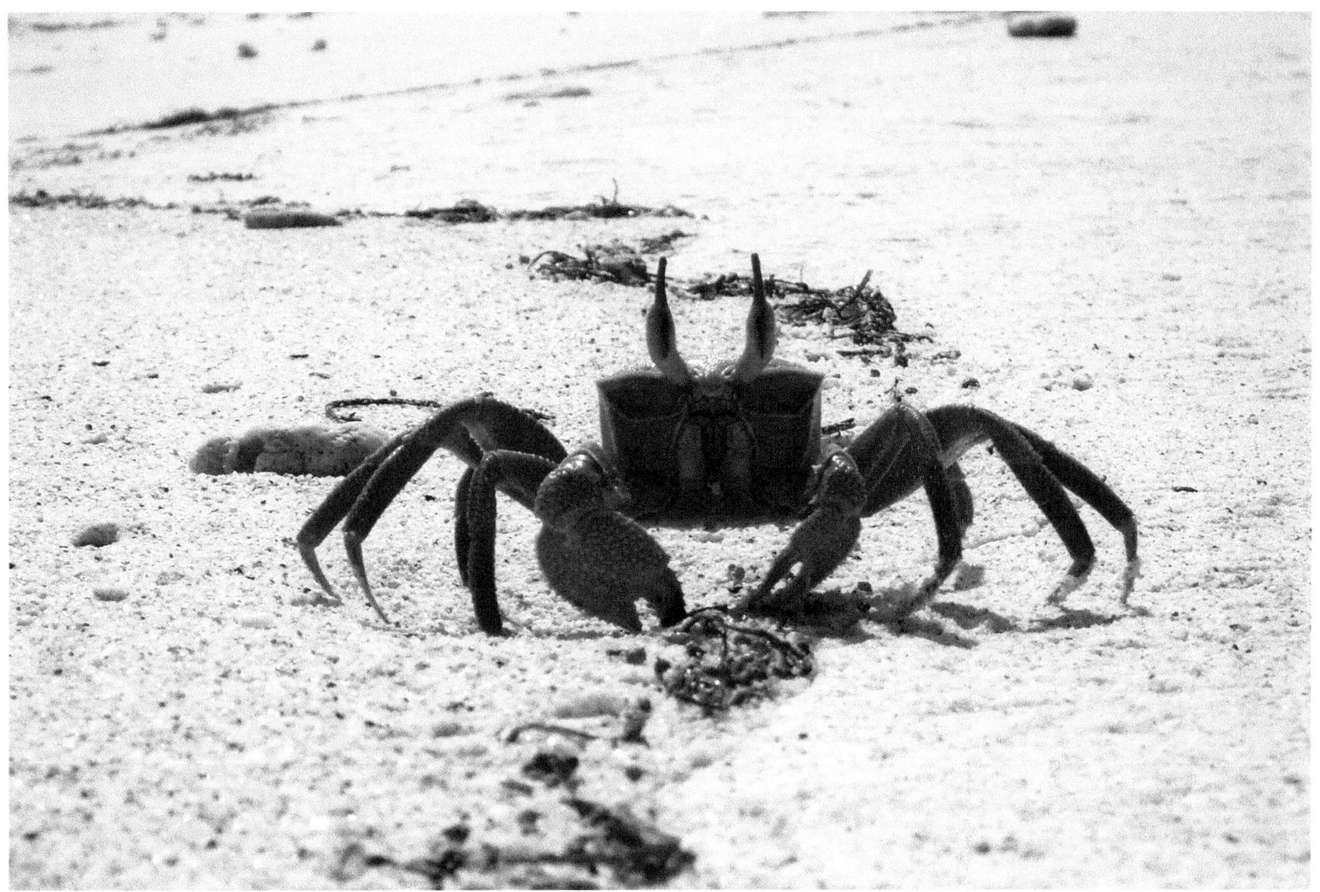

*© Chloe Prehn-Arnold*

I had forgotten about the details of Aride, from the scurrying crabs, the noise, the light, to the warm sand beneath my feet. It felt like I was experiencing the island for the first time all over again. It was worth the time away just to feel like this, to be able to rediscover the place that demanded my attention, which made me take notice; I couldn't wait to explore this amazing island once more.

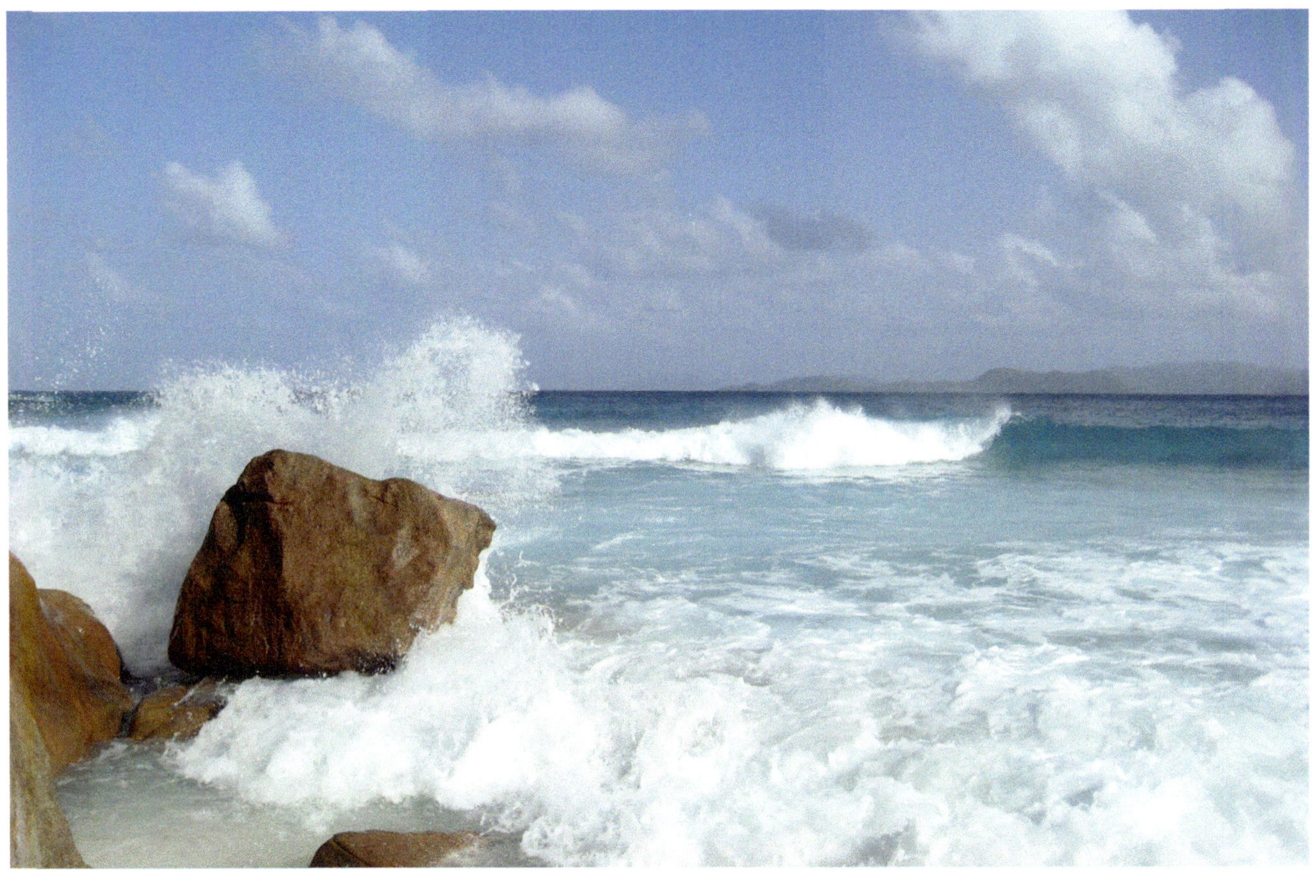

Stepping foot on Aride for a second time seemed to heighten my awareness. It constantly stimulated the senses. The light was exceptional; with no pollution, it was forever changing and at times quite breath-taking. The island was a place where you needed to have time, not just to think but to absorb and enjoy, just to sit, watch and breathe in whatever was in front of you.

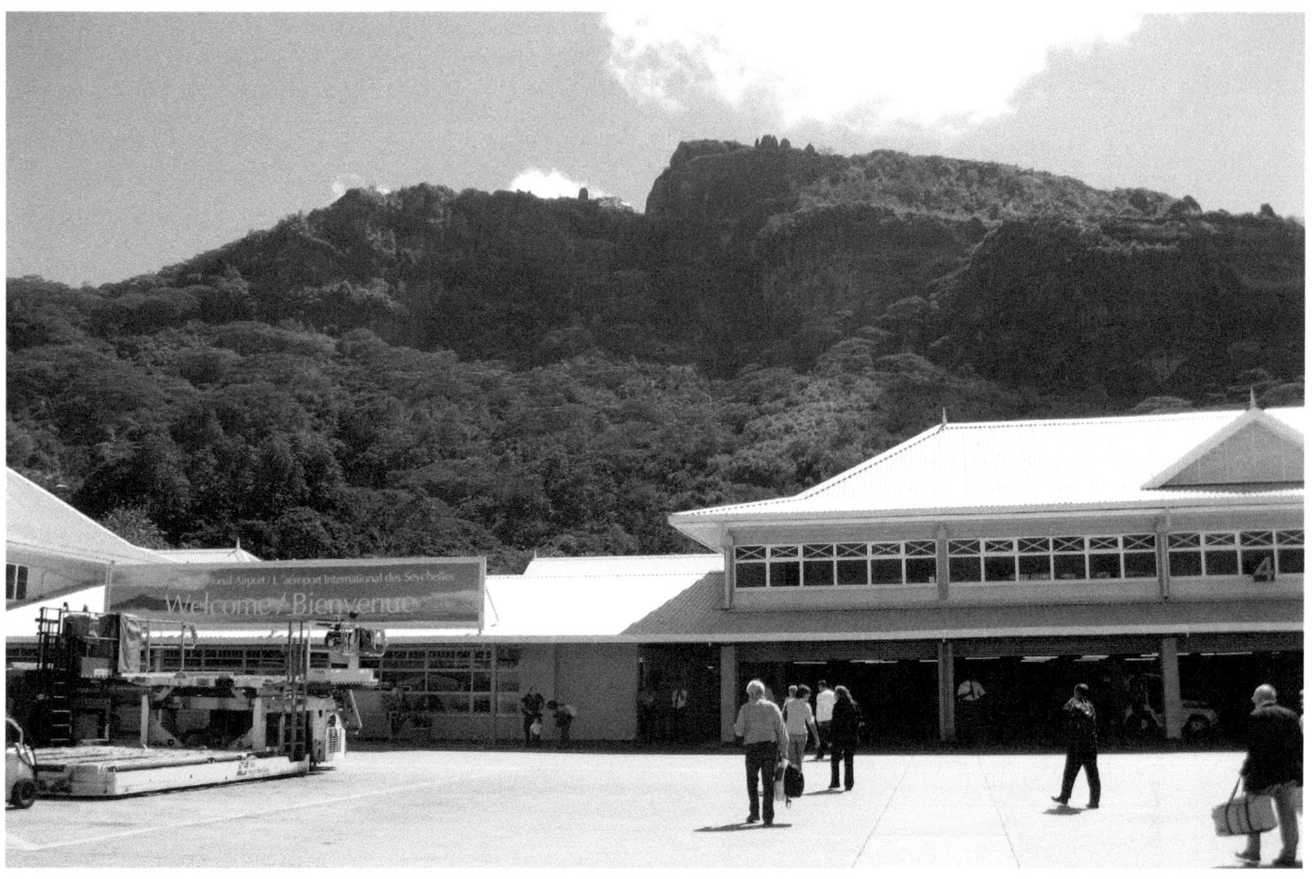


When my dad suffered from a stroke I found myself unexpectedly heading back to the UK once again. The time I spent with my parents was emotionally taxing, the days filled with visits from speech therapists, physios and stroke specialists. They were very special days, but they went quickly, and I soon found myself back walking down the steps onto the Mahé runway. I stared up at the pure blue skies and the backdrop of the lush tropical vegetation, as the heat and humidity took my breath away.

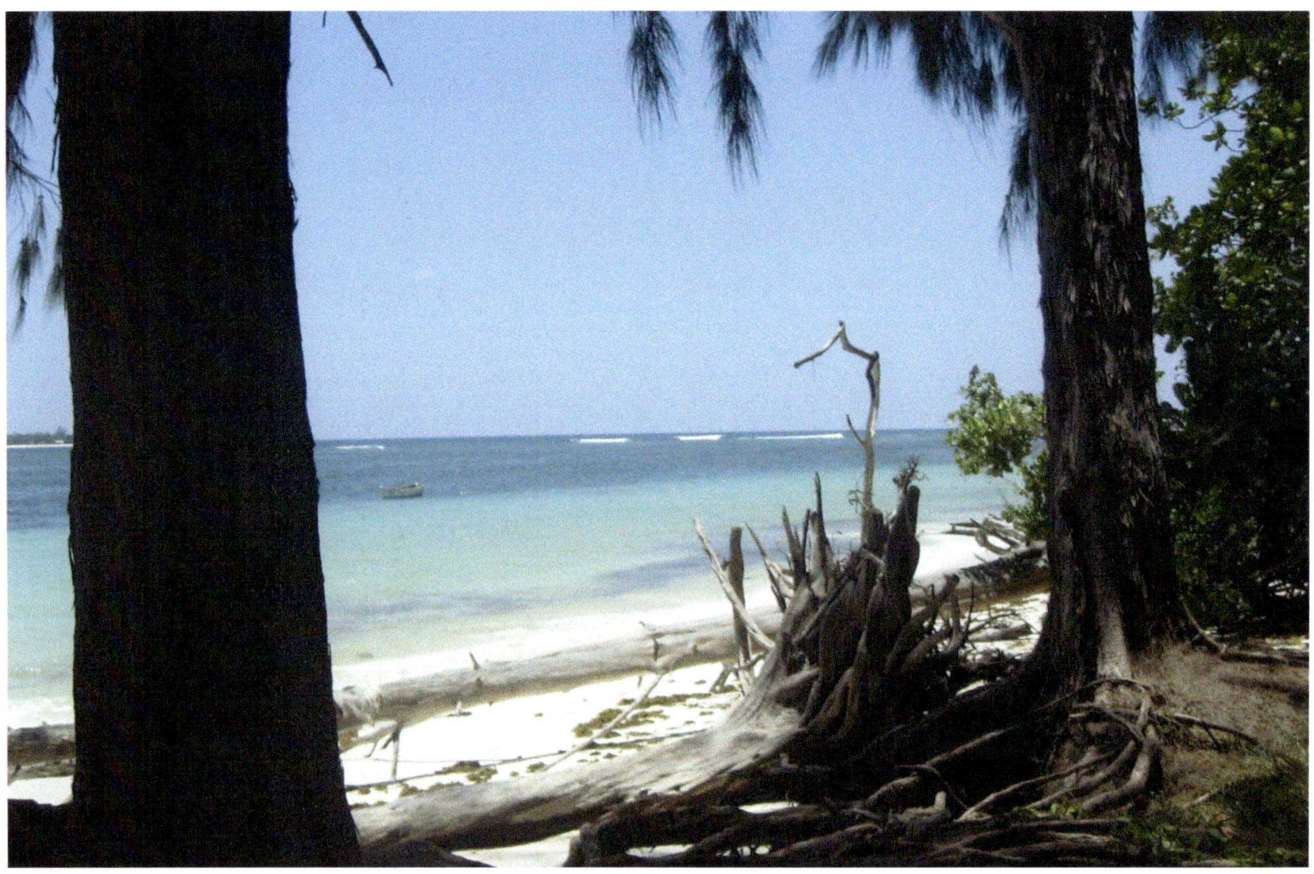

As I looked out onto the islands of Cousin and Cousine from the beach on Praslin, the blues of the sky and the sea were intense, so intense they hurt my eyes, forcing me to squint. It felt great to discard my shoes and t-shirt and paddle as I waited for the sound of the engine to come around the coast. Once the boat arrived, we were soon on our way across the calm sea, and as Aride poked its head around the northwest corner of Praslin, I smiled. I was heading home.

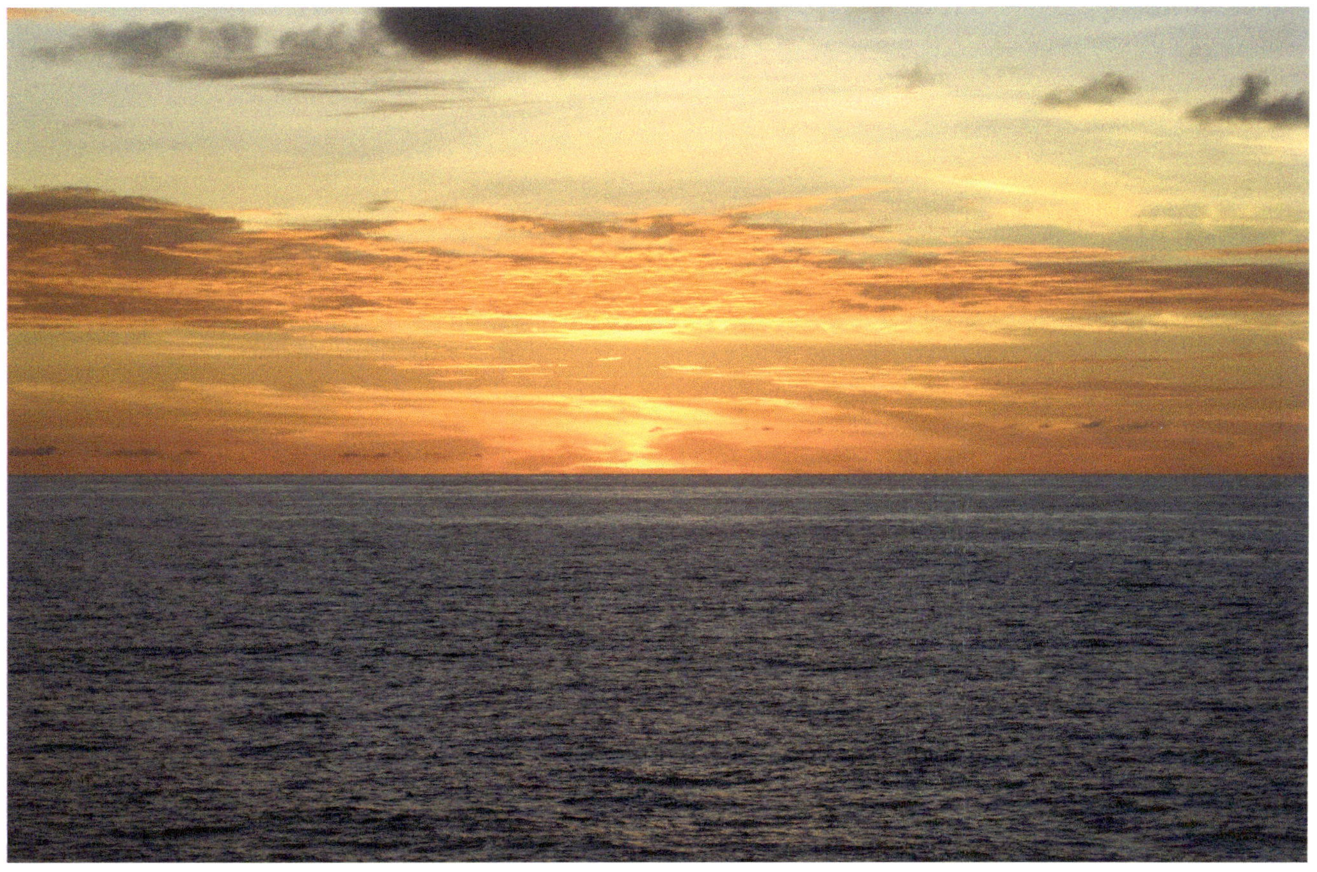

On the evening of my return, we sat with a beer on the beach crest and watched the sun set, the stars twinkling against a dark, clear sky. We talked excitedly, exchanging stories from the last two weeks. We both had a renewed confidence about our remaining time in this special place, as we knew we could rely on and get strength from each other. With the knowledge that my dad was on the road to recovery and mum was OK, it felt lovely to be back.

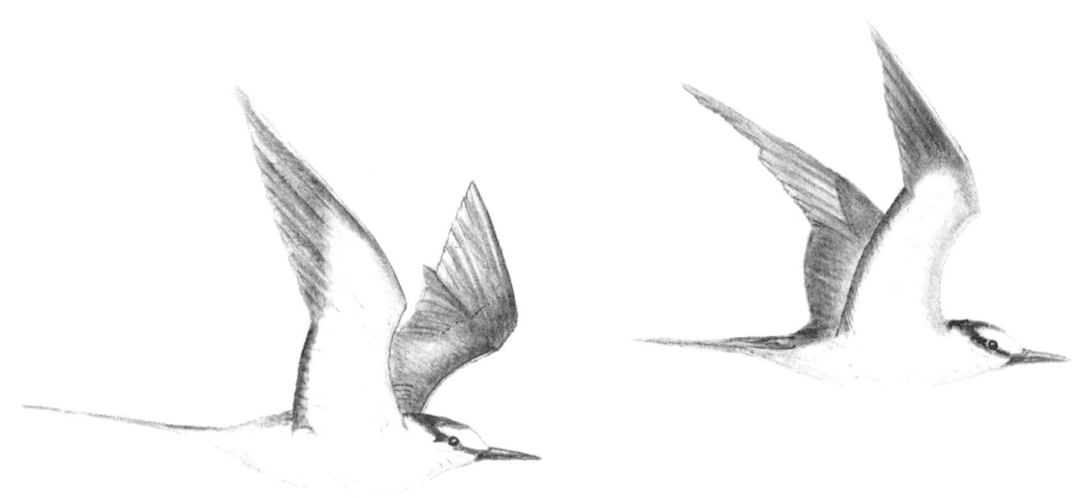



# Chapter 15

## History Repeats

During my time on Aride, I came to realise that living on a small island with a handful of people meant that trying to understand what made people tick was important. There was one thing that had become very clear since our arrival – culturally, we were extremely different from the Seychellois.

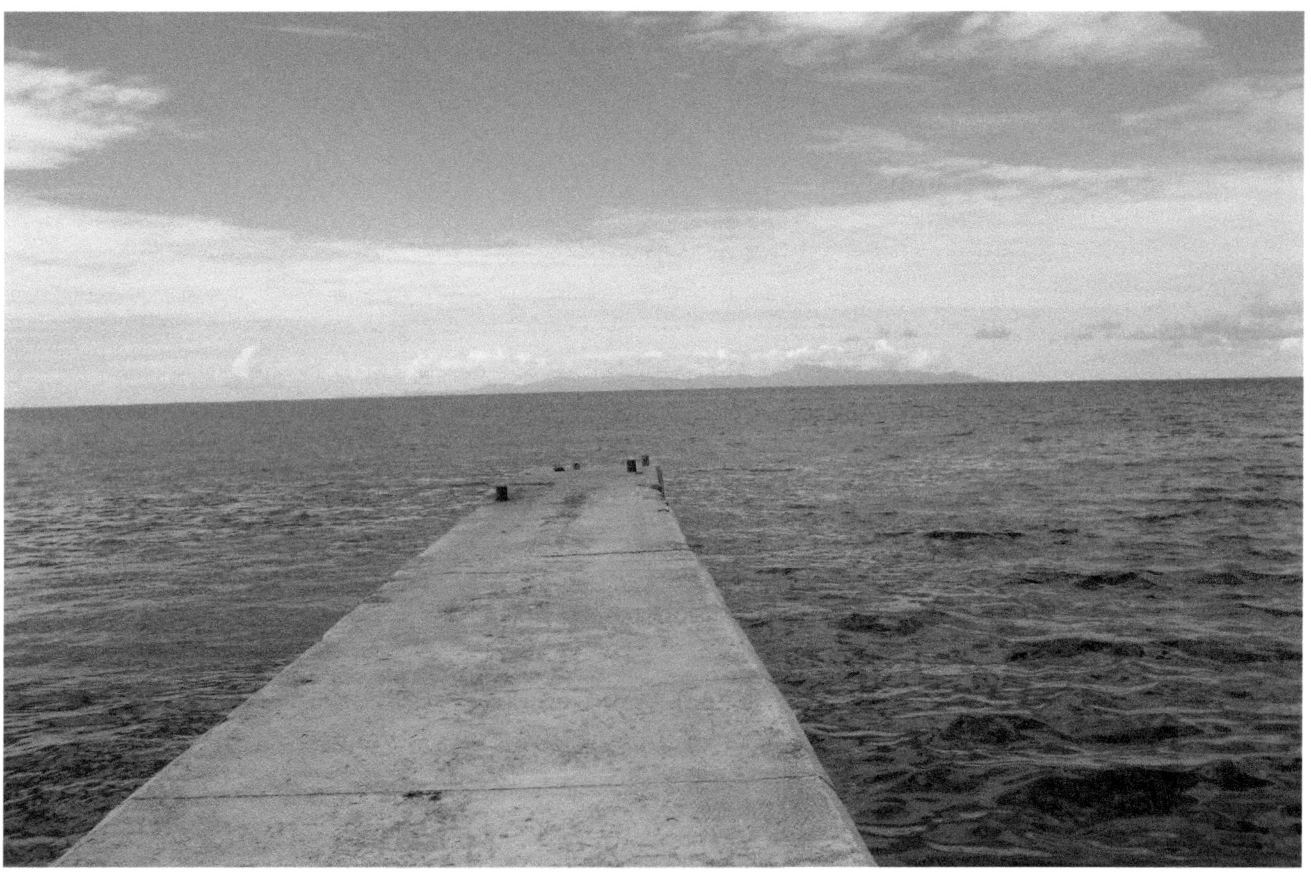

Working in a different culture was a constant challenge; though we had the same objectives, we often had different agendas and ways of doing things. This was illustrated during an episode of confrontation on Praslin, which marked a significant turning point in relationships. We depended on our boat drivers for literally everything, including survival, but on this occasion they simply downed tools and refused to take us back to Aride, leaving us stranded on Praslin with a cruise ship waiting for us.

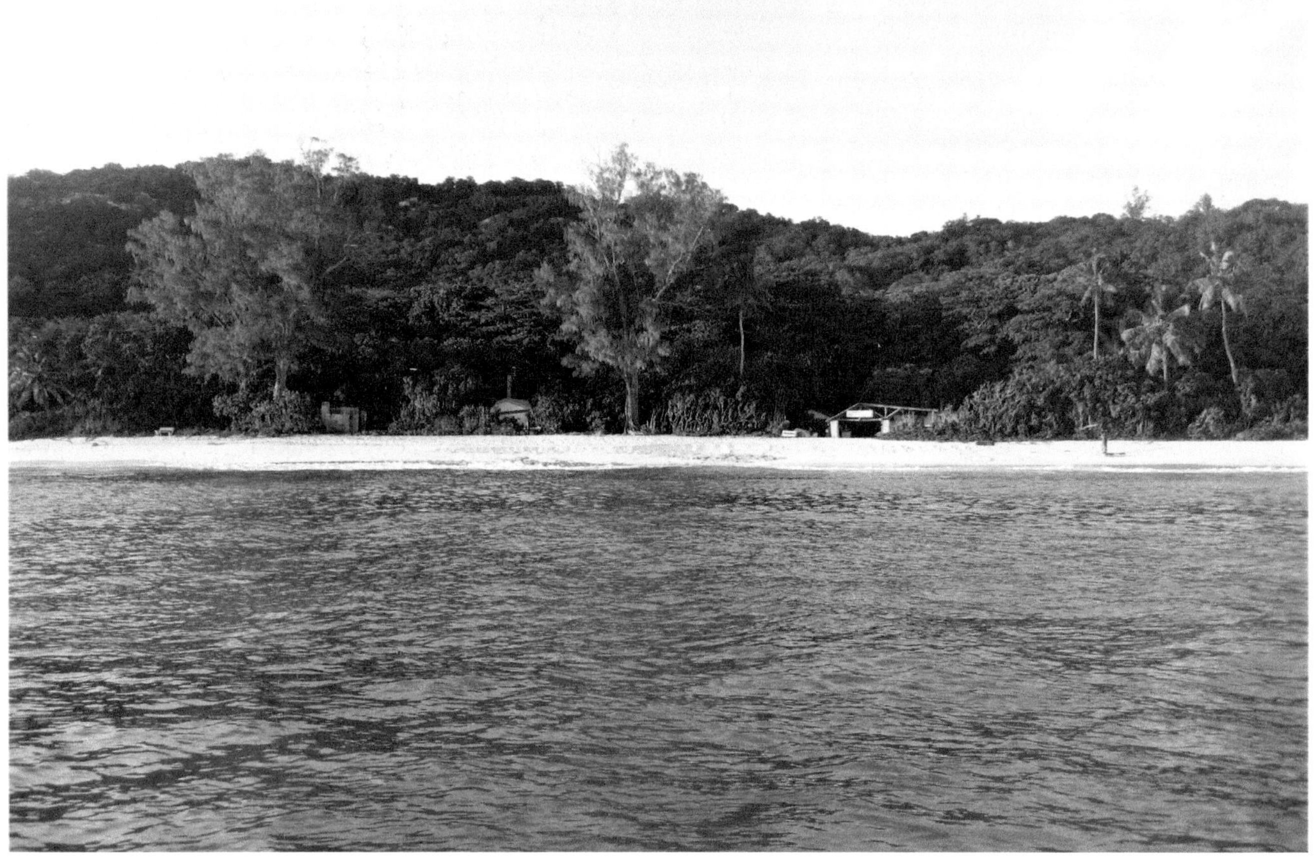

Fortunately, after a long debate, we managed to turn one of the boatmen around, and as Aride opened out before us, we saw the cruise ship in the distance. It was heading to the island – we powered on. It was a race against time. Thankfully, our beach landing was straightforward and, as we cleared the boat of its contents, the cruise ship moored up. The island was ready, it looked tidy and smart and amazingly it turned out to be a successful afternoon. The sea was calm and all went smoothly. No one would have known that, just an hour before, our two boatmen had resigned.

## *Fairy tern*

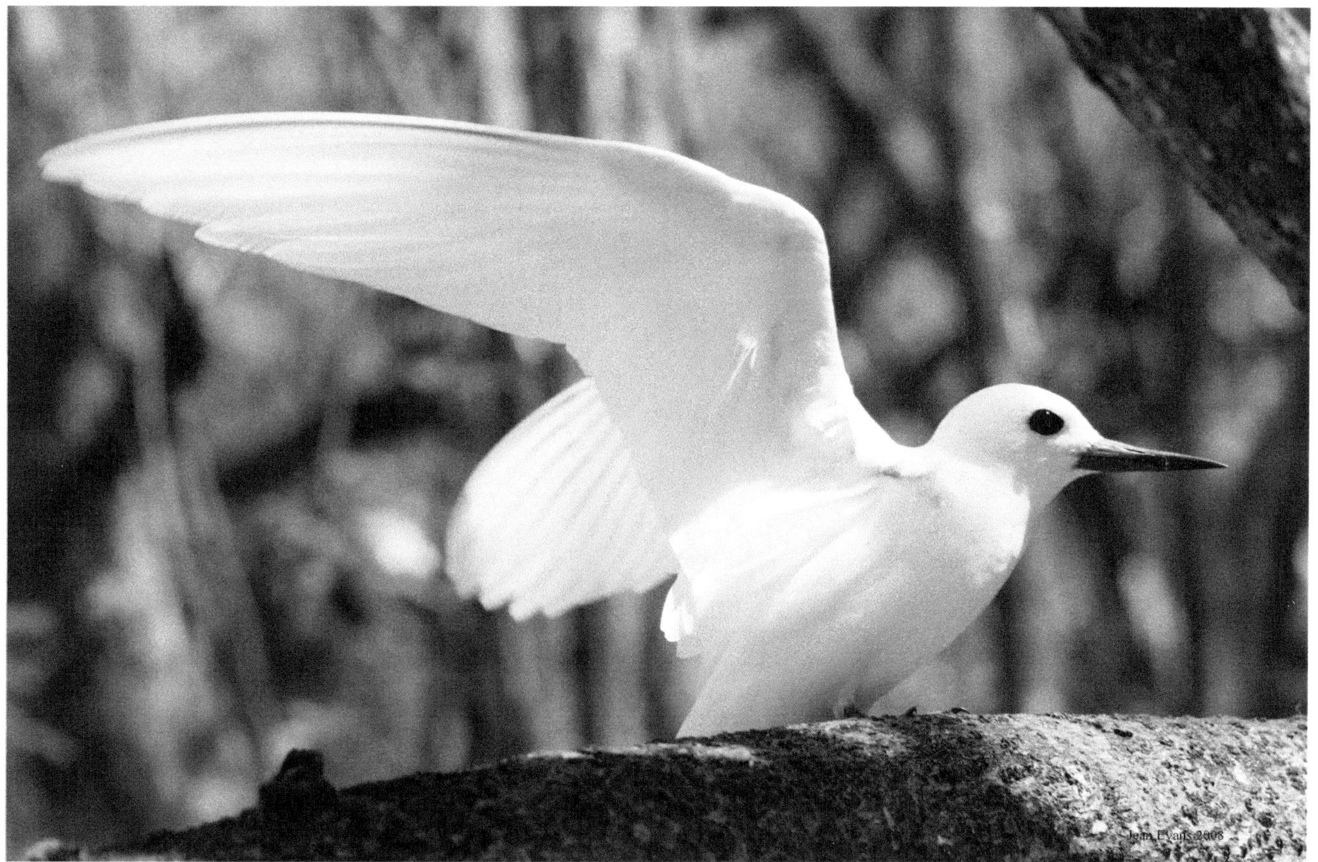

© *Jean Cheadle*

After a testing day, I would often walk to the eastern end of the beach crest and watch the fairy terns, the smart little white birds clinging on to their branches, resisting the brisk breeze. As I walked closer to the sea, the soft sand felt like talc beneath me, and as I watched the bridled terns fishing out in the surf, stooping down to make their catch off the surface, slowly, my head would start to clear.

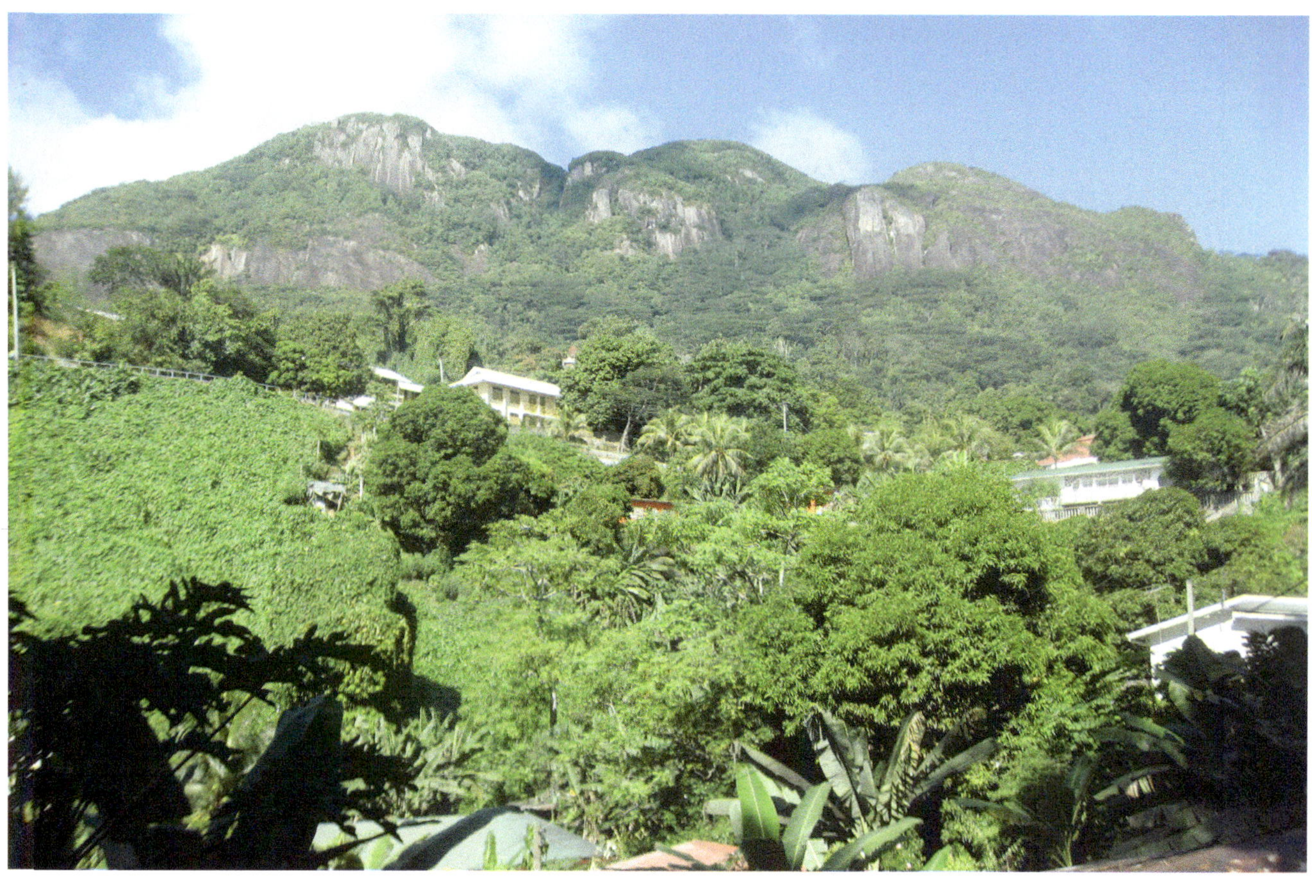

It was always striking to me how tropical, lush and green Mahé looked whenever we visited. As we walked down into the city from our accommodation, the slopes either side were dotted with bananas, standing proud, their large, elongated, waxy olive-green leaves glossy in the humid air. Trips to the mainland were infrequent, and often staff related. On this occasion our Head Ranger/Boatman was facing dismissal.

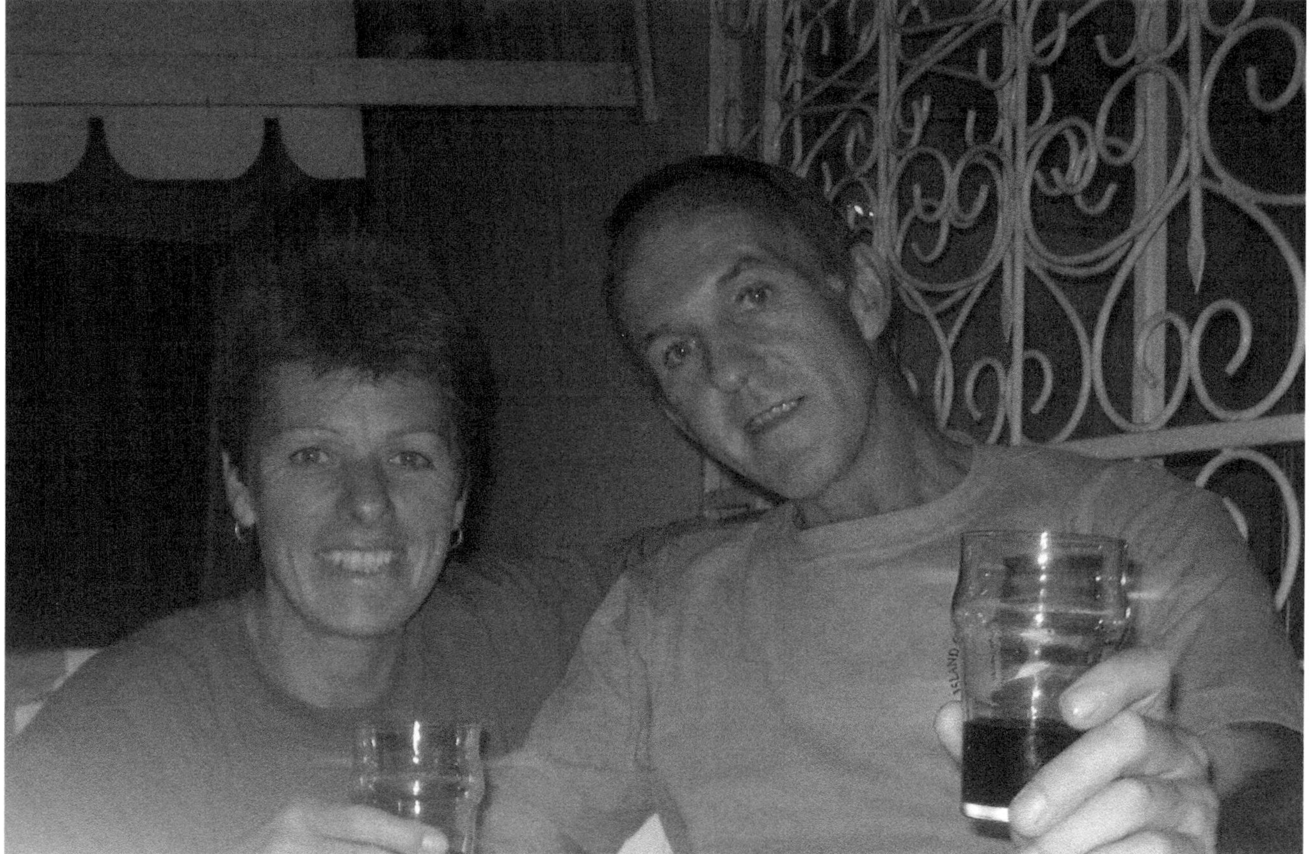

Sitting on the veranda with a glass of wine, overlooking the illuminated boats in the floodlit port of Mahé, we knew that even with only two rangers we would be OK. We had learnt through all the highs and lows that a depleted stable team was better than a troublesome one.

*Threadfin butterflyfish*

# Chapter 16

## Best Friend and Worst Enemy

From a practical perspective, the sea was a place to cool down and be invigorated; although the water was warm, it was cooler than the hot sun and it regularly served to take the sting out of sunburn and mosquito bites. Both emotionally gratifying and physically satisfying, I never took for granted or failed to value the significance that living next to the ocean brought to our lives.

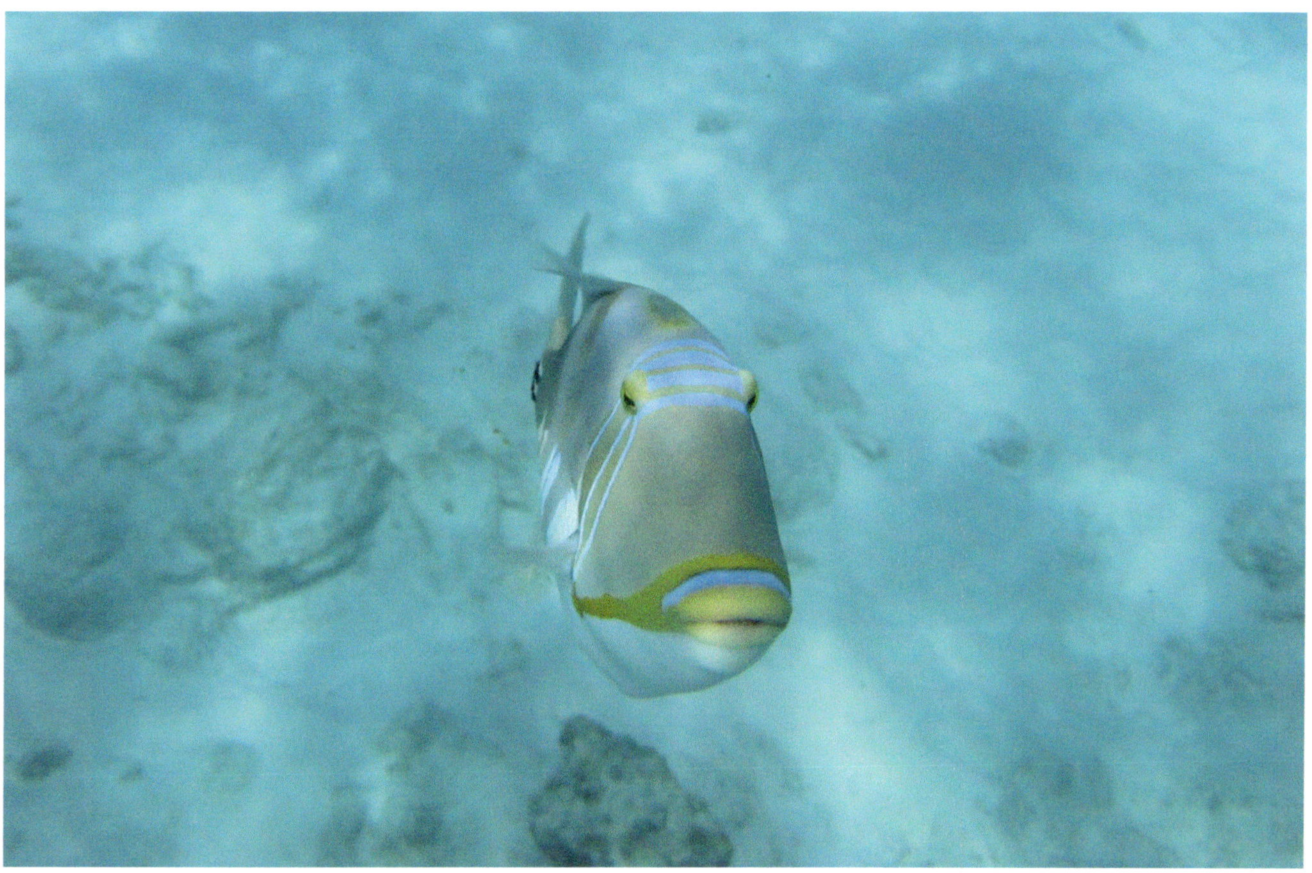

Snorkelling off the coast of Aride was superb. It was like entering another world as soon as you peeped through the surface. The underwater colours were fantastic and if the water was calm the sun would shine brightly through, lighting up the reef below. Seeing a turtle was a real bonus, but the usual residents were species such as powder blue surgeonfish, moorish idols, Picasso triggerfish, scissor-tail sergeants and threadfin butterflyfish, to name a few.

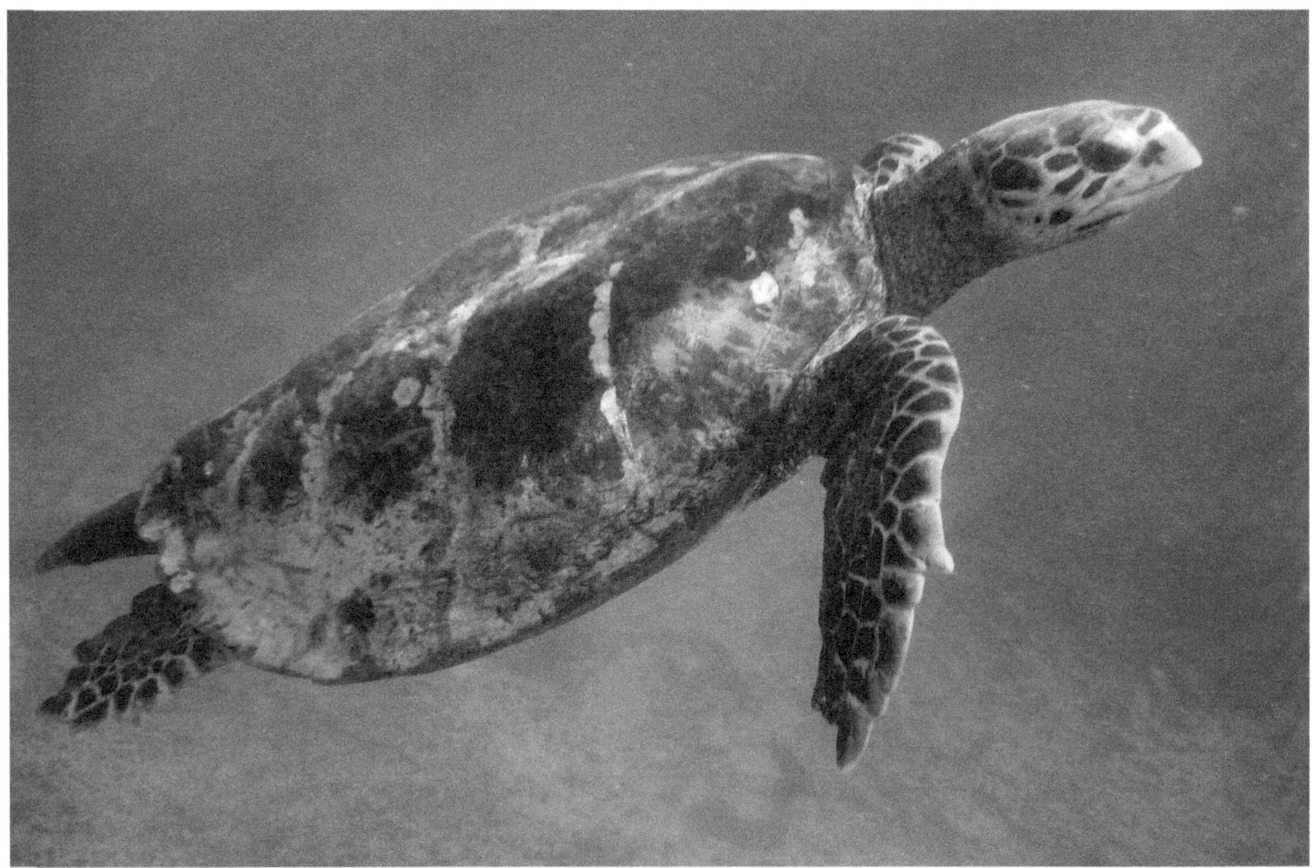

*© Chloe Prehn-Arnold*

Whilst snorkelling, the sight of a hawksbill turtle was always captivating, as they would inquisitively drift towards me for a closer look. Truly beautiful creatures, they glide through the water gracefully, so strikingly different to how they clumsily drag themselves up the beach.

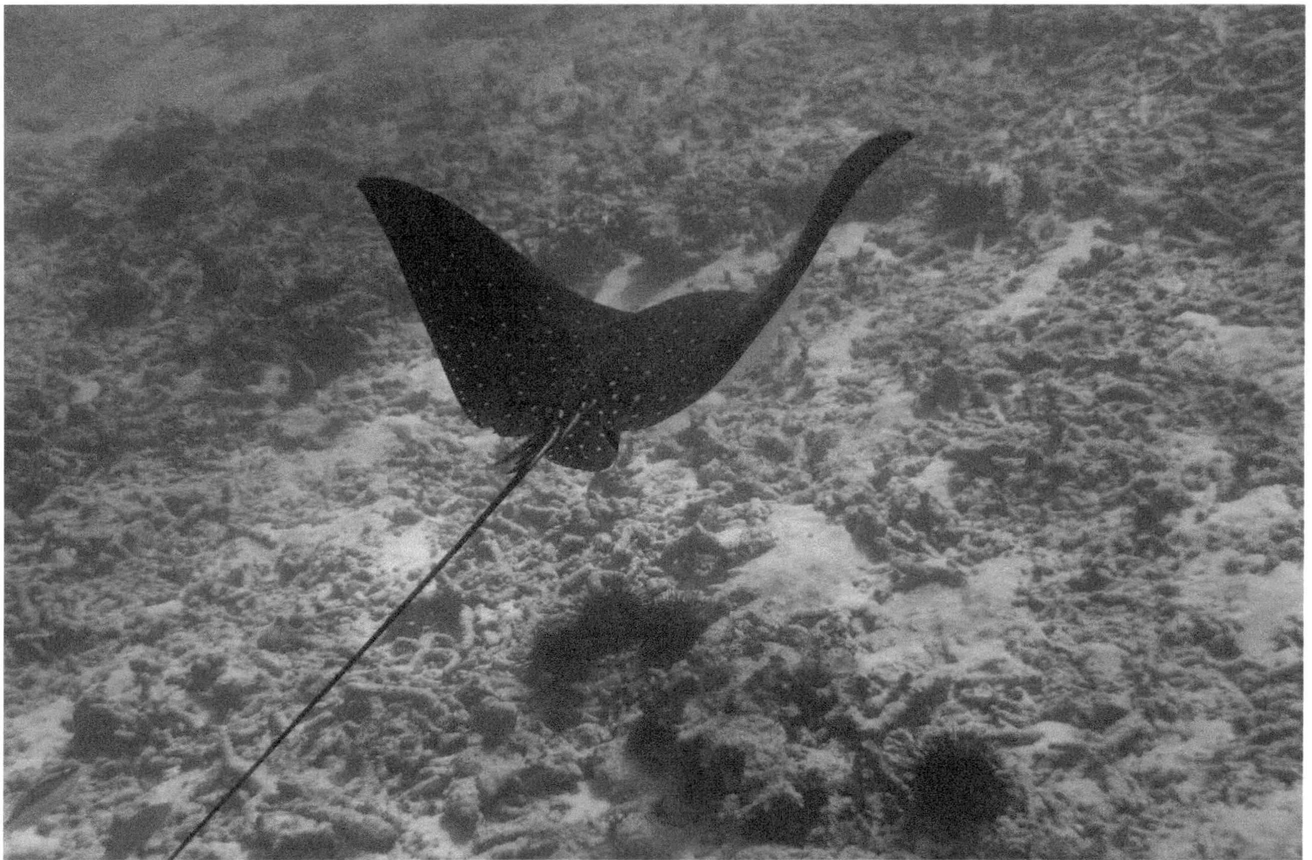

© Chloe Prehn-Arnold

From the beach crest we often watched marine life playing in the water, surfing, skimming, breaking the water's surface with the flick of a tail, or using the surface tension to propel themselves along. Bottlenose dolphins caught the sunlight as they surfaced and spotted eagle rays glided in the surf like black shadows.

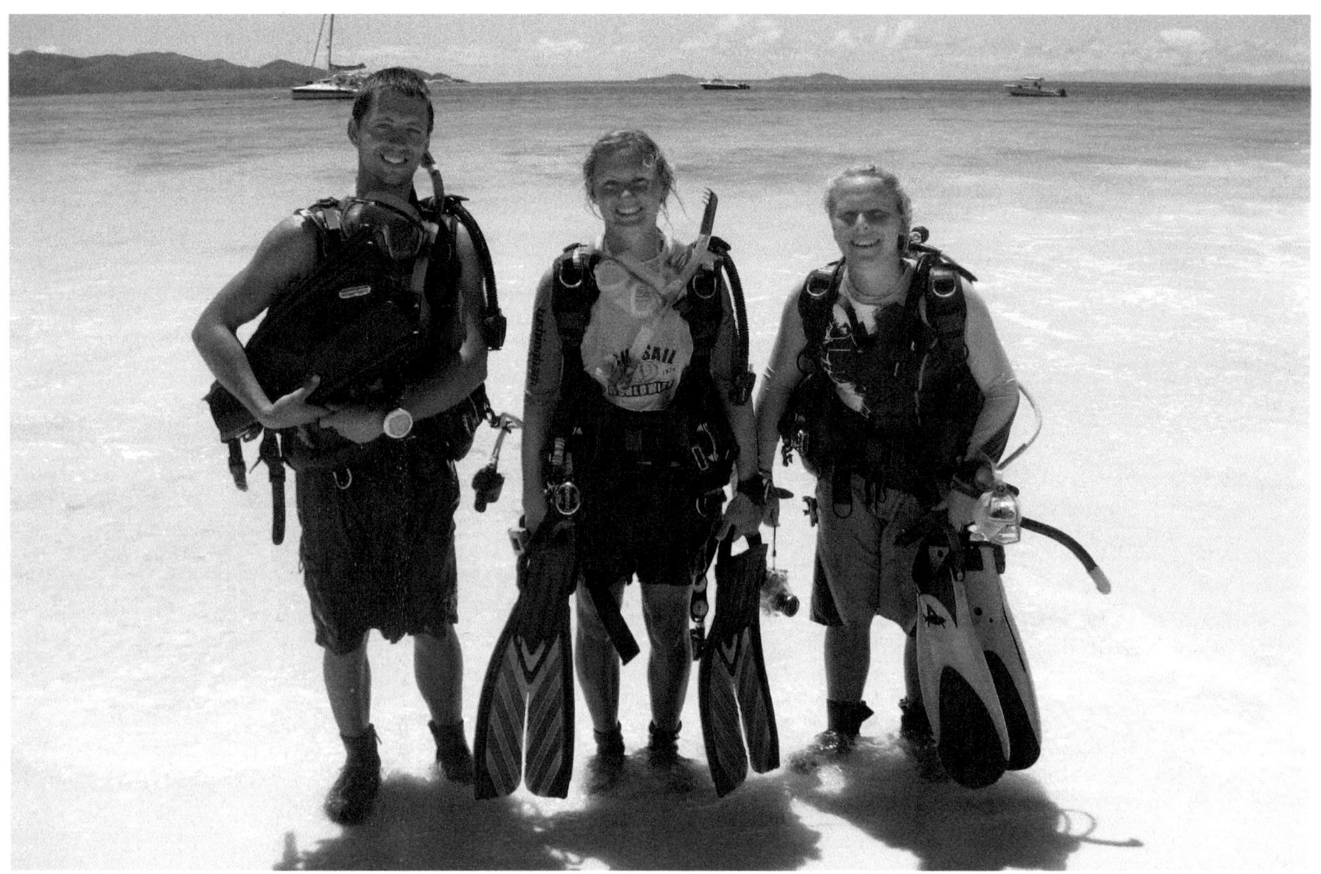

Marine work was a gap in the historical knowledge and management of Aride. The focus had always been on terrestrial, with a full set of data about the bugs and beasties on land, but very little about those in the water. Prior to coming to Aride, I wouldn't have put myself in the bracket of 'marine enthusiast'; I often thought about diving, but never really knew if it was for me or how I would feel going down into the depths of the ocean. But then, I don't think anyone really knows until they give it a go.

*__Sunset across the water, Aride__*

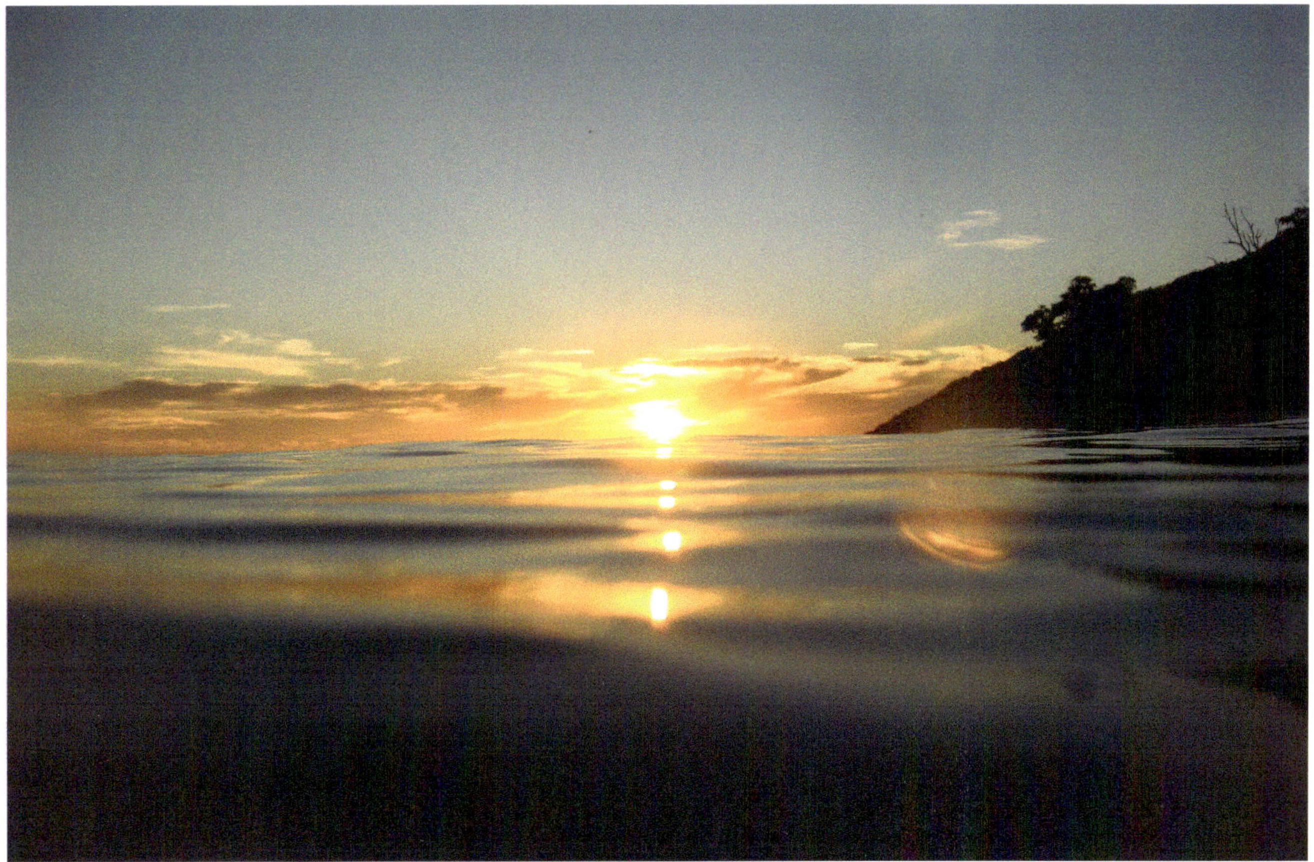

*© Chloe Prehn-Arnold*

In the enormity of the Indian Ocean, conditions could change in an instant, with a bright, clear, tropical horizon being replaced by one heavily shrouded in mist and cloud. The strong currents, deep swells and silver cresting waves were unforgiving, and they showed no mercy to anything or anyone, however vulnerable. There were numerous occasions when this was demonstrated to be the case, not least a significant diving incident.

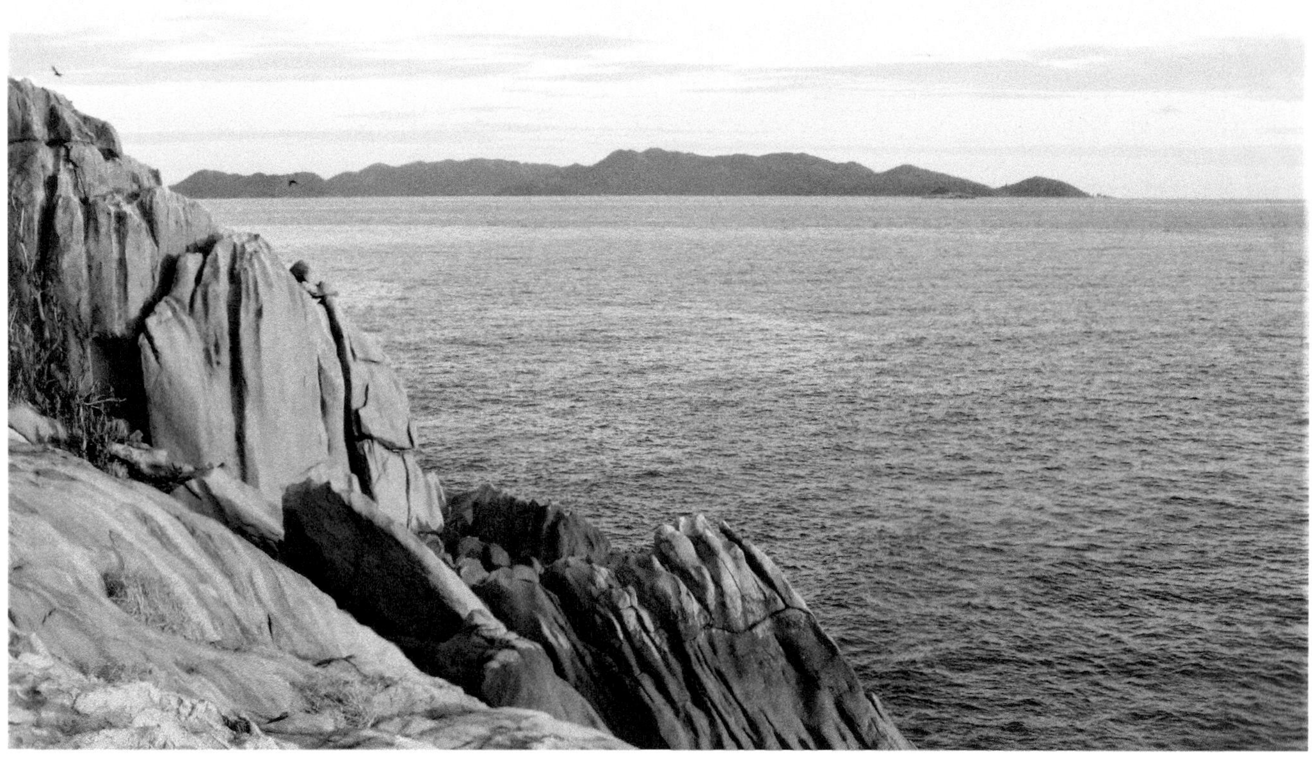

The western end of the island was also a favourite haunt when I needed time to think, as I knew the breeze would be stronger and cooler there. I would sit for a while and feel for my precious white conch shell in my pocket, its bold, rounded form soothing to the touch.

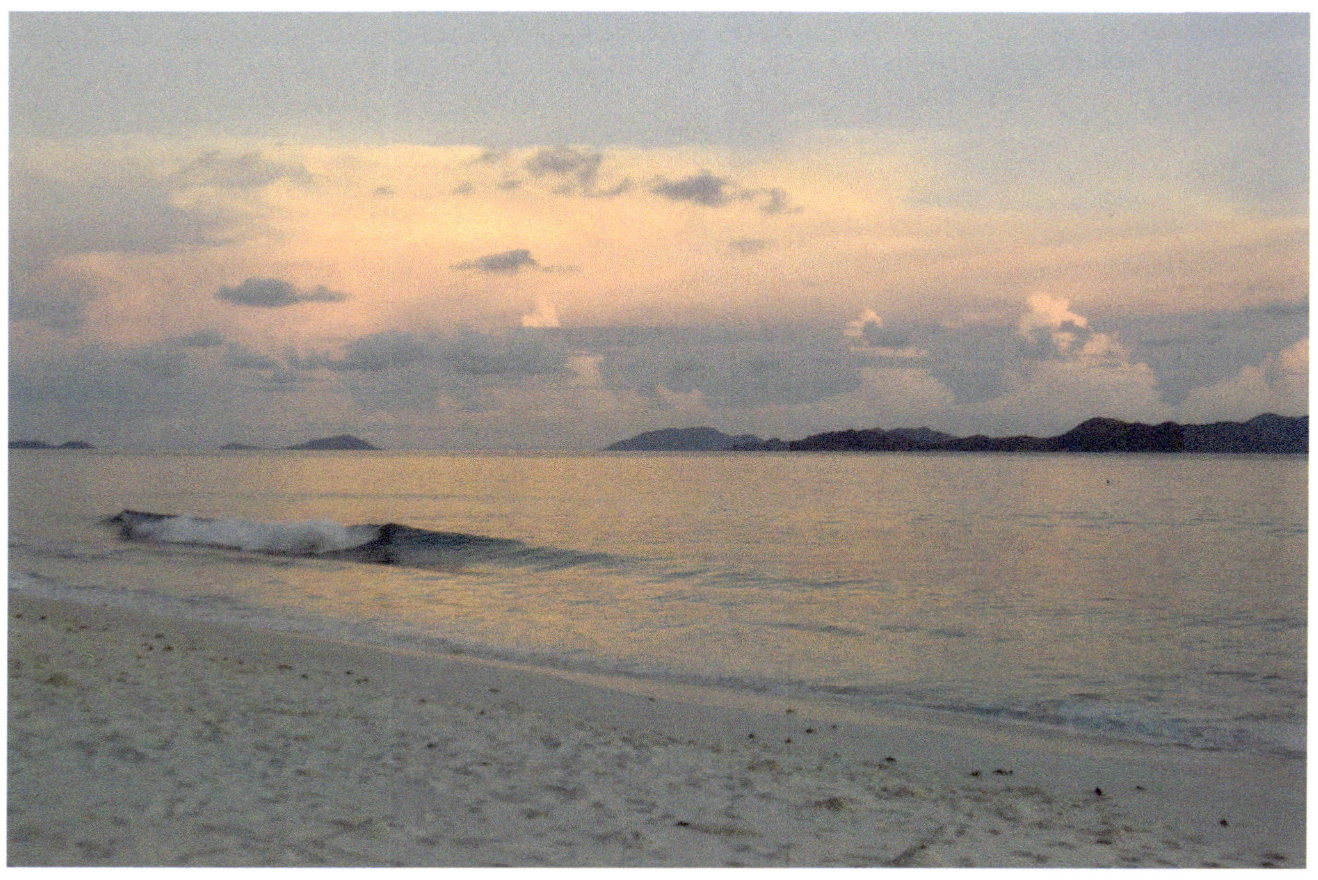

The sunsets were incredible on Aride, however, after the trauma of the diving accident, we knew that the romantic perception of living on a remote tropical island in the middle of the Indian Ocean needed always to be laced with a degree of realism... if required, it was OK to apply a bit of UK rationale – even if it was born of another culture, if it helped to keep us safe...

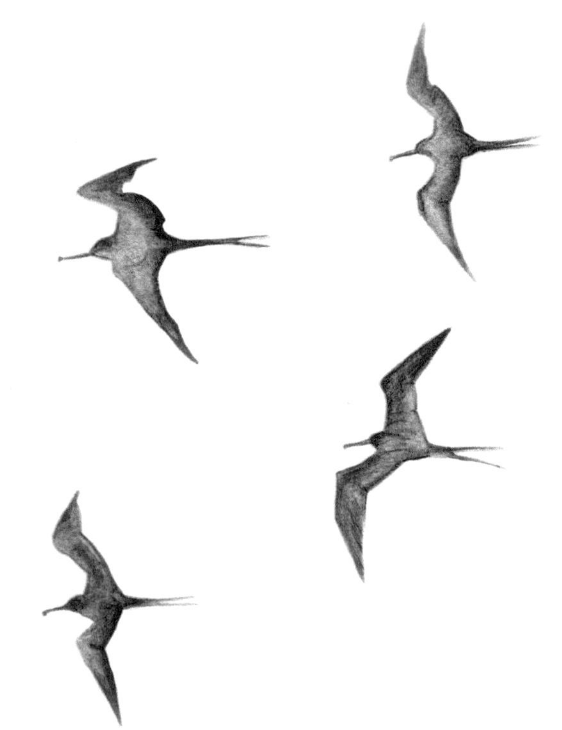

*Frigate birds*

# Chapter 17

## On the Edge

Living in a culture with different beliefs and ways of life was a continual upward learning curve, just to be able to toe the appropriate line. I don't think I could have ever fully appreciated how difficult it would be before coming to Aride. I never imagined that working in a different culture would be so challenging, so different and so emotionally draining.

*Burnt out generators*

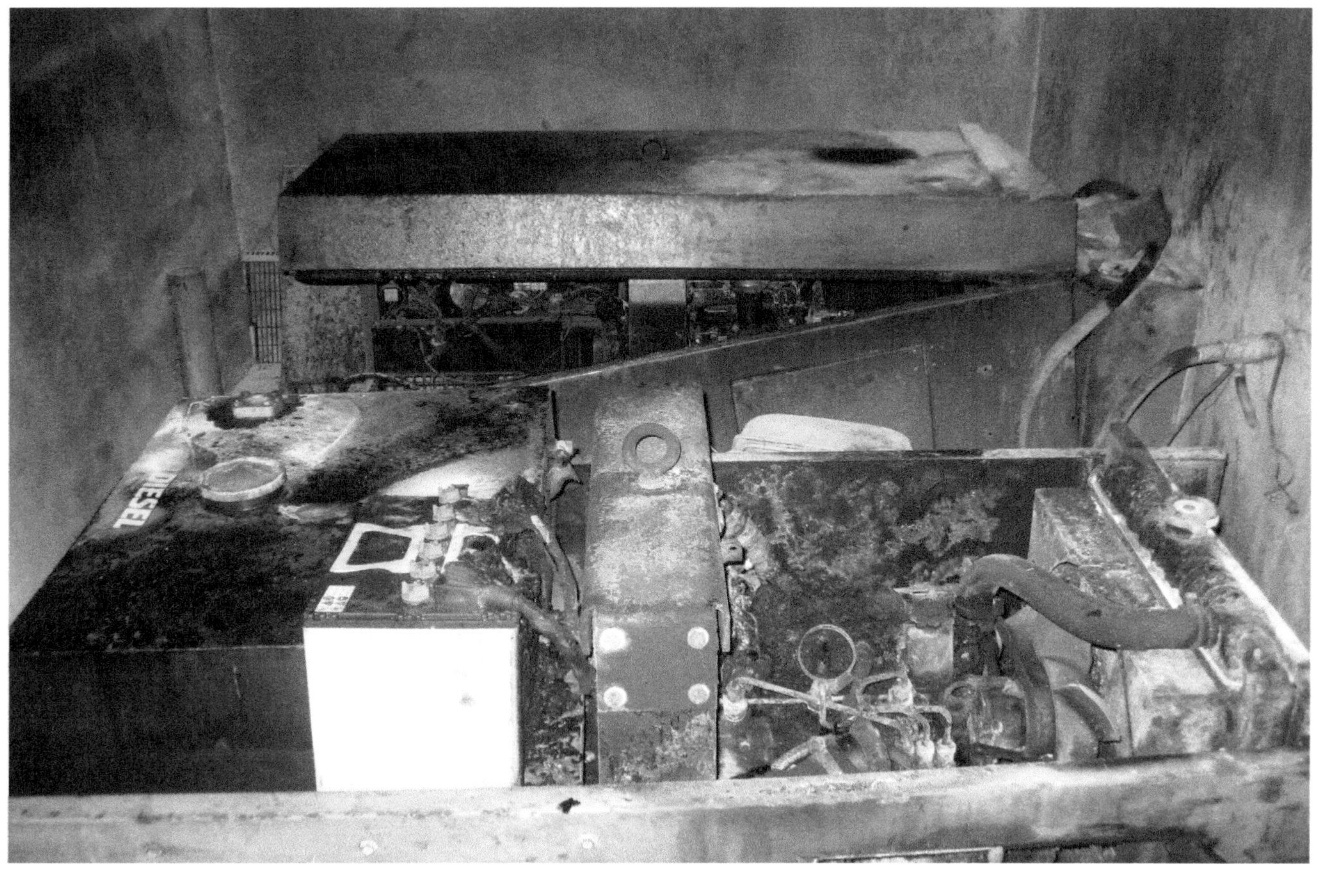

The generator was a constant battle and at times we both felt that we would be better off without it rather than limping on with it the way we did. Predictably, it was dangerous to tempt fate. Despite the irreparable damage to the generators themselves, we were lucky that the block construction of the shed had helped to prevent a much larger explosion. The fire was the final straw that broke the back of any power provision for a while… until the day of the big Aride delivery.

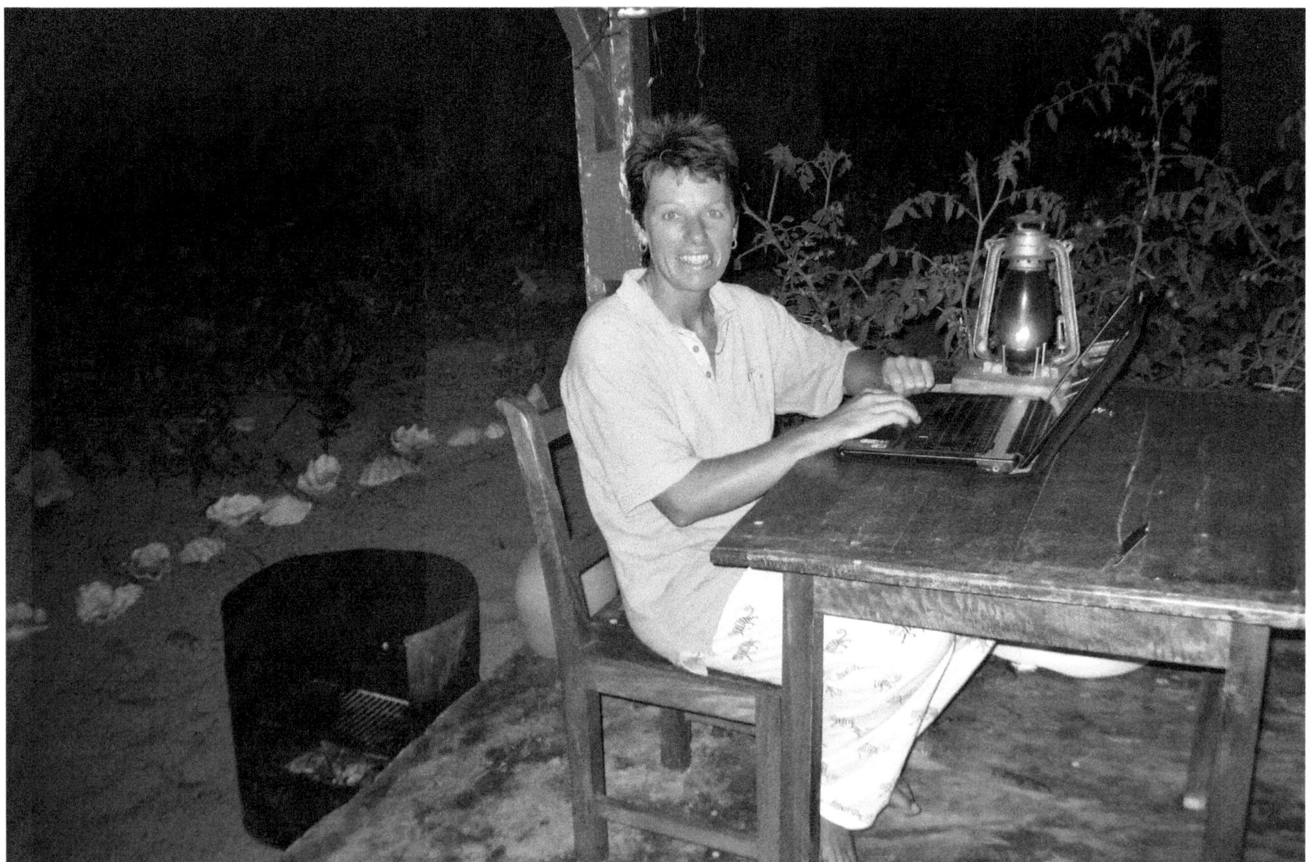

*© Melvyn Yeandle*

Once candles were 'all finished' on Praslin, Melv rose to the challenge and made a lantern fuelled by burnt candle wax that we had gathered from all the used candles. Constructed from bits of old lanterns in the hoard of 'might be useful rubbish', it meant we had some light to eat and drink by. The makeshift lantern provided a softer light and one not so attractive to flying creatures, and of course it didn't need batteries.

186

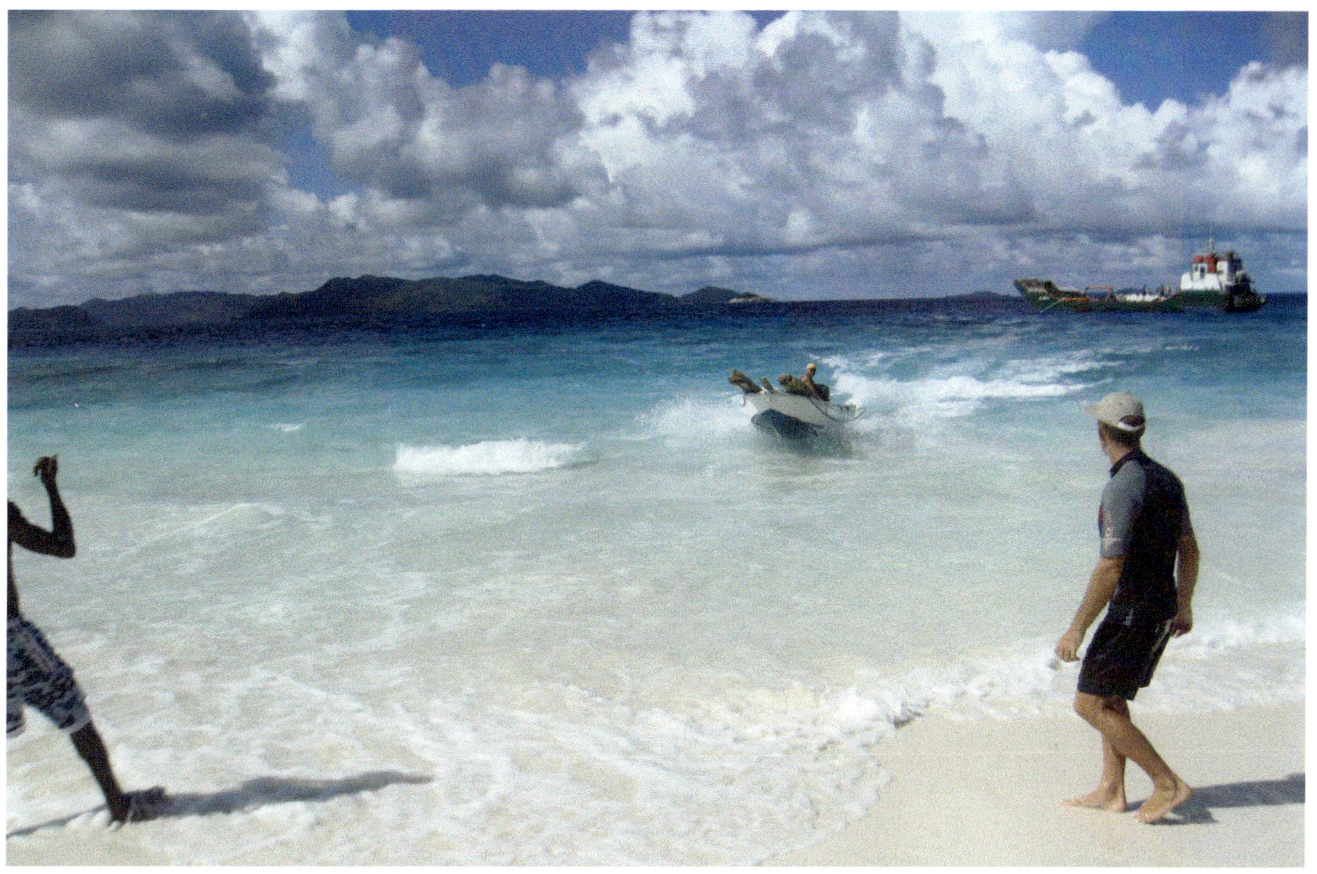

The delivery was the largest Aride had ever received. We were expecting twenty-five barrels of fuel, six tonnes of aggregate, fifty bags of cement, two thousand blocks, three tonnes of timber and several miscellaneous things like a new boat, pipe and freezer – oh, and a generator. The three tonnes of timber and assorted goods were landed on the beach, with crews on the shore ready to grab the boat and its contents as it arrived, empty it, and turn the boat around to launch for the next trip.

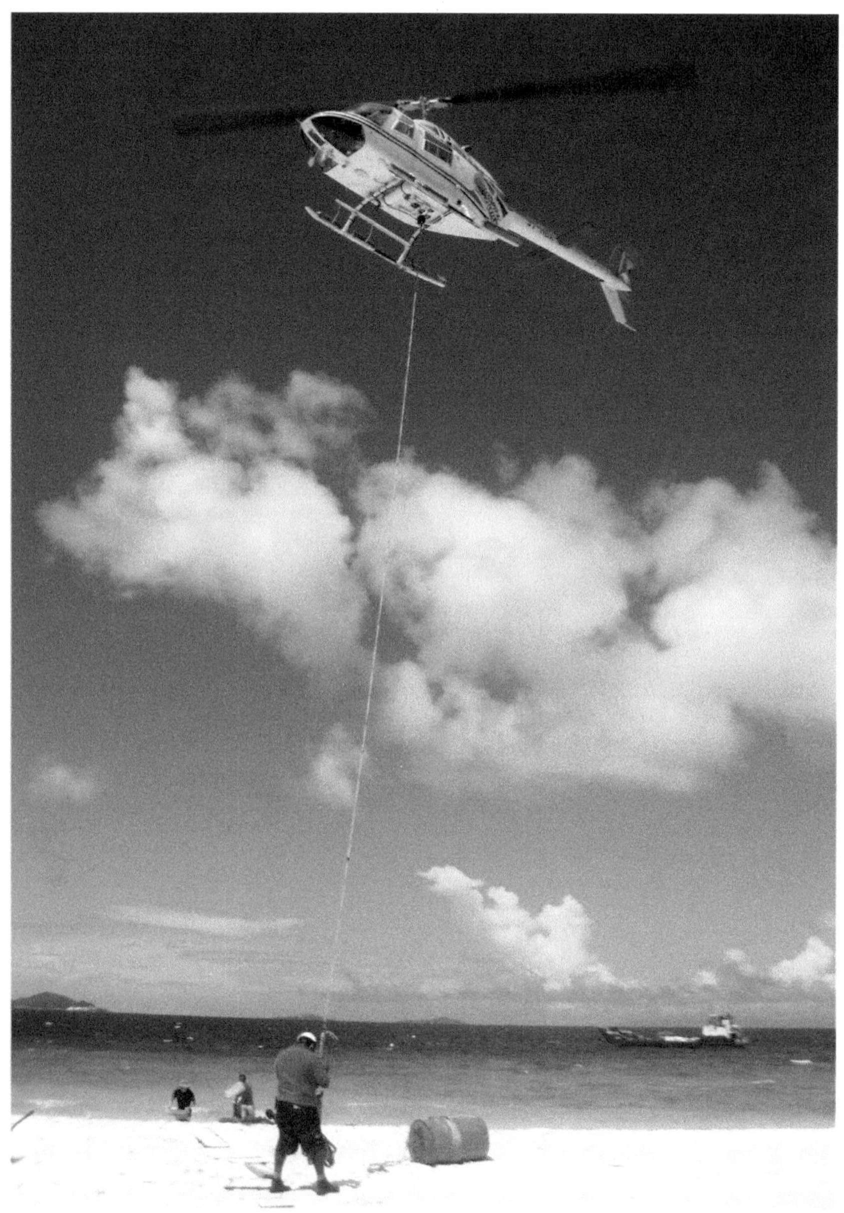

A helicopter was used to carry the generator fuel across in massive barrels, each containing 200 litres. The barrels were landed on the beach in nets on ropes, and we needed to ensure they were moved as quickly as possible up to the safety of the beach crest and away from the water. The nets, once emptied of the fuel, then had to be loaded with the empty barrels and rubbish from the island, so that the return helicopter trip was not wasted.

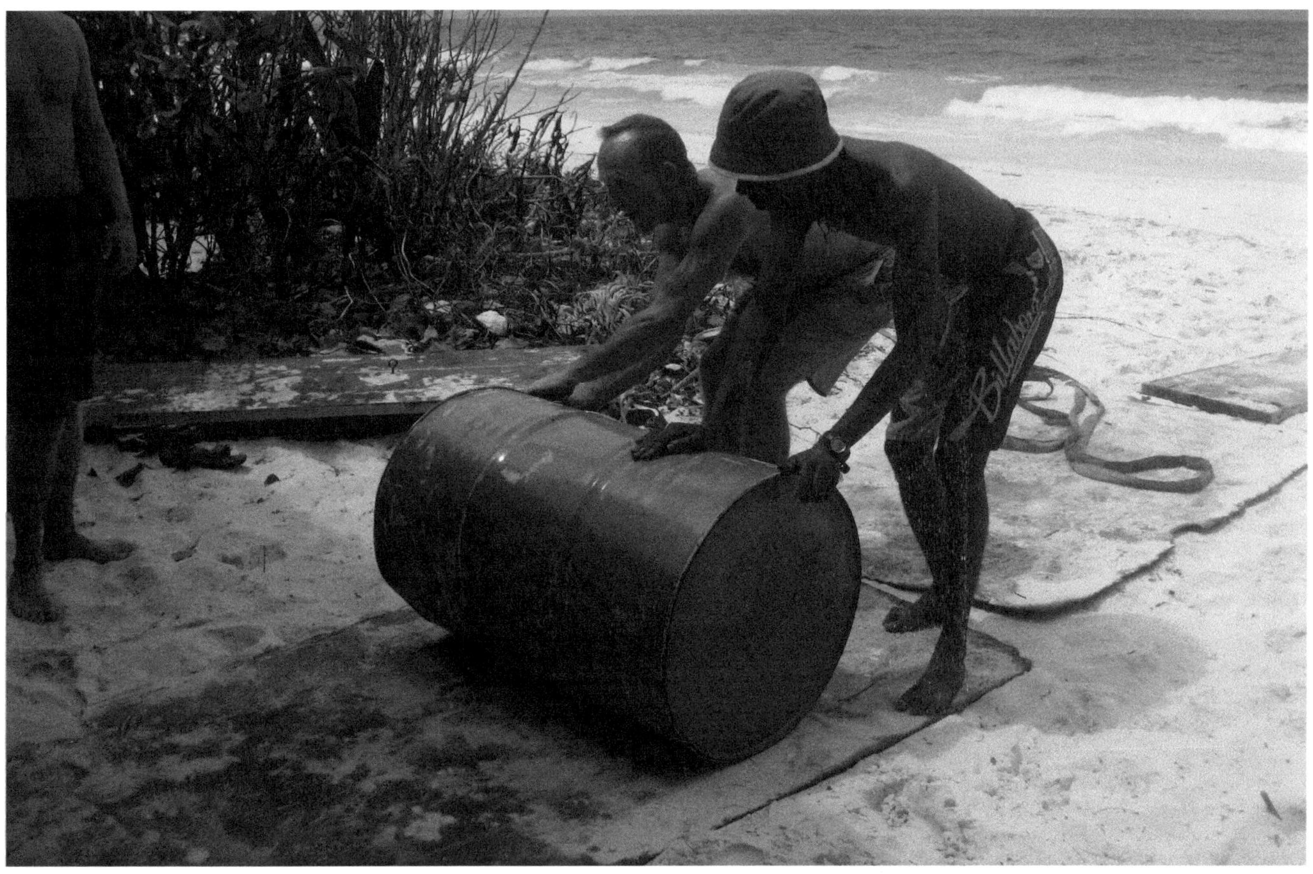

As each barrel of fuel came in, we prepared a net of rubbish and empty barrels to go out, working like this until all the rubbish and barrels had gone. Watching a net holding two rusty, old, dilapidated fridge freezers go flying through the air was very satisfying. We even managed to roll all the full barrels up the beach and back to the safety of the boatshed.

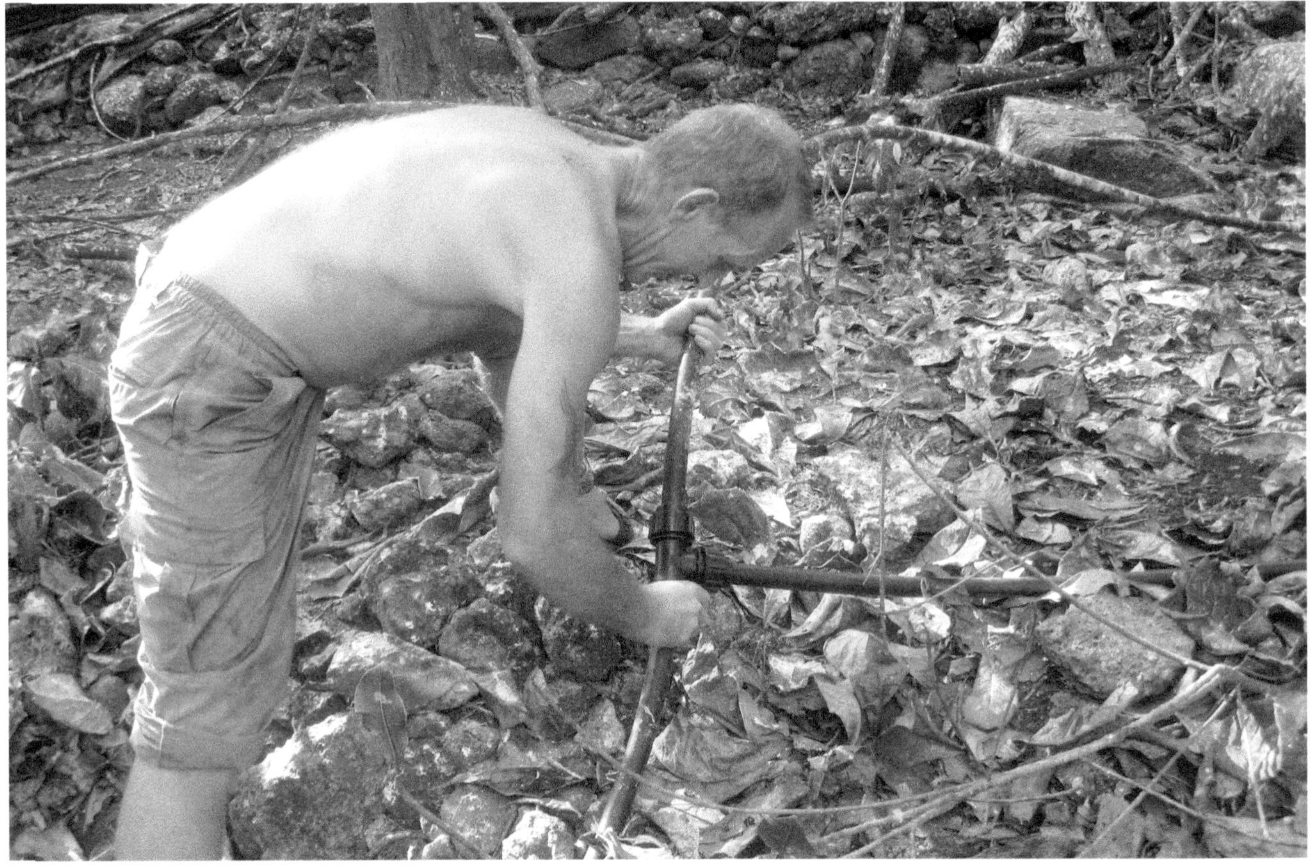

The shipment was also the catalyst for another major convenience — running water — as it brought the pipe we needed for the water project. The pipe in question was a flexible hose that would be used to take water from the well to fill a tank on the hill. Like many things, the water project had been ongoing on Aride for a long time, but without any real belief that it would happen. However, with Melv's doggedness and determination, we finally cracked it.

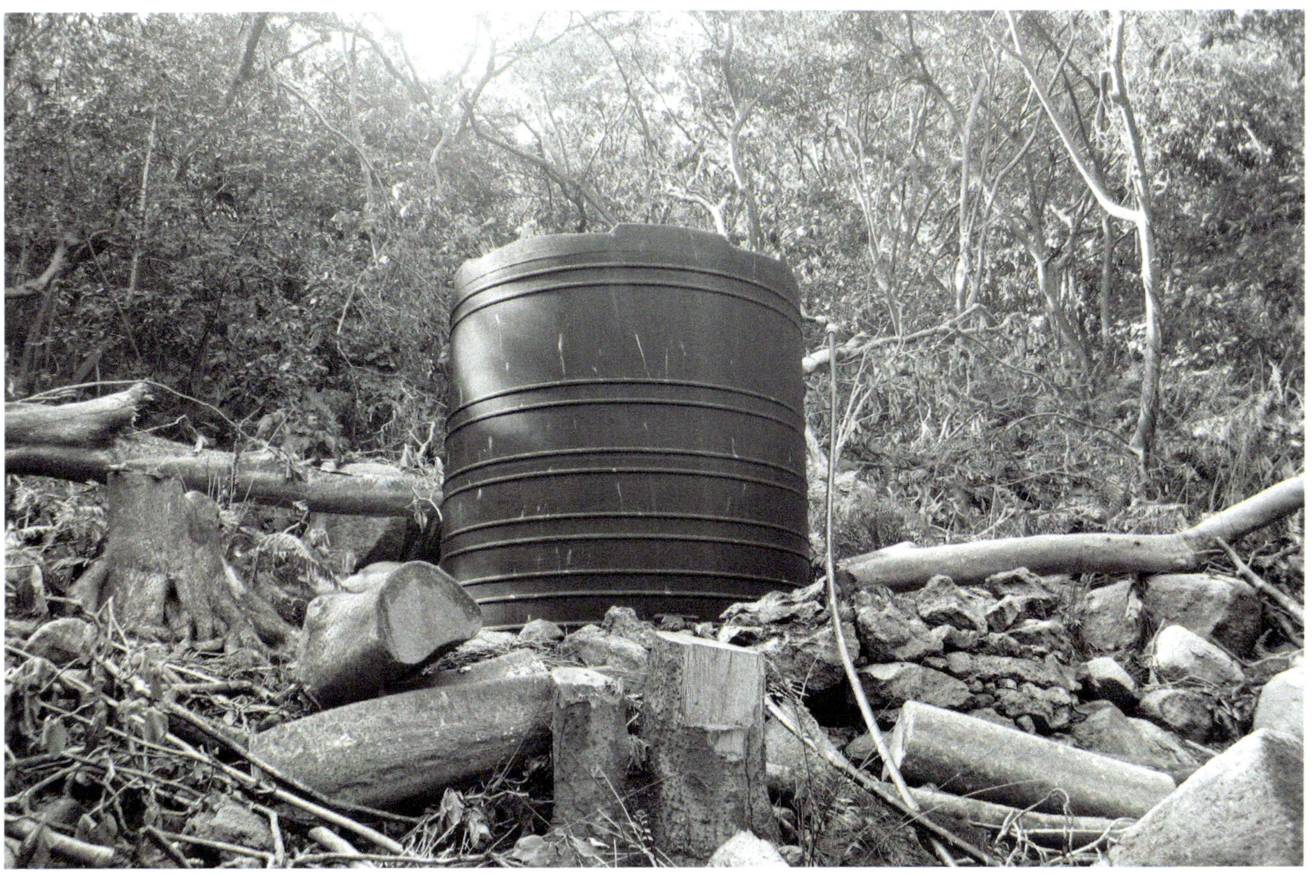

Achieving running water all started with moving the tank, which had to go up the hill to provide the head of water we needed to feed the houses by gravity. From the tank, Melv laid the pipe, which was to take water to each of the properties. We made good use of the plumbing fixtures we had brought back with us from our trip home to the UK; our suitcase had been massively over the weight limit as we were compelled to sacrifice chocolate for a bag of copper fittings and a bit of flux!

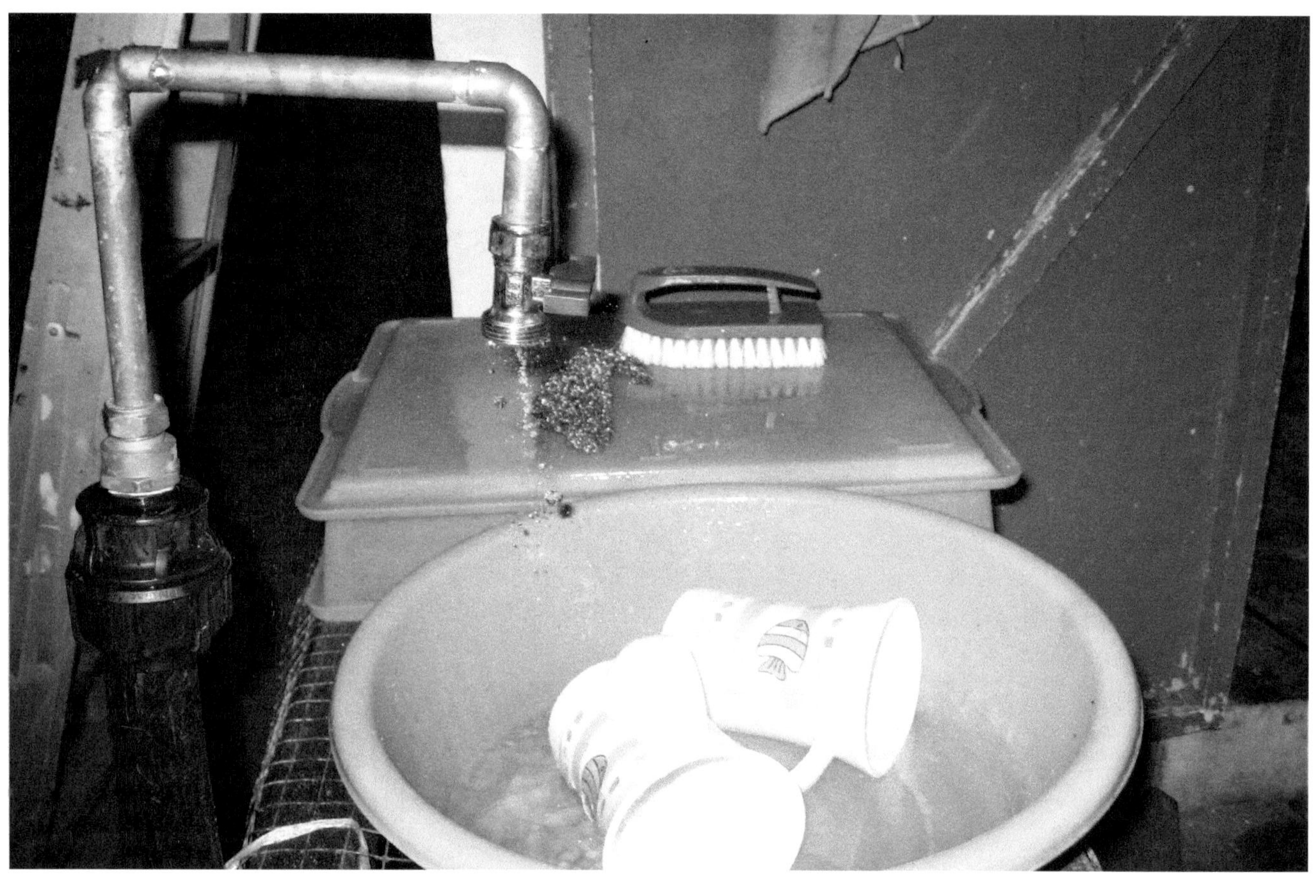

After the shipment had finally brought the last and most critical bit of kit for the water project, it was such a novelty to have running water coming out of our own 'tap' over the washing up bowl. We could wash our hands – I remember thinking, "Blimey! We might even become hygienic." Even though it was only fashioned out of a bit of copper pipe, with the touch of a lever, we had water on demand - fantastic.

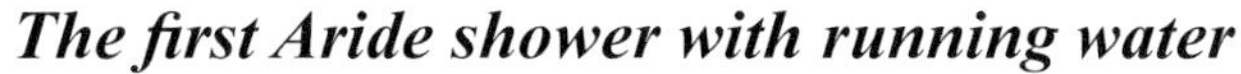

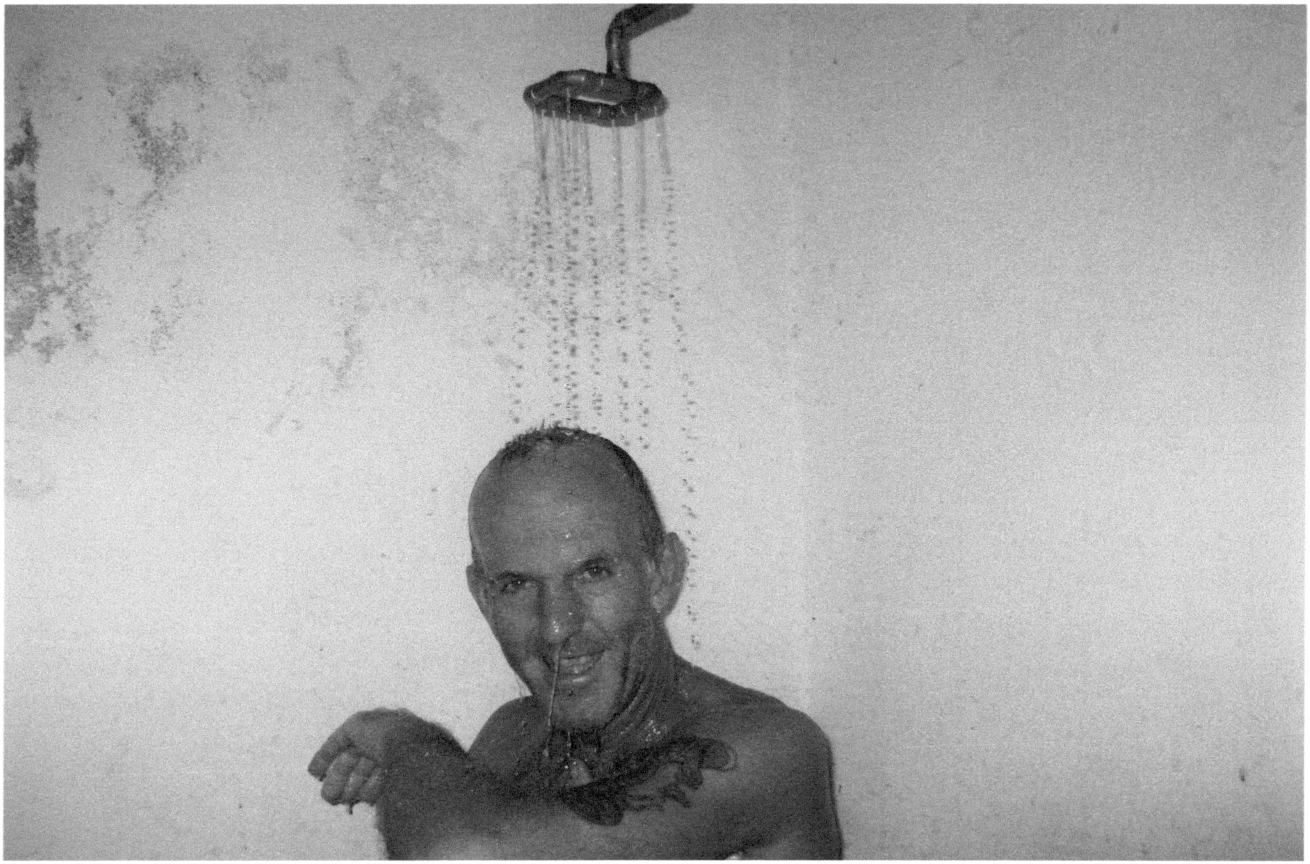

The water project didn't stop with the tap, as not long afterwards, we had a working shower. No more pouring a bucket over one's head; no more sand left in your hair; no more trying to make a bucket of water stretch far enough to make sure all the soap and sand had gone – we had a shower!

## *Plumbing in the washing machine*

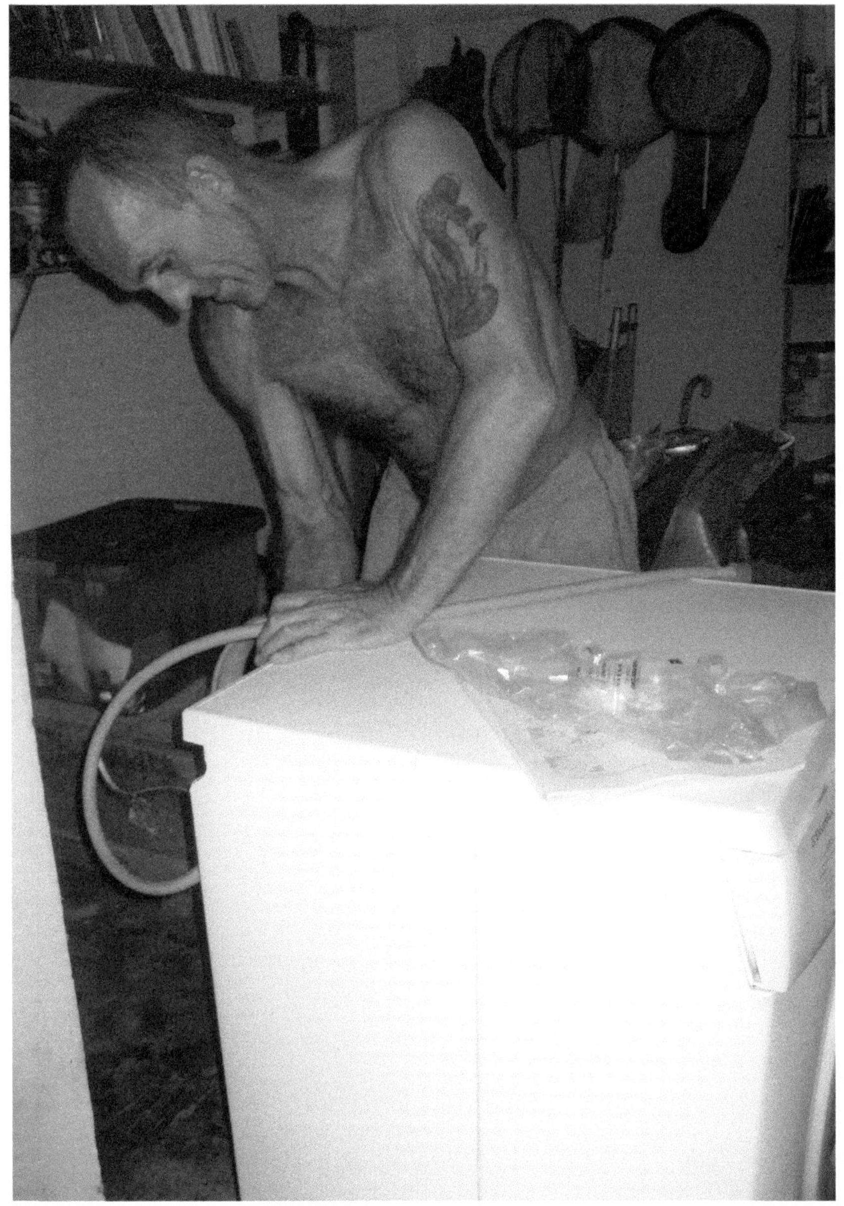

There was more! The washing machine, which had been nothing more than an additional work surface for six years, was finally plumbed in. Melv had created a water system with enough capacity and pressure to service a WASHING MACHINE… A WASHING MACHINE. It was goodbye scrubbing brush, hello Electrolux and clean clothes. The thought of wearing clothes that did not exude the smell of wet dog, even after they had been 'washed' brought a massive grin to my face.

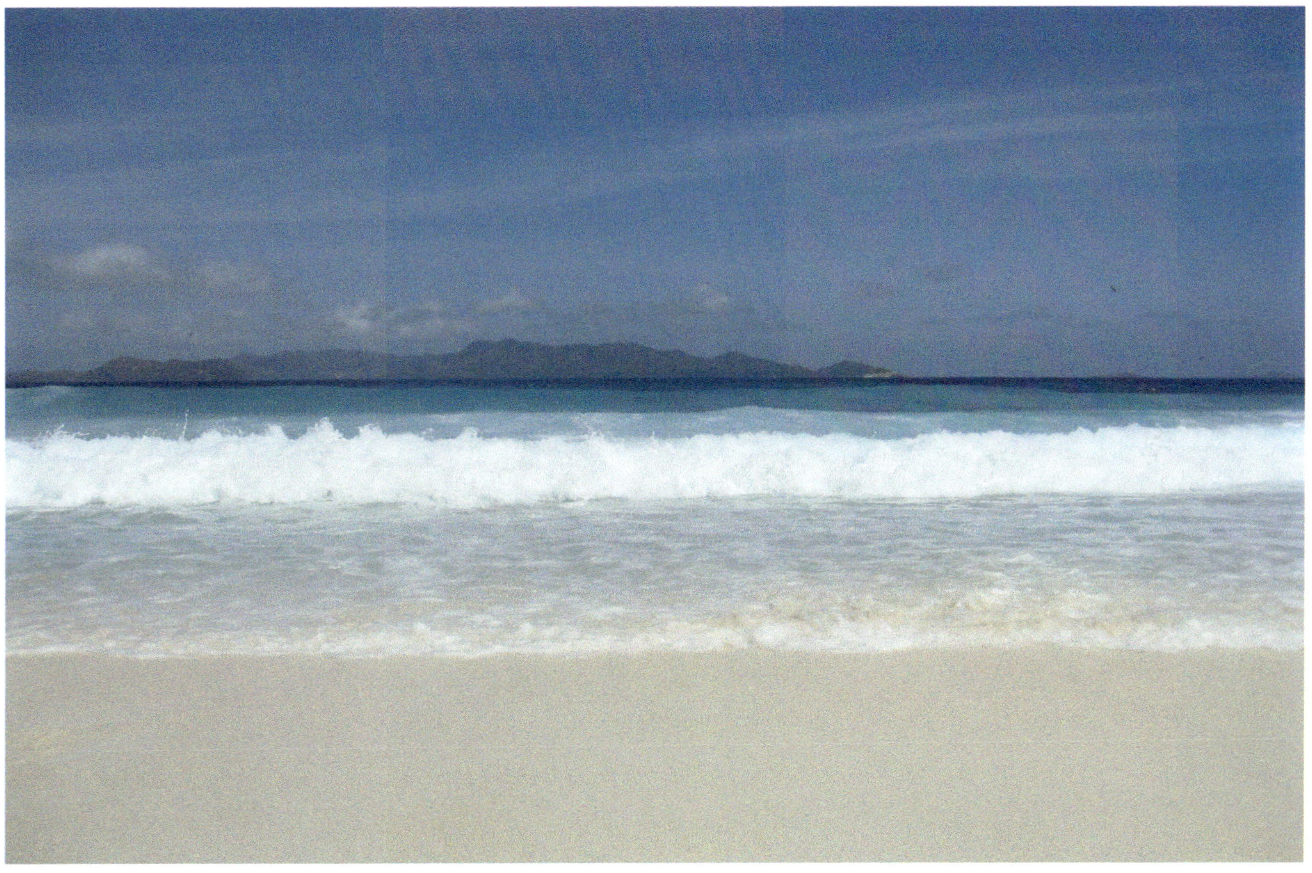

Unfortunately, our elation at the new water system was cut short by the news that my dad was really struggling with his cancer treatment. On receiving the news, I remember walking to the eastern end of the beach. I watched the turquoise water lapping the silver sand, the lush green undulations of Curieuse and Praslin and the blue sky, not a cloud in sight, just electric blue holding the sun that had lit up my life for the last twenty months. I was on the verge of talking to Melv about leaving this breath-taking place.

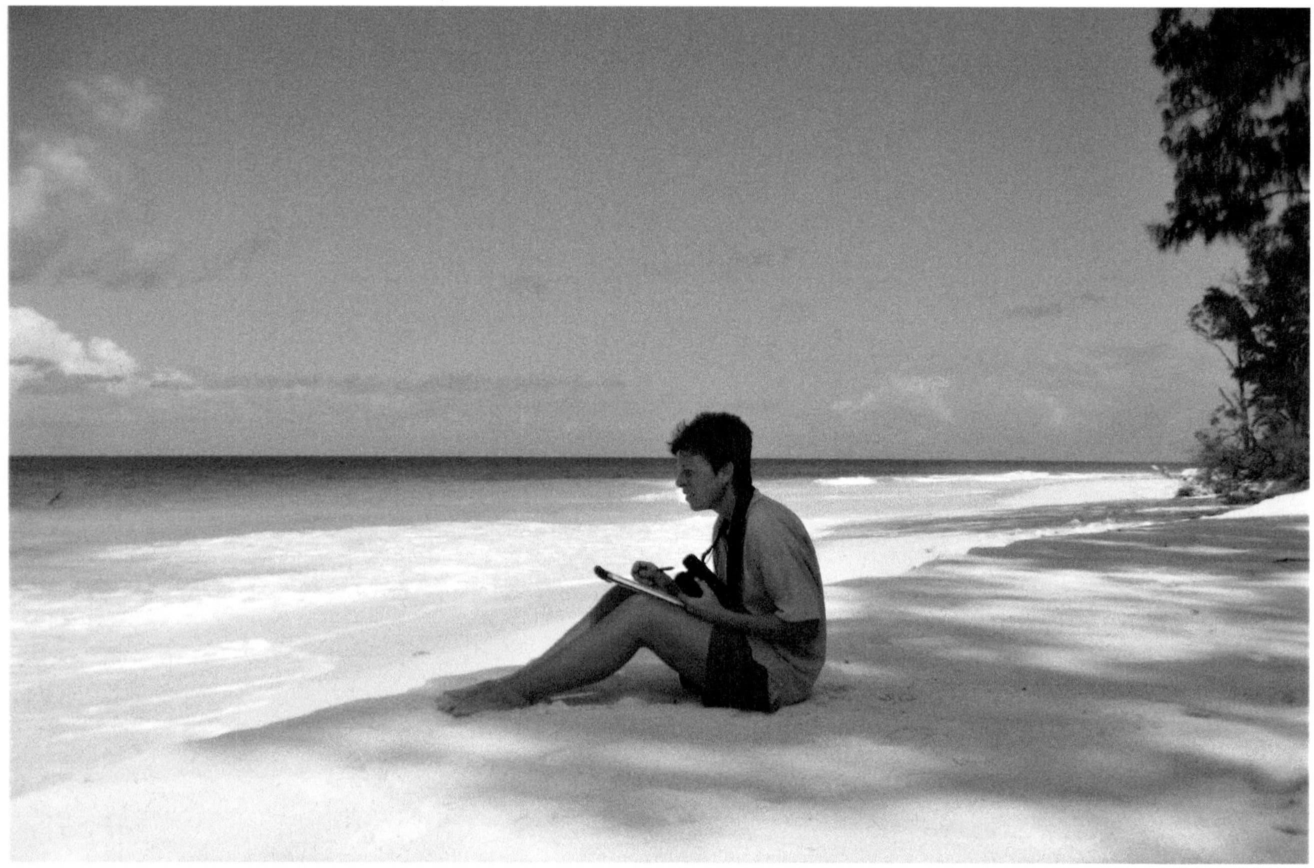

*© Melvyn Yeandle*

That day, I sat on the beach with my sketchbook and admired the frigates above my head. It was beautiful, warm, although a little breezy; the sea had calmed and there was hardly a white horse on the horizon. It had been a day of distraction, and one completely disrupted by our resignation. Realistically, it was always going to be: leaving Aride to try and pick up our lives in the UK was never going to be easy.

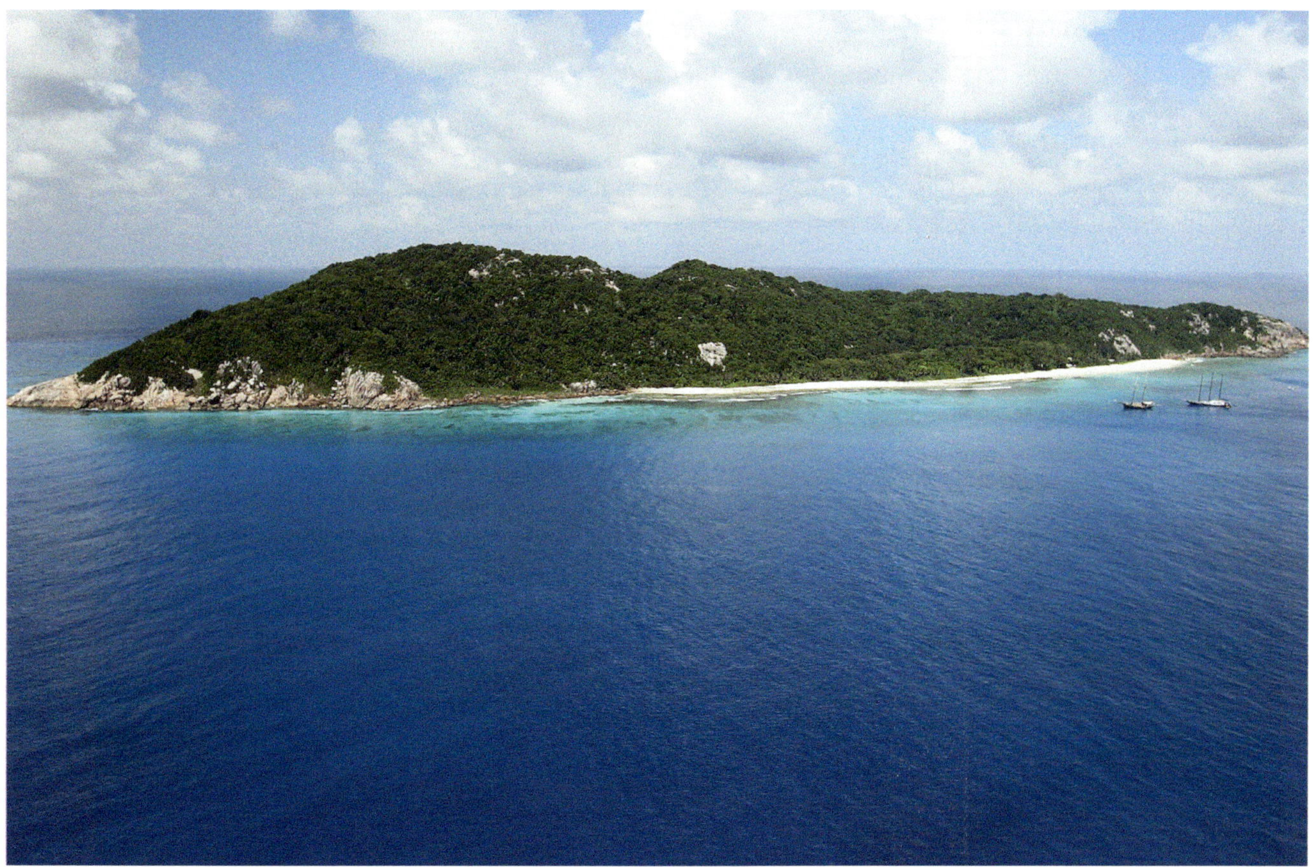

*© Colin Bell*

Our time on Aride ultimately came to an end, and as we made our final boat launch into some difficult surf and rough sea, it was impossible to comprehend that our time in the tropics was over. As I looked back to see the pairs of fairy terns and tropicbirds flying along the beach, the frigate birds soaring overhead, and the noddies and sooty terns flying alongside us, I had to wipe away a tear. I was saying goodbye to what had been an amazing period in my life; although very difficult at times, it was full of experiences that will stay with me forever.

## *The Photographers Behind the Photographs*

**Melvyn Yeandle**

Born in a small Somerset village in the UK, Melvyn completed a diesel fitter apprenticeship on leaving school and subsequently worked for many years in the building trade, running his own plastering business. With his extensive practical background and range of skills to match, there is nothing he can't turn his hand to. In later years, he followed his boyhood passion and pursued a career in nature conservation, through which we met 28 years ago. Both captivated by the environment, the job of Aride Wardens was a dream come true and we relished the unique challenge of living and working on one of the most renowned tropical island nature reserves in the world. Now semi-retired, we run a small horticultural business together in Somerset.

**Jean Cheadle**

After working as a North Wales Coastal Partnership Warden in the UK, Jean came to Aride as a 3-month volunteer. Her passion for the natural world came to the fore and is most evident in the photographs she captured during her short stay. As a qualified diver she was inspired by and contributed to both marine and land-based work and settled into island life admirably. The environment and photography are still very much a feature in her life, and Jean currently works for Hart District Council as a Senior Countryside Ranger. She is now married and lives in Hampshire with her husband and two children.

**Kate Wright**

Kate was a neighbour for many years from a time when we both lived in rural southwest England. A good friend, she was rather envious of our Seychelles venture, although it must be said, highly entertained, if not perplexed, by the eccentric preparations deemed necessary to leave Somerset security for the tempestuousness of the tropics. Shortly after our departure though, she too, together with her husband Steve, left for warmer climes. Although a little safer and not quite as exotic, they have now both comfortably retired and are enjoying a laid-back life in the Andalusia National Park, Spain.

**Chloe Prehn-Arnold**

A young 25-year-old from Yorkshire in the UK, Chloe arrived on Aride as a 3-month volunteer. Incredibly adaptable to change, she embraced island life comfortably and welcomed the opportunity to stay for a further 12 months. With all the personal attributes that a remote, spartan existence demanded – strong, determined, motivated, yet sensitive – she became my right-hand girl, whose depth of character kept me sane on many occasions. A local tour operator, *Silhouette Cruises*, brought her future husband to the island, who was Dutch, and they are now happily married with two children living in the Netherlands. Chloe currently works for a Dutch manufacturing business, Seed Processing Holland, as a Service Coordinator.

**Colin Bell**

Based in South Africa, Colin has co-founded three successful specialist wildlife safari enterprises. Firstly, Wilderness Safaris in 1983, followed by The Great Plains Conservation Project in 2005, both born with the ethos of building sustainable partnerships between safari companies and impoverished remote rural communities. Although it never came to fruition, he also considered the potential of Seychelles for green tourism opportunities which included a visit to Aride. Remaining African focused, in 2017 he co-founded Natural Selection, a conservation-driven tourism company through which he now works independently as a specialist guide.

**Caroline Arnold**

Then a student nurse from the UK, Chloe's younger sister Caroline came to stay on Aride for a week over Christmas. She arrived with her luggage bordering on the weight limit, bulging with gratefully received Western gifts and additions to our festive fayre. She sacrificed personal items and caringly carried memorable presents such as Christmas chocolates and jars of *Branston Pickle* and even *Hellman's Mayonnaise*! She now works as a Specialist Nurse for Parkinson's disease and lives in Leeds with her partner and two sons.

**Colin Taylor**

After being a Field Conservationist in Mauritius, Colin was employed as the Warden on Aride in September 1992 for 12 months, following which he worked as a UK Police Officer in Devon and Cornwall for 27 years. On retirement, he returned to Aride as Island Manager for a 3-month stint in April 2022. He now lives in a Devon village on the east side of Dartmoor with his wife and two children and currently works for Natural England as an Enforcement Lead Advisor. After the time spent on Aride he feels a unique bond and association with the island and still actively keeps in contact and abreast of progress.

## *Acknowledgments*

Aride Island secures a special place in many hearts, and I hope you agree that this is most apparent in the photographs from which this collection comprises. I would like to thank all the photographers for sharing the images they managed to capture, which illustrate how meaningful their time on Aride was. The photographs give a true and honest reflection of island life seen through the eyes of people who all had the opportunity to experience a truly unique existence, whether gained from a fleeting insight or over a significant length of time.

I must acknowledge separately three people who have supported all my literary endeavours to date. Firstly, Melvyn and Chloe, whom I shared the emotional rollercoaster of life on Aride with and who, in addition to providing photographs, kindly took time to review several drafts of different compilations. Secondly, my mum, who throughout my life has provided endless and unconditional support, and now latterly is a much-valued listening ear and critic for all my writing and creative ventures.

Finally, a general thanks must be extended to all those who made it possible for me to live and work on Aride Island, for giving me the opportunity to have that once in a lifetime experience that very few people are lucky enough to ever get the chance to enjoy.

BV - #0026 - 110823 - C41 - 210/210/14 - PB - 9781803781426 - Matt Lamination